TEXT AND CONTEXT
SERIES EDITOR: FRANK COULSON

enaissance
Postscripts

RESPONDING TO OVID'S *HEROIDES* IN
SIXTEENTH-CENTURY FRANCE

PAUL WHITE

THE OHIO STATE UNIVERSITY PRESS | COLUMBUS

Copyright © 2009 by The Ohio State University.
All rights reserved.

Library of Congress Cataloging-in-Publication Data
White, Paul, 1978–
  Renaissance postscripts : responding to Ovid's Heroides in sixteenth-century France / Paul White.
    p. cm. — (Text and context)
  Includes bibliographical references and index.
  ISBN-13: 978-0-8142-0744-4 (cloth : alk. paper)
  ISBN-10: 0-8142-0744-8 (cloth : alk. paper)
  1. Ovid, 43 B.C.–17 or 18 A.D. Heroides 2. Ovid, 43 B.C.–17 or 18 A.D.—Appreciation—France. 3. Ovid, 43 B.C.–17 or 18 A.D.—Translating into French. 4. Epistolary poetry, Latin—History and criticism. I. Title.
  PA6519.H7W48 2009
  871'.01—dc22
                          2008036182

This book is available in the following editions:
Cloth (ISBN 978-0-8142-0744-4)
CD-ROM (ISBN 978-0-8142-9191-7)
Paper (ISBN: 978-0-8142-5701-2)
Cover design by Fulcrum Design Corps.
Text design by Juliet Williams
Type set in Adobe Garamond Pro

CONTENTS

List of Illustrations — vii
Acknowledgments — ix
Note on Transcription of Latin and French Texts — xi

INTRODUCTION — 1
CHAPTER 1 Responding to Ovid's *Heroides* — 11
CHAPTER 2 Uses of the *Heroides* in Education — 43
CHAPTER 3 Editions and Commentaries — 87
CHAPTER 4 The *Heroides* in Translation — 144
CHAPTER 5 Replying to the *Heroides* — 187
CONCLUSION — 244

Bibliography — 251
Index of Passages from Ovid's *Heroides* — 265
General Index — 269

ILLUSTRATIONS

FIGURE 1. *Les XXI épîtres d'Ovide* (Paris: H. De Marnef, 1580), p. 14. Bibliothèque Nationale de France/Gallica — 5

FIGURE 2. *Epistolæ heroides Publij Ouidij Nasonis* (Lyon: J. David, 1528), fol. viii[r]. Cambridge University Library — 99

FIGURE 3. *Heroides epistolæ* (Venice: Hieronymus Scotus, 1543), p. 21. Cambridge University Library — 100

FIGURE 4. *Les XXI épîtres d'Ovide* (Paris: H. de Marnef, 1580), p. 31. Bibliothèque nationale de France/Gallica — 102

FIGURE 5. *Epistolæ heroides Publij Ouidij Nasonis* (Lyon: J. David, 1528), fol. xxxiiii[r]. Cambridge University Library — 104

FIGURE 6. *Les XXI épîtres d'Ovide* (Paris: H. de Marnef, 1580), p. 117. Bibliothèque nationale de France/Gallica — 105

FIGURE 7. *Les XXI épîtres d'Ovide* (Paris: H. de Marnef, 1580), p. 257. Bibliothèque nationale de France/Gallica — 132

FIGURE 8. *Les XXI épîtres d'Ovide* (Paris: H. de Marnef, 1580), p. 278. Bibliothèque nationale de France/Gallica — 133

FIGURE 9. *Heroides epistolæ* (Venice: Hieronymus Scotus, 1543), p. 119. Cambridge University Library — 134

ACKNOWLEDGMENTS

THIS BOOK is a revision of my doctoral thesis. My research was funded by the UK Arts and Humanities Research Council, and by a Domestic Research Studentship from the University of Cambridge. The award of a British Academy Postdoctoral Fellowship enabled me to undertake the revision.

I owe an immense debt of gratitude to Philip Ford for all the advice, support, and friendship he has offered me over the years. I am grateful also to Ann Moss, whose work in many ways inspired this project.

I would like to thank Robert Cummings for his help in refining the material for chapter 4, parts of which were published in modified form in *Translation and Literature:* "Ovid's *Heroides* in Early Modern French Translation: Saint-Gelais, Fontaine, Du Bellay," *T & L* 13.2 (Autumn 2004): 165–80.

In revising the thesis I benefited enormously from the comments of Neil Kenny, Ingrid de Smet, Frank Coulson, Carolin Ritter, and the two anonymous readers for the press. My ideas were also informed by discussion with the participants of the Birkbeck London Renaissance Seminars on the *Heroides;* and, on numerous occasions, with those attending the seminars of the Cambridge Society for Neo-Latin Studies.

Special thanks also to my family, and Aristea.

Images from the Cambridge University Library are reproduced by kind permission of the Syndics of Cambridge University Library. Images from the Bibliothèque Nationale are reproduced by permission of the BnF.

NOTE ON TRANSCRIPTION OF LATIN AND FRENCH TEXTS

IN TRANSCRIBING titles of works and in quoting passages I have for the most part retained the original orthography; I have however consistently replaced 'v' with 'u' in Latin texts. Where necessary, I have inserted punctuation in Latin passages quoted from early printed editions. Conventional abbreviations are resolved without indication.

All translations, unless otherwise stated, are my own.

Introduction

Une lettre arrive toujours à destination.

—Jacques Lacan

WHY DOES a letter always arrive at its destination? Slavoj Žižek's readings of Lacan's "Séminaire sur *La Lettre volée*" respond to Derrida's commonsensical objection that the letter might also fail to arrive. For Žižek, the letter's true addressee is the symbolic order, "which receives it *the moment the letter is put into circulation*."[1] The exemplary case of the letter that always arrives is the message in a bottle, cast into the sea by the marooned sender and addressed to nobody in particular. Abandoned on Naxos, Ariadne does not even have access to an intermediary or messenger to support the illusion that her letter might complete its trajectory. Unlike Penelope, she cannot pass her letter on to an itinerant stranger in the hope that it will somehow find its addressee. Her situation demands a message in a bottle, a letter cast out to sea and put into circulation at random, aimed at no single predestined reader. The intended recipient of Ariadne's letter is, of course, Theseus. But the logic of her situation dictates that its true addressee can be none other than the symbolic order itself, made flesh in the figure of the 'external reader': whoever occupies that place in the letter's itinerary temporarily stands in as its addressee.

Ovid's heroines write letters that will, in most cases, never be read by their intended recipients. Some will never even be sent: one wonders whether Deianira will send her missive on its way having just heard of the death of its addressee, Hercules. In the untypically evocative language of French postal

---

1. Žižek 2001, 10. Žižek draws extensively on Barbara Johnson's account in chapter 7 of *The Critical Difference: Essays in the Contemporary Rhetoric of Reading* (1980).

bureaucracy, they are letters "en souffrance." Of course, the truth is that these letters will be read, and that their intended recipient is none other than the "external" reader, we who intercept the message and, in the act of reading, confer upon it the status of literature. The letter arrives at its destination simply because its destination is wherever it arrives.

The first letter in the collection, read as a "programmatic gesture,"[2] brings out some of the implications of this epistolary logic. An inattentive reader might judge at first glance that Penelope has no means of sending her letter to her wandering husband, given that her motivation for writing is precisely that she does not know where he is. A closer reading of her letter reveals that she does in fact have access to a postal service of sorts. Penelope entrusts her letters (she has written more than one) to passing sailors, in the hope that their peregrinations might lead them, by chance, to an encounter with Ulysses:

> quisquis ad haec uertit peregrinam litora puppim,
>   ille mihi de te multa rogatus abit,
> quamque tibi reddat, si te modo uiderit usquam,
>   traditur huic digitis charta notata meis.[3]

> Whenever a foreigner turns his ship to these shores, he goes away interrogated at length about you, and this letter written in my hand I give to him, to deliver to you, should he ever see you.

Immediately, then, in the first letter in the collection, we are presented with a third party, an intermediary, complicating the classical definition of the letter as the transmission of information to an absent person (*absentis ad absentem sermo*): the letter's trajectory from author to addressee is by necessity circuitous, not direct. These intermediaries are themselves potential readers: indeed, it seems much more likely that Penelope's letter will be read by its retainer than by Ulysses himself. In this way, the narrative seems to demand what Effrosini Spentzou calls "interceptive readings."[4]

---

2. Kennedy 2002, 217–32.

3. 1.59–62. For quotations from and references to the *Heroides*, I shall use the "Cambridge Greek and Latin Classics" texts edited by P. E. Knox (1995) and E. J. Kenney (1996); Heinrich Dörrie's text (1971) will be used for the poems not included in Knox. The base text of editions printed in the fifteenth and sixteenth centuries varies considerably. Where textual variants have caused significant divergences in the readings favored by different authors, and where the modern texts used differ significantly from the texts encountered by sixteenth-century readers, this will be indicated in the footnotes. Except where otherwise stated, translations are my own.

4. "The stranger to whom Penelope is about to entrust her letter . . . is a powerful reminder of

Early modern readers of the *Heroides*[5] intercept Ovid's letters in order to recuperate the heroines' "messages" even as they participate actively in the dissemination of the text. There is a double movement of advancement and "drawing-back": read in terms of Ovid's intentions, the meaning of the text need not exceed the grasp of the reader, even if the heroines' aleatory discourse threatens to. As we shall see in the course of this study, in the humanists' institutionalized readings of the *Heroides,* Ovid can be read "against the heroines," but the heroines cannot easily be read "against Ovid." The heroines can be figured as vain, imprudent, excessively passionate, and irrational as long as there is a moral intention on the part of the author that affirms the text's utility, draws the text's meaning back into itself. Thus the intermediary, the interceptive reader, perceives the void left by the absent, unreachable "true" addressee, and actively fills it. In actualizing the text's meaning, drawing the text back into itself, the interceptor takes the place of the true addressee, becomes the true addressee himself: the letter arrives at its destination: how could it not?

Penelope's postal problems, at this stage, provide us with a rather crude model for our study of Ovid's respondents. However, when we begin to unfold the implications of the situation described in Penelope's letter, the model looks more adequate. Duncan Kennedy, reading *Heroides* 1 in conjunction with its most prominent intertext, the *Odyssey,* has made a persuasive argument concerning the identity of the stranger to whom Penelope entrusts her letter.[6] An examination of the chronology of events in Homer's epic leads the reader to conclude that Ovid's Penelope must be writing her letter at a time when her husband has already arrived in Ithaca. More than that, Penelope's own description of her usual technique of interrogating any stranger that passes through Ithaca as she entrusts her letters to them leads us to suppose that a certain Cretan beggar is likely to come in for the

---

the collection's eager need for intermediaries, contingent 'extra-diegetic' addressees whose readings can further disperse the messages of this collection" (Spentzou 2003, 28). For another reading that makes the connection between Barbara Johnson's account of the Lacan seminar and Penelope's intermediaries in the *Heroides,* see Victoria Rimell (2006, 131).

5. Ovid himself never uses the word "heroides" when referring to the work; the word "epistola" is used to denote any one of the poems in the collection in the *Ars Amatoria,* 3.345. Nevertheless, Peter E. Knox suggests that Ovid probably gave the title *Heroides* or *Heroidum liber* to the work, at least in its first edition (Knox 1995, 5). Most printed editions in the Renaissance use the titles *Epistolae/Epistulae Heroidum, Epistolae Heroides* or *[Epistolarum] Heroidum Liber;* references often abbreviate the title to *Epistolae Ovidii.* The collection is occasionally referred to simply as *Heroides* by neo-Latin authors. That title was in use as early as Priscian (Purser, ed. by A. Palmer, 1898, x). Since that is the title by which it is most commonly known today, I shall refer to the work throughout as "the *Heroides.*"

6. Kennedy 1984, 413–22.

same treatment. We are led to the satisfying conclusion that "all unknowing, Penelope is about to deliver this letter into the hands of its addressee" (418). The intermediary and the true addressee are one and the same: they occupy the same place in the symbolic circuit.

A further perspective on "a letter always arrives" is afforded by the idea that the heroines anticipate responses to their words even as they write. They can be said to be constructing the letter's addressee as they compose their text: the act of writing inscribes the reader into the text.[7] There is a sense of the 'present moment,' an immediacy that is, outside of the theater, peculiar to the epistolary form. In the words of W. S. Anderson, we are "peeking over the woman's shoulder as she is writing."[8] Penelope writes to Ulysses because he is absent; but her words conjure his presence. The reader is made present in the performance of letter writing.

An illustration to Charles Fontaine's mid-century translation of the first epistle depicts Penelope (Figure 1). She is, to all appearances, weaving her web; though in the context her action can surely be imagined to figure the act of letter writing.[9] On her left-hand side an old man approaches to hold Penelope in an embrace; he seems to be reading the letter over her shoulder. Her work, then, is supervised by a male presence: she is restricted in her physical movement by his proximity; his controlling gaze limits her freedom to work. Penelope's right arm is engaged in the action of weaving; or else it holds out the writing implement as if to prevent the man taking it from her, her arm poised as if wielding a weapon. The bearded man depicted in this illustration is most likely Laertes, the father of Ulysses, described as a "senex," "inutilis armis" by Penelope in her letter (98, 105), and mentioned by Fontaine in his preface: Laertes is too old, just as Telemachus is too young, to defeat the suitors. However, if we suppose that this figure is Ulysses himself, finally returning to Ithaca disguised as the Cretan beggar, it opens up new possibilities for reading.[10] Ulysses stands over Penelope even as she weaves, even as she writes; he "peeks over her shoulder," the reader in the text. The letter reaches its destination the very moment it is written.

---

7. Victoria Rimell touches upon this point when she brings Johnson's remarks on "The Purloined Letter" to bear on the *Heroides:* "The reader is comprehended by the letter; there is no place from which he can stand back and observe it" (131).

8. Quoted by Kennedy (1984, 416).

9. The equivalence of writing and weaving is pointed up elsewhere in Ovid's work, most notably in the Philomela episode in the sixth book of the *Metamorphoses*. One important development in the early modern story of Ovid's heroines, as we shall see, is the tendency for their epistles to take on forms other than the written: they become oral laments, dramatic monologues, visual artworks.

10. The composition of the image bears some similarity to Pinturricchio's "Return of Odysseus," which also depicts Penelope in the act of weaving.

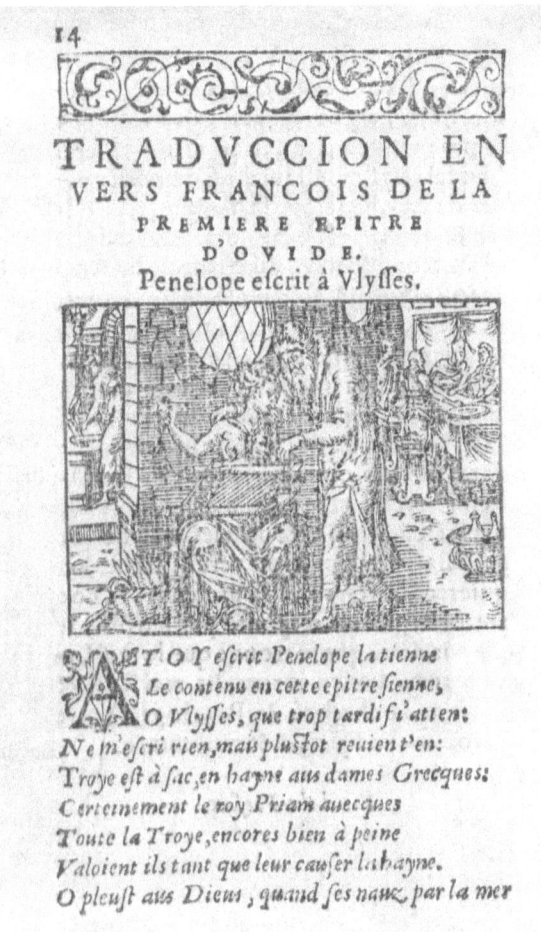

Figure 1. *Les XXI épîtres d'Ovide* (Paris: H. De Marnef, 1580), p. 14. Bibliothèque Nationale de France/Gallica

Similarly, the extradiegetic reader is invited to read the heroine's words as if in the very moment of writing. At the same time, however, that reader is party to information "outside the frame." Much of the dramatic tension in the *Heroides* derives from this clash of perspectives. From the reader's point of view, the heroines' narratives always overreach themselves: temporally, they extend far beyond the moment of composition, through the devices of dramatic irony and foreshadowing. As privileged overseers of their mythological destinies, readers of Homer, Virgil, and the mythographers, we—and their early modern readers—cannot help imposing a retrospective teleology onto the heroines' discourse. The reader's response is inscribed into the text in advance.

The heroines' stories are always already written: the destination of the letter is always bound up with the destiny of the heroine who writes it. There is a productive tension between immediacy and known destiny, between "writing to the moment"[11] and reading "out of" the moment. There is, though, at the same time a resistance to the imposition of ends: whereas the 'masculine' rhetoric of Ovid's heroes (especially that of Paris in *Heroides* 16) is focused single-mindedly on an end goal, the heroines of the collection write without an end in sight: their discourse flails onward, unchecked, aleatory. Their versions of their own myths often contradict or undermine the dominant narrative.

This tension underwrites early modern responses to the text as a whole; it has the potential to destabilize any reading that relies on a logic of cause and effect. It is perhaps for this reason that medieval and early modern commentators spilled so much ink in interpreting Phyllis's response to the words of the Thracian countryman at *Heroides* 2.85, "exitus acta probat" (the outcome is the measure of the deeds). It is a phrase that was very often underlined and annotated in *Heroides* editions, to be copied down in personal miscellanies and commonplace books. It remains a well-known Latin tag today, and is often taken to be saying "the end justifies the means," though that is not the sense of it here: but, as we shall see, the exact meaning of the line in context is open to interpretation. The context is an argument between Phyllis and one of her fellow Thracians, who would condemn her love affair with the Athenian Demophoon. I give the lines unpunctuated as they appear in early printed editions; my translation clarifies the sense as it is generally understood by modern commentators and translators.

> atque aliquis, iam nunc doctas eat, inquit, Athenas:
>   armiferam Thracen qui regat, alter erit.
> exitus acta probat: careat successibus, opto,
>   quisquis ab eventu facta notanda putat. (2.83–86)

And somebody says: "Let her go now to learned Athens; another will reign over warlike Thrace in her stead. The outcome is the measure of her deeds." May he come to a bad end, I pray, whoever thinks that actions should be judged from their result!

---

11. The phrase is Samuel Richardson's. See Kennedy 2002, 222.

"Exitus acta probat": the outcome, or interpretation arrived at, confers meaning upon the act of reading and retroactively shapes it, just as, according to T. S. Eliot's conception of tradition, a new poem alters the existing order of the past—this is one perspective on the reading and writing of literary texts, which is brought into sharp focus by the case of the *Heroides*. Ovid's heroines write themselves into literary history, modifying and reconceptualizing the canonical versions of their myths; and subsequently they become part of the corpus, they shape responses to their stories, their versions become accepted. Modern critics such as Alessandro Barchiesi have drawn attention to the intertextual ironies of the *Heroides:* Ovid situates his heroines in a past that predates their literary precursors, and endows them with a future that is already written. It has been suggested that the *Heroides* should be read as letters to be retroactively inserted into the texts that preceded them, as if (as Jean-Christophe Jolivet argued in a recent study) *Heroides* 9 really were the letter written by Deianira in Sophocles' *Trachiniae*, or if *Heroides* 7 really were a page missing from the fourth *Aeneid:* such an act of interpolation would necessarily change the reality of the myth. This is a prominent feature of Ovidian poetics, what Laurel Fulkerson has called "Ovid's own Hegelian drive to rework all of previous literature in order to show that it leads directly to him."[12]

The complications bound up with the phrase "exitus acta probat" are not limited to questions of moral philosophy: they involve the general question of the interpretation of texts. For early editors, dealing with an unpunctuated text, further complications arose from the indeterminacy of *who speaks* the words, and from that ever-present threat to a reader of an author's intention, irony. "Exitus acta probat" is perhaps the most telling *locus* to be found in the collection; the phrase could stand as a fitting epigraph to a study of the work's early modern reception. It may even help us understand just why "a letter always arrives at its destination."

THIS BOOK gives an account of responses to the *Heroides* in the domain of humanist education, in the works of Latin commentators and French translators, and as a particular mode of imitation, the reply poem. Our focus will be on authors writing in Latin as well as in the vernacular. Despite the differences in treatment, the interests of Latin language authors often coincide with those of vernacular poets. The comparison of the Latin elegiac *epistula* with the French *épître,* for example, viewed from the perspective of

---

12. Barchiesi, chapter "Future Reflexive," 2001. Jolivet 2001. Fulkerson 2005, 18.

their shared Ovidian models, will provide insights into the symbiosis of the two cultures. Very often, the works of authors writing in French have direct counterparts in the compositions of Latin language poets: chapter 5 will provide an opportunity for direct comparison between d'Amboise on the one hand, and Sabinus and Boyd on the other. The sections dealing primarily with Latin works will of necessity take a pan-European perspective. Humanist commentaries and pedagogical and theoretical texts will be studied in detail only where there is evidence that they were published and read widely in France. The most influential theorists, from the quattrocento humanists, through Erasmus and Vives, to Justus Lipsius, all had a major presence in France. In studies of the sixteenth century it is often difficult, and usually undesirable, to isolate national currents from international trends. The story of the French reception of the *Heroides* is in large part the story of its European reception.

The first chapter establishes the extent of the text's influence in the sixteenth century throughout Europe, with special attention to France. An assessment of theoretical perspectives proposes to situate the *Heroides* in the context of epistolary and related poetic traditions in Latin and vernacular literatures. Each generation of readers and writers has viewed Ovid's work from a different perspective, and measured the text by different standards according to the particular possibilities for reading available to them. In this process the text itself has been altered and reformulated countless times: it is a different text that is handed on to the next generation of readers. It was in the early stages of formal education that many authors had their first encounter with the *Heroides*. Chapters 2 and 3 will therefore focus on educational works and the commentaries penned by the humanists of the late quattrocento and the scholars of the generation of Erasmus, which continued to be used throughout the century. The chapter on the uses of the *Heroides* in humanist education examines methods used to accommodate the discourse of Ovid's heroines and heroes to pedagogical purposes. The work had practical applications in epistolography and in the teaching of rhetoric and poetic composition. Here we will find the clearest response to the question: to what ends was the text of the *Heroides* being used? By what criteria and in which disciplines was the text "approved"? Close readings of Latin commentaries on the *Heroides* published in France throughout the sixteenth century focus on treatments of the epistles of Phyllis, Dido, Paris, and Helen (*Heroides* 2, 7, 16, 17). The text was valued for the historical and mythological material it furnished, and for its rhetorical and ethical utility. Commentary is often viewed as constraining and limiting readings of a text; but we shall see that the humanist practice of commentary contradicts its putative goal of finality, and dispenses with 'ends' to favor a more open approach. The concerns of vernacular authors were similar but framed differently. Chapter 4 will follow Ovid's translators as they take us forward into the middle of the century and into the middle of French literary controversies. It incorporates comparative readings of versions of the Phyllis and Dido epistles ranging through a period which witnessed important shifts in attitudes to the text and to poetic translation in general. These translations may either approve or challenge Ovid's versions of the heroines; but they are more obviously in competition with each other, and each represents an engagement with the question: what are the ends of poetic translation? In Chapter 5 the scope of our treatment of *Heroides* imitations will be limited to those that demonstrate a distinct and sustained indebtedness to Ovid's text. The reply poem, a mode of imitation taken up by authors in both Latin and the vernacular, carries the concept of a literary "response" to the text to its natural conclusion. In tracing the development of this mode, we advance further forward in time, first taking in the responses to Ovid's work of the 1540s, and then the responses to those responses in the latter part of the century. Such compositions, once again, intrude to disrupt the dynamic of Ovid's text: they are intended as supplements to be interpolated into the narrative, supplying an "end" at the points where the text remained troublingly open. But in this attempt they expose the very open-endedness of the Ovidian text, to which such limits cannot easily be set. The reply poems themselves are subject to repeated recomposition; the formal complications to which they give rise touch upon the paradoxical core of the poetics of imitation.

CHAPTER 1

Responding to Ovid's *Heroides*

Quae uoluit legisse, uolet rescribere lectis
(Whoever was willing to read, will want to write back.)

Ovid, *Ars Amatoria* 1.481

Situating the *Heroides*

Great works demand a response, and the story of the Renaissance reception of the *Heroides* proves in more ways than one that "a letter always arrives at its destination." The humanists knew that ancient literature was always written *for them,* and that they were the rightful heirs to the classical tradition. In commentaries, translations, and imitations, sixteenth-century authors were able to rediscover a text that had never been lost. Uses of the text of the *Heroides* within the domains of education, of rhetoric, of moral philosophy, and of literary theory must be figured as so many responses to a text that communicated something important to its early modern readers, something that, they believed, had been lost on previous recipients. Just as Petrarch and Coluccio Salutati rediscovered Cicero's letters and in the process became the very people to whom they were addressed, so the Renaissance writers responding to Ovid's heroines—responses of many different orders—stand in place of the mythical heroes for whom the letters are provisionally destined.

Petrarch himself even wrote reply letters to the classical authors with whom he felt most intimate. He opens his "Letter to Cicero" thus: "I read with the greatest enthusiasm your letters, which I had been seeking for so long all over, and which I found where I least expected" (*"Epistolas tuas diu multumque perquisitas, atque ubi minime rebar inuentas, auidissime perlegi"*). Of this reply Petrarch wrote in the *Praefatio* to the edition of his correspondence: "I could not stop myself writing to him as to a friend and contemporary, with all the familiarity I had with his genius, as if the passage of time meant nothing" ("... *temperare mihi non potui quominus ... sibi tamquam coaetaneo amico, familiaritate quae mihi cum illius ingenio est, quasi temporum oblitus, scriberem ...*").[1] Similarly, the 'respondents' to the *Heroides* must also be figured as writing subjects themselves, putting their own 'letters' into circulation. In so doing they receive the letter back from its addressee *in its inverted, true form*, to use Žižek's formulation (13). At the intradiegetic level of Ovid's text, one instance of this idea is furnished by the epitaphs that close the heroines' letters in *Heroides* 2, 7, and 14. Such epitaphs function as a sort of signature, a message that the heroine is sending back to the hero. As Barbara Johnson comments in a different context: "What the addressee of the violence is going to get is simply his own message backwards" (117). At the level of the 'external reader,' the formula may be glossed as "there is no metalanguage": no mode of communication that stands outside the text to describe a value-free system. The respondents are themselves the proper addressee of the letter they send out. Again, Johnson's remarks on Poe's "The Purloined Letter" can also be predicated of the *Heroides:* "A literary text that both analyzes itself and shows that it actually has neither a self nor any neutral metalanguage with which to do the analyzing"; "no analysis ... can intervene without transforming and repeating other elements in the sequence" (110). Moreover, "the frame is always framed by part of its content" (Žižek, 14ff.). There is no point of view that is not framed by the historically determined horizon of possible points of view; but we can invert this by saying that the 'horizon of meaning' is always linked to a point *within* the field disclosed by it. In much the same way, the cultural grounding or horizon of expectations that gives form to any response to a literary text is simultaneously defined by the text itself, or rather, by textuality. Barchiesi, in his discussion of the 'future reflexive' mode in the *Heroides,* makes a salutary point about the nature of literary self-consciousness: "We are superior to the heroines, we know the unavoidable ends—but while we look at their illusions from the vantage point of irony, we are framed too: our ironical vantage point is built on the acceptance of a master fiction which controls it as we control intertextual ironies" (114).

The trajectory of the letter toward its destination also figures the trajectory of interpretation toward 'truth' (a truth which is already posited in the movement itself).[2] This trajectory is also figured as a 'circulation,' a circular

---

1. Petrarch 1863, vol. III: 262 and vol. I: 25. The relationship may be figured differently; when Petrarch wrote in his letter to Homer: "Penelope did not wait more eagerly or longer for your Ulysses than I did for you" (*"non hercle avidius neque diutius Ulyxem tuum sua Penelope expectavit quam ego te"*), it was to identify himself instead with the heroine suffering in wait of a response (III: 293).

2. See Derrida 1980, 439ff.

motion, because it returns to its proper place—where it started. This is the idea that the process of interpretation already contains its own truth: it finds what it sets out to find. Letters circulate. The responses can be figured as various ways of 'short-circuiting' the motion of the letter, as we shall see in chapter 5.

The conceit I have adopted here—the idea that Ovid's editors, translators, and imitators are the true recipients of his heroines' letters—is suggested by the very language of the critical discourse. We speak of orders of reception of classical texts, readers' 'responses,' 'dialogues' with the literary tradition. The text of the *Heroides,* of course, is particularly suited to this kind of 'double' reading; as Duncan Kennedy put it: "*Mutatis mutandis,* what is said of the heroine or hero and their readers can be interestingly predicated of Ovid and his, and vice versa."[3] All the texts written by authors studied in this book represent different types of response to the *Epistulae heroidum.* These responses to the text each say something important about the reading practices particular to distinct categories of knowledge that define possibilities for writing in the French Renaissance. They each belong to different disciplines: in the first place, pedagogy; overlapping with this, the humanist learning and its deployment in textual commentary; translation and its theorization; and the range of contexts encompassed by the concept of *imitatio,* represented by the reply poems.

The umbrella term 'paratext' may usefully designate the body of commentaries, translations, and imitations that concerns us here, whether they serve to "bring the reader to the poem" or to "bring the poem to the reader." Paratext is simultaneously both within and outside the text; but it is also the boundary itself. It is secondary to the text "like a guest to his host, a slave to his master," but is at the same time equivalent in status, on the same level.[4] Every type of text that served to present, mediate, or adapt the *Heroides* for a sixteenth-century audience can be considered as part of the paratext. Our use of the term is therefore rather broader than Genette's, whose study focuses primarily on the book as object, on the elements that frame the text on the page, and on the epitext as a function of the primary author and his editors (interviews, biographical details, etc.); Genette does, however, acknowledge that every context can be considered a paratext.

Hans Robert Jauss provides a theoretical framework to distinguish the different levels of reception that determine the cultural identity of any text. The immediate encounter with the text is mediated through institutional-

---

3. "Epistolarity," 222.
4. Genette 1987, 7. For Genette, 'paratext' includes both 'peritext,' elements within the book such as prefaces and notes, and 'epitext,' which exists around or outside of the book proper.

ized readings: its pedagogical uses, commentaries, and to a certain extent its translations. As we shall see, however, the developments in literary theory and practice as the century progresses take translation beyond what might be termed the institutionally approved reading. At the next level are situated imitations and literary readings of the source text: the 'dialogue' between authors.

> [T]he concept of a literary history of the reader . . . certainly represents a necessary corrective to the kind of history which has prevailed up until now: that of genres, styles, authors, and works. [. . .] Pascal as a reader of Montaigne, Rousseau as a reader of Saint Augustine, Lévi-Strauss as a reader of Rousseau are examples of the highest level of individual dialogue between authors, a dialogue which may be epoch-making in literary history owing to the assimilation and re-evaluation of the predecessor whose influence has been recognized as crucial. [. . .] In [the] middle level of institutionalized reading, the power of literature to transgress norms is again co-opted and transformed into traditionalized and authorized meaning. However, the need for reading, like any other aesthetic pleasure, cannot be totally channeled or manipulated. [. . .] [The] need for admiration or sympathetic identification, for protest and for new experience, fall into the lower, or shall we say prereflective, level which represents a subversive process of canon formation. In this way institutionalized thought may become equally subject to change, as much by the lower level of subversive canon formation as by the highest level of dialogue of 'great authors.'[5]

Jauss makes the "dialogue of 'great authors'" the highest level of textual reception, and situates 'prereflective reading' at the lowest level. This hierarchy, predicated as it is on an implicit value judgment, is difficult to sustain. As Charles Martindale points out,[6] "any division between immediate response and reflective critical activity is . . . easily deconstructable"; there are, moreover, no tenable criteria to define the point at which an 'institutionalized' reading becomes a 'great' one. It will be necessary for our purposes to imagine orders of response as distance from the source text in less rigidly hierarchical terms: there is no easily sustainable hierarchy that would account for all levels of commentary, translation, and imitation. Charles Martindale's reading of Dryden's threefold scheme of metaphrase, paraphrase, and imitation, elaborated in his 1680 "Preface to Ovid's *Epistles*," highlights some of

---

5. Jauss 1978, 137–47; 139.
6. Martindale 1993, 15.

the difficulties bound up with such schematic textual hierarchies. If we were to use Dryden's scheme as the framework for a study of *Heroides* paratext, we would soon encounter difficulties. We could make the general category of translations broadly equivalent to Dryden's 'metaphrase' as the closest to the source; the commentaries would fall into the next level of distance from the source (Dryden's 'paraphrase'); and the imitations at the outermost level. Alternatively, we might choose to situate the commentaries at the first level, since they represent a direct engagement with the text in its original form. In this case, translations would be placed at various points along the line demarcated by the next level of distance from the original. We are then faced with further problems. What criteria should we use to distinguish translation from imitation? Should imitations written in Latin be considered closer to Ovid than imitations written in French? Is the distinction between commentary, translation, and imitation really a qualitative one, rather than one of degree? Does commentary "bring the reader to the poem" where imitation "brings the poem to the reader" (Martindale, 83)? The spatial metaphor breaks down.

We are faced with further difficulties when we consider, with Martindale, that the source text is not in itself a fixed point; the heroines' letters are in a sense always 'in circulation': "The signs—and even these change their shape—have to be read, and *every* reading . . . is an act of translation. So we have no final 'text,' but rather an ever widening fan of 'translations,' which can always be supplemented by another translation" (100).

The commentaries, translations, and imitations under scrutiny here must be understood not only as responses to the *Heroides,* but as responses to the responses of others. Every 'translation' of the text is shaped by forces beyond its immediate relation to the source. The choice to write in the vernacular or in Latin will affect the treatment of the text according to the nature of the implied audience. Attitudes toward classical scholarship and its purposes, to the possibilities for 'translation' of knowledge from one culture or language to another, will shape responses. H. R. Jauss identifies two ways of 'salvaging' a text when it is no longer directly accessible to a certain culture: grammatical interpretation and allegorical exegesis.[7] The former poses as a preservation of the past as past; but it really "seeks to reconstruct past meaning in order to translate it into a form understandable in the present" (54). The latter is a process of adaptation of the text to present meaning, which nevertheless seeks to preserve the text's literal meaning. The two procedures are two sides of the same coin. Similarly, the humanists' attempts to revive antiquity

---

7. Jauss 1990, 53–73.

can be seen on the one hand as an effort of 'pure philology,' a preserving of the past as past, and on the other as an 'applied study,' adapting texts to mean something for the here and now. Both of these possible approaches are aspects of the same effort to 'make familiar' the texts of antiquity, to accommodate what they mean and how they mean to the way meaning is constructed in the present.

Jauss further comments: "It is not until the transitional period between the Middle Ages and the modern age that this move from passive to active reception, from merely receiving to producing, is seen in the history of the concept itself" (55). I intend to treat the commentaries, translations, and imitations as three complex ways of responding actively to the text of the *Heroides*. They represent differing degrees of engagement with the source text; each discloses something about the conditions of its production and the immediate concerns of its author, and about the 'potential for meaning' of Ovid's text itself. Our authors write back to Ovid, just as Sabinus had done in the months after Ovid's publication of the work. To pursue the conceit, we might characterize this study as a survey of selections from the correspondence of Ovid's respondents. Our intention, however, is not to indulge the fantasy of a personal correspondence between the great authors of the Renaissance and the Roman poet, nor to figuratively adopt the role of biographer in 'editing their correspondence.' Rather, it is to investigate how the concerns of Ovid's respondents can illuminate the process of making the text of the *Heroides* familiar.

These concerns manifest themselves in certain tendencies in treatments of the text. First, there is the disposition toward moralizing, the vestige of medieval traditions which, although less present in the commentaries, translations, and imitations published in the sixteenth century, persists, especially in the domain of Protestant humanism. The text may be used in education as a sort of handbook of moral philosophy and as a *locus classicus* of female exemplarity; such uses are not without their complications. Second, and closely bound up with the ethical utility attributed to Ovid's studies in psychology, would be the interest in the rhetorical dimension of the work: the *Heroides,* viewed as the work in which the poet's ingenuity and artifice are best displayed, were recommended for study within the humanist curriculum both for their moral content and as a rhetorical learning tool. The influence of the text goes beyond dry school exercises in *suasoria* and *ethopoeïa:* the *Heroides,* being in many cases the first poetic text to which boys were exposed in the schoolroom, is responsible for shaping trends in French poetry. This happens in the first place indirectly, most notably through Octavien de Saint-Gelais's translation of the work, which had considerable influence on French poetry before the Pléiade. There is also a direct line of influence: poets seize upon the *Heroides* as models for imitation, since the form itself seems to provide the perfect opportunity for the rhetorically minded poet to give free rein to his genius. The popularity of replies to and parodies of Ovid's letters was perhaps at its height in the sixteenth century.

The shifts in focus that inform sixteenth-century responses to the *Heroides* correspond to broader cultural trends. Ann Moss identifies a pattern in the reception of the *Heroides* which neatly encapsulates the changing fortunes of Ovid studies in France in the sixteenth century:

> [F]irst, those [commentaries] of the first third of the century with their encyclopædic erudition and their interest in Ovid's description of the psychology of passion, more or less adapted to the conventions of contemporary morality; then, beginning in the 1530s, the obsession with rhetoric which makes the mid-century editions read like manuals in the art of literary imitation; and lastly, when these seem to lose their relevance after 1570, the narrowing-down of literary studies to problems of textual criticism.[8]

Reading the *Heroides*: Trends in Scholarship

The reputation of the work reached its height in the seventeenth and eighteenth centuries, an age when the editor of a London edition of the *Heroides* could claim, without fear of ridicule, that it is "the greatest work of the great Naso" (*"magni Nasonis maximum opus"*), and that all of the qualities to be found in Ovid's other works shine through with the greatest clarity in this, his *chef-d'œuvre* ("Si quis autem maximas Nasoniani ingenii dotes inspexerit, has non uspiam magis splendere comperiet"). The *Heroides* rightly and deservedly win first place, ahead of all his other works ("Præstantissimum illius opus . . . jure meritoque reliquis eius operibus palmam præripit").[9]

In the nineteenth century the work's popularity declined: by the twentieth century the *Heroides* had come to be viewed as suitable texts to be read selectively in the schoolroom, but undeserving of serious attention. Despite

---

8. Moss 1982, 15–16.

9. "Whoever has considered the greatest qualities of Ovid's talent, will not find them displayed more brilliantly anywhere else. [. . .] His most outstanding work . . . rightly and deservedly snatches first place ahead of the rest of his works." From the anonymous introductory note to the reader in *Epistolarum Heroidum Liber: Interpretatione & Notis Illustravit D. Crisp. Helvetius* (London: C. Rivington, 1775).

the occasional attempt to 'rescue' the *Heroides* in the intervening years, the revival of interest starts properly with Howard Jacobson's book-length study of the work,[10] which focuses in some detail on the role of perspective and on Ovid's intertexts. These two points of interest have dominated *Heroides* criticism since the 1980s. Jacobson's study prepared the ground for subsequent work on the complications of the gendered voice, and on the ways in which Ovid makes his heroines engage with other texts to generate meaning. Florence Verducci's study of the *Heroides* emphasized the wit and irony of Ovid's text, privileging its intertextual dimension; the heroines' violations of classical decorum were shown to be features of Ovid's parodic intent. The *Heroides* obey only "the rule of indecorum."[11] Marina S. Brownlee, similarly, saw the *Heroides* as the site of interanimation of a plurality of discourses, but placed emphasis also on the pathetic dimension, and on subsequent influence on the Spanish *novela sentimental*.[12] The intertextual approach is exemplified by the work of Alessandro Barchiesi; two of his essays on the *Heroides* appear in chapters 2 and 5 of the compilation *Speaking Volumes* (2001). In a book published in the same year (*Allusion et fiction épistolaire*), Jean-Christophe Jolivet deployed a number of particularly suggestive readings in this vein, based largely on the premise that the heroines' letters might be imagined as being retroactively inserted into preexisting texts.

Recently in *Heroides* criticism, a trend has emerged that recasts the discourse of Ovid's heroines in terms of its radical otherness, the irruption of the feminine voice into the male-authored space. There is an 'incompleteness principle' built into the epistolary form, and this principle operates most radically in the discourse of the heroines. The heroines' act of writing certifies absence; their discourse is stumbling, directionless, aleatory; desire is never fulfilled. The female voice is only allowed to speak as long as it fits a culturally approved role (the abandoned lover, the seductress, the faithful wife) and as long as it is defined in relation to the male voice: that of the addressees, but more importantly, that of the male author, Ovid himself. Suzanne Hagedorn, in her study of the characterization of abandoned women in Chaucer, Dante, and Boccaccio,[13] applies to the *Heroides* Lipking's idea that abandoned women are necessarily 'outside the law,' both in a spiritual sense and in terms of the rules that govern literary representation.[14] Other critics

---

10. Jacobson 1974.
11. Verducci 1985.
12. Brownlee 1990.
13. Hagedorn 2004.
14. The letter, in this case, as it resists being read becomes a 'stain.' Žižek, 8: "is not the letter itself ultimately such a stain—not a signifier but rather an object resisting symbolization, a surplus, a mate-

have reacted against the view of the male author's dominance to emphasize the ways in which the heroines gain some degree of authorial autonomy themselves. Effrosini Spentzou reads the heroines' discourse in terms of the Platonic *pharmakon*, "writing's dangerous supplement" (143); she attempts to recuperate the text's female voices by presenting the heroines as sometimes eluding or opposing Ovid's authorial control. Sara H. Lindheim's Lacanian analysis focuses on the heroines' self-construction as desired objects.[15] Laurel Fulkerson's recent study marries the two trends in *Heroides* scholarship: her approach endows the heroines with some degree of autonomy as readers and writers of each other's texts, and examines the ways in which intratextual allusions construct a community of authors. Victoria Rimell takes a somewhat similar approach, but focuses on the "Epistula Sapphus" and the six 'double letters': her interest is in the ways in which intertextuality performs intersubjectivity: in doubled, relational identities engaged in a "complex dialectic or exchange which seems itself to fire and propel desire" (1).

The other version of the idea of the excess is the notion that Ovid is 'too much himself' in the *Heroides*, that he does not know when to let well alone. The idea that Ovid's chief failing in the *Heroides* is an excess of wit is a persistent one in criticism, from Seneca Rhetor (whose "nescit quod bene cessit relinquere" is often quoted as a reproach directed at the *Heroides*), through John Dryden, to L. P. Wilkinson. Dryden's judgment of the *Heroides*, that in that work Ovid is "frequently witty out of season" did not, however, diminish his enthusiasm for translating Ovid; the eighteenth-century French critic Élie Catherine Fréron, even while praising the richness and variety that characterized Ovid's text, acknowledged that the work suffered from "trop d'esprit"; and Wilkinson memorably described the single *Heroides* as a plum pudding that becomes less appetizing with each slice.[16]

Florence Verducci, writing on the twentieth-century reception of the *Heroides*, notes that for modern critics the temptation to make Ovid's surface wit and his 'serious' intent mutually exclusive has been too great: "Lying behind all this, but nonetheless clearly discernible in it, is the inevitably value-laden opposition between the two functions of imaginative literature: *aut doceat aut delectet*. This is an opposition which has not yet suffered its last

---

rial leftover circulating among the subjects and staining its momentary possessor?" In Žižekian terms, this study could be seen as a survey of various attempts to deal with this disturbing surplus (*objet petit a*). How can the excessive element of the lover's discourse be accounted for in the sixteenth-century sphere of knowledge?

15. Lindheim 2003.

16. For Fréron see R. Carocci 1988, 43. For the plum pudding reading, see Wilkinson 1955, 106.

obsequies, even in the era of 'the irreality of reality'" (304). This tendency in modern critical judgments of the *Heroides* could not be further removed from the attitudes that predominate in Renaissance evaluations of the work. Guy Morillon, writing the preface to his edition of the *Heroides* in the first decade of the sixteenth century, quotes the Horatian dictum to which Verducci alludes:

> ... in Heroidas illas Ouidianas forte incidi: dii boni quam multiplici eruditione refertas, quam lepidissimis salibus concinnatas. Omne tulit punctum (ut inquit Flaccus) qui miscuit utile dulci. Quod quidem aut nemo (ut puto) aut noster hic Naso est assecutus, qui ita seria mellitis figmentis, figmenta seriis miscet, ut satis nescies, plusue utilitatis, an uoluptatis præ se ferat.[17]

> By chance I came across those *Heroides* of Ovid: great gods, how crammed they are with complex learning, how cleverly and wittily they are put together! He has won every vote (as Horace says) who has mixed the useful with the pleasurable. Which indeed, either nobody (in my opinion) or else this Ovid of ours, has achieved; he mixes the serious with honeyed fictions, and fictions with the serious so well that you will not know what he exhibits more of, utility or pleasure.

For Morillon, Ovid has been the most successful of all poets in bringing together the art of rhetoric and the moral component proper to literature. Even if in practice no poet can truly fulfill the Horatian dictum, Ovid's art in the *Heroides* is such that the reader can never separate the work's utility from the pleasure it brings. The honeyed strains of the poetry are so skillfully intermingled with the 'serious' intent of the poet that no critic could suggest the work's 'superficiality' detracts from its educative impact.

What does it mean for the *Heroides* to be the text in which Ovid is too much like Ovid? It is doubtful that a Renaissance audience would have seen the point of this criticism; still more doubtful that it would have been acknowledged as a failing. For Ovid's sixteenth-century commentators, translators, and imitators, the *Heroides* is more likely to be the work in which Ovid's qualities are most brilliantly and abundantly deployed. Guy Morillon certainly judged the *Heroides* to be the work in which Ovid is most like himself; but for him, it seems, this was unequivocally a good thing. Morillon reads into the *Heroides* a breaking down of the opposition between

---

17. Ovid, ed. Morillon, 1545, sig. A2ʳ.

'serious' and 'witty,' the very opposition that polarized critics up until the late twentieth century. It is clear to him that Ovid has included nothing remotely lubricious or lascivious in the work: Phaedra is the one responsible for promoting a detestable kind of incestuous love in *Heroides* 4, not Ovid. Even where there is a possibility of reading the heroines 'against Ovid,' a Renaissance reader may rely on the notion that Ovid's authorial control will reassert itself to correct deviant perspectives.

The idea that Ovid can be 'too much himself' has been used to refute authenticity: an imitator or interpolator can be 'more Ovid' than Ovid himself: he might 'out-Ovid' Ovid. The established text of the *Heroides* has a particularly complex history.[18] Debates about the inclusion of certain letters have often hinged on the question of interpolations in the work and elsewhere in the Ovidian corpus, most notably in *Amores* 2.18. Disputed passages in the text itself, the inclusion or exclusion of interpolated titles or salutations, the question of the proper order of the letters in the collection and of its structural divisions, as well as the broader question of whether certain letters should be included at all; all these points of contention have posed problems for Ovid's editors. Of course, these problems to some extent affect the editor of any classical text; but the *Heroides,* more than most, poses intractable difficulties. The *Heroides* has been transmitted and published in so many different versions that its unity must always be undermined by questions of authenticity. Even the part of the work that has the best claim to be its inviolable core, the letters numbered 1–14, has been rejected by some modern critics.[19] Some critics, following Karl Lachmann, accept as genuine only the letters mentioned by Ovid in the undisputed parts of *Amores* 2.18, that is to say, 1–2, 4–7, and 10–11. Knox adds *Heroides* 3 to this list.[20] It must be noted, however, that no fifteenth- or sixteenth-century editor of the work excluded these fourteen letters, although some thought of them as being divided into two or three books. The edition of Antonius Volscus and Ubertinus Clericus, for example, originally divided the whole collection into five books: 1–5; 6–10; 11–13; 14 (mistakenly listed as 13) and 16–17; 18–21; with the *Epistula Sapphus* (15) not numbered, and listed

---

18. Joseph Farrell suggested that the authenticity issue ought to be integrated into purely 'literary' readings of the text: "I would argue that the *Heroides*, in virtue of the ways in which they represent the production, transmission, and reception of texts, thematize both the philological and hermeneutic issues to which I have referred and that they do so in such a way as to draw the two types of interpretation together" (Farrell 1998, 308–9).

19. For an account of the case made by Otto Zwierlein and Wilfried Lingenberg for the inauthenticity of the *Heroides,* see J. A. Richmond's review of "Wilfried Lingenberg, *Das erste Buch der Heroidenbriefe,*" (27 August 2003).

20. Knox, introduction to *Select Epistles,* 5ff.

separately. In his introduction to Palmer's text and commentary, Purser notes that the MSS. often divided the work into two, three, four, or five books, the contents of which varied. It has been suggested that Ovid's first series of letters (1–15) must have consisted of three books (see Palmer's edition, xlii). As Knox points out, Ovid's original book would not have fitted on one papyrus roll (11–12).

In the next textual layer, at a greater distance from the textual 'center,' we might situate the double letters (16–21 in modern editions, usually 15–20 in Renaissance editions); the authenticity of these has been doubted since the beginnings of textual criticism.[21] Even if these letters are authentically Ovid's, they further problematize textual unity when we recall that most critics now consider them to have been written by Ovid at a later stage of his career, and published separately.

In the third layer is the *Epistula Sapphus,* not transmitted as part of the work in the Middle Ages, but generally granted authenticity in the Renaissance, although usually published in an appendix. The *Epistula Sapphus* and its reception have been the focus of many recent studies.[22] It stands out, for modern critics, as the point in Ovid's œuvre at which the poet engages most explicitly with gender issues and the problem of female eloquence, and for this reason its problematical reception remains a focal point for feminist critics. Joan DeJean writes that "Sappho is a figment of the modern imagination. During her recovery by early modern scholars, she was completely a French fantasy."[23] The Sappho epistle only starts to have an impact on the poetic imagination in the second half of the sixteenth century, most notably in poets like Louise Labé,[24] although it does get translated by Octavien de Saint-Gelais as early as 1492, and Michel d'Amboise, for instance, includes the reply from Phaon in his *Contrepistres.* The discovery of the Sappho fragments perhaps raised questions about the authorship of *Epistula Sapphus.* In the Renaissance there was even a popular notion that it was a translation

---

21. On certain points of contention in the double letters, see Kenney 1979, 394–431. Kenney considers letters 16–21 to be authentic however, and concludes that the two disputed passages (in letters 16 and 21) are unlikely to be the work of an interpolator.

22. The case for inauthenticity was made by R. J. Tarrant (1981, 133–53). For a critique of Tarrant's methodology and a discussion of the complications involved in philological approaches to the question of authenticity in general, see S. Hinds, 1993, 44.

23. DeJean 1989, 1.

24. Silver 1994, 170–74. See also F. Rigolot 1997, ch. 1, "Retrouver la voix de Sappho," and Daniel Martin 1999, 174–85. A recent study by Mireille Huchon (2006) suggests that Labé, too, might have been a figment of the modern imagination. Huchon contends that Labé's works were penned by a group of male collaborators; the creation of many *Heroides*-inspired texts seems to have taken place under the sign of imposture.

into Latin of a Greek original by Sappho herself.[25] By the seventeenth century, the voices of "Sappho and Ovid [had] become completely intertwined" (DeJean, 54).

The fourth, outermost layer would comprise the Sabinus replies: never considered an authentic work of Ovid, but often included as part of the text by Renaissance editors more or less confident of their status as genuine works of antiquity, endorsed by Ovid himself.

The text of the *Heroides* is, then, fundamentally incomplete, both in its formal basis, and in the indeterminate status of the 'authentic book.' The 'core text' of letters 1–14 seems to provide a stable point around which to arrange the outer textual layers; however, it too has been undermined by modern critics. Once the core is denied, the edifice of authenticity starts to collapse, causing a domino effect that leads one to dispute passages elsewhere in the Ovidian corpus: if the *Heroides* are not by Ovid, then the references to them at *Amores* 2.18.21–34 and *Ars Amatoria* 3.345–46 must also be forgeries. Thus there is no single point upon which to base a comprehensive argument for authenticity. The strategies employed by Renaissance editors and readers of the work to engage with and to resolve this difficulty, to 'give body' to the text, will be examined in the following chapters. The problematic of authenticity and completeness is reflected in responses to the text from the Middle Ages onward: in the words of Duncan Kennedy (2002), 218: "Literary imposture is written into epistolary heroinism from the start."

Writing the *Heroides*: A Brief Overview of *Heroides*-Influenced Texts[26]

The *Heroides* were, it seems, much imitated in antiquity. Ovid himself mentions the imitations penned by his friend Sabinus. Persius, writing just over half a century after Ovid, disapproves strongly of a contemporary vogue among terrible poets for imitations of the *Heroides*:

> hic aliquis, cui circum umeros hyacinthina laena est,
> rancidulum quiddam balba de nare locutus

---

25. See A. Fritsen 2005, 41–58; 44–49.
26. The classic work on *Heroides* reception is Heinrich Dörrie's 1968 bibliographical study *Der heroische Brief*. Indispensable as a reference work, though necessarily not exhaustive, it is the broadest and most thorough study yet undertaken of the influence exerted by the *Heroides* on the literature of the modern era, both in Latin and in the major vernacular languages.

Phyllidas, Hypsipylas, uatum et plorabile siquid,
eliquat ac tenero subplantat uerba palato.
adsensere uiri: nunc non cinis ille poetae
felix? non leuior cippus nunc inprimit ossa?
laudant conuiuae: nunc non e manibus illis,
nunc non e tumulo fortunataque fauilla
nascentur uiolae? (*Satires* 1.32–40)

Dryden renders these lines thus:

One, clad in purple, not to lose his time,
Eats and recites some lamentable rhyme:
Some senseless Phyllis, in a broken note,
Snuffling at nose, or croaking in his throat.
Then graciously the mellow audience nod;
Is not th'immortal author made a god?
Are not his manes blest, such praise to have?
Lies not the turf more lightly on his grave?
And roses (while his loud applause they sing)
Stand ready from his sepulchre to spring?[27]

The list of *Heroides*-influenced vernacular texts in the Middle Ages is a long one. Rudolph Schevill remarked in the medieval Spanish reception of Ovid the dominance of what he called the "Ovidian tale," which has its origins in the *Heroides*.[28] For Schevill, the influence of Ovid in the Middle Ages was "less tangible and direct than that of Virgil," more a matter of ideas suggested or inspired by Ovid than direct imitation of any particular work of his. Still, the *Heroides* had a major presence in the vernacular literature of medieval Europe. In her study of representations of abandoned women (cited above) Suzanne Hagedorn traces Ovid's influence in some of the major authors of the period: Dante; Boccaccio's *Teseida, Amorosa Visione*, and *Fiammetta;* Chaucer's *House of Fame* and *Legend of Good Women;* and, briefly, John Gower's *Confessio amantis*. As well as being indebted to Ovid's *Heroides,* these texts also contributed to the formation of an identifiable tradition of abandoned women's writing. The medieval text that is most influential on that tradition is probably the letters exchanged by Heloise and Abelard, and the legend surrounding them. That story, of course, was

---

27. Dryden, ed. G. R. Noyes, 1950, 359.
28. Schevill 1913, 1–268.

to inspire the best-known of all *Heroides* imitations, Alexander Pope's *Eloisa to Abelard*. It was to exert an important influence, too, on the French eighteenth century. The poem that set off the vogue for poetic love letters in the latter half of the century was Colardeau's 1758 *Lettre d'Héloïse à Abelard*. The original letters had first appeared in a printed edition in France in 1616, edited by François d'Amboise (Carocci, 140). The influence of the Heloise and Abelard letters on *Heroides* imitations in the sixteenth century is for the most part indirect and by no means as dominant as it was to become later.

It was in the eighteenth century that the fortunes of the poetic genre known as the 'héroïde' were at their peak in France. Renata Carocci locates the brief flourishing of this phenomenon in the decade and a half following 1758, with a particular concentration of activity in the years 1764–65 (35). Among its chief practitioners were Colardeau, Dorat, La Harpe, and Blin de Sainmore. These authors were not interested in direct imitations of Ovid, and the genre was generally asserted to be independent of that tradition, owing more in style and tone to tragedy than to Ovidian elegy.[29] Even where these poets adopted characters and situations from Ovid's collection, the differences in treatment are obvious (68). It will probably come as no surprise, for example, that Louis Sébastien Mercier's Medea has more in common with Racine's Phaedra than with her Latin model (75).

The influence of the *Heroides* on the French literature of the seventeenth and eighteenth centuries has been studied in some detail. Joan DeJean comments that it was only in the early seventeenth century that "[the *Heroides*] began to play its most important role in the development of the French tradition," *viz* the Sapphic tradition (61). Daniela Dalla Valle affirms that it was in the first part of the seventeenth century that the *lettre héroïque* flourished as a genre or subgenre (the 1620s was the beginning of the period in which "ces Epîtres étaient en leur plus grande chaleur" in the words of Ogier); and that its success continued throughout the century (379, 381). This period witnessed a great proliferation of *Heroides*-inspired texts, particularly in Jesuit literature, and the birth of the epistolary novel. But the presence of the work in sixteenth-century literary culture, and its role in the prehistory of the epistolary novel, is equally deserving of attention.

In his study of the origins of the epistolary novel,[30] Charles E. Kany charts the evolution of the ancient tradition of fictional letter writing, focusing in particular on the love letter; the vernacular traditions beginning in

---

29. Already in the seventeenth century a certain relationship between the *héroïde* and the theatrical monologue had been established in Tristan l'Hermite's 1642 *Lettres héroïques;* see D. Dalla Valle 2003, 371–84; 382.

30. Kany 1937, 1–158.

medieval France and culminating in the epistolary novel proper recapitulate this development in almost parallel fashion. Ovid's *Heroides* might be placed at the origin of both traditions: the single-letter collection prompted replies by Ovid's friend Sabinus, and by Ovid himself, if we assume the second part of the collection (the 'double letters') to be authentic; after this came the works of Greek Sophists (Alciphron, Aristaenetus), incorporating model letters penned by several correspondents; love letters also featured prominently in the Greek romances of late antiquity. Since these novels were usually stories of separated lovers, epistolary exchanges resembling those of the *Heroides* were often central to the narrative. Among those romances that employ epistolary conceits, Laurent Versini follows Kany in listing Chariton's *Chaereas and Callirhoe* (first century AD), Iamblicus' *Babylonian Story* (second century), Achilles Tatius' *Leucippe and Clitophon* (second century), Xenophon's *Ephesian Tale* (second century), Heliodorus' *Ethiopian Story* (third century).[31] At this point Kany sees an end to the development of the form among the ancients. The vernacular tradition of the love letter also began with poetic forms: the Provençal *Salut d'amors* (twelfth and thirteenth centuries) probably owed some debt to Ovid's *Heroides*.[32] Kany cites Scheludko's claim that half of all poems from the Charlemagne period onward were written in epistolary form (11). Later came poetic correspondences in other forms: the sonnet in Italy, *ballades* and *rondeaux* in France; then came the epistolary romance in verse, culminating in Christine de Pisan's *Cent balades* (around 1400). Kany traces the tradition into the fifteenth century, identifying first prose letters inserted into verse romances (Machaut, Froissart) or prose romances (Aeneas Silvius, the *Càrcel de Amor*); and then the sixteenth-century romances that were indebted to the Greek novels of late antiquity and the Byzantine period.

Kany pays little attention to the sixteenth-century *épître* genre, judging that, for example, the sonnet correspondences of the Pléiade poets "merely continue the tradition of such poetry" (*saluts,* Italian sonnets and French *ballades*) and "can be summarily dismissed with other forms of the letter that mark no advance over earlier achievements." It might well be the case that the sixteenth-century poetic letter forms played no significant role in the development of the epistolary novel; but the overwhelming popularity of this form in the first half of the century makes it impossible to ignore. Furthermore, the direction taken by the *épître amoureuse* in this period, and

---

31. Versini 1979, 10. With the exception of the Iamblicus which survives only in fragments, all the novels are available in translation in B. P. Reardon, ed. and trans., 1989. See also A. Lesky 1966, 857–70.

32. Alfred Jeanroy, however, denies all classical influence on the troubadours; see Kany, 13.

in particular by those *épîtres* conceived as close imitations of Ovid's *Heroides* and their replies, does in fact prefigure later developments in the epistolary novel.

According to Kany, the first 'novelistic' epistolary fictions were being produced during the very period that is the focus of this study. These texts came from Spain and Italy for the most part, but they were translated into French and enjoyed considerable success in France.[33] Octavien de Saint-Gelais translated into French verse Aeneas Silvius Piccolomini's *Historia de duobus amantibus,* one of the first and most successful examples of narrative by letters.[34] Versini stresses the importance of this work in the development of early novelistic forms in France: French romances incorporating epistolary elements in the sixteenth century—and in particular Helisenne de Crenne's *Les Angoisses douloureuses qui procèdent d'amours* (1538)—betray a threefold influence: Ovid's *Heroides,* Aeneas Silvius' *Eurialus and Lucretia* and Boccaccio's *Fiammetta* (Versini, 18). The fact that Saint-Gelais was also the author of the most prominent translation of the *Heroides* is significant: he binds together the origins of two traditions whose later developments were to be intertwined: the Ovidian *épître amoureuse* and the continuous epistolary narrative that was to reach its height in the eighteenth century.

Bernard Bray singles out another important influence on the epistolary tradition after the sixteenth century: the vernacular letter-writing manuals that began to be produced at the end of the century and then in greater numbers in the seventeenth century, influenced by the Italian manuals and their obsessions with artifice and aesthetic propriety.[35] These manuals did not, for the most part, find their model love letters in the courtly chronicles, but in literature: the three main sources were Ovid's *Heroides,* the letters of Heloise and Abelard, and Italian letters by such authors as Isabella Andréini (13–14). Interestingly, Kany considers collections of fictional love letters such as Parabosco's *Lettere amorose* (translated into French in 1546) almost as letter writing manuals themselves, claiming that the letters in which the lady responds to her suitor "may have been intended as model replies" (59). From this perspective, similar collections of letters by French poets might also be seen as letter writing manuals of a sort: Kany mentions the *Epistres veneriennes* (1532) of Michel d'Amboise in this context, as does Bernard

---

33. The first epistolary novels proper were Juan de Segura's *Processo de cartas de amores* (1548) and Pasqualigo's *Lettere amorose* (1563). See Kany, 69–75 and Versini, 21ff. These were the only *romans par lettres* of that period.

34. On this translation and its influence see, for example, B. Bray 1977, 136–37.

35. Bray, 1967. The influence of the Latin humanist letter manuals will be examined in more detail in the next chapter.

Bray, along with d'Amboise's *Secret d'amours* (1542). Also of interest is the series of prose letters contained in the *Jardin amoureux* (1530–35) of Christophe de Barrouso. Later in the century, texts such as Etienne Pasquier's *Lettres amoureuses* (which first appeared in 1555) begin to blur the boundaries between the different modes of letter writing, *recueils,* manuals, and the epistolary narrative fictions that later developed into the epistolary novel.[36]

The link between the literary fiction of the love letter and letter writing manuals intended for practical use demonstrates that, in the sixteenth century, the boundary between literature and discourses of everyday communication was not well defined. As Laurent Versini observes:

> La démarcation se fait mal entre lettres fictives, lettres authentiques dont les préoccupations évidentes de style, le souci d'un public, voire une dose certaine d'artifice, font de la littérature, lettres morales, recueils de modèles épistolaires . . . et lettres en vers parmi lesquelles . . . les héroïdes tiennent une place capitale. (9)

> It is difficult to make the distinction between fictional letters, authentic letters made literature by their obvious stylistic concerns, awareness of audience, or by a certain degree of artifice, moral letters, collections of epistolary models . . . and verse letters, among which . . . "heroides" feature prominently.

In his study of the development of epistolary fiction from the sixteenth century onward, Thomas Beebee mentions Ortensio Lando's popular letter collections, the *Lettere di molte valorose donne* (1549), and the *Lettere della molto illustre Sig. La Sra Donna Lucretia Gonzaga* (1552), both of which purported to reproduce the private correspondence of contemporary personalities.[37] But both collections were, it is thought, composed entirely by Lando himself, ventriloquizing the female subject just as Ovid had done in the *Heroides.*[38] These letters cannot be said to be authentic records of sixteenth-century epistolary practice in the feminine mode, but at the same time cannot be reduced to the status of a literary *divertissement.* As Beebee comments: "The letters of Lucretia, whether real or fictional, escape the Ovidian model and present their author as a social agent acting on and interacting with every level of her culture" (112). By this stage, the highly artificial discourse

---

36. Bray 1977.
37. Beebee 1999, 109–12.
38. Mireille Huchon (267) makes the connection between Ortensio Lando and Maurice Scève, with Lando as a possible model or inspiration for the publication of the works of Louise Labé.

of Ovid's fictional heroines has been integrated into everyday social contexts. In the *Heroides,* Ovid had created a genre that remains "antigeneric and anticanonical," claims Linda Kauffman: "it engulfs and is engulfed by other languages and other cultures, and it assimilates other genres"; it brings about a "blurring of the boundaries between letter and literature."[39]

Letter Writing Fictions in the Sixteenth Century

The boundary between the rhetoricity of poetic fictions and the practically applied rhetoric of everyday life was always a permeable one for the humanists; and the dividing line was even less sharply defined in the domain of letter writing.[40]

Various letter-writing traditions interacted with the *Heroides* tradition in the sixteenth century. The Ciceronian-Petrarchan-Erasmian tradition of the 'familiar' prose letter, and the Senecan tradition that developed somewhat later, were central to humanist self-fashioning.[41] In the familiar prose letter the humanists constructed a space in which to pit fictions of the self against fictions of the other, a space in which allies could be recognized and enemies excluded, as the runaway success of such collections as the *Epistolae virorum obscurum* (1515–17) demonstrates. The Latin Horatian-Ovidian tradition (by which is meant the Ovid of the *Tristia* and the *Epistulae ex Ponto*) of the personal or satirical epistle influenced the development of the moral or familiar *épître* in the vernacular. The love *épître* owed much to medieval lyric forms such as the *salut d'amour;* it became associated in particular with the Marotic tradition.

One feature of the *Heroides* which might account for its popularity in the sixteenth century is the work's overt rhetoricity, the prominence of the role of language in the construction of character. The construction of the self in the text, the fashioning of a persona and the way that the role of the addressee just as much as the role of the writer are defined by language are concerns common to all types of letter writing in the early modern period. In the case of the *Heroides,* the distinction between the voice of the author and the assumed persona of the poet is at its clearest. In Latin poetry this distinction already exists to some extent in subjective elegy and in the Horatian

---

39. Kauffman 1986, 32, 34.
40. On the tensions between the concepts of 'private' and 'public' when applied to early modern epistolography, see Rice Henderson 2002, 17–38.
41. See, in particular, Heinrich Dörrie's discussion (1966, 51–52) of Petrarch's adaptation of the *Heroides* form to contemporary political themes.

and Ovidian epistle, but is much more prominent as performance in the *Heroides*. There is a progression in Ovid's elegiac poetry from the relatively consistent and self-identical subject which speaks in the *Amores* toward the formal duplicity which is the discursive basis of the *Heroides*. As Howard Jacobson comments:

> When Ovid turned from the *Amores* to the *Heroides*, he was again working within the framework of traditional subjective elegy while rejecting it at the same time. For here the dichotomy between the subjective 'I' and the poet, merely implicit in the *Amores*, becomes a necessary function of the form. (6)

Far from being simply the concern of modern critics steeped in narratology, the work's 'duplicity' has interested readers since the Middle Ages. The writer of an *accessus* to a twelfth-century manuscript edition of the *Heroides* makes the distinction between the authorial *intentio* and that of the letter-writer herself: "In qualibet epistula habetur duplex intentio actoris et mittentis"[42] (In each of the epistles there is a double intention, of the author and of the sender). Here, the primary focus is not on the rhetorical dimension of Ovid's text, but on the edifying moral content of the work, its suitability for use as a pedagogical tool. However, the doubleness that underwrites every utterance in the text—the basis for much of the linguistic ingenuity and wit in the *Heroides*—will not escape the attention of Renaissance writers better disposed to the rhetorical subtleties of Ovid's work.

The *Heroides* in the French Renaissance: Épître, Élégie, Epistula, Elegia

Establishing to what degree the text of Ovid's *Heroides* is a presence in the French verse epistle is no simple task. The *épître* form, which in practice overlapped greatly with the *élégie*, was capable of incorporating diverse poetic traditions: whether the verse epistle constituted a self-contained genre at all in the sixteenth century is arguable. Even within the more narrowly defined category of the *épître amoureuse*, it is difficult to distinguish all of the thematic, structural, and rhetorical features it has in common with Ovid's

---

42. Cited by R. J. Hexter 1986, 163. Some medieval commentators showed more interest than others in the rhetorical dimension of the text. Hexter gives an account of different applications of the 'duplex intentio' scheme in three commentaries dating from the twelfth and thirteenth centuries (Hexter 2002, 212–38).

collection.[43] A cursory survey of the major poetic theorists of the sixteenth century[44] reveals that the genre was—for the most part—neither well defined nor well thought of. Sebillet has difficulty separating the *épître* from the *élégie,* but he does state that the *élégie* is simply a love letter in verse (LeBlanc, 46–47). In the *Deffence et illustration de la langue françoyse,* Du Bellay mentions the vernacular *épître* genre only to reject it on the grounds that it is too closely identified with the Marotic tradition:

> Quand aux epistres, ce n'est un poëme qui puisse grandement enrichir nostre vulgaire, pource qu'elles sont voluntiers de choses familieres et domestiques, si tu ne les voulois faire à l'immitation d'elegies, comme Ovide, ou sentencieuses et graves, comme Horace.[45]

> As for epistles, this type of poem could not enrich our vernacular in any great measure, because they are generally about familiar and domestic matters, unless you wanted to make them in imitation of elegies, as Ovid does, or sententious and serious, as Horace does.

It seems likely that here Du Bellay is referring to Ovid's exile poetry and not to the *Heroides*. Scollen, however (15), sees a contradiction in Du Bellay's simultaneous rejection of the *épître amoureuse* and recommendation of Ovid's *élégies* (*Heroides*). In any case, it is clear that despite the best efforts of sixteenth-century authors of *arts poétiques,* the questions of genre, influence, and correct practice remained confused.

Within the heroical epistle there are several variables in subject matter and treatment which it will be useful to outline here. First, considerations of voice and gender: who is writing or speaking in imitations of the *Heroides,* and how does this choice relate to Ovid's text? The question of gendered

---

43. For an attempt to define the verse epistle from both synchronic and diachronic perspectives, see Y. LeBlanc 1995. Daniela Dalla Valle focuses more specifically on the vernacular 'lettre héroïque'; her article concludes that by the seventeenth century (*pace* Roger Duchêne) the 'lettre héroïque' had emerged as a well-defined subgenre, albeit one that had developed quite far beyond its Ovidian origins. For a brief survey of Ovidian influence on the *épître* genre as practiced by the 'rhétoriqueur' poets, see Joole 1997, 47–53. Joole discerns a specific influence on the French *épître* genre in the Italian 'epistola eroica,' as practiced by Galeotto. The 'epistola eroica' derived from the *Heroides* via O. di Montichiello's fourteenth-century translation (48–49).

44. Undertaken in more detail by C. M. Scollen 1967, 13–17; LeBlanc, 44–58.

45. Du Bellay 1948, 115–18. To counter Du Bellay's claim that the *épître* cannot contribute to the enrichment of the vernacular, the author of the *Quintil Horatian* cites, among others, the work of Octavien de Saint-Gelais (whose verse translations of the *Heroides* contributed in large part to the popularity of the *épître* genre in France), and of 'Philistine' (by which he presumably means the *Heroides* imitations of André de La Vigne, discussed below). See Du Bellay, ed. Chamard 1948, n. 2, 116.

discourses is closely bound up with the issues of fictionality and dialogism mentioned above; it also seems to fit neatly with another generic consideration which is discussed by LeBlanc:

> The *Heroides* inspired two major epistolary paradigms in French poetry which we will refer to as the narrative and the lyric. The epistles in the narrative group present specific individuals from unique backgrounds writing under singular conditions to their absent lovers.... The lyric group transposes the basic elements of the *Heroides* into a more familiar, native idiom which echoes the style and many of the themes of the traditional French love lyric. (176)

In this scheme, the 'narrative' group is mainly concerned with the abandoned female lover—and is therefore most closely related to the original *Heroides*[46]—whereas the 'lyric' group speaks in a predominantly male voice, removing in large part the textual 'duplicity' which underlies Ovid's epistles. LeBlanc goes on to define her 'lyric' group more fully:

> These epistles set the correspondent-addressee relationship within the intimate, subjective world of the emotions. The correspondents are not related in any significant way to the spatio-temporal context; instead they exist and express themselves within the universal, timeless realm of the heart. (183)

This group owes as much to medieval courtly lyric as it does to the *Heroides*, and, LeBlanc argues, is the model for the genre that will later be called the *élégie marotique*.

The division of texts according to the scheme that equates narrative to the female subject and lyric to the male subject holds true for the most part. There are, however, many exceptions, not least of which would be the male-authored letters in the second part of Ovid's own work and the many replies inspired by letters 1–15, all of which would fall into the narrative group. The lyric group, moreover, would have to include Louise Labé's *Elégie II*, a poem that presents shifting perspectives on the gendered voice.[47] *Heroides*-inspired texts also straddle the distinction made by Henri Guy

---

46. This is not to suggest that the *Heroides* themselves are primarily narrative poems. As Marilynn Desmond observes, "... the *Heroides* are rhetorical rather than narrative poetry"; they deploy "rhetorical commentary on past events which have already been recorded and represented in other texts" (1993, 60). On the rhetoricity of the *Heroides*, see chapter 2.

47. See Silver for a discussion of this poem in the light of Ovid's *Heroides*, and in particular the Sappho epistle.

between 'artificial' and 'natural' epistles.[48] The 'épître naturelle' would be one in which the poet writes in his own name, addressing friends or courting a lover. The 'épître artificielle' designates a letter with a mythological or historical subject, or an abstraction or dead person addressing an individual or generalized audience.

Another consideration in distinguishing different degrees of proximity to Ovid's text in *Heroides*-type poems is the *mise-en-scène* of the act of letter writing. This is of significance only for the 'narrative' texts which are grounded in a spatial and temporal context. In the *Heroides* a knowledge of the mythological context is essential for an understanding of the rhetorical features of the text: the perlocutionary function of each of the letters, the dramatic irony, the subjective manipulations of events and all the textual effects which rely on the differing perspectives of writer and reader. The objective structures of myth are subjected to a process of internalization, in which past, present, and future all become functions of the emotional perspective.[49] This textual dynamic is not present in all imitations of the *Heroides:* differences in contextualization produce very different effects. The immediate context which occasions the writing of a letter might be either a well-known myth (classical or, as in the case of Marot's *Epistre de Maguelonne,* domestic); an obscure or unknown narrative framework (as in La Vigne's *Epistres d'Ovide*); or a setting which is historical rather than mythical (Macé de Villebresme's *Epistre de Cleriande la Romayne à Reginus son concitoyen*).[50] In each of these cases the narrative treatment will be very different.

Other formal elements which may be present in all verse *épîtres* are those "epistolary-enhancing elements" examined by LeBlanc (9–58). These include the superscription and subscription, which stand outside the main body of the text ("Penelope écrit à Ulysses"; "Fin de l'Epître"), and the salutation and complimentary close (not so complimentary in some cases) contained within the text. In addition to these we find references to the act of letter writing or to expected response, and references to the spatiotemporal context. Also, specifically within the context of *Heroides* imitations, the inclusion of a self-penned epitaph is a common feature, as the heroine imagines her own death (as in *Heroides* 2, 7, and 14).

Many of Marot's *épîtres* are of the moral or familiar Horatian type, rather than the Ovidian elegiac type. Some of his output, however, bears certain

---

48. For this distinction, see C. E. Mayer's introduction to *Les Epîtres / par Clément Marot: édition critique* (1958), 32.

49. On the role of perspective see Jacobson, 349–62.

50. On the differences in treatment necessitated by the extraction of narrative from the framework of myth, see LeBlanc, 183.

traces of a link to the *Heroides,* often through allusion or, occasionally, direct imitation (on the *Epistre de Maguelonne,* see below). Jean Bouchet's *Epistres morales et familieres* (1545), similarly, seem to take Horace as their model more obviously than Ovid: they are "sentencieuses et graves" more than they are elegiac. The *Heroides* are not particularly influential on Bouchet's work.[51]

Michel d'Amboise (the self-styled "esclave fortuné") and Christophe de Barrouso have already been mentioned in the context of *épître* collections that furnish model letters. Other poets to publish similar collections of *épîtres* in the same period include Gilles Corrozet, and Gilles d'Aurigny (in *Le Tuteur d'amour,* 1546). These collections generally mix pieces written in the author's own persona (in the 'lyric vein') with more 'artificial' pieces written in the person of a fictional character. The latter type of letter or letter sequence uses for the most part contemporary rather than historical or mythological situations, and reduces background narrative to a bare minimum: this type is not to be included in the 'narrative' group. Charles Fontaine, who was later to publish an important translation of the *Heroides,* also produced a large number of works of this type, for example in *La Fontaine d'amour* of 1545 and in *Les Ruisseaux de Fontaine* of 1555. The latter work contains, among others, an "Epître philosophant sur la bonne amour, à une dame," an exchange of letters between the poet and a fan of his, "E. H.," as well as others addressed to real people.

Helisenne de Crenne's *Epistres invectives* (1539), which consists of prose letters rather than verse *épîtres,* along with Louise Labé's *élégie,* represent an interesting case, in that they might be broadly defined as belonging to the 'lyric,' personal grouping, but at the same time involve an overt construction of 'artificial' poetic identity modeled on Ovid's heroines. We are touching upon issues of performative identity and *écriture féminine* which are too complex to be dealt with satisfactorily here, especially in the light of recent scholarship which proposes that Labé's works were an elaborate hoax perpetrated by a group of male poets headed by Olivier de Magny and Maurice Scève. Mireille Huchon's claim that Labé's works were in fact written by male poets, if true, aligns Labé's elegies yet more closely with the *Heroides* as works in which the feminine voice is ventriloquized by a male author. The hoax, Huchon claims, took its cue from Marot, and involved many of the poets I have mentioned in connection with the *épître* genre and the *Heroides* (most notably Charles Fontaine).[52] Whether or not Labé's

---

51. But to the contrary, see Morisset 1934, 143ff, for a brief account of possible echoes of the *Heroides* in Bouchet's *épîtres.*

52. It seems unlikely, however, that Charles Fontaine was involved in the composition of Labé's

works were indeed composed by male poets, it is nevertheless instructive to remark what Huchon identifies as a particular "Lyon tradition" of male poets ventriloquizing women: "une tradition lyonnaise . . . des hommes qui font entendre une voix féminine."[53]

Philibert Bugnyon also had a hand in the publication of Labé's works; in this connection his 1557 *Erotasmes de Phidie et Gelasine* is worth mentioning, chiefly because it begins with an *épître* from the poet, the self-styled "Phidie" to his beloved Gelasine, concluding with a request for a reply. The rest of the book is really a sequence of love poems in the style of Scève's *Délie*.

Du Bellay himself, despite his prescriptions in the *Deffence,* wrote several epistolary love elegies that could easily be characterized as *épîtres amoureuses,* two of which appear in the *Divers Jeux rustiques*. These poems are certainly not of the type recommended in the *Deffence,* and they do not resemble the *Heroides* in subject or execution. The unusual case of his translation-imitation of *Heroides* 7 will be discussed at length in chapter 4. Ronsard, for his part, composed at least one *épître* closely modeled on the *Heroides* type, as well as on *Ars Amatoria* 125–42: "Les parolles que dist Calypson" (1569).

François Habert, author of the Christian *Epistres héroïdes* (1551), had earlier published several collections of *épîtres*. In the *Jeunesse du Banny de Liesse* of 1541 ("le Banny de Liesse" being Habert's own poetic persona), letters addressed by the poet himself to patrons, friends, and mistresses are interwoven with pieces based in more artificial situations. The sequel, entitled *Suytte du Banny de Liesse,* published around the same time, contains more of the same; it also includes an *épître* written in the person of a mythological character, Oenone: this piece, clearly directly modeled on the *Heroides* (Habert calls it "tant par imitation d'Ovide que de l'invention de l'auteur") brings us closer to our immediate field of inquiry.

Elégies (as Huchon implies): Michèle Clément (December 2004, 65–77) demonstrates that it is Octavien de Saint-Gelais's translation of the *Heroides,* and not Fontaine's 1552 version, whose influence can be traced in Labé's *Elégies.*

53. Huchon mentions a number of works in this tradition (267–68): the 1547 Lyon collection entitled *Déploration de Vénus sur la mort du bel Adonis* included several poems written in the person of women; in the same year the *Opuscules d'amour, par Heroët, La Borderie, et autres divins Poètes,* which contained poems relating to the so-called "querelle des amyes," saw Héroët write in the voice of "La Parfaicte Amye," La Borderie in the voice of "L'Amye de Court," and Charles Fontaine as "La Contre amye de Court." The 1545 *Panegyric des demoyselles de Paris sur les neuf Muses* included several female 'complaintes.' Gilles d'Aurigny's *Tuteur d'Amour,* mentioned above, contains several poems written in the person of wronged women; Etienne Forcadel's 1548 *Le chant des Seraines* includes among others a "Chant triste de Medée abandonée de son aymé Jason"; Pontus de Tyard in his *Oeuvres,* which were published in 1573, had an elegy "d'une dame enamourée d'une autre dame."

Chiefly narrative *épîtres* which set mythological and fictional characters in outlandish situations are usually more easily identifiable as being modeled on the *Heroides*;[54] they are less common than the more broadly defined types discussed above. Jean Lemaire de Belges is one of the authors of the early sixteenth century most clearly interested in imitating the *Heroides*. His *Epîtres de l'amant vert* (1509), for example, betray a strong Ovidian character even if the narrative setting is not derived directly from the *Heroides*.[55] His *Illustrations de Gaule* includes a prose version of Oenone's epistle, *Heroides* 5 (Ch. XIII livre II). Of particular interest, too, among works directly modeled on the *Heroides*, are the *Epistres d'Ovide* of André de La Vigne, four letters composed around 1497 and first published in 1534 in the same volume as Octavien de Saint-Gelais's translation of the *Heroides*.[56] These letters use quasi-mythological characters and situations obviously intended to emulate those used by Ovid in the *Heroides*, if a little more given to extravagance. If Ovid's poems had been noteworthy for their lack of respect for verisimilitude, La Vigne's compositions went a step further. The first epistle, penned by an Arabian princess, Philistine, is addressed to her lover, Elinus. When her father discovered their affair, Philistine was thrown into prison, where she befriended a lizard, and Elinus was captured and killed. It is revealed that at the time of writing Philistine is floating on a raft in mid-ocean with only the corpse of Elinus (to whom she is writing the letter) as company. Even more bizarre is the conceit that Philistine is writing her complaint using her tears as ink and Elinus' body as paper.

Marot's "Epître de Maguelonne" (1517–18) would also fall into this category of narrative epistles that use legendary settings and characters.[57] In the poem Marot establishes Maguelonne's connection with the Ovidian heroines first through allusion and then by naming them directly, as when Maguelonne recalls her lover comparing their courtship to that of Paris and Helen. She later styles herself as "la seconde Médée," with Pierre taking on

---

54. An exception: the *Epistres héroiques amoureuses aux Muses* of Ferrand de Bez (1579) are broadly speaking mythological in subject matter, since they are letters addressed by the poet to the nine Muses, but they are nonnarrative in execution. They are effectively moral letters. Despite their title, they do not bear a resemblance to the *Heroides*.

55. On the hybrid character of this text, which intermingles fiction with the real world of the writer, combining an Ovidian sensibility with the conventions of medieval courtly lyric, see LeBlanc 193–95.

56. See F. Lestringant 1988, 65–83. Patrick Joole (49) suggests that La Vigne was influenced by Andrelini's *Livia*.

57. Morisset (150–51) senses an affinity between the "waking-up scene" as described in La Vigne's "Amazone" letter and a similar scene in Marot's "Maguelonne" (152). Both are, of course, based on Ariadne's awakening at *Heroides* 10.9–10.

the role of "l'aultre Jason." The *rondeau* with which she ends her letter suggests a greater debt to the Dido of *Heroides* 7 than to Virgil's creation:[58]

Comme Dido, qui moult se courrouça,
Lors qu'Eneas seule la delaissa
En son Païs: tout ainsi Maguelonne
Mena son dueil: comme tressaincte; et bonne,
En l'hospital toute sa fleur passa.
Nulle fortune oncques ne la blessa:
Toute constance en son cueur amassa,
Mieulx esperant: et ne fut point felonne,
Comme Dido.

Aussi celluy, qui toute puissance a,
Renvoya cil, qui au boys la laissa,
Où elle estoit: mais quoy qu'on en blasonne,
Tant eut de dueil, que le Monde s'estonne,
Que d'un cousteau son cueur ne transpersa,
Comme Dido.

Like Dido, who was greatly angered when Aeneas left her all alone in her land: so too Maguelonne spent her mourning: most holy and good, she passed all her youth in a convent. From that time on no ill fortune touched her: she filled her heart with constancy, hoping for better: and was in no way wicked, like Dido.

And so He who is all powerful sent back the man who abandoned her in the wood, to the place where she was: but however much they sing her praises, she was so sorrowful, that the world marvels that she did not run through her heart a knife, like Dido.

HEINRICH DÖRRIE's bibliographical study *Der heroische Brief* lists a number of neo-Latin imitations of the *Heroides* by European humanists. Such imitations either took the form of epistolary elegies, such as those of Petrus Lotichius Secundus (*Helicana Mario suo* and *Eadem ad eundem* [1551]),[59]

---

58. The figure of Dido was of course the most prominent of all the heroines in the literature of the Middle Ages and the Renaissance. Between Ovid and Marot there stretches an important tradition of texts written from Dido's point of view: for a brief list, with references, see Desmond, 67, n. 11.

59. These poems are not, however, mythological in setting. The 'realistic' setting of an epistle written by a concerned wife to her traveling husband is perhaps to be aligned more closely with Prop-

or they took the form of poems neither epistolary nor elegiac, but which borrowed situations and characters from the *Heroides*. Joachim Camerarius's Oenone complaint (1568), written in hexameters rather than elegiac couplets, and closer in style to a Virgilian eclogue than an Ovidian elegy, fits into the latter category.[60]

The above examples are isolated poems: they do not lead one to assume any particular, sustained interest in Ovid's *Heroides* on the part of the imitator; but several authors published entire collections of *Heroides* imitations, among them Eobanus Hessus, Claude d'Espence, and Mark Alexander Boyd. In the domain of Latin-language imitations of the *Heroides*, there is a preponderance of two types, which might deserve to be called subgenres: the Christian adaptation and the reply poem. The form of *Heroides* imitation practiced most widely in Latin during the sixteenth century was the reply poem, penned in the person of the heroes to whom Ovid's heroines had originally addressed their letters. The reply poem will be discussed more fully in chapter 5.

The epistolary form of the *Heroides*, with its perceived emphasis on suasive and hortatory rhetoric, lent itself well to the presentation of exemplary narratives of the lives of famous women. The Christianization of the amatory discourse of Ovid's heroines had begun long before with Heloise and Baudri of Bourgueil's Constance, but it was the sixteenth century that saw the first poetic epistles written in the person of Christian heroines, known as *Heroides sacrae*. The formal structures of Ovid's text were thought by many humanist authors to be able to accommodate sacred subjects, and to be adaptable to devotional purposes.

The German Protestant author Eobanus Hessus was the first to adapt the heroine's epistle to sacred themes in his 1514 *Heroidum Christianarum epistolae*. Heinrich Dörrie sees a precursor to this work in Mantuan's *Parthenices*, epic poems in which the Carmelite had reacted against the tendency of works such as Boccaccio's *Clarae mulieres* to present pagan heroines alongside Christian saints as models for virtuous conduct. For Mantuan, only the celestial love of Christian martyrs, and never the worldly love of the tragic heroines of pagan antiquity, was a suitably exemplary subject for a heroine's narrative.

Eobanus Hessus agreed; indeed, he went further. Dörrie (369–74) charts the effects of the changing attitudes of the Reformation on his work and its

---

ertius 4.3 and with the elegiac *propemptikon* poem generally than with the *Heroides* specifically.

60. See H. Dörrie 1968, 108, on the fusion of Ovidian subject matter and Virgilian form and style: "Kurz, die Grenzen der imitatio im strengen Sinne sind erreicht" (In short, the limits of *imitatio* in the strict sense are reached).

revision: Protestant antipathy to non-Scriptural sources meant that certain stories were no longer suitable subjects. In 1532 Hessus reissued the work, having removed several of the more dubious letters, rearranging the collection into sections to reflect the poems' proximity to the truth of the Gospel ("Heroides historicae," "mixtae," and "fabulosae").

The work went through several editions, and the revision was published in Paris in 1546, ensuring that it reached a French readership.[61] Indeed, it prompted at least one work in the vernacular, François Habert's *Les epistres heroides, tres salutaires, pour servir d'exemple a toute ame fidele* (1550). Habert was a popular and prolific poet, and this work proved successful enough to be reprinted several times over the next decade. Dörrie (384) notes that Habert's "Epistre de Dieu le Pere a la vierge Marie" owes much to Eobanus Hessus both in its execution as well as in the choice of subject. In fact, Habert's poem is more like a translation than an imitation, a fairly thorough—though unacknowledged—rendering into French decasyllables of Eobanus Hessus's opening epistle.

Around the same time another Latin work in this tradition by a Northern European author was gaining an audience in France. Petrus Nannius (Peter Nanninck), a Catholic, published his *Dialogismi Heroinarum* in Louvain, 1541. In the same year it was reprinted by Chrétien Wechel in Paris, and, like Hessus's work, it too prompted a French translation.[62] Amédée Polet[63] observes that despite their title, Nannius's *Dialogismi* are closer in form and theme to tragic monologues than to the Lucianic or Erasmian dialogue. The work, being in prose and not in epistolary form, does not quite belong to the category of *Heroides sacrae;* but Polet characterizes the monologues as "poèmes en prose," and they have in common with the Ovidian epistle a particular interest in the emotions and individual psychologies of the heroines. Unlike Hessus, Nannius does not exclude non-Christian models: of the five heroines, two are from Roman history (Lucretia and Camma), two from the Old Testament (Susanna and Judith), and one a Christian saint (Agnes). Nannius published two more *Dialogismi* in 1550, written in the persons of Saint Agatha and Saint Lucy. These are more obviously concerned with the themes that were to motivate the heroines portrayed in Claude d'Espence's *Sacrarum Heroidum liber:* the defense of female chastity, a steadfast resistance to paganism and to sex, and a commitment to Christian martyrdom.

---

61. *Heroidum libri tres, nuper ab authore recogniti* (Paris, 1546).
62. *Dialogismi Heroinarum* (Paris: Chrétien Wechel, 1541); *Cinq dialogismes, ou Délibérations de 5 nobles Dames, à sçavoir Lucrèce, Susanne, Judith, Agnès, Camma Galathienne; traduits du Latin de Petrus Nannius par Jean Millet* (Paris: Arnoul l'Angelier, 1550).
63. Polet 1936, 43.

By the time the Catholic theologian Claude d'Espence issued his own *Heroides sacrae* in Paris—the preface is dated December 1563—he was writing between two traditions. On the one hand his work was written in the shadow of two prominent precursor texts, one of which had been written from within a Protestant tradition; and on the other he was overseeing the beginnings of a new kind of Catholic poetry, which was to flourish in the post-tridentine context of 'feminized' devotion and meditative practices. What began as a Protestant genre would come eventually to be associated with the Counter-Reformation; Claude d'Espence, who was active in the development of the new devotional poetry, stands at the turning point.[64] In the seventeenth century the heroine's epistle form appealed especially to Jesuit authors (see Dörrie, 389ff).

Andrée Thill suggests that Christian adaptations of *Heroides* were often little more than superficial formal imitations.[65] Nevertheless, such adaptations can function as something more than a flattening-out of the complexities of Ovid's text: the Christian appropriation of the heroines' amatory discourse broadens out the field of meaning and linguistic exchange. The elegiac lexicon of epistolary heroinism is given a new bias in its alignment with the rhetoric of devotion, martyrdom, and religious ecstasy. Further work remains to be done on the link between the early *Heroides sacrae* and the emergence of a 'feminized' devotional literature in the vernacular. Catherine d'Amboise, the aunt and patroness of Michel d'Amboise, composed before 1542 a collection of *Heroides*-influenced devotional poems (see below, chapter 5). There is a connection, too, between Claude d'Espence and female devotional poetry: he maintained a close literary friendship with the Dominican nun and poet Anne de Marquets.[66] A full treatment of the origins and influence of Christian imitations of the *Heroides* is the work of a separate project.

Conclusion

Nowhere was the sixteenth-century renewal of interest in Ovid more pronounced than in the publication and reception of the *Heroides* in France.

---

64. D'Espence, a moderate reformer and proponent of Gallicanism, was one of the *moyenneurs* at the 1561 Poissy colloquium. A further contribution from a Northern author to the *Heroides sacrae* genre came in 1574, when Andreas Alenus published at Louvain a lengthy collection of seventy-seven epistles written from the point of view of biblical and saintly personages.

65. Thill 2003, 368.

66. See Gary Ferguson's introduction to the critical edition of her *Sonets spirituels* (1997).

Even the *Metamorphoses*, a perennially popular work valued throughout the Middle Ages for its encyclopedic mythological content and for the facility with which it lent itself to allegorical interpretation, did not enjoy the same degree of success. Between 1499 and 1580 forty-two editions of the *Heroides* were printed in France; this figure, moreover, does not include complete editions of Ovid's amatory works (*Amores, Heroides, Ars Amatoria, Remedia Amoris*).[67] In the same period the *Metamorphoses* was printed thirty-five times in its entirety. Admittedly, this does not include editions of extracts or of prose paraphrases of the work, but judging by the core criterion of editions printed, the *Heroides* was at least as widely read as Ovid's most famous work.

The body of literature which grew up around the *Heroides*—translations and imitations both vernacular and neo-Latin—was, moreover, considerable, as Heinrich Dörrie showed in his classic pan-European study *Der heroische Brief*. Interestingly, though, the rise in popularity of the text as an educational tool within the humanist curriculum does not seem to correlate with the rate of production of imitations. Henri Lamarque asserts:

> En ce qui concerne les *Héroïdes*, le succès, moins prompt à se déclarer [que celui des *Métamorphoses*], ne se démentira jamais, sans nul fléchissement notable (26 éditions s'échelonnent de 1529 à 1588). Si les *Métamorphoses* dans le premier tiers du siècle ont été l'ouvrage d'Ovide le plus lu, la tendance est inversée ensuite au profit des *Héroïdes*. (24)

> As far as the *Heroides* are concerned, their success, slower to become evident [than that of the *Metamorphoses*], would never be challenged, with no noticeable falling away (26 editions spread out from 1529 to 1588). If the *Metamorphoses* in the first third of the century was the most widely read of Ovid's works, this trend is subsequently reversed in favor of the *Heroides*.

Ann Moss, on the other hand, comments that, although the text remained prominent in education throughout the period, its popularity as a source for literary imitation was largely confined to the first half of the sixteenth century:

> In spite of this [familiarity of school editions], there are not many direct imitations of the *Heroides* in French in the years between 1549 and 1590, perhaps because the work had so obviously shaped the fashions of the earlier

---

67. Source: H. Lamarque 1981, 18.

years of the century that it had become identified with an outmoded sensibility, and more especially with the despised genre of the 'epistre amoureuse.'[68]

Chief among the reasons for this decline was the association of the *épître* genre with the *marotiques:* imitation of the *Heroides* played an important part in the formation of the *élégie*,[69] a genre invented by Marot and therefore *infra dignitatem* for the Pléiade. A cursory examination of *Heroides*-related texts being published in France reveals a distinct concentration of material in the first half of the century.

It is certainly the case that at this stage the *Metamorphoses* had overtaken the *Heroides* in popularity, with many more editions and commentaries being published. *Heroides* imitations, however, continue to be published up to the end of the century, and beyond. As a model text for vernacular French poets, it may well have fallen out of favor, but in the sphere of neo-Latin literature it persisted, probably because the Latin elegiac epistle did not have the same negative associations as the French *épître*. For that reason the scope of this study extends beyond the period in which the *Heroides* were at their most influential (1500–49) to take in texts—principally in Latin—up to the close of the century.

The foregoing survey of *Heroides*-influenced texts in the sixteenth century gives a partial impression of the extent and diversity of the material under scrutiny. It is beyond the scope of this study to give a full account of the presence of Ovid's text in sixteenth-century literature; such an account might begin with the narrative, artificial type of verse epistle whose setting is mythological, historical, or religious, before taking in the nonnarrative, 'natural' or lyric type of verse epistle, the prose letter, proto-novelistic forms, and so on. It is not my intention in the chapters that follow to pursue a detailed analysis of specific points of contact between Ovid's text and the various manifestations of the verse epistle. Rather, I intend to examine the treatments of the *Heroides* that shaped possibilities for reading the text in sixteenth-century France, by limiting my focus chiefly to theoretical works, manuals, commentaries, translations, and to a particular mode of imitation, the reply poem.

---

68. Moss 1982, 14.
69. Scollen, 17.

CHAPTER 2

Uses of the *Heroides* in Education

The letter, like the dialogue, should abound in glimpses of character. It may be said that everybody reveals his own soul in his letters. In every other form of composition it is possible to discern the writer's character, but in none so clearly as in the epistolary.

Demetrius, *On Style,* 227

Il se mit aussitôt à transcrire cette première lettre d'amour; c'était une homélie remplie de phrases sur la vertu et ennuyeuse à périr; Julien eut le bonheur de s'endormir à la seconde page.

Stendhal, *Le Rouge et le noir*[1]

"More Rhetorician than Poet"

Seneca Rhetor gives an account of Ovid's rhetorical education under Arellius Fuscus. Seneca's pronouncement on Ovid's rhetorical proclivities is very often taken as alluding to the *Heroides*: "Ouidius nescit quod bene cessit relinquere" (Ovid is incapable of leaving off what has ended well). Perhaps most tellingly, Seneca relates that Ovid had little interest in *controversiae,* unless they were to do with ethics; and that he preferred *suasoriae,* because he did not like having to engage in argumentation: "Declamabat autem Naso raro controuersias et non nisi ethicas: libentius dicebat suasorias: molesta illi erat omnis argumentatio" (Ovid would perform *controuersiae* only rarely, and only those to do with character: he preferred to recite *suasoriae:* all kinds of argumentation he found tiresome).[2]

Suasoriae were the first kind of declamation practiced in rhetorical schools. Although modern critics have doubted that the *Heroides* owe much

---

1. "He immediately set about transcribing this first love letter; it was a homily stuffed with phrases about virtue, and deathly boring; Julien had the good fortune to fall asleep by the second page."
2. Quoted in Purser's introduction, xv, fn. 1.

to such declamatory exercises,[3] the text was certainly read in these terms in the sixteenth-century schoolroom. If the *Heroides* were originally composed by Ovid as rhetorical exercises of this kind, then it is only appropriate that they should, in turn, be recuperated as educational texts, models for schoolroom compositions. The *Heroides,* as we shall see, are studied and imitated by students at a very early stage of the humanist education.

L. P. Wilkinson reads the *Heroides* primarily in the context of the *ethopoeïa* exercise of the *paideia:* Ovid, the pupil of Arellius Fuscus, explores every facet of any given situation, and "proceeds to make every point that can be made." He introduces all the familiar *topoi,* and supplements them with motives. He analyses the situation and back-story of any given character, in search of rhetorical points to be scored. "It is they [the *Heroides*], no doubt, which have given Ovid the reputation of being more rhetorician than poet" (*Ovid Recalled,* 95ff).

Wilkinson's comment that "we may be fairly sure that his audience read these poems as connoisseurs of rhetoric" is as relevant to a sixteenth-century humanist context as it is to a first-century Augustan context. Sixteenth-century readers would certainly join with Wilkinson in appreciating "the terse, quotable aphorisms" and the "fine expressions of *ethos,*" and in admiring Ovid's "ingenious tricks" of language and dextrous manipulation of mythological and historical details. They would, however, part company with the judgment that "psychological subtlety is not one of the characteristic excellences of ancient literature" (97).

Since Wilkinson, the idea has been widespread in modern criticism that the *Heroides* demonstrate the failure of rhetoric when it is applied to emotional realities. Joseph Farrell, writing here about the Byblis of the *Metamorphoses,* casts the problem in terms of gendered rhetoric:

> Try as she might to follow Ovid's advice about the letter of seduction, she finds that this is an essentially masculine form, that the woman writer is not sufficiently duplicitous to carry it off; that her writerly gift is not persuasion, but rather exquisitely, even painfully accurate self-disclosure.[4]

A Renaissance audience would be more likely to see in them the failure of feminine logic, the inability of the emotional heroines to express themselves rhetorically without betraying their moral failings. Their fractured rhetoric

---

3. See Jacobson, 325, with references.
4. Farrell, 323.

is entirely symptomatic of their levity and fickleness of mind, and lack of emotional restraint, rather than a failure of language.[5]

Not all of the heroines' letters have the object of persuading the addressee to follow a particular course of action through concealed eloquence: in fact, Phaedra's is perhaps the only one that is a straightforward rhetorical exercise in persuasion. The object of Dido's letter, for example, is not to persuade at all. Jodocus Badius Ascensius makes this point in his commentary on *Heroides* 7: Dido's opening lines, comparing her writing to the final song of the swans on the banks of the Maeander, must be read as an answer to the hypothetical questions: why write, Dido, if you are certain and utterly resolved to kill yourself? Why sing as you die? This can be read as Dido explicitly stating from the outset that there is no rhetorical purpose to the letter. Of course, such a claim is not to be taken at face value. Every one of the letters employs suasive rhetoric in one way or another.

There is more to the poems of the *Heroides*, though, than suasive rhetoric: they are also narrative poems. Long sections of the work are narrative, as the heroine tells her story "in her own words." Much modern criticism, especially feminist criticism, emphasizes the narrative features of the work, the heroines' 'reclaiming' of their stories. But it must not be overlooked that the heroines' narration of past events, the rewriting of their own stories, is always a part of a wider rhetorical strategy of persuasion.[6] Sara H. Lindheim argues that the heroines do not in fact seize the opportunity to shape their narrative to their rhetorical purposes—although in developing the argument she shows that they do achieve a kind of empowerment through language in their "narrative fusion" with the beloved, and in their realization of feminine desire (*Mail and Female*, 14). Their rhetoric is often weak and ineffective. This leaves the way open for Ovid to 'reassert' his voice in the text. For

---

5. For a concise and well-researched account of Renaissance conceptions of woman in the spheres of theology, medicine, moral philosophy, and law, see Maclean 1980. Despite a slight tendency in the theological or mystical discourses to associate women with greater potential for virtue (longsuffering, humility, patience), the mass of women remain overwhelmingly associated with "weaker reason, stronger passion and greater inherent vice" (22). Although the Aristotelian account of the inherent inferiority of woman (woman as 'botched male') becomes discredited in the course of the sixteenth century, certain dualities always remain associated with sex difference: action/passivity, eloquence/silence, command/obedience (54). It is sometimes doubted by moral philosophers whether women, being passive and in possession only of "consilium invalidum et instabile" (weak and wavering judgement) (Aristotle, *Politics* 1.13), are even capable of moral action (50ff.).

6. Cf. Dalla Valle's comments on the 'lettre héroïque' in the sixteenth century: because the situations depicted, whether historical or literary in origin, are usually well known to the audience, "l'intérêt de ces lettres n'est presque jamais narratif, mais il est surtout rhétorique" (371) (the appeal of these letters is hardly ever narrative, but is above all rhetorical).

sixteenth-century readers a failure of the heroines' rhetoric is a triumph of Ovid's rhetoric (Phaedra): the author has been successful in persuading the reader of the wretchedness and hopelessness of the heroine's desire. The inverse does not prove true: triumph of the heroines' rhetoric is still a triumph of Ovid's rhetoric (Penelope): exemplary female conduct is endorsed by the male perspective.

We must also acknowledge that when sixteenth-century readers encounter references to the *Heroides* or *Epistulae heroidum,* it is understood in spite of the title that this includes the letters by male authors as well. Although controversy over the authorship of the double letters raged on, they were generally published alongside the single letters; they were not considered to constitute a separately published work produced by Ovid at a later point in his career, as they are today. The double letters do not conform to the *suasoria* model; from a formal point of view they are *controversiae.*[7] However, far from being mere exercises in argumentation on both sides of an issue, they interest readers as studies in psychology, moral philosophy, and gender differences. Although *a priori* distinctions are not made in humanist readings between the 'male' rhetoric of Paris, Leander, and Acontius and the 'female' rhetoric of the heroines, such distinctions often make themselves felt in rhetorical analyses of the text, where 'male' rhetoric is treated in purely analytical terms and 'female' rhetoric is treated in predominantly ethical terms.[8] In instructional texts where rhetoric is primarily instrumental, something to be employed to a specific end, the chief models are the seducers, the manipulators, the male voices, whose rhetoric can always be shown, in one way or another, to succeed. In texts where the focus is on edification, on exemplarity, the chief models are the wronged women, the foolish women, the wicked women, whose rhetoric can always be shown, in one way or another, to fail.[9] Indeed, to demonstrate the failure of the heroines'

---

7. See Ovid, ed. Kenney, 1996, 2, with references.

8. Patricia B. Phillippy stresses the importance of the *Heroides* as rhetorical models for young men making the transition from the domestic, female sphere to the male world of active engagement with public life (Phillippy 1998, 31).

9. A perplexing counterargument is advanced by Linda Kauffman, who suggests that, in Dido's case, "suicide is depicted as a threat, a rhetorical strategy she uses merely to persuade Aeneas to return.... She doesn't die at the end but remains alive, discoursing about her desire" (48). A more considered argument is advanced by Fulkerson, who asks what might happen if we imagine that the heroines *can* change the end of their stories ("if we do not assume that, where master narrative and heroine diverge, the latter must be getting it wrong," 6); this approach enables some particularly powerful readings. For two different perspectives on the heroines' taking control of their rhetorical self-representation as desiring subjects and objects of desire, see Spentzou (especially chapter 1, "Getting Down to Essentials?" 1–12); and Lindheim, 177–84. For the view that the "blatant rhetorical machinations" of Dido are to be read in the spirit of Ovidian wit, and that this irony works to

rhetoric is the avowed motivation for the composition of reply epistles by Ovid's imitators. Even when the letter is shown to have met with a degree of success (in that the recipient has undertaken to write back), the motive of the respondent is always to break down and contain the feminine lover's discourse. On some of the complications bound up with the discourse of exemplarity in the reply epistles, see below, chapter 5.

The single letters imply a similar distinction between masculine and feminine speech. Perrine Galand-Hallyn comments:

> Une sorte de dialectique s'établit dans chacune des lettres simples: la parole mensongère, celle des amants, présentés par Ovide comme les 'beaux-parleurs' intéressés, les faiseurs de faux-serments, apparaît *efficace* (les jeunes femmes ont été séduites); en revanche, l'éloquence de la sincérité, qui déploie pourtant ses artifices les plus variés au long de chacune des épîtres, tandis que les jeunes femmes cherchent à reconquérir leur bien-aimé, *aboutit à l'échec*.[10]

> A kind of dialectic is established within each of the single letters: deceitful speech, that of the male lovers, presented by Ovid as self-interested 'smooth-talkers' making false promises, appears *effective* (the women have been seduced); by contrast, the eloquence of sincerity, which nevertheless deploys its whole range of devices throughout each of the epistles, as long as the women are seeking to win back their beloved, *ends in failure*. (emphasis in original)

However, Galand-Hallyn concludes, the third term in the dialectical movement between deceptive male speech and 'sincere' female speech is the "parole poétique," which aestheticizes, transfigures, and sublimates the heroines' suffering. So, for example, Sappho's rhetoric must not be categorized as suasive, but as transfigurative or sublime (356).

Therefore, to characterize the heroes' rhetoric as 'strong' and effective and the heroines' rhetoric as 'weak,' ineffectual, and self-cancelling does not tell the whole story. It is in the domain of *poetic* eloquence that the heroines excel. This is what enables the heroines' 'true,' 'sincere' eloquence to overwhelm the lying words of the men's suasive rhetoric. But is it not possible—indeed, is this not precisely what the early modern readers do?—to detach poetic eloquence from the agency of the heroines and restore it to

---

"undermine the traditional rhetoric of heroic speech," see Gross 1978–79, 308–14. Verducci makes a similar claim of the *Heroides* as a whole in her book.

10. Galand-Hallyn 1991, 352.

the male poet who ventriloquizes their suffering? This is the problem of the "duplex intentio" writ large.

Moreover, the dichotomy does not always hold. It is possible for female voices to become masculine (Phaedra, Helen), and to function, temporarily at least, as morally neutral rhetorical models. Indeed, it makes no sense to characterize the heroines' discourse as typically 'feminine,' inexpert, ineffectual rhetoric. In this connection Kathryn L. McKinley, in her study of commentaries on the speeches of heroines from books 7 and 10 of the *Metamorphoses*, makes a salutary point. She argues that much modern criticism unquestioningly accepts that medieval and Renaissance readings of the feminine functioned only on the basis of moral dichotomies. In fact, the medieval and early modern commentaries on Ovid's heroines did not rely exclusively on a praise-blame hermeneutic: the discourse on the feminine was more complex and heterogeneous than that.[11] The women's letters do not simply represent 'soft' feminine rhetoric and the men's 'hard' masculine rhetoric. Marina S. Brownlee offers a view contrary to Linda Kauffman's gender-focused readings of the poems: the distinction between the single and double letters is "not a gender distinction but a discursive one."[12] W. S. Anderson even claims that it is the female respondents, and not the male writers, who are in the "dominating position" in the double letters; and that, in terms of the textual dynamic, "the poet has subordinated the man's letter to the woman's."[13]

Recent criticism has focused on the extent to which the heroines are in control of their own rhetorical self-construction. Three recent studies, by Sara H. Lindheim, Effrosini Spentzou, and Laurel Fulkerson, bring this feature of the work to the fore; their approaches and conclusions differ significantly, however. The feminist recuperation of the *Heroides* has more in common with sixteenth-century rhetorical approaches to the text than one might assume. Fulkerson writes of the 'authorial self-fashioning' (49) of the heroines in the light of their reading of each other's stories, and imputes considerable rhetorical skill to the heroines themselves. Lindheim reads the heroines' texts in terms of their self-construction as objects of male desire. Her reading focuses, in the first place, on points in the text where the heroines construct themselves as foolish or naïve, as role-playing masqueraders, and as weak-minded passive entities: "Like Phyllis, Dido also conjures herself up for Aeneas as impotent, a role she chooses because, as Phyllis did before her, she calculates her helplessness will render her desirable

---

11. McKinley 2001.
12. Brownlee, "Hermeneutic Transgressions," 1990, 97, n. 8.
13. Anderson 1973, 49–83; 71.

in the eyes of the hero" (107). In the second place, Lindheim distinguishes a tendency of the heroines to portray themselves as powerful agents. Their self-representations alternate between these two irreconcilable poles.

The analytical technique of medieval and Renaissance readers of the text is in some ways similar: it focuses on the points in the text at which the heroine reveals herself as *stulta, mutabilis, debilis,* and analyses how they function rhetorically. Crucially, however, the theoretical basis, the determinant question of agency or intentionality, differs. Where some modern feminist critics distinguish an assertion of female multiplicity either independently of considerations of Ovid as author, or even *despite* Ovid's best efforts to suppress it, earlier readers usually adduce the male author as the ultimate authority.

Rhetorical analysis in humanist readings of the text is, however, not always limited by ethical-moral judgments. Significantly, the rhetorical purpose of the author does not always run counter to the heroine's rhetoric: the two may coincide. As we shall see in the next chapter, commentators are capable of admiring Ovid's rhetorical skill *as if it belonged to the heroine* without having to impute a moral purpose to the author.

THERE ARE three prominent strands in the exegesis of the *Heroides* in the context of formal education. First, there is the explanation and interpretation of the poems' mythological and historical content: the presentation to schoolboys of the 'facts' of ancient history and myth. Second, there is the use of the text to provide edifying moral examples; this touches too on the question of humanist education of women and the construction of the woman's role in society. Third, there is the attention to stylistic and formal aspects of the text. At the most basic level it is used as a textbook for the learning of the Latin language: parsing, construing, and so on; and the study of prosody. Next comes its use in the teaching of rhetoric, including the formation of letter-writing style. These three strands are not necessarily distinct from one another: the commentators by turns draw them apart or bring them together, giving greater prominence to one or other of them. Each of these aspects assumes a greater or lesser degree of importance depending on the text's intended audience. The presentation of the text in early education differs from its presentation in editions prepared for a wider audience, or for the scholarly élite; however, the different levels of presentation are not entirely separable: they merge into one another, and their concerns are broadly similar.

How, then, did the *Heroides* fit into the humanist curriculum? One possible response may be found in Shakespeare's parody of schoolroom teaching methods in *The Taming of the Shrew*. Lucentio uses a couplet from Penelope's letter (*Heroides* 1.33–34) in the lesson he gives to Bianca:

BIANCA Where left we last?
LUCENTIO Here, madam:
   "*Hic ibat Simois; hic est Sigeia tellus;*
   Hic steterat Priami regia celsa senis."
BIANCA Conster them.
LUCENTIO "*Hic ibat,*" as I told you before, "*Simois,*"
   I am Lucentio, "*hic est,*" son unto Vincentio of Pisa,
   "*Sigeia tellus,*" disguised thus to get your love,
   "*Hic steterat,*" and that Lucentio that comes a-wooing,
   "*Priami,*" is my man Tranio, "*regia,*" bearing
   my port, "*celsa senis,*" that we might beguile the old pantaloon.
[. . .]
BIANCA Now let me see if I can conster it:
   "*Hic ibat Simois,*" I know you not, "*hic est Sigeia tellus,*" I trust you not, "*Hic steterat Priami,*" take heed he hear us not, "*regia,*" presume not, "*celsa senis,*" despair not. (3.1.26–37, 41–5)[14]

The way the passage is construed is—formally at least—typical of sixteenth-century teaching methods.[15]

The educative utility of the *Heroides* was not universally acknowledged: Ovid's works went in and out of favor, and did not necessarily have the entrenched position of a Cicero or a Virgil.[16] However, certain prominent

---

14. *The Riverside Shakespeare*, ed. by G. B. Evans, 1974, 124.

15. Jonathan Bate remarks that "the chief effect of this device is to take the Latin text out of the schoolroom and make it a means of fulfilment of desire" (1993, 127). Phillippy suggests that Shakespeare's take on the pedagogical uses of the *Heroides* in this passage marks out the text as "subversive literature"; and observes that the *Heroides* is alluded to in the context of complication of gender roles elsewhere in the play, when Lucentio casts himself as Dido to Bianca's Aeneas (40–42). Warren Boutcher also cites this passage to illustrate the humanist tendency to use rhetoric, especially the discourse associated with the erotic and the feminine, to explore different moral and affective situations (Boutcher 2000, 11–52; 27).

16. There was little consensus among educators on the appropriateness of the *Heroides* as an educational text. Ann Moss 1982, 9, mentions that Noël Béda saw fit to ban the *Heroides* from the curriculum of the Collège de Montaigu, and Lefèvre d'Étaples excluded it from Christian education. Augustin Renaudet cites from the statutes of the Collège de Montaigu, drawn up by Béda in 1508 (1509 n. s.): "Quia tales prohiberi debent: Terentius, Martialis, Juuenalis, Naso in Epistolis et similes" (These authors should be excluded: Terence, Martial, Juvenal, Ovid's epistles [*Heroides*] and the like) (Renaudet 1916, 466). It must be noted, however, that at Montaigu the pupils were not exposed to

educators clearly considered the *Heroides* an essential text. At the Collège de Guyenne, for example, it was introduced to the pupils at a young age. The 1583 "programme d'études" composed by Elie Vinet, which was based on the curriculum devised by André de Gouvéa in the 1530s, prescribes that in the *quintus ordo,* Ovid's letters ("aliqua Ovidii epistola") will be studied "sub anni finem."[17] In all likelihood this refers to the *Heroides,* since the *Tristia* and *Pontics* are mentioned specifically in the fourth class; this makes the *Heroides* the first poetry to be studied. Indeed, according to Quicherat, Ovid's first appearance in the classes coincided with the pupils' first attempts at verse composition:

> En cinquième on commençait à composer des vers, et l'explication d'Ovide était ajoutée à celle des prosateurs. On n'abordait Virgile qu'en seconde, et Horace qu'en première.[18]

> In the fifth class they would begin to compose verses, and analysis of Ovid was added to the prose authors. They would not approach Virgil until the second class, and Horace until the first.

Given that Gouvéa's curriculum was based on the Paris colleges (and he was also principal at Sainte-Barbe) it seems reasonable to assume that Guyenne was not the only educational establishment where Ovid was given pride of place. The *Heroides* therefore occupied a privileged position, influencing the formation of style in younger students even before the formalized teaching of prosody and rhetoric (which comes later, in the third class). In Jesuit education, Ovid would come to occupy a similar position. The 1599 *Ratio studiorum* prescribes the *Heroides* (in expurgated form)—along with some of Ovid's other elegiac works—as the first poetry to be studied in the first semester of the highest grammar class (followed by some Catullus, Propertius, Tibullus, and Virgil in the second semester).[19]

The teaching of letter-writing technique had a prominent place in all humanist educational programmes. Might this training have made use of rhetorical models furnished by Ovid's heroines? How could the *Heroides,* which are prized as highly artificial, literary works—and 'written' by women,

---

full texts of works by even Virgil or Cicero: the teacher might dictate a few lines from those authors, taken from Alexander's *Doctrinale,* but no more than that. On disapproving attitudes toward Ovid in the sixteenth century see also Lamarque, 35.

17. Massebieau 1886, 20.
18. Quicherat 1860–64, I: 235.
19. *The Jesuit Ratio Studiorum of 1599,* trans. Allan B. Farrell, 1970, 84.

to boot—fit into the epistolary genre: a genre defined by the way it relates 'biographically' and historically to the writer and addressee? In fact, the *Heroides* were often treated in education primarily as letters rather than poetry. In his study of Shakespeare's Latin sources, T. W. Baldwin describes a 1566 edition of the *Heroides* that proves its hands-on use in the schoolroom as a letter-writing text.[20] On the title page, the original owner of the book, one James Butler, had written:

> Est familiaris amicorum absentium et quasi mutuus sermo. In exponendis authoribus sex sunt consideranda.
>
> 1. Authoris uita
> 2. Titulus operis   quare inuenta est epistola.
> 3. Dicendi qualitas   Ut faceremus amicos absentes certiores si quid
> 4. Scribentis intentio   esset, aut nostra aut ipsorum interesset.
> 5. Operis diuisio
> 6. Eusdem explanatio

> It is the familiar and, as it were, reciprocal conversation of absent friends. For the explanation of authors six things must be taken into account:
>
> 1. The life of the author
> 2. The title of the work
> 3. The nature of the language
> 4. The intention of the writer
> 5. The division of the work
> 6. The interpretation of the work.
>
> Why the letter was invented.
> So that we might inform absent friends whenever there was anything that was important for them to know, whether to do with us or themselves.

These notes, setting the outline of the basic method for reading a literary work alongside the classic definitions of the letter, would have been copied down from the master's dictation. The first sentence is the definition of the letter given by Erasmus, after Turpilius, in his letter-writing treatise *De conscribendis epistolis*. There follows a version of the standard formula for the exposition of texts which appeared in varying forms in ancient and medieval

---

20. Baldwin 1944, 2: 423.

commentaries: it is used, for example by Servius to introduce his commentary on the *Aeneid*.[21] The note on the invention of the letter is drawn from a different source: it corresponds to Cicero, *Epistulae Ad Familiares* 2.4.1: "Epistularum genera multa esse non ignoras sed unum illud certissimum, cuius causa inuenta res ipsa est, ut certiores faceremus absentis si quid esset quod eos scire aut nostra aut ipsorum interesset." This definition often featured in humanist letter-writing manuals: it appears, for example, at the head of Badius's *De epistolarum compositione compendium* (1502).[22] Baldwin goes on to describe the markings made by the same pen in the text of the first epistle, highlighting useful rhetorical figures. The *Heroides* were clearly used in the schoolroom as a sort of letter-writing handbook.

Epistolography in the Renaissance

The *Heroides* is a text particularly well suited to schoolroom use, for a number of reasons. First, it is relatively short and neatly structured. The individual poems are short enough to study individually, and the work as a whole can be read as so many variations on a single ethical theme. Second, it lends itself readily to moral-didactic readings. As Ralph Hexter comments, the relatively straightforward situations depicted in the *Heroides*, unlike the more problematical episodes of the *Metamorphoses*, had no need for complex allegorical schemes (*Ovid and Medieval Schooling*, 141ff). Third, it is an aphoristic work, rich in rhetorical material. Finally, it is a collection of letters, and letters formed the core of the texts studied in the early stages of the humanist education.

That the *Heroides* can properly be said to belong to the epistolary genre has been doubted by modern critics. Some have preferred to emphasize the poems' elegiac lineage.[23] L. P. Wilkinson denied that the epistolary features of the poems were anything but incidental: "The choice of the epistolary form for what are really tragic soliloquies was not entirely happy" (86). More recent criticism has emphasized epistolarity as an integral feature of the collection. To be sure, early modern readers did think of the *Heroides* as

---

21. The medieval *accessus ad auctores* generally incorporated some or all of the following elements: "uita auctoris," "titulus operis," "intentio scribentis," "materia operis," "utilitas," and "cui parti philosophiae supponatur." On the various applications of the scheme, see Quain 1945, 215–64. Quain discusses its uses in introductions to literary texts, with a particular focus on the twelfth-century *accessus* to Ovid's *Heroides* (216–228).

22. On this work, which appeared under various titles in editions of Cicero's *Epistulae ad Familiares*, or grouped together with other letter writing treatises, see Renouard 1908, vol. 1: 109–10.

23. See, for example, Spoth 1992.

letters, even if often in practice the epistolary formal features and settings were treated as adventitious elements.

Luc Vaillancourt excludes the love letter from his study of the theorization of the Renaissance familiar letter; this decision, the author acknowledges, is somewhat arbitrary.[24] Lecercle argues that the vernacular love letter owes more to the Petrarchan tradition than to other letter-writing traditions as formalized in epistolographical works.[25]

Our review of literature concerning the love letter's status as precursor to the epistolary novel (ch. 1) argues for placing it more firmly in that more straightforwardly literary tradition than in the context of formal education and the *epistola familiaris*. However, despite the resistance of certain theorists—in particular Erasmus—to the inclusion of the love letter in theories of letter writing, there is a tradition of amatory epistolography. The following section will attempt to situate the *Heroides* somewhere in the complex web of classical and medieval epistolographical traditions. With Petrarch comes a departure from the formulaic rigidity of the *ars dictaminis*. Quattrocento humanist epistolography stresses that letters should be tailored to meet the expectations of the recipient. With the humanist practice of publishing letter collections as models of style and self-presentation, there is a rising awareness of letter writing as a social practice. The hybrid public-private space which letters occupy prevents us from conceptualizing them purely as "absentis ad absentem colloquium" (as Erasmus does, after Libanius, in his *Epistolarum formula*): the letter privileges the creation of a self and its presentation to the world. Vernacular letter-writing manuals in turn were influenced by various traditions: Italian manuals dominate in the early sixteenth century; the French manuals follow later in the century and become massively popular in the seventeenth century. French epistolography in the Renaissance is almost entirely based on Italian traditions: both the Latin works of the quattrocento humanists and the Italian vernacular manuals. Theorists are never quite sure how to categorize the amatory epistle, nor what exactly its usefulness might be; but the presence of the love letter in theoretical works of the period testifies to the pervasiveness of the influence of the *Heroides* in particular.

The indeterminacy of the text's role in Renaissance epistolography is evident in its contrasting treatments in Niccolò Perotti's *Rudimenta grammatices* (1473) and Filelfo's *Novum epistolarium* (1482), two influential texts in French humanism.[26] Filelfo lists around eighty types of letters, among

---

24. Vaillancourt 2003, 25.
25. Lecercle 1984, 213–25.
26. See Vaillancourt, 148–51. A measure of the popularity of these texts in the early stages of

them "amatoria honesta." The chapters on each letter type are divided into "familiaris," "familiarissima," and "grauis." The sample letter under the heading "amatoria honesta grauis" makes mention of various ancient authors' writings on the subject of love from Homer through Sophocles to Seneca.[27] The 'author' of the letter quotes directly from various authorities to lend credence to his arguments. His quotation from Ovid comes from *Heroides* 5, used to illustrate the concept of unrequited love: "quid harenae semina mandas? non profecturis litora bubus aras" (Why sow seeds in sand? You are ploughing a shore with oxen that are of no use). It is not entirely clear what practical purpose this sample love letter is meant to serve. Because the work was considered the most 'moral' of all Ovid's works on love, authors were more likely to use extracts from the *Heroides* than from Ovid's other amatory works when writing on the subject of love. Here the extract is not identifiably 'epistolary' despite being used as part of a sample letter.

A contrasting treatment is to be found in the section of Perotti's work entitled *De componendis epistolis*. As Judith Rice Henderson comments, Perotti is more concerned with the general question of style than with the distinct genres of letter writing: he does not even distinguish the verse love letter from all the other types of familiar prose letter, for example. Ovid's *Heroides* is quoted and alluded to alongside Cicero's letters: both are used as epistolary stylistic models. The introductory section names the preeminent letter writers among the ancients (Pliny, Cicero), including Ovid as the exemplary 'poetic' letter writer. No distinction is made at this stage between the fictional status of Ovid's letters and the status of the Ciceronian letter:

> Reperitur quoque aliquando pro epistola apud poetas duntaxat: ut Ouidius: *Quam legis a rapta briseide littera uenit.*[28]

> Sometimes one also finds pieces written as letters in the poets, for example Ovid: "The letter you read comes from abducted Briseis."

The line quoted is from *Heroides* 3. Perotti goes on to list the many types of letters that can be found in the works of ancient authors, again making little distinction between 'artificial,' fictional works and nonfiction. He lists:

French humanism is given by the record of editions printed in Paris and Lyon: Perotti's *Rudimenta* was printed at least twenty times in Paris, and a further six times in Lyon, all before 1500. Filefo's *Novum epistolarium*, narrower in scope than Perotti's work, was first printed in Paris in the 1480s, and there were at least two further editions by 1511. See Green and Murphy 2006.

27. Filelfo 1489, fol. liiii^r.
28. Perotti 1479, sig.1.viii^v.

letters on divine matters, such as Plato's; on religion, such as Paul's; on morals (Seneca, Jerome, etc.); on current events; letters that console, commend, exhort; love letters, which are mostly by the poets ("Aliæ amatoriæ quæ magis poetarum sunt, ut sunt epistolæ Nasonis"); letters on familiar and domestic matters; and humorous letters.[29] It seems strange that the verse love letter should be included in this list alongside prose nonfiction letters. They are simply treated as different types of letter, rather than as fundamentally different categories of writing.

In Latin humanist culture, the *Heroides* was a text that came to be treated as a rhetorical model; but it never ceased to be considered *as poetry*, for the simple reason that Ovid was a poet: he did not write prose. In vernacular culture, on the other hand, the text of the *Heroides* would come to be seen primarily as a source for rhetorical models for epistolary composition in prose. Translations of the work in the seventeenth century were mostly in prose, not verse: in French vernacular culture, the *Heroides* would cease to be a poetic text.[30]

The use of prose translations of the *Heroides* in French eloquence manuals bespeaks the interpermeability of the boundaries between poetic fiction and practical rhetoric. Translations of the *Heroides* by various authors appeared in the 1605 *Fleurs de bien dire*; in the 1615 *Fleurs de l'éloquence française*; and in the 1624 *Bouquet des plus belles fleurs de l'éloquence*; in Pierre Deimier's *Lettres amoureuses* of 1612; and in Jean-Baptiste de Croisilles's 1619 *Héroïdes, ou Epîtres amoureuses*.[31] The tensions between public and private, between 'literary' and practical rhetoric addressed in chapter 1, had to a large extent dissolved as the *Heroides* became assimilated into vernacular culture as prose texts.

---

29. The 1553 "Style et maniere de composer, dicter, et escrire toute sorte d'Epistres ou lettres missives," which was the first widely circulated French vernacular letter-manual, duplicates this passage, mentioning the same categories and authors. See Vaillancourt, 173.

30. See Dalla Valle, 375: "Dans les premières décennies du XVIIe siècle, on commence à considérer les *Héroïdes* comme des modèles rhétoriques de lettres, plutôt que comme des compositions poétiques: alors que le genre de la lettre en prose commence . . . à être codifié dans la civilisation française et à remporter un remarquable succès, même les *Héroïdes* ovidiennes sont insérées dans cette mode et commencent, elles aussi, à être traduites en prose" (In the first decades of the seventeenth century, the *Heroides* begin to be considered as rhetorical models for letter writing, rather than as poetic compositions: at a time when the genre of the prose letter is beginning . . . to be codified in French civilization and to meet with remarkable success, even Ovid's *Heroides* get included in this trend, and begin also to be translated into prose).

31. Ibid.; and Jensen, 1995, 22–23. Jensen comments that the inclusion by François des Rues, editor of *Les Fleurs de bien dire*, of women's love letters based closely on the *Heroides* "functions to close the gap between fiction and life."

Erasmus

The most successful work of epistolography in the first part of the sixteenth century was the *De conscribendis epistolis* of Erasmus. It went through a huge number of editions throughout Europe, and particularly in the North, beginning with the first pirate edition issued in 1521 (the authorized Froben edition appeared in 1522). The *Renaissance Rhetoric Short-Title Catalogue* records thirteen Paris printings in a twenty-year period from 1523. Lyon printers matched this figure, and it continued to be printed there up until 1551. Erasmus' *Brevissima maximeque compendiaria conficiendarum epistolarum formula* was printed separately at Paris at least six times from 1521, and it continued to be printed in combination with other epistolographical works. It is to these works that we turn in order to establish the position held by the *Heroides* in humanist education.

Erasmus doubts whether fictional letters composed in order to show off or exercise the author's skills belong to the epistolary genre at all. He acknowledges their existence in the section entitled "Peculiaris epistolae character":

> Fortassis erunt qui quasdam epistolas semouebunt ab hoc ordine, quod genus sunt epistolae ad exercitationem, uel ostentationem ingenii confictae: [gives examples] ad haec heroinarum, autore Nasone, aliaeque consimiles, quas si quis malit appellare declamatiunculas, equidem non admodum refragabor.[32]

> There will, perhaps, be some who would separate certain letters from this category, of which type are letters composed for practice or for showing off one's talent. To this class belong the *Heroides* written by Naso, and others like them, which, if anyone prefers to call them "little declamations," I for my part will not demur at all.

So the *Heroides* fit into that category of letters that are first and foremost rhetorical: they are to be read as "declamatiunculae," useful primarily in education as little exercises in rhetoric. Erasmus goes on to dismiss the *Heroides* from closer consideration; he also specifically mentions that his work will not consider the composition of metrical verse letters, which ought to be left to the experts.

---

32. Erasmus 1971, 1–2: 224.

Although the *De conscribendis epistolis* was composed as a reaction against the formalism of contemporary Italian epistolography, Erasmus nevertheless includes a typology of letter forms, each form fitting one of the four rhetorical genres. Erasmus' four genres have their basis in the three oratorical genres (deliberative, demonstrative, forensic), with the addition of a fourth: the 'familiar.' A cursory survey of the letter forms named by Erasmus (310–12) reveals the difficulty of fitting the *Heroides* neatly into any scheme of this type: the Ovidian epistle is, broadly speaking "amatoria" (and therefore 'suasive' or deliberative), but it is also "exhortatoria," "dehortatoria"; on occasion "invectiva" and "deprecatoria" (belonging to the forensic genre); and also "lamentatoria" or "conciliatoria" or even "nunciatoria" (*genus familiaris*). The writing heroes and heroines themselves seem to be intent on disrupting rhetorical categories, and the dual character of the text (including as it does letters penned by both men and women) further complicates the matter. Acontius, for example, is able to make ironic reference to his 'suit' of Cydippe in terms of forensic oratory:

> nunc reus infelix absens agor et mea, cum sit
>   optima, non ullo causa tuente perit. (*Her.* 20.91–92)

> Now I am tried in my absence, my testimony is no use, and my case, though it is excellent, is lost because no one defends me.

This is a strategy that seems to be unavailable to the heroines, since it would constitute an egregious transgression of gender boundaries.[33] However, Cydippe herself handles forensic terminology adroitly in her reply. For example:

> consilium prudensque animi sententia iurat,
>   et nisi iudicii uincula nulla ualent. (*Her.* 21.137–38)[34]

> Only counsel and the prudent reasoning of the soul can make an oath, and without the bonds of judgement, no oath has value.

---

33. In the *Metamorphoses*, however, Byblis uses just such a strategy in the opening lines of her letter. As Farrell comments (321, n. 24), Ovid here shows "that Byblis is transgressing an important gender boundary—that she has, in effect, 'misread' the *Ars amatoria.*" The latter recommends 'forensic' style training in the writing of love letters for men but not for women.

34. "Sound moral and legal doctrine, weightily expressed through theme and variation," writes Kenney (in Ovid, ed. Kenney, 1996, 233). There are other examples of Cydippe's legal *savoir faire* throughout lines 133–50.

Erasmus goes on to define two main types of love letter: the "honesta" ("conciliatoria") and the "turpis" ("amatoria"). The adjective "amatoria" is therefore rather sloppily applied to both types, serving at the same time to distinguish the 'immoral' type from the moral. To illustrate the "epistola conciliatoria," Erasmus supplies a model letter written by Fausto Andrelini to Petrus Santeranus. It is a letter from one friend to another which treats of matters to do with love, and alludes to Ovid's *Ars Amatoria;* but it is by no means itself a 'love letter.' Erasmus does not deal with letters addressed to women. The extracts he includes in the so-called "Amatoriae Sylua" are expressions of nonsexual love or friendship taken from the familiar letters of Cicero, Pliny, and Politian. The "epistola turpis" is thereafter passed over in silence. Other authors of letter manuals before and after Erasmus are not so reluctant to treat immoral matters, as we shall see.

Erasmus defines the love letter, the "epistola amatoria," as belonging to the *genus deliberativum,* presumably because it has as its aim to persuade and encourage a certain course of action. This is the love letter of masculine desire: it is not the love letter of endlessly flowing tears (Hermione), of bitter reproach (Phyllis, Dido, Ariadne), or of pure expression of desire (Laodamia) that is the female type in the *Heroides.* Erasmus does not analyze the strategies and aims of the love letter in any detail, but we can be sure that whatever type of love letter he has in mind, its main feature is its focus on whatever is "utile" and "honestum," and not on the corruption of young women:

> In primis uero notandum, deliberatiuum genus, quod suasorium dici potest, utilitate ac honestate definiri. Quamquam cum utile dicimus, honestum etiam uolumus intelligi, quando nihil utile dici potest, quod idem honestum non sit.[35]

> First then we should note that the deliberative genre, which can also be called 'suasive,' is defined by usefulness and moral goodness. To be sure when we say something is useful, we mean to suggest that it is also morally good, since nothing can be said to be useful which is not at the same time morally good.

In the brief section entitled "De Amatoria Epistola" (509), the author acknowledges that not all love letters fit into a single genre: "Aliae enim petunt, aliae expostulant, aliae queruntur, aliae blandiuntur, aliae purgant" (For some entreat, some demand, some complain, some flatter, some justify).

---

35. Erasmus 1521, sig Bii'.

This might as well be a typology of the single *Heroides*. In excluding letters of this type from further consideration, Erasmus suggests that study of the rhetoric of the female letter writers *as rhetoric* would be neither "utile" nor "honestum."

Erasmus does not often quote the *Heroides* in this work: where he does, it is to criticize the heroines' foolishness. He contrasts the admirable attitude to death exemplified by Socrates with the common, stupid notions of Oenone in *Heroides* 5. He quotes lines 7–8 of her lament, to the effect that well-deserved adversities are more easily borne than unmerited ones. When Erasmus comments (437): "uulgi ista sententia est et stulticiae plena" (This is a vulgar sentiment, and full of foolishness), can we be sure that the sentiment being denounced is Oenone's and not Ovid's?

In his chapter on practice and imitation ("Exercitatio et imitatio"), Erasmus recommends that schoolboys be given practice exercises in various short epistolary themes ("breuibus et epistolaribus argumentis," 231). These should be targeted to be of appropriate interest to boys of whatever age: the more enjoyable they are, the more useful they will prove. Usually these topics should be taken from poets and historians, but they may also come from current events. However, subjects taken from historians are more worthwhile even if less entertaining. In the first category are topics from Ovid's *Heroides,* (and later, Lucian's dialogues), but only for older boys ("in quibus fortasse totum non sit, rudem aetatem exerceri," 232 [which perhaps are not wholly appropriate to be used as exercises for young inexperienced boys]). The emphasis is on appropriateness of style to matter and target audience. It is entirely appropriate that the *Heroides* be used as models for these exercises, since they are effectively *ethopoeia,* bearing all the features of Ovid's training under Arellius Fuscus. Erasmus focuses primarily on *inventio*: he does not talk about the style of the *Heroides,* nor about what elements of the text ought to be imitated. Indeed the text itself is not really central to the educational program Erasmus envisions. It is noteworthy also that Erasmus does not refer at all to the education of girls or women in this work.[36] Erasmus goes on to demonstrate how Ovid's text might properly and chastely be used as a source for such exercises:

> Quanquam heroinarum sunt castiores, neque quicquam uetat et hoc genus caste uerecundeque tractari. Ueluti si procus blandis literis ambiat nuptias puellae; si Helena Paridem ab amore non permisso deterreat. Nam Pene-

---

36. See Sowards 1982, 77–89.

lopes ad Ulyssem epistola tota pudica est, quemadmodum et Acontii ad Cydippen. (232)

And yet some of the heroines are chaste enough, and nothing prevents this type of epistle being handled chastely and modestly. For instance, a suitor might propose marriage to a girl in a flattering letter; or Helen might deter Paris from a forbidden love. For indeed Penelope's letter to Ulysses is wholly modest, as is that of Acontius to Cydippe.

Erasmus suggests possible themes the *Heroides* might furnish: a suitor writing to a girl to solicit marriage; Helen dissuading Paris from a love that is forbidden. These summaries allude to *Heroides* 16–17, but hardly tell the whole story. In the first instance, Paris has everything but marriage in mind; in the second Helen vacillates between mock outrage and manipulative flirtatiousness. Evidently Erasmus is not recommending for study the full text of *Heroides* 16–17, but extracts or perhaps prose summaries of the text. At this stage, it seems, Ovid's versions of these mythological stories do not supply material at the level of *elocutio:* they are of primary interest for the themes and situations they furnish. They are not recommended by Erasmus as rhetorical or stylistic models, to aid schoolboys in their compositions; but as generic examples of certain typical themes.

The other *Heroides* mentioned by Erasmus in this context are the letter from Penelope to Ulysses, which is "morally sound in all respects," and that of Acontius to Cydippe. It seems somewhat strange that these two letters should be yoked together. Acontius is a persuasive suitor and an expert rhetorician, but his methods are hardly above reproach: the ploy Acontius had used (the oath written on the apple) to deceive Cydippe into pledging herself to him taints his rhetoric with the mark of dishonesty and disingenuousness. Indeed, in the section on seducers' letter-writing techniques in the *Ars Amatoria,* Ovid prized the deceptive eloquence of Acontius as a model for the aspiring cad:

littera Cydippen pomo perlata fefellit
    insciaque est uerbis capta puella suis. (*Ars Amatoria,* 1. 457–58)

A letter delivered in an apple fooled Cydippe, and she, unwitting girl, was trapped by her own words.

Penelope's letter, on the other hand, is traditionally exemplary because her language speaks of feminine guilelessness, and the course of action she commends—that her husband return immediately—is morally unproblematical.[37] Acontius's letter is exemplary because he achieves perlocutionary success through strategic cunning; a strong, 'masculine' rhetoric.

There are any number of letter-themes to be taken from the mythological background of the *Heroides* in this way. Erasmus also suggests letters from Nestor or Phoenix to Achilles, persuading him to be magnanimous about the rape of Briseis; the idea for this is taken from *Heroides* 3. One might also explore other variations on *Heroides* 16–17, for example, writing in the person of Antenor to Priam to persuade him to return Helen to Menelaus. Erasmus alludes to the Paris of *Heroides* 16 when he suggests that the letter denounce the disgraceful conduct of Paris, that effeminate half-man ("turpissimum effoeminati iuuenis et uix uiri Paridis amorem" [that disgusting love of the effeminate youth and half-man Paris]). Erasmus also suggests a letter from Menelaus to Paris, upbraiding him for his violation of hospitality. He does not relate this specifically to the *Heroides;* but one can imagine an outraged Menelaus intercepting *Heroides* 16 and writing a letter to charge Paris with the written evidence of his crimes.[38] The suggestion of a letter from Agamemnon to Menelaus, encouraging him to forget about Helen the "mulierculam uita indignam" (silly woman undeserving of life), perhaps tells us more about Erasmus' view of the Helen of *Heroides* 17 than the first suggestion he had given ("si Helena Paridem ab amore non permisso deterreat" [if Helen might deter Paris from illicit love]).

A contrasting treatment of the *Heroides* as model letters is to be found in the *De conscribendis epistolis* of Juan Luis Vives (1534).[39] Though less successful than Erasmus' work of the same title, it too found an audience in France, and it was printed in Paris by Mathieu David in 1547. In a departure from the usual practice in humanist epistolographical works, Vives does not relate letter writing to the oratorical genres at all. He is more interested in the *Heroides* at the level of *elocutio*. In his miscellany of useful epistolary phrases, under the heading of "Resalutandi," he cites *Heroides* 1.2:

---

37. That this is Erasmus' reading of Penelope's letter is hinted at in the following sentence, when he recommends that schoolboys compose a letter that a wife might write to her absent husband, persuading him to hurry home ("Si uxor marito peregre cessanti scribat, uti domum properet," 232). Erasmus seems to have in mind here a more generalized situation; but the obvious model is Penelope.

38. It is difficult to imagine Menelaus writing a letter to Paris *after* the rape of Helen. Menelaus must surely write to Paris from abroad while the latter is still in Sparta, having got wind of his ungentlemanly intentions.

39. Vives, ed. by C. Fantazzi, 1989.

Renuntia ei non exspectare me ab eo salutationes, sed epistolas, aut quod matrona illa castissima marito scribit:
Nil mihi rescribas, attamen ipse ueni.[40]

Reply to him: I do not expect greetings, but letters, or else what that most faultless of wives writes to her husband:
Do not write back to me, but instead come in person

And, if an especially clever or witty greeting is sought, then the *Heroides* might supply it:

Sunt apud Ouidium genera quaedam salutationum festiua et arguta ut:
Quam nisi tu dederis caritura est ipsa salutem
    Mittit Amazonio Cressa puella uiro.

Mittit et optat amans quo mittitur ire salutem. (99)

In Ovid there are some particularly amusing and expressive types of salutation, such as:
Greetings and health, which, unless you grant it, she will lack, the Cretan girl sends her man, the Amazon's son.
[Laodamia] sends greetings and health, and wishes with love for it to go where it is sent.

The first of these is Phaedra addressing Hippolytus (a greeting not without erotic undertones); the second is Laodamia. Elsewhere, in the preface to the *De institutione foeminae Christianae*, Vives would denounce Ovid as a "corrupter of virtue"; here, it seems, Ovidian wit is judged to be separable from ethical considerations. Both the given examples pun on "salus" / "salutatio,"[41] furnishing the prospective letter writer with a ready-made witticism

---

40. Knox reads "nil mihi rescribas attinet: ipse ueni."
41. This grammatical structure ("salutem" occupying the end of the hexameter, the rest of the couplet bulked out by a relative clause) is employed in the opening lines of a great many verse epistles. See also *Metamorphoses* 9.530–31 (Byblis's letter to Caunus): "quam, nisi tu dederis, non est habitura salutem, / hanc tibi mittit amans" (Greetings and health which, unless you grant it, she will not have, your lover sends to you). The "salus" conceit is also common in prose epistles. For example, Eurialus in Aeneas Silvius Piccolomini's *Historia de duobus amantibus* (1444) begins his first letter to Lucretia with the words: "Salutarem te Lucrecia meis scriptis si qua mihi salutis copia foret. Sed omnis tum salus tum uite spes mee ex te dependet" (I would greet you/send health, Lucretia, in writing, if only I had the strength. But all my well-being, all my hope of life depends on you) (Piccolomini, ed. by E. J. Morrall, 1988, 101). On the construction "salutem mitto" (used by Ovid alone among classical authors) and its punning treatment by Christian-era authors ("salus" also means "salvation"), see

which will be appreciated both at a surface level—for its ingenuity—and at the intertextual level: the recipient will no doubt recognize the allusion and bring the Ovidian context to mind.[42]

OVID HIMSELF had provided a breakdown of techniques for composing love letters. The main points of reference are the *Ars Amatoria* 1.437–86, in which men are schooled in suasive strategies, and 3.469–98, in which women are instructed to be coy and subtly flirtatious.[43] The letter-writing advice given to men is of necessity different from that given to women. Men are advised to cloak their eloquence in a seemingly plain style; women, too, are encouraged to write in the plain style, but only because they lack the rhetorical mastery of men. Joseph Farrell comments:

> Accordingly, men and women approach the ideal of good, plain latinity from very different perspectives—men from that of a linguistic and rhetorical mastery of their native tongue, women from one of strangeness and unfamiliarity that can only aspire to mere functionalism. (313)

Furthermore, although the writing of love letters is "a duplicitous art" (315) for both women and men, the man's aim is to deceive his addressee, whereas the woman aims only to deceive those standing between her and her addressee. Men's and women's love letters are practically "altogether different genres" (317).

In the *Ars*, Ovid specifically warns against being overtly rhetorical in a love letter, for who but a guileless fool would see fit to *declaim* to a beautiful

---

Lanham 1975, 31–35.

42. In his study of the epistolary character of Du Bellay's *Regrets*, Marc Bizer comments (2001, 36–37) on the tension between clarity and obscurity of style in Erasmus' definition of the letter. Erasmus writes that the letter, more than any other literary genre, may contain allusions comprehensible only to the addressee and not to a wider audience. For Erasmus, the humanist letter is a space for the playing of erudite games. Vives picks up on this (see Bizer 2001, 37–38 and 210 n. 98) in defining the letter as a vehicle for secrets, which ought not to be understood by everyone—and it would surely not have escaped his readers' notice that Phaedra in her letter does precisely this: she writes down secrets it would be dangerous to speak aloud. Vives recommends that a writer should insert into his letter allusions to myth, to history, to proverbs, and quotations from the best authors, not for the sake of advancing an argument, but merely for making a point and attracting attention to it. He sees this as a way of 'encoding' sensitive information intended only for a particular readership (38).

43. Medieval commentators had certainly made the connection between the advice on letter writing Ovid gave in the *Ars Amatoria* and the practical demonstration of epistolary rhetoric offered in the *Heroides*: the author of one twelfth-century *accessus* suggested that one of the author's intentions in writing the *Heroides* had been to provide the reader with examples of model love letters, to supplement the theoretical advice given in the *Ars Amatoria*. The text is printed in Quain 1945, 219–20.

girl ("Quis, nisi mentis inops, tenerae declamat amicae?"). Renaissance epistolographers, where they instruct in the art of the love letter, conspicuously fail to heed this advice.

Francesco Negri

An important early influence on French humanist epistolography was Francesco Negri's *Opusculum epistolarum familiarum* (1487). Paris printers produced ten editions of it in as many years from 1490, and it came to be a significant source text for French vernacular epistolary theory. Negri's treatise on the "epistola amatoria" includes a chapter entitled "Amatoria turpis," which instructs the reader on how best to compose a declaration of love, and on how to write a letter recommending an immoral course of action(!): "Amatoria epistola: quae turpis appelatur: est illa quae ad aliquam amicam uel pulchram puellam scribitur ab amore suo: pro amoris declaratione: cuius epistolae talis est regula."[44] (The love letter which is called immoral is one which is written to some girlfriend or pretty maid by her lover, as a declaration of love. The model for such a letter is as follows.) Negri defines the "epistola amatoria turpis" as a letter written to a woman as a declaration of love. He does not explore the moral implications of including practical instructions of this kind in the work, nor does he attempt to answer the question of what would constitute 'fair use' of the information that follows.

> Si amatoriam epistolam quae turpis dicitur ad aliquam puellam scribere uoluerimus: illam potissimum in partes quattuor diuidemus. In quarum prima beniuolentiam captabimus ab ea persona: ad quam scribimus: laudantes ipsam triplici laude. primo scilicet a uirtute uel morali uel litterali: si litteris fuerit imbuta: secundo a genere si fuerit generosa. uel a fortuna et diuitiis: si ex humili genere nata fuerit. tertio a pulchritudine quae maiorem habet commendationem & efficatiam in amore. In secunda uero beniuolentiam captabimus a persona nostra demonstrantes primo sine aliqua arrogantia: conditionem nostram propter quam etiam ipsa puella incitetur ad amorem nostrum: deinde ei quantum honeste poterimus declarantes amorem & beniuolentiam. qua in ipsam afficiamur. In tertia autem rogabimus ipsam ut penitus uelit acquiescere precibus nostris: & nos similiter amare quemadmodum eam amamus: laudantes hunc amorem: & dicentes: ipsam

---

44. Negri 1500, sig. b.i^v.

esse rem potius diuinam quam humanam: simulque adducentes aliquod exemplum aliarum puellarum: quae in amore positae foelicem uitam sunt consecutae. In quarta et ultima: adducemus ipsam puellam in timorem alicuius damni si noluerit talem amorem sequi: & simul confirmabimus per exempla aliquarum feminarum: quae nolentes amori adherere: crudeliter uitam finierunt: deducentes ipsam amicam nostram in talem timorem: & conclusiue inducentes ipsam ad amorem: ne aliquid mali ei contingat: cui etiam offeremus omnem operam nostram: cum omni honestate ei paratam. (sig. b.i^v)

If we want to write an amatory epistle (which is known as 'immoral') to some girl, first of all we shall divide it into four parts. In the first part, we shall win approval by commending the personal qualities of the girl we are writing to, praising her in three stages. First comes praise of her qualities, whether moral or literary (if she happens to be well-read): second comes praise of her social standing—if she is noble—, or of her fortune and riches—if she is of humble birth. Third comes praise of her beauty, which in matters of love is more advantageous and effective. In the second part, we shall win approval on the basis of our own character, demonstrating first (without arrogance) our good standing, on account of which the girl might be persuaded to love us; then declaring (as decently as possible) the love and good will we feel towards her. In the third part we shall ask her to willingly cede to our imprecations, and to love us in the way we love her, praising this kind of love and saying that it is truly a thing more divine than human. At this point, we invoke some example of other girls who have been in love and have led a happy life. In the fourth and final part, we shall lead the girl herself into fearing some punishment if she should refuse to follow our love; and we shall confirm this point by invoking examples of some women who refused to love and came to a bad end, provoking fear in our girlfriend and conclusively leading her to love, lest any harm should come to her: against which we shall offer our full protection, ready to defend her in all matters of honor.

Negri goes on to provide a model letter: "Pyramus writes to Thisbe to declare his love, and to seduce her" (sig. b.ii^r). The Pyramus-Thisbe narrative was a popular one among imitators of Ovid.[45] Here the narrative element is

---

45. Its widespread use for classroom exercises in rhetoric during the twelfth and thirteenth centuries is discussed by Glendinning 1986, 51–78. The story was very well known by the time Shakespeare parodied it in *A Midsummer Night's Dream*. For an account of the various ways in which Renaissance commentators interpreted the story, see Doran 1964, 44–62.

suppressed; indeed, the letter is a generic prose piece intended merely to exemplify the principles set out in the foregoing section: "Pyramus" does not make any reference to the story told by Ovid in the *Metamorphoses*. Thisbe is duly praised by Pyramus for her moral and physical beauty, and her nobility; Pyramus goes on to describe his love for her, remembering to praise love as "more divine than human"; and finally he follows Negri's advice in giving *exempla:* Daphne to dissuade resistance and Penelope as a paragon of wifely love.

The *Ars Amatoria,* especially the section on letter writing in book 1, is an important model here, along with the tradition of Ovid-influenced "arts of love" from the Middle Ages. But a more specific model suggests itself, and the composition scheme broadly resembles *Heroides* 16, the letter from Paris to Helen. The praise of Helen's qualities, her nobility and beauty (135–44 and *passim*), is balanced by Paris's self-promotion: the praise of his own beauty, nobility, and wealth (51–88 [the Judgement]; 89–106; 179–212). This is followed by the plea for Helen to requite his love (271–80) and the praise of love's divinity (281ff). He follows this with *exempla* of women whom love has benefited, or of women whose abduction has brought no undesirable consequences (341–52). He closes his letter with an attempt to allay Helen's fears, and a reassurance that he is capable of protecting Helen from reprisals (353–78). The commentaries on the Paris epistle bring out the parallels. The humanist commentator Ubertinus Clericus, for instance, in his remarks on the overall structure and the strategies of persuasion deployed, aligns the epistle closely with Negri's model letter. Paris' rhetorical technique (in which commentators find much to fault as well as to praise) will be analyzed in more detail in the following chapter.

Pierre Fabri

Pierre Fabri's *Grand et vrai art de pleine rhétorique,* first published in 1521,[46] includes a chapter on "Lettres missives" which adapts material from the major Latin epistolographical works. Most of the material comes from humanist sources, but Fabri is also influenced by the medieval "artes," especially in his attention to hierarchical divisions and levels of writing. Negri's work is a conspicuous influence: long sections of the work are fairly close translations from the Latin. These chapters of the work stand as the founding work of vernacular epistolography in sixteenth-century France. Much of the material

---

46. Vaillancourt, 168ff.

included in the text was recycled by later compilers of vernacular manuals. These manuals, chief among which were the many versions of *Le Style et manière de composer . . . lettres missives,* were distinct from the *dictamen* tradition and the formularies of chancelry in that their intended audience was a literary élite: they were not intended primarily for professional use. The first successful French epistolary manual, Jean Temporal's 1553 *Style et manière,* reproduced Fabri's two chapters on letter writing.[47]

Fabri begins his section on love letters by posing a problem:

> Le langage françoys n'a point encore mis de différence entre amour vertueuse et amour vitieuse; mais indifferentement vse de ce terme cy "amour," tant en aymant son pere en vertu que sa paillarde en lubricité.[48]

> The French language has not yet established a difference between virtuous love and wicked love; but uses without distinction this term "amour," whether loving one's father virtuously or one's mistress lecherously.

What follows has the appearance of a non sequitur: Fabri seems to ignore the first category, adding a parenthetical note to inform the reader that "amour" is conventionally feminine in French though masculine in Latin: he does, however, concede that it would be correct to say "bon amour" or "vertueux amour." The examples he gives for linguistically 'masculine' love are, pointedly, virtuous and good; sinful love implicitly remains a feminine concept, both linguistically and ethically.

Fabri goes on to describe the proper procedure for composing 'virtuous' love letters. The first stage in the tripartite process is the *captatio benevolentiae;* second is the declaration of love; and the third stage is to offer incentives to the beloved. He then provides a model letter entitled "N. rescript a N. l'amour de quoy il l'aime," with each of the sections clearly marked.

Fabri is more anxious than Negri had been to justify the inclusion of 'immoral' advice in his manual. His version of the section on "immoral amatory letters" is closely based on Negri's, but the French author adapts it slightly. Fabri's disclaimer for including this material seems somewhat self-conscious, if not wholly disingenuous:

> Quand on veult rescripre d'amour vitieuse a quelque belle ieune fille pour luy desclarer son amour,—combien que i'aye esté deliberé de ne bailler point

---

47. Vaillancourt, 172.
48. Fabri, ed. Héron, 1969, 227.

de exemple de cecy ne de vitupere, ne de invective, etc., veu que la malice des hommes en sçayt trop, touttesfoys, pour aggreement et assouuissement de mon liure et par conseil ie l'ay faict—il fault diuiser ses lettres en trois. (p. 229)

When we wish to write of immoral love to some beautiful young girl in order to declare our love to her—even though originally I was determined not to give any examples of this, or of abusive or invective writing, etc., given that the wickedness of men knows all too much about it, for the sake of amenity and completeness of my book, after some consideration, I have done so—we should divide our letters into three parts.

The mid-sentence *volte-face* might strike the modern reader as amusing. The author is at pains to stress his obligation to the moral health of his audience—something that had been much less emphatic in the Latin work—but this concern is quite clearly subordinate to his primary interest in rhetorical technique. The three divisions Fabri proceeds to outline are broadly the same as the stages of the procedure for writing virtuous love letters. The main difference is that Fabri goes into the techniques for writing "d'amour vitieuse" in greater detail, following Negri closely. The rhetoric of vice is more appealing than the rhetoric of virtue. The first stage, the *captatio benevolentiae,* is itself now divided into three: first the praise of the addressee's morals or her learning (if she has any); second, praise of her nobility or riches (if she has any); and third, praise of her physical beauty (no parenthesis). Fabri adds that if the beloved is deficient in any of the above, one should write something like:

"Combien que tu ne soys pas noble ne de grans parens, si es tu en meurs, en courage plus noble que les aultres, ou semblable, etc." (230)

"Though you are not noble, and have no great ancestors, still you are, in morals and in spirit, more noble than others, or comparable, etc."

In the second part of the letter, the writer lists ("sans arrogance") his good qualities, such as his youth, nobility, and riches, as incentives for the beloved. He goes on to declare his love, "le plus honnestement que l'en pourra."

Fabri's instructions for the third section are even more specific:

En la tierce partie, nous luy prierons qu'il luy plaise nous accorder nostre requeste, en nous aymant ainsy que nous l'aymons, disant que l'amour est plus diuin que humain, en admenant quelque exemple de celles a qui bien est venu par bien aymer. Et puis fault declarer quelque crainte de dommage la ou elle pourroit venir, se elle ne veult aymer, en confermant de exemples d'aulcunes qui non voullant aymer sont mortes miserablement, en luy suadant non cheoir en tel inconuenient, luy promectant honnestement et secretement la garder et luy faire tout seruice et playsir. (230)

In the third part, we beseech her to kindly grant our suit to love us as much as we love her, by saying that love is a thing more divine than human and adducing some example or other of women who have benefited from loving well. And next we should declare some fear of the harm she might come to if she refuses to love, corroborating this with examples of certain women who, in refusing to love, died miserably, all the while persuading her not to fall into such a disadvantageous state, promising her honorably and confidentially to protect her and to do all we can to serve her and bring her happiness.

Fabri collapses Negri's third and fourth stages into one. This technique, to persuade by advancing examples of women who gained advantages by ceding to love and negative examples of women who met miserable deaths as a consequence of their refusal of love is entirely in tune with the seductive techniques recommended by Ovid in the *Ars Amatoria* and put into practice by Paris or Acontius in the *Heroides*, but entirely at odds, one would assume, with the Christian discourse of female martyrdom.

Fabri departs from Negri's text at this point, replacing the Pyramus model letter with one based on Aeneas Silvius' popular semi-epistolary narrative *Eurialus and Lucretia*. The epistolary parts of this work are based in large part on the rhetoric of the *Heroides*. It owed its popularity in France to Octavien de Saint-Gelais's verse translation, composed in the 1490s some time before his verse translation of the *Heroides*. The model letter included here is clearly not taken directly from the Saint-Gelais translation, since it is in prose. The letter Fabri presents is divided into parts corresponding to the scheme sketched out above; it follows this scheme very closely indeed. Eurialus begins by praising Lucretia's qualities: her "grandes vertuz," her "richesses" and "noblesse," and her "plus diuine que humaine beaulté." The latter is described in greater detail. In the second part, Eurialus declares his love and modestly alludes to his own good qualities. In the third part he praises love, using the examples of Daphne and Syrinx to prove that those who refuse love often meet with a cruel end; and Penelope to show love's benefits. This model letter could not be more abstract and formulaic; but it is based on a well-known work of fiction, and it uses well-known characters. It is telling that Fabri cast as an exemplary love letter a piece whose situation and characters derive from a *Heroides*-influenced text that had been translated by the *Heroides* translator. The rhetoric of the love letter in the French vernacular had by this point become inextricably bound up with the rhetoric of the *Heroides*.

The Rhetorical Utility of the *Heroides*

In his 1481 preface to the *Heroides,* the commentator Antonius Volscus[49] privileges style above all else. First he stresses that Ovid's poetry is not simply for entertainment or relaxation, as some have claimed: his decision to "take on" Ovid's text in "gladiatorial combat" was not lightly undertaken. The utility of the work is to be sought in Ovid's excellence in "inuentione . . . facilitate . . . ingenii ubertate et uerborum copia" (in invention, fluency, the fertility of his genius, and linguistic abundance). Quintilian judged that Ovid bettered all other Latin poets in these areas.[50] He concludes:

> Opus enim uarium est: disertum, multiplex, copiosum, ubi multe non solum exquisitæ reconditæque sententiæ uix satis explicantur, sed etiam locorum historiarumque et fabularum obscura et perdifficilis hactenus allucinationem præbuit appositio.[51]

> For the work is various: eloquent, manifold, copious; in it not only are there many rare and abstruse expressions that are not easily explained, but also the obscure and difficult use of geography, history, and myth has up until now brought about confusion.

The value of the work, then, resides in two areas of study: rhetorical instruction and general factual detail: the educational utility of the *Heroides* is as much in its difficult geographical, mythological, and historical detail as in its copious language. This emphasis on the *difficulty* and *density* of the work—on the difficulty of the language as well as the obscurity of the allusions—is, in the first place, a way to justify the existence of Volscus' own

---

49. The commentaries to which I refer in this section will be dealt with in greater detail in chapter 3.
50. Evidently here Volscus does not have in mind Quintilian's much-quoted description of Ovid: 'lascivus . . . et nimium amator ingenii sui' (*Inst. Or.* X.1.88).
51. Ovid 1492, sig. a.ii^v.

commentary: its aim is to shed light on recondite references and convoluted turns of phrase. At the same time, though, it highlights an aspect of the *Heroides* that might strike the modern reader, accustomed to consider the text as relatively straightforward and linguistically uncomplicated, as unusual. For many early modern readers the *Heroides* led a double life, as an entertaining, easy text suited to recreational reading and to study at an early stage of education, and as a densely rhetorical work, packed with *recherché* details and brimming over with precious jewels of eloquence.

Guy Morillon's dedication, probably written in the first decade of the sixteenth century, places emphasis on the recreational value of the *Heroides:*

> Idcirco cum superioribus diebus a dialecticorum mæandris mentem relaxarem, sacrum illud Musarum diuersorium repetens, in Heroidas illas Ouidianas forte incidi: dii boni quam multiplici eruditione refertas, quam lepidissimis salibus concinnatas! (sig. A2ʳ)

> And so some days ago, when I was taking time off to relieve my mind of the twists and turns of the logicians, making for the sacred resting-place of the Muses, by chance I came across Ovid's *Heroides:* great gods, how crammed they are with complex learning, how cleverly and wittily they are put together!

Again, it must be acknowledged that the author is striking a rhetorical pose here. Indeed, the conceit that the author fell upon the work by accident while looking for something to occupy his mind is a common enough one: Octavien de Saint-Gelais had used the very same device to introduce his *Heroides* translation.[52] The author then feigns surprise at his discovery that the text is not in fact merely a trivial *divertissement*, but is "crammed with manifold knowledge" and "put together with the utmost charm and wit." Again, the emphasis is on the density and complexity of the work; but not at the expense of harmony and wit and lightness of touch. The *Heroides* is a text that is both easy and difficult at the same time.[53]

---

52. " . . . apres avoir tournoye la petite librarie de mon entendement et visite les angletz de mon gazophile, ung jour entre les autres assez curieux et embesongne de scavoir ne [*sic*] en quel endroit dresser mon oeuvre, le [*sic*] trouvay par my le nombre des autres volumes les epistres heroydes par le treseloquent et renomme poete Ovide, iadis compilees en forme latine doulce et mellifluë,' *Les XXI Epistres D'Ovide* (Paris: G. de Bossozel, 1534), fol. iᵛ [After having ranged through the little library of my intellect and visited the corners of my gazophile, one day when I was feeling rather curious and occupied with the question of where and on what ground to build my work, I found among a number of other volumes the *Epistulae heroidum* by the most eloquent and renowned poet Ovid, composed long ago in a smooth and flowing Latin style]. The unusual word "gazophile," meaning a treasury or storehouse, derives ultimately from the Greek *gazophylakion*.

53. For a discussion of what is at stake in the characterization of the *Heroides* as a work that

The rhetorical character of the *Heroides* can be defined yet more specifically. Ubertinus Clericus situates the text precisely in a classical rhetorical scheme:

> Genus autem orationis humile est: quia tali carmini conuenit. hoc est elegiaco: quod: ut uidimus: exiguum appelauit Horatius. quamquam inter elegiaca Nasonis carmina hoc maxime et sententiis: quantum materia ipsa patitur: et uerborum proprietate uidetur assurgere. (sig. a.iii^v)

> The style is low, because it suits such poetry—that is, elegy, which as we have seen Horace called "small." And yet among the elegiac poems of Ovid most of all this [style] seems to rise above that, as far as the matter permits, both in ideas and in the language itself.

Ovid is successful in using the 'low' style to bring out the substance of his poetry. Morillon agrees: "Contextus autem humilis atque facilis, utpote elegiaco carmini peculiaris, nec propterea minus florentissimus" (sig. A3^r) (It is composed in a low and easy style, as far as befits elegiac poetry; but it is no less brilliantly elaborate for that).

That it is written in the low style does not make the text any the less dazzlingly abundant in the flowers of eloquence. Again, simplicity of style (which the genre demands) does not preclude textual richness and complexity. Florence Verducci reads the avoidance of the high style in the *Heroides* as an implicit challenge to the values that belong to epic and tragedy: "In the *Heroides* Ovid subjects traditionally lofty subjects to the 'middle level' of style, and the result proves 'very dangerous' to his subject, a subject by definition in the arena of 'the passions and the sublime'" (294). In the humanist commentaries, however, there is no sense at all that the elegiac treatment of 'heroic' subjects contravenes the rule of *decorum*.

Morillon in his preface comments that anyone who reads the *Heroides* will find himself unable to resist imitating Ovid's rhetoric in his own writing:

> Nemo est enim usque adeo languidus, usque adeo ieiunus, qui non aliquid deliciarum atque argutiarum illinc hauriat. Nullus insuper tam frigidis præcordiis, cui non se offerant fœcunda ad excogitandum adminicula. Denique non existimo aliquem tam ceruicosum, tamque durum, qui minima epistolarum perlecta non statim concipiat similis conscribendæ copiosissimam farraginem. (sig. A3^r)[54]

---

reconciles the *dulce* and the *utile*, that is, both entertaining and serious, see above, chapter 1.

54. Morillon here borrows heavily from Badius's dedicatory epistle. Badius had written: " . . . tam

For there can be nobody so feeble-minded and lacking in taste that he would not absorb at least some of the work's charm and liveliness. No one, moreover, could be so insensitive that this rich aid to thought would not appeal to him. Finally I do not think there could be anyone so stubborn and so dense, that having read even the least of these epistles, he would not immediately adopt this most copious mixture in his own writing.

The virtues of the text are as much in its language as in its moral content: just as the ethical *exemplum* necessarily leads the individual to moral improvement, so exposure to rhetorical mastery brings about a similar change for the better in his character. Stylistic imitation necessarily brings ethical improvement in its train.

In his 1551 *Epître-préface,* Charles Fontaine also has more to say about style than moral considerations. Fontaine first praises Ovid as a "singulier poëte en invencion, grace et facilité," and goes on to affirm that the *Heroides* "ont tousiours esté, au iugement de tous savans, estimées de tregrand artifice." They are "briefves, utiles, et recreatives," three essential qualities in a poetic work "selon le iugement d'Horace." They also compare favorably with the *Metamorphoses:*

> Et combien que la Metamorphose soit estimée de tresgrand artifice et grace ... si est ce toutefois que pour sa longueur elle peut sembler estre moins plaisante, ioint qu'elle se montre plus fabuleuse que historique, et que ces Epitres, au contraire, plus historiques que fabuleuses.[55]

> And although the *Metamorphoses* is judged to be a poem of very great skill and elegance ... nevertheless because of its length it can seem less enjoyable, along with the fact that it appears more fabulous than historical, whereas these Epistles, by contrast, are more historical than fabulous.

Fontaine places the recreational value of the *Heroides* on a par with its educational utility. Here the utility is not in the realm of morality but in the 'historical' details contained in the narratives. His individual letter prefaces, on the other hand, do make occasional reference to the moral lessons to be learned from the stories (Phyllis and Phaedra). The section entitled "Le translateur aux lecteurs" which follows the tenth epistle, moreover, has a

---

fecunda praebeant ad excogitandum adminicula, ut nemo sit tam frigidis praecordiis qui minima epistolarum lecta non statim habeat consimilis scribendae plenissimam ferraginem." The full text of Badius' preface is usefully reproduced in Renouard, vol. 3: 102.

55. Fontaine 1580, 8.

detailed discussion about the utility of the translation in terms of both rhetoric and morals (see chapter 4).

The rhetorical character of the *Heroides* makes it an important source text for printed commonplace books. This is an aspect of humanist education whose importance in the shaping of the early modern literary mind cannot easily be overstated.[56] The texts of ancient authors would not have been presented to pupils for study in their entirety; the first experience of Ovid's works, for most, would have been either in the form of expurgated passages or excerpted segments arranged according to theme or part of speech in commonplace books. Usually these books mixed quotations from various classical authors according to schemes relating to *res* or *verba;* some presented the works of a single author or group of authors for easy consumption. One such text is Georgius Fabricius' *De re poetica libri VII* (first printed in its entirety at Basel, 1574),[57] the second book of which is essentially a commonplace book which presents lines culled from poets under various headings. It is entitled "Liber secundus exemplorum varietatis et copiae, ex Ouidio, Tibullo, Propertio"; the vast majority of the quotations are from Ovid, but Propertius and Tibullus also feature. The *Heroides* feature prominently, especially, appropriately enough, in the sections devoted to letter-writing formulae. Clearly, Ovid's epistolary poetry was used to generate forms of expression one might use in one's own letters: the *Heroides, Tristia,* and *Pontics* have a copious supply of formulae that fit into epistolary categories: "salutandi"; "formulae quibus initio literarum utimur"; "formulae quibus utimur ante uale"; "ualedicendi" (salutations, formulas we use at the start of a letter, formulas we use before signing off, valedictions). The list of possible greetings, to take an example, includes extracts from Penelope, Hypermnestra, Phaedra, Laodamia (the two quoted in Vives), Paris, Leander, Hypsipyle, and Hero (149–52). As well as supplying material for the sections on basic epistolary composition, excerpts from the *Heroides* also appear under more specific headings: "optandi" (prayers), "blanditiarum" (compliments), and the made-to-measure "in hominem asperum et immitem" (against a harsh and unfeeling man). The latter uses choice insults from Dido (2), Ariadne (2), Phyllis, Sappho, Phaedra (2), Canace, and Briseis (2). Fabricius does not venture too far into impropriety, however: the section on curses ("vitu-

---

56. For an extensive analysis of the role of the commonplace book in the Renaissance, see Moss 1996.

57. Here we are moving away from the chiefly Italian editions of the *Heroides* toward Northern Protestant treatments of Ovid's works. See Moss 1996, 199–200. Fabricius' work appeared in an Antwerp edition of four books in 1565 and was later reprinted in seven-book form (Paris 1584; Leipzig 1589); my references are to the latter edition.

perandi," 105) is disappointingly short and does not include any female-authored maledictions (which are hardly in short supply in the *Heroides*).

The specific interest in the epistolary rhetoric of the *Heroides* demonstrated by Vives and in the printed commonplace books appears to be a relatively new development. In the Middle Ages, the *Heroides* is less likely to be treated as a model for epistolary composition. The twelfth-century *Florilegium gallicum*, for example, contains many excerpts from the *Heroides;* but they are not obviously epistolary in nature: they do not draw attention to the "epistolary enhancing elements" (salutations, valedictions, references to the act of writing, etc.) of the collection. Only one of the excerpts refers explicitly to letter writing (*Her.* 4.20); excluding that, the reader has no way of knowing that the excerpts come from letters at all.[58] As we have seen, humanists were more interested than their medieval precursors had been in the formation of epistolary eloquence through the imitation of literary models.

The age of humanism saw a new kind of enthusiasm for integrating the rhetorical and ethical learning of classical texts into everyday contexts. In some ways, the editions of Ovid used in Jesuit education represent a culmination of this development. A notable text in this regard is Jacobus Pontanus' *Hortuli Ovidiani*.[59] Although printed a little later than the period which interests us (1610), the work affords a useful insight into contemporary ways of organizing knowledge. The text presents the works of Ovid to schoolboys in the form of excerpts listed under various categories. Unlike the commonplace book of Fabricius discussed above, the headings focus on *res* rather than *verba:* the subjects range from the morally neutral ("agricultura") to the prescriptive ("amor honestus/lasciuus" [honourable/licentious love]); "poena merita/immerita" [deserved/underserved punishment]). Obviously these headings are intended to teach the schoolboy—in a much more forceful way than the humanist commentaries—how Ovid's poetry ought to be read. Pontanus is highly selective in the choices he makes. It is relatively unsurprising that the only examples of "amor honestus" come from Penelope and Deianira, but the omission in the "amor lascivus" section of everything but two half-lines from the *Heroides* is more like censorship. Pontanus includes nothing more lascivious than Phaedra's "Quid deceat, non uidet ullus amans" (What is right, no lover ever sees), and Hypsipyle's singularly inoffensive "Credula res amor est" (Love is a credulous thing). The limited use of Phaedra as a model for imitation in these texts demonstrates how

---

58. Rackley 1992, 125–35.

59. Pontanus is responsible for the editions of Virgil and Ovid used in all Jesuit schools in the period; see Moss 1996, 221, n. 6.

much the basis for moral interpretation of the *Heroides* has changed since the Middle Ages. In the *Florilegium gallicum,* excerpts from Phaedra's letter predominated, above all others: it was *Heroides* 4 that occupied the most text on the page (19 lines in all). As Sally A. Rackley observes (132–33), none of the excerpts contains any direct reference to incestuous love: they are carefully chosen to be detachable from their erotic context. Humanist readings of the text had definitively shifted the ground upon which moral readings of the *Heroides* could be built: Jesuit educators recognized the absolute importance of rhetoric in the shaping of the moral individual. The Phaedra of *Heroides* 4 became a potentially dangerous voice, not just for the immoral *content* of her letter, but for the problems posed by her mastery of rhetoric.

Moral Edification

There is a problem with the rhetorical-moral axis upon which study of the *Heroides* turns which goes to the very heart of humanist educational theory: how could the rhetorical skill of Ovid's heroines be squared with their moral deviance? Quintilian's model of the "uir bonus dicendique peritus" (a good man, skilled at speaking) is inadequate: there is an implicit separation of rhetorical education from moral education. How could Phaedra represent a model of 'good' rhetoric (as she does in Vives)? To what extent was the rhetorically skilled woman a threat? To answer to this question in part, Kathryn L. McKinley adopts the idea that in antiquity and in the Middle Ages and Renaissance, male writers found that the feminine was "good to think with" (16). On the use of Ovid's female characters as models for effective rhetoric in the medieval schoolroom, she remarks: " . . . for the all-male students of the medieval *studium* or university, the feminine is not only good to think with, but is also presented as a model good to 'speak with'" (89); "From the twelfth through seventeenth centuries, when it was applied in the classroom to the speeches of Ovid's heroines, rhetoric offered a means to project an alternate view of the feminine: one linking feminine speech with acts of deliberation, judgment, and fine discrimination" (64).

The general introductory remarks of Ubertinus Clericus on the moral utility of the work as a whole are very much in the tradition of the medieval *accessus,* and they make no explicit comment on the problem of feminine eloquence.

> Materia uero est ethica, id est moralis, quia describit uarios uirorum mulierumque mores. Intentio poetae est exercendo ingenium et quaerendo

> famam amoris affectus demonstrare & ostendere quantum hi differant in mulieribus pudicis & impudicis: quia in aliis casti amoris pietatem, in aliis libidinis et furoris incontinentiam probant. Itaque aliae ad laudem & imitationem: aliae ad libidinis & impudiciciæ detestationem memorantur. (sig. a.iii^v)

> The matter is, then, ethical, that is to say moral, since it describes the diverse morals of men and women. The poet's intention is, in exercising his talent and seeking fame, to demonstrate the affects of love and to show how much they differ in virtuous and immoral women: since in some they demonstrate the devotion of chaste love, in others the excesses of lust and madness. Therefore some of their stories are told to make us praise and imitate them, others to make us despise lust and immorality.

The twofold scheme that Clericus outlines here is entirely characteristic of medieval and early modern critical approaches to the *Heroides*. The heroines are either paragons to be imitated or wicked specimens to be despised. This scheme does not account, however, for those pieces that do not obviously fall into either category. Clericus evidently considers that of little consequence, since he does not give examples at this point, nor does he refer back to this scheme in his commentaries on the poems themselves.

The approach of Clericus differs, however, from the medieval approach in one respect: it is primarily rhetorical.[60] Craig Kallendorf writes of the rhetorical approach to poetry:

> As O. B. Hardison and Brian Vickers have shown, the principles of epideictic rhetoric became entangled with the principles of literary criticism in late antiquity, so that praise of virtue and condemnation of vice came to be seen as a legitimate goal of poetry and criticism as well as speechmaking.[61]

Elsewhere, Kallendorf demonstrates that Boccaccio was the first prominent humanist to apply the epideictic approach (bound up by that time with the concerns of moral philosophy) extensively to the study of poetry, and in

---

60. However, see McKinley on the continuities between medieval and humanist approaches to commentary in the case of the *Metamorphoses*. It is important to acknowledge that the medieval commentary tradition was by no means homogeneous, and certain commentaries of the High Middle Ages (for example the "Vulgate" *Metamorphoses* commentary) display a sophistication and an interest in rhetoric similar to that associated with Renaissance humanism.

61. Kallendorf 1998, 355.

particular to Virgil's Dido.⁶² The rhetorical construction of Dido in terms of praise and blame, in particular as a way to dispose of the ambiguities of Ovid's text, will be discussed in more detail in the following chapter.

Clericus adds that it is in this work that Ovid expresses the effects of love most successfully; and that the *Heroides* instruct us on how best to conduct ourselves in practising the art of love in the same way that Cicero's speeches instruct us in the art of speaking. In these examples, both Ovid and Cicero teach by example; in other works they are more explicitly didactic (the *Ars* and *Remedia* on the one hand; and the many Ciceronian theoretical works on the other). In asserting the equivalence of Ovid, the "praeceptor amoris," and Cicero, the "magister eloquentiae," Clericus affirms the primacy of rhetoric, and especially its epideictic dimension, in his approach to the text.

Superficially, Clericus' reading of the work resembles closely the medieval scheme that addressed in turn the *intentio auctoris* (to commend legitimate love), the *pars ethica* (the work instructs good morals and uproots bad ones) and the *finalis causa* (that we will flee both legitimate and illegitimate love and devote ourselves to chaste love). A representative example of this method of reading the *Heroides* is a twelfth-century *accessus* quoted by Suzanne C. Hagedorn, 29.⁶³ Hagedorn also quotes a twelfth-century poem that neatly summarizes the main points of this approach to the *Heroides:*

> Actoris intentio restat, condemnare
> Amores illicitos fatuos culpare
> Et recte feruentium mentes commendare:
> Utilitas nostra sit iustum pignus amare. (28)

> The author's intention remains to condemn illicit love, blame the foolish, and commend the souls of the ardently righteous: the utility for us is to honor legitimate pledges.

This attitude had written itself so deeply into the tradition of *Heroides*-interpretation that humanist commentators could not fail to acknowledge it at least. Even Guy Morillon, writing a generation after Clericus, thought it necessary to preface his edition with a section entitled "Poetae intentio, et quid frugis afferant Heroidum Epistolae, necnon cui parte philosophiae

---

62. Kallendorf 1985, 401–15.
63. See also Shaner 1999, 25–31. Shaner highlights some subtle differences in the "intentio" sections of separate *Heroides* commentary traditions; the approach is, however, broadly similar in each case.

debeant supponi." Morillon here fits the work into a moral framework, almost identical to the one used in the medieval *accessus*. The poet's intention, he writes, was to show, in a variety of different narratives, in what consists the duty of a wife, and to let the reader know what sort of women love their husbands chastely and what immodestly.

> In aliis enim casti amoris pietatem extollit. In aliis uero libidinis atque incontinentissimos amoris æstus subinde taxat. Itaque (ut duas pro reliquis accipiamus) Penelopes castitatem ad imitationem, Phedræ uero incestum amorem ad detestationem proponit. Propterea opus istud non immerito morali philosophiae (quam Graeci Ethicen uocant) supponi debet: quandoquidem & mores hominum, & uitia docet. Non enim aliud nobis illæ amantium querimoniæ, lamentationes, ultimæque desperationes clamitant, quam ut suis exemplis cautiores effecti, uetitos indecentesque amores deuitemus. Et profecto quamuis Ouidius in nullis aliis uoluminibus amoris affectus ardentius expresserit, quam in epistolis, nulla tamen lubricitas, nullaque lasciua (si modo aequum sortiantur interpretem) inuenitur. (sig. A3ʳ)

> For in some he extols the devotion of chaste love. In others he reproaches lust and the unbridled passions of love. So—to take two representative examples—he holds out Penelope's chastity to be imitated, and Phaedra's incestuous love to be despised. For this reason this work ought to be categorized as moral philosophy (what the Greeks call "ethics"), because it teaches of the morals and vices of men. For these lovers' complaints, laments, and final cries of despair demand nothing other of us than that we, forewarned by their examples, avoid forbidden and indecent love. And indeed, although Ovid in all his other works has never represented the passions more violently than in these epistles, even so nothing dangerous or wanton can be found here (assuming they get a fair hearing).

Although Morillon's *argumenta* to the individual poems continue to be printed well after the sixteenth century, this introductory section does not. Here, Morillon emphasizes the moral utility of the work in the well-established terms of example and negative example: "Penelopes castitatem ad imitationem, Phedrae vero incestum amorem ad detestationem proponit," and in the last two sentences he follows the earlier Badius preface quite closely. The moral interpretation is, however, taken no further than this. Ann Moss observes that specific moralizing is rare in sixteenth-century editions of the *Heroides*:

Despite the commentators' interest in the ethical questions raised by the *Heroides,* they make little or no attempt to illustrate in detail from the poems the edifying conclusions they had drawn in their introduction to the work. . . . Suasive rhetoric and descriptive psychology are closely linked, but it is to be left to the reader's good judgment to draw out the moral implications. . . . [64]

The interest in moral condemnation and exemplarity professed in the prefatory comments does not continue to be applied in the main body of commentary, in the annotations on the individual letters. This was often true of medieval commentary practice also. As McKinley demonstrates, there was often a "hermeneutic gap" between the stated aims of the *accessus* and the content of the commentary itself (55). Other humanist commentators pay lip service to the established interpretative scheme, but pass over in silence the specifics of its application.[65] Badius, like Antonius Volscus, pays little attention in the body of his commentary to the work's moral utility, though in his prefatory letter he rejects the charge of immorality with an affirmation that the heroines' stories stand as cautionary examples.[66] The *intentio auctoris* part of his preface simply states: "intentio poetae est, si non fallor, uberrimum ingenium suum ostentare" (The poet's intention is, if I am not mistaken, to make a show of his fertile genius). As we have seen, Erasmus came to the same conclusion in the *De conscribendis epistolis.*

Among the writers that do attempt to demonstrate how the interpretative scheme is meant to work, most see fit to mention only Penelope and Phaedra to illustrate the dual "exemplum"/"exemplum ex negatiuo" scheme. This is typical of the medieval "intentiones," where these two heroines are almost always the examples mentioned. Penelope and Phaedra are seen as the

---

64. Moss 1982, 10–11.

65. Theory and practice did not always fit well together in humanist education. On the disconnect between the humanists' stated aim of moral education and the actual classroom practice of formal textual analysis, see Grafton and Jardine 1986, ch. 1. McKinley demonstrates how this applies in the case of Raphael Regius' *Metamorphoses* commentary (130–31).

66. ". . . cognouique nihil in epistolis lubricum, nihilque lasciuum quod ad amores hortetur reperiri; contra quae illinc dehortentur quamplurima. quid enim aliud illae amantium querimoniae atque lamentationes et supremae desperationes nobis clamitant quam 'Apagite amores, fugite hinc adolescentes, fugite iuuenes! nostris exemplis cautiores effecti, uetitos proscribite amores!'" (I know that in these letters nothing can be found that is dangerous, and nothing licentious that encourages love; on the contrary, very many points would discourage it. For what else do these lovers' complaints and lamentations and final cries of despair proclaim to us but: "Be off, love! Get away youths! Away, young people! Take caution from our examples, and let it be known that such love is forbidden!") Quoted by Lamarque, 37, n. 34; Renouard, vol. 3: 102. Note that Badius mentions men as well as women in his scheme. In the commentary tradition beginning with the twelfth-century Munich manuscript analysed by Hexter, both men and women are mentioned. See Shaner, 29.

two most extreme epitomes of Ovid's ethical intention. Penelope stands at the head of the collection, and it is she who always stands at the head in the order of exemplarity: she is the archetypical example of wifely fidelity. Clericus, at the end of his commentary on the first poem, concludes: "Penelope usque ad ultimum spiritum pudice uixisse dicitur: unde pro exemplo pudicitiae a poetis proponi solet "(sig. b.iii^r) (Penelope is said to have lived chastely until her last breath: so she is usually set forth as an example of virtue by poets). Although, as I have said, it is not shown how this exemplarity functions specifically in Ovid's version.[67] Indeed, in *Heroides* 1, Ovid perhaps hints at the countertradition that makes Penelope into a devious adulteress. This tradition is known in the sixteenth century: Charles Fontaine, midcentury translator of Ovid, is aware of it. The *praeteritio* in the closing sentence of his preface to the first poem dismisses the slander, lest elements of *that* Penelope be read into (his translation of) Ovid: "Ie me tais de ce que ie trouve que le seul Lycophron, ancien auteur, ha mal senti & escrit de la chasteté de Penelope, contre la commune opinion & renommee" (13) (I pass over in silence what I find in the ancient author Lycophron alone, who thought ill and wrote slightingly of Penelope's chastity, in disagreement with the common opinion and repute).

Phaedra, on the other hand, always stands at the opposite pole: it is her letter that is adduced most often as a negative example. Phaedra is often seen as the most 'rhetorical' of the heroines. This is usually seen by modern critics as a failing. Joseph Farrell, for instance, sees Phaedra as the least 'spontaneous' heroine; she does not "speak from the heart"; her intention is solely to deceive. However, Phaedra's letter is *not* representative of women's writing strategies in general: " . . . a character like Phaedra should not be considered normative for the collection as a whole: rather she should be evaluated against the generic expectation that the written word of a woman in love is a truthful utterance."[68]

The fact that Phaedra, so obviously an exception to the rule of women's writing in the *Heroides,* should be used as a representative example demonstrating Ovid's intention to edify by negative example, shows that the ethical commendation-condemnation scheme is not being applied rigorously to the collection as a whole. The *Heroides* cannot easily be made to fit universal ethical categories. Marina S. Brownlee suggests that the emphasis on moral exemplarity in medieval editions is basically at odds with the character of the text itself, which is resistant to such readings:

---

67. In chapter 5, I explore the question of why the Ovidian poetic is resistant to such 'exemplary' readings.
68. Farrell 1998, 318, n. 19.

If Ovid programmatically dismantles the exemplary function which initially accorded his heroines their legendary status, the Middle Ages effected a reversal of this hermeneutic procedure. [. . .] Unlike the epoch in which it was written, [sic] medieval readers no longer view Ovid's text as a politically and discursively transgressive artifact.[69] (104)

That is why the humanist readings, even as they extol the moral utility of the work and invoke the tradition categories of exemplarity in their preliminary comments, do not impose moral readings on the text itself with any consistency. The *Heroides* is a text that seems to lend itself well to moral-ethical judgments *grosso modo;* but it resists systematic application of such readings.

Vives's use of the salutation from *Heroides* 4 proves that Phaedra *can* be used as a morally neutral stylistic model. This had been impossible in the Middle Ages: the only way that Phaedra could be presented as a model for imitation was in *florilegia* that presented her words *in vacuo,* isolated from the wider context. Sally A. Rackley observes that the *Heroides* 4 excerpts in the *Florilegium gallicum* suppress the context, so that Phaedra's words can be read without the knowledge that what motivates them is an incestuous desire.[70]

On the other hand, *Heroides* 4 still poses problems for authors of serious epistolographical works, even where it is not mentioned directly: there is a sense that all allusion to the strategies of Phaedra in *Heroides* 4 is to be avoided. In the Siberich version of his *De conscribendis epistolis,* Erasmus had included some comments about the personal dimension of the familiar letter. Expanding on Demetrius' idea that letters expose to the addressee something of the individual letter-writer's soul, Erasmus noted that we write things in a letter that we would be ashamed to say in person.[71] This observation recalls Phaedra's "dicere quae puduit, scribere iussit amor." It is perhaps partly for this reason that Erasmus suppressed this section of his introduction in later printings.

The preface to the Phaedra letter by Clericus is surprisingly neutral:

---

69. One might object that the idea that Ovid's audience in the Augustan period would have read the *Heroides* as a transgressive text is pure speculation.

70. Rackley, 132–33.

71. Fantazzi 2002, 39–56; 45. Conrad Celtis had also made this observation in his treatise on epistolography, quoted in Bizer (209, n. 92): "Epistola nuncia mentis, et uelut quidam est uector atque internuncius sermonis nostri, desideriique, & conceptus unius ad alterum absentem, rubore aut alio casu loqui certioremque reddere nequeuntis significatio, uel qua cum amicis & inimicis tacitas nostras cogitationes uoluntatemque communicamus."

> Itaque hac epistola ei amorem suum indicat, conaturque multis rationibus eum ad libidinem suam deflectere; nitens persuadere nullum esse crimen in concubitu priuigni et nouercæ. (sig. c.v^v)

> So in this letter she reveals her love to him, and tries with many arguments to bend him to her lust; striving to persuade that there is no crime in a stepson and his stepmother sleeping together.

The language used by Volscus is only slightly more moralistic: "Epistola Hippolytum ad amorem flectere nititur phædra: sed cum turpe sit priuignum a nouerca in amore sollicitari: principium ex insinuatione sumitur" (sig c.v^r) (With her letter Phaedra strives to bend Hippolytus to her love: but since it is immoral for a stepson to be propositioned by his stepmother, she begins by trying to gain his favor). Volscus recognizes that Phaedra begins her letter in a rhetorically subtle way, using insinuation and innuendo to skirt around the immorality of what she is proposing. But his description of the technique does not draw out the moral implications any further.

Phaedra presents herself as a master of 'strong' rhetoric: Amor himself guarantees the success of her suit:

> Ille mihi primo dubitanti scribere dixit:
>   'Scribe! Dabit uictas ferreus ille manus.' (*Her.* 4.13–14)

> He said to me when at first I was hesitating to write: "Write! That iron-hearted man will hold up his hands in surrender."

Hippolytus, iron-hearted though he is, will surrender to the persuasive power of Phaedra's eloquence. However, as Giovanna Malquori Fondi observes, Amor's words carry a secondary meaning, a subtext that denies the heroine's writing perlocutionary success.[72] "[M]anus" can be read as a metonymy for the messages Hippolytus receives from suitors: the phrase therefore hints at the inevitable defeat of the written word; and, of course, the reader knows that Phaedra's advances *will* be rebuffed, and that the story will end in tragedy.

It is only at the end of the commentary that Clericus explicitly condemns Phaedra (as he had promised the reader at the start: "Qui fuerit finis utriusque dicetur in fine epistolae"). Moreover, this sort of intervention

---

72. Malquori Fondi 1995, 257–70. .

is very unusual in the commentaries. Clericus relates the outcome of the narrative: the death of Hippolytus and the suicide of Phaedra; then he draws the conclusion:

> Phædram uero audita morte hippolyti alii gladio alii laqueo uitam finisse dicunt. Quo exemplo deterrentur mulieres omnes ab illicito detestabilique amore: ne uel idem, uel et miserabilior finis eas sequatur. (sig. d.iv^r)

> Indeed some say that Phaedra, having heard of the death of Hippolytus, ended her life by the sword; others say by hanging. By this example all women are deterred from illicit and abominable love: lest the same fate, or an even more wretched one, should await them.

Here Clericus uses the categories of 'amor' familiar from the medieval commentaries;[73] the judgment is rather peremptory: he does not attempt to make it relevant to the schoolboys using his work in the classroom, addressing it instead to "mulieres omnes." Moreover, the moral is drawn from other sources which give the final outcome of Phaedra's story; the commentators make no effort to read the moral *into* the epistle itself; it is entirely detachable from the heroine's rhetoric.

THE ATTEMPTS by humanist editors and commentators to make Ovid's text 'readable' meet with several difficulties, not least of which is the impossibility of categorizing the *Heroides* definitively. As we have seen, Erasmus in his treatise rejected it because he was unable to fit the heroines' epistles anywhere into his epistolary scheme; yet he returns again and again to the text. Compilers of partial editions of the text (commonplace books and rhetoric manuals) faced problems, too. Excerpting sections of the text is a way of reshaping it, of controlling its potential applications; but any attempt to present the 'characteristic' face of Ovid's text risks becoming entangled in its own contradictions. That is why moral readings of the text by humanist authors tend to stay as general and superficial as possible. In part, humanist editions prepared for use in the schoolroom reduced the text to the level of a rhetorical exercise. Even then, however, it continues to pose problems: is it possible to attribute each element of discourse to Ovid or to the heroines?

---

73. See Hexter 1986, 160 for the division of "amor illicitus" into the categories of "stultus," "incestus," and "furiosus" in a twelfth-century Munich manuscript.

Can a poetic text be fixed within a rhetorical scheme? Such questions are further complicated by the fact that Ovid's text itself plays on the merging of modes of writing, of genre and gender. 'Rewriting' the text of the *Heroides* for pedagogical uses becomes a way of 'writing back,' or 'writing *against*': against the heroines; against Ovid; against the grain of the text.

CHAPTER 3

Editions and Commentaries

Tout est parti de ce principe: qu'il ne fallait pas réduire l'amoureux à un simple sujet symptomal, mais plutôt faire entendre ce qu'il y a dans sa voix d'inactual, c'est- à-dire d'intraitable.

[. . .] Si je pouvais contraindre le signe, le soumettre à une sanction, je pourrais enfin trouver le repos.

Roland Barthes[1]

OVID'S HEROINES pose a problem for their humanist commentators: the fact of a discourse that resists integration into the systematized procedures of humanist rhetoric and moral philosophy. Nevertheless, as we have seen, the rhetoric of the letter-writing heroines, orchestrated as it is by the poet schooled in the discipline of *ethopoeïa*, is not intractable in the same way as the "lover's discourse" of which Barthes writes. Grammarians, rhetoricians, and moral philosophers had at their disposal a number of ways to accommodate the text to the concerns of an early modern readership.

The commentaries on the *Heroides* that were most influential in France in the sixteenth century were not those penned by the greatest humanist scholars of the scholars of the day.[2] The notes by Politian and other famous

---

1. Barthes 1977, 7, 192. "Everything stemmed from this principle: that we must not reduce the lover to a straightforward symptomatic subject, but rather make heard in his voice whatever is untimely, that is, intractable.[. . .] If only I could constrain the sign, submit it to a sanction, I might at last find repose."

2. For my account of commentary editions of the *Heroides,* I rely on Ann Moss's bibliographical survey and "check-list of editions" in *Ovid in Renaissance France,* 8–16 and 66–79. A resurgence of interest in the general subject of textual commentary has seen the recent publication of several collections of essays on commentary, from the classical era to the Middle Ages and Renaissance: Mathieu Castellani and Plaisance (eds.) 1990; Besomi and Caruso (eds.) 1992; Most (ed.) 1999; Goulet-Cazé (ed.) 2000; Gibson and Shuttleworth Kraus (eds.) 2002; Pade (ed.) 2005. This latter volume poses the question of whether there is, in fact, a "Renaissance commentary" as distinct from a medieval commentary. Commentary's essentially tralatitious nature meant that the form, and in many cases the content, of commentaries changed very little over the centuries; but Renaissance commentators did often distinguish themselves from their predecessors by their methods, and by their interest in different aspects of the text.

contemporaries of his, including Quintianus Stoa, were often printed alongside the main commentaries in editions from 1518 onward; but it was the notes by Antonius Volscus, Ubertinus Clericus, and Jodocus Badius that always formed the core text of this first wave of commentary editions. Volscus and Clericus belonged to the generation before Politian, and their style is undeniably different from that of the great humanist scholars of his generation.[3] Yet their commentaries dominated in editions of the *Heroides* printed throughout Italy and France in the late fifteenth and early sixteenth centuries. When the more sparsely annotated Guy Morillon edition took over in popularity from the 1530s onward, the abundant notes by various famous humanists, often included throughout the century in handsome Venice editions claiming comprehensive coverage, ceased to be reproduced by French printers. Those editions had flourished from 1518 and throughout the 1520s: Ann Moss lists six French editions that incorporated the full range of annotations. The core commentary text of these editions was still provided by Clericus, Volscus, and Badius; this was augmented by the annotations of Italian humanists of the next generation.[4]

The edition that dominated in the first half of the sixteenth century in France, as Ann Moss demonstrates, was the one prepared by Jodocus Badius Ascensius (Josse Bade), which incorporated his own commentary alongside those of Antonius Volscus and Ubertinus Clericus; it first appeared in 1500[5] and was reprinted fifteen times in Lyon by 1536. Thereafter, the combination of Guy Morillon (Guido Morillo) and Johannes Baptista Egnatius (Cipelli), which first appeared in 1533, superseded it. The focus of this chapter will therefore be on the texts of the commentaries that formed the core of the two most popular commentary editions printed in France in the sixteenth century. They will not be read in the context of advances made

---

3. For Politian's 'historical' approach and the advances in philology made by him, see Grafton 1977, 150–88. The 'encyclopaedic' approach of the likes of Volscus and Clericus differed greatly from the historicist approach of Politian: the former was not concerned with making philological judgments on the text. It aimed primarily to offer help with matters of rhetorical style, and to amass large volumes of information about ancient literature and culture, without making much of an effort to discriminate between sources. On the different approaches, see also Grafton 1991, 23–46.

4. Notes by the following scholars are included, in various capacities, in six French editions from 1518: Politian, J. B. Pius, Crucius, Egnatius, Quintianus Stoa, Domitius Calderinus, G. Merula. Added to that list in four editions (1526, '28, '29, '36) are the names Scoellius, Bartolitanus, Zarotus. The Morillon edition incorporated notes by Nizolius (1567), and the emendations and textual criticism of Navagero appeared in editions from the 1570s. I have come across notes by the following scholars in various Venice editions which do not appear in any French editions: Janus Parrhasius, Aaron Battaleus, I. Scoppa.

5. Paris, Jean de Vingle for Etienne Gueynard, 1500. This is the earliest surviving edition. Renouard reasons that there must have been an earlier edition, since Badius' preface appears to have been written in Lyon in 1499 (Renouard, vol. 1: 149).

in philology by the great humanist scholars from Politian onward; nor will they be related to the wider context of the conditions of their composition. It is in the reception of these texts that the greatest interest resides: how they came to be popular; what aspects of them were valued by their readership; and what their popularity tells us about the interest in the *Heroides* and the applications to which the text was put by amateurs, poets, and scholars alike.

The edition that first brought together the commentaries of Antonius Volscus and Ubertinus Clericus was printed at Casale in 1481.[6] In the decade following their first publication, the two commentaries were mostly printed separately; from 1491 they were often published together, along with the commentaries of Calderinus and Merula.[7] Many Venice editions followed, and this format continued to be printed at Venice and elsewhere very frequently up to the end of the century and well into the next.

Antonius Volscus was a member of the Roman Academy of Pomponio Leto, and sometime Professor of Rhetoric at the university at Rome. He collaborated with Leto in preparing the 1472 *editio princeps* of Nonius Marcellus. As well as the *Heroides* commentary, which first appeared in print in the 1481 Casale edition, Volscus also published his notes on the *Satires* of Persius, and a 1482 commentary on the elegies of Propertius. The latter was often reprinted in editions containing the complete works of Catullus, Tibullus, and Propertius.

The *Heroides* commentary was the first work of scholarship that Volscus had published.[8] B. M. Mariano compares two manuscript versions of the commentary, 'r' and 'ed,' the first of which resembles a set of notes for the lessons given orally by the *magister:* it is more diffuse and more obviously didactic in style than the other version. The notes in 'ed,' which is evidently the basis for the printed text of 1481, are less fragmentary, and more carefully constructed (107). Mariano goes on to describe the general technique of Volscus, contrasting his approach with the great scholars of the late quattrocento: Volscus intended his commentary to serve students as a kind of compendium of mythological, historical, geographical information, at a time when such compendia were not widely available (108).

Ubertinus Clericus Crescentinas (Ubertino Clerico da Crescentino) was born in the first half of the fifteenth century at Crescentino, a small town in Vercelli. In the 1470s he was professor of rhetoric at Pavia; his best-

---

6. Mario Cosenza informs us that this book has the privilege of being the only known book printed at Casale in the fifteenth century. See the entry on Volscus in Cosenza 1962–67.

7. See the article on Clericus in the *Dizionario biographico degli italiani*.

8. See Mariano 1993, 105–12.

known work dates from this period, a commentary on Cicero's *Epistulae ad Familiares*, first published in 1480 at Venice. This work was printed at least twenty-three times in the next two decades.[9] In a prefatory letter to this work dating from 1476, Clericus also mentioned having prepared commentaries on the first book of the *Metamorphoses* and Cicero's *De Officiis;* these were probably never published.[10] Around 1477 he went to Casale di Monferrato to take the post of professor of the "ars dicendi."

His commentary on the *Heroides,* composed some time during his stay there, is dedicated to Guidone di San Giorgio, conte di Biandrate. The words of gratitude and praise that Ubertinus Clericus showers upon the latter in his preface, in the judgment of Vinay, "vengono su dal cuore e sono aliene da servilità" (144). Vinay informs us that the printing expenses were defrayed in part by canonico Stefano de Ulmo, although Clericus does not mention him in the preface.

Clericus says that he decided to publish his commentary owing to popular demand ("multorum efflagitatione compulsus" [compelled by the insistence of many]). This leads Vinay to suspect that the text was probably a rehashed version of a course of lessons. But Clericus had a broader audience in mind than just students: the work was intended for anybody who "wished to become learned." The colophon to the 1481 Casale edition insists that the work had been published by Clericus "non ad ostentationem ingenii aut doctrinæ: sed ad communem utilitatem" (not in order to show off his talent or his learning, but for the common good) (sig. o.ii^r). Clericus reserves special scorn for those who "deal in obscure allegories in order to appear more learned" (sig. a.iii^r). Vinay claims that the commentary of Clericus is of primary interest because it "pone sott'occhio il pane quotidiano di cui si alimentavano le persone colte di Casale" (145). The interest is hardly limited to the culture of a small northern Italian town, however: the commentary, along with that of Volscus, enjoyed huge popularity throughout Europe well into the sixteenth century.

The focus of the commentary is more on the form than on the content of the work. The stated objective of the author was simply to see to it that: "si qua, aut in uerbis aut in sensu, obscuriora essent, diligenter explanarentur" (anything obscure in the words or in their meaning should be carefully explained) (sig. a.iii^r). Clericus generally does not depart much from this aim: to aid comprehension and to avoid pedantry ("in hoc nolim tamen esse contentiosus aut pertinax" [In this undertaking, I do not wish to be

---

9. Cosenza, "Clericus."
10. Vinay 1935, 144.

argumentative or stubborn]). He does not go into great detail on contentious points, and rarely adopts a firm stance; Vinay comments: "Questo metodo fa, talora, l'impressione di metter da parte anzichè risolvere le difficoltà" (This method gives the impression, at times, of setting aside difficulties instead of resolving them).

Vinay notes that here Clericus is more inclined to allegorical interpretation (than he had been in his previous commentaries), but only when it is supported by a classical authority. He concludes that Clericus did not enjoy his work on the *Heroides* as much as he had the Cicero commentaries, and that the former is generally duller, and less lively. The *Heroides* work was never "destined to live long," in Vinay's judgment. But it is certain that Clericus' work *was* destined to live on in humanist circles, at least for a few decades after his death (probably around 1500): it continued to be printed in many editions throughout Italy and France in those years.

Jodocus Badius (1461–1535), or Ascensius, often supplied his own commentaries for his printed editions of the classics. He also composed a number of textbooks for use in the grammar classes; as we have seen, he wrote a short letter-writing manual, the *De epistolarum compositione compendium* (1502), which went through a dozen editions in the first third of the century, often grouped together with other humanist epistolographical treatises. Though Flemish by birth and upbringing, Badius spent most of his career in France, and he probably prepared his commentary on the *Heroides* during his time in Lyon teaching Latin in the school of Henri Valluphinus. At that time he was also preparing editions for the press of Johann Trechsel. After the death of the latter, Badius had come to Paris (in 1499) to work alongside Jean Petit, but it was not until 1503 that he established his own press, which was to become so famous as the "Praelum Ascensianum." As is the case with all his commentaries, his notes on the *Heroides* are intended for schoolroom use or as a learning aid for beginners. Badius continued to write commentaries of this type throughout his career under the rubric "familiaris explanatio" or "facilis explanatio"; he usually supplemented them, in the editions he prepared, with commentaries aimed at a more learned audience—as he had done in the case of his *Heroides* edition, with the commentaries of Volscus and Clericus. The essential source for information on Badius' life and work is Renouard's 1908 three-volume study, cited above. Usefully, all of the prefaces Badius wrote for the editions he prepared are reprinted there.

The commentary of Domitius Calderinus (1446–1478) on the *Epistula Sapphus* dates from 1476; it was usually included at the end of the main *Heroides* text in sixteenth-century editions, and very often published alongside his *Ibis* commentary. The earliest printing of this commentary alongside the Clericus and Volscus commentaries seems to be the Venice edition of 1492; editions prior to that seem to contain only the *Ibis* and not the Sappho letter, although the latter had previously been printed on its own. Calderinus argues for the authenticity of the *Epistula Sapphus*, using *Amores* 2.18 as his chief authority. Unlike many critics who had set the *Epistula Sapphus* apart from the other *Heroides* (it was transmitted separately), or even considered it a translation into Latin of a poem penned by Sappho herself, Calderinus judges it to be a genuine work by Ovid, and an integral part of his *Heroides*.[11] He even asserts that the letter's proper place in the collection is immediately following the Dido letter. Later in the commentary he returns to the question of authorship, arguing that none of the "double letters" is by Ovid: the replies cannot be by him, since he mentions only the replies penned by his friend Sabinus in *Amores* 2.18; and the initial letters cannot be by Ovid, since the men write first, and Ovid testifies only to having written in the person of heroines.

Calderinus differs in his commentary style from Volscus and Clericus: he is quite clearly a more accomplished scholar than either of them. He marshals his sources more adeptly than the other commentators, and always supports his usage notes with examples from Latin and Greek authors. He uses Greek words in their original form, something done only rarely by Volscus, and not at all by Clericus. His glosses are fewer in number and less basic than those furnished by the main commentators: Calderinus seems to have in mind a better educated readership.[12] He is sensitive to the uses of irony and rhetorical subtleties of Ovid's text. Nevertheless, as is characteristic for scholars of his generation, Calderinus is rather undisciplined in deciding where to set the limits of relevancy to his observations. There are frequent long digressions on the mythological, etymological, and literary background to words used only in passing by Ovid, such as the lengthy explanation of "Typhoidos" in line 11, or the discussions of avian behavior in Aristotle prompted by the allusion at 38–39. He refers often to his previous commentary on Statius's *Silvae*. Calderinus is more inclined than Clericus or Volscus had been to court controversy and to join battle with rival scholars: he argues

---

11. Politian would agree; his notes on the *Epistula Sapphus*, prepared for students around 1481, are available in a modern edition (Poliziano, ed. by E. Lazzeri, 1971).

12. Indeed, Grafton claims that Calderinus was one of the first to depart from the standard commentary method, and to concern himself with difficult textual problems, writing for an audience of advanced scholars rather than for students. However, he was also guilty of misusing and inventing sources to corroborate erroneous readings, a practice for which Politian attacked him ("On the Scholarship of Politian," 155–60).

the case for his favored textual readings with the utmost conviction. Mario Cosenza informs us that Perotti used to call Calderinus "Timon," "after the famous misanthrope of Athens, meaning that D. C. hated all men." This argumentative nature sometimes emerges in the Sappho commentary, as when he rails against those scholars whose Greek is so poor that they rely on a particularly deficient Latin translation of Plutarch for their citations; however, he archly refuses to name the victim of his attack.[13] Elsewhere in his writings he had been less restrained, and it was against his archenemy Angelus Sabinus that Calderinus directed much of his vitriol: this dispute occupies an important place in the history of the *Heroides* reception.[14]

The notes of Johannes Baptista Egnatius (1478–1553) are included in many editions from the second third of the century onward.[15] Also known as Giovanni de' Cipelli, Egnatius studied at Venice under Benedetto Brognoli and Francesco Bragadin. At the age of seventeen he opened a private school of grammar in his own house; he continued teaching privately until 1520. Between 1520 and 1549 he occupied the chair in humanities in the School of San Marco. Egnatius edited many works for Aldus Manutius, including Valerius Maximus (1502), Suetonius (1516), Aulus Gellius (1515), Lactantius (1515), and Pliny's letters. He himself wrote a work entitled *De Caesaribus* (Lives of the Caesars), first published in 1516; his *De exemplis* was published in 1554. Ross comments:

> We have no definitive list of the works he edited or composed but we have sufficient evidence to characterize his learning as broad rather than deep, as primarily Latin rather than Greek, as historically oriented but essentially biographical and anecdotal, and as formulated primarily for popular and academic audiences rather than for the world of scholars. (553)

The "observationes" of Egnatius, advertised prominently on the title pages of the Morillon-Egnatius editions, are in fact rather meager. In the Antwerp 1545 edition, they are printed at the beginning of each poem, alongside Morillon's *argumenta,* and not in parallel with the text. The "observationes" generally occupy only a few lines and address textual questions rather than

---

13. "omitto infinitos pene illius errores tum in hac uita Thesei tum in aliis: non enim eum accusabo quem nolo nominare" (I omit to mention the almost infinite number of mistakes he makes in that "Life of Theseus" and in the other "Lives": for I will not accuse somebody whom I do not wish to name). The "Theseus" translation in question is probably the one by Antonio Pacini, which appeared in the earliest printed editions of the *Lives.* Lapo da Castiglionchio had also translated the "Theseus." See Pade 1995, 169–83; and Pade 1998, 251–87.

14. See below, chapter 5.

15. See Ross, Winter 1976, 521–66.

the elements of rhetoric, historiography, and mythography that interest the commentators.

Guy Morillon's entry in the *Biographie nationale de Belgique* describes him as a distinguished humanist, sometime secretary to Charles V and Eleanor of Austria, and friend of Erasmus.[16] Morillon was originally from Burgundy, but spent most of his life in the Low Countries. He was schooled at Paris; while there he edited the *Epistles* of Horace and the *Heroides* (1507), and published an annotated edition of Suetonius in 1509.[17] Thereafter he moved to Louvain, where he spent the rest of his life, excepting stays at the court of the emperor in Spain, notably between 1525 and 1531. He is said to have taken the chair in Greek at the newly established *Collège des trois langues* in Louvain, but this is unsubstantiated.[18] Petrus Nannius informs us in his *Miscellanea* (1548) that Morillon spent the last years of his life working on Livy, but refused the former's pleas to publish his work. Morillon died at Louvain in 1548.

Erasmus held Morillon in high esteem, as the extant correspondence between the two scholars proves.[19] Perhaps the most interesting of the letters the two men exchanged is the short note, dated 5 June 1517, sent by Morillon to inform his friend of his recent marriage: it begins with the words: "Helena suo obtigit Paridi."[20] It seems likely, given the tone of the letter, that this allusion is to the courting of Helen by Paris in Ovid's *Heroides*. Erasmus would, of course, have been well aware of the work of Morillon's youth, his commentary on the *Heroides:* the jocular reference is typical of those scholarly games beloved by humanists.

The *argumenta* and scholia for the editions of the *Heroides* and *Ibis* were composed by Morillon in his youth. According to P. S. Allen, they were written "for the use of pupils living in his house," and printed by D. Roce in August of 1507. They were used in a great many French editions from the 1530s on.

The commentaries differ from one another in methods and aims: different target audiences demand different treatments of the text. Volscus' com-

---

16. The information in this article also appears, in expanded form, in another article by the same author (van Even 1877, 136–68).

17. See the note on Morillon in P. S. Allen's edition of the correspondence of Erasmus (Erasmus, ed. by P. S. Allen, 1906–58, 2: 475).

18. See van Even, 138.

19. In a letter of 1524, for example, Erasmus writes: "Et tamen curabimus ut si quid mearum lucubrationum merebitur posteritatem, ut mecum uiuat candidissimus Morillonus" (But I will see to it, if any of my own works deserve to live on, that the brilliant Morillon will live on with me) (V, 419). Morillon's fame, however, was not destined to equal his friend's. Egnatius, too, corresponded with Erasmus and helped edit the *Adagia* in 1508.

20. Vol. 2: 587.

mentary had its origins in lecture notes adapted for a wider audience. The text of Clericus, on the other hand, had not been prepared in the context of formal education: it was aimed not at "learned men" but at those members of the upper classes of Casale who sought to become more cultured. Badius' and Morillon's notes belong to a third category: they had been written with a significantly younger audience in mind.

Volscus adopts a schoolmasterly tone, providing extensive glosses to the text, ironing out grammatical difficulties, naming rhetorical techniques and giving mythological, historical, and geographical detail; his references tend to be to prose writers: historians and mythographers. Volscus is an antiquarian with an encyclopedic instinct. Clericus is slightly different: he likes to supply literary references, mostly poetry—and not only to lend authority to 'facts.' He occasionally comments on Ovid's style and prosody, and suggests his own readings of corrupt parts of the text. At one point in the Phyllis commentary, he brings moral issues to the fore by initiating discussion that moves away from the text itself. Once or twice he even allows his literary judgment to come into play: for example, in his appreciation of Phyllis' last lines. Badius mainly concerns himself with glosses of the text, prose paraphrases of lines whose word order or vocabulary is particularly difficult; many of his glosses begin with the formula "ordo est . . . ". He also discusses, where relevant, aspects of Roman life (superstition, auspices, religion, curses, attitudes to chastity) and mythology (conventional representations of the gods, etc.), usually referring the reader to Virgil and other ancient authors for examples. In the case of the Dido and Phyllis poems the vast majority of these citations—unsurprisingly—come from *Aeneid* 4. Morillon's edition is aimed at a still younger audience of schoolboys; however it certainly had a wider appeal. The marginal notes in his edition are brief and to the point; they stay close to the text, providing information on mythology, geography, and rhetorical figures.

Analysis: *Heroides* 2 and 7

The epistle from Phyllis to Demophoon takes its story from a mythological narrative with few literary precedents. The fifteenth- and sixteenth-century commentators are certainly not aware of any sources prior to Ovid.[21] Demo-

---

21. Callimachus' version of the story, a single line-fragment of which survives, might have served as a model for Ovid. See Jacobson, 58–59 and Knox, 111–13. Other later versions of the legend include: *Remedia Amoris* 55–58, 591–608; Boccaccio's *Genealogia*, 11, 25; Chaucer's *Legend of Good Women* 2394–561; and Gower's *Confessio amantis* 4.731–878.

phoon, son of Theseus, was shipwrecked as he was returning to Athens after the Trojan war; the Thracian queen Phyllis welcomed him, and they embarked on a love affair. Having promised to return within one month, Demophoon left for Athens and never returned; and Phyllis committed suicide by hanging herself. Since the Phyllis myth itself has few sources prior to Ovid, readings of the text are less likely to be contaminated by dominant traditions. There is, however, evidence that Ovid deliberately suppressed certain aspects of the myth.[22] At the same time Ovid's text enters into dialogue with the *Aeneid* and, in the *Heroides,* Dido, Ariadne, and Phaedra. This provides the commentators with many parallels and verbal echoes to draw upon in their explications of the text. The Phyllis story bears a striking similarity to the Aeneas-Dido narrative; indeed, Howard Jacobson argues that Ovid "approaches Virgil's Dido episode and adapts it two times in two different ways, once in the person of Dido herself, a second time in the guise of the Thracian heroine, Phyllis" (65). The mythological background to *Heroides* 7—the love affair between Dido and Aeneas—is much better known than the Phyllis-Demophoon narrative, and the commentators have no difficulty in tracing Ovid's poem back to a single source text: the *Aeneid,* in particular the first, second, and fourth books of Virgil's epic.[23]

Both the Phyllis and Dido epistles will serve as fine representative examples for a comparison of the commentators' treatments of the text. They typify many of the thematic and formal characteristics of the collection as a whole: the host-guest theme; the lament of the abandoned heroine; the opposition of *cultus* and *rusticitas,* duplicity and simplicity; the discursive ambivalence between devotion and invective, between eroticism and the threat of death. The epistle's formal structure betrays the writer's psychological instability. The heroine's discourse oscillates, aleatory, between hope and despair; paradoxical oppositions are drawn out in complex verbal structures. Finally, both the Phyllis and the Dido letters dwell heavily on the heroine's projection of her own death, and both feature a crowning "epitaph."

Woodcut Illustrations

Visual representations of the heroines' narratives influence the way the text is read and learned. It is in these visual narratives that the boundaries

---

22. Jacobson suggests that the Phyllis myth "was of great popularity in antiquity" (58). The variant traditions (the magic box; the metamorphosis into a leafless tree) are found in later mythographers and commentators: Apollodorus, Hyginus, Servius, Tzetzes. For Apollodorus' account of the magic box, see the commentary by Knox (111–12).

23. For Ovid's Dido as a "skeptical reader" of Virgil's *Aeneid,* see Desmond, 56–88.

between text and commentary are at their most permeable. Ann Moss observes that the illustrators used the commentaries as a source as much as the text itself.[24] Often, though, the illustrations are obviously taken from the printer's stock of generic woodcuts: they bear little relation to the text and are used more than once to head different poems.[25] In the 1534 edition of Saint-Gelais's translation (Paris, Guillaume de Bossozel), for example, the battle scene which illustrates the Phyllis poem reappears at the head of the Oenone letter. However, certain editions enjoy higher standards of presentation, featuring custom-made woodcuts which are of good quality and highly detailed.

Two aspects of the Phyllis story omitted in Ovid's version feature often in the illustrations: they are mentioned by both Clericus, in his introduction, and Volscus, in his commentary on the final lines. Clericus narrates the details of Phyllis' suicide and transformation into an almond (or "filbert") tree:

> Phyllis amoris impatentia et doloris impulsu quod se spretam crederet: et eius [Demophoontis] reditum iam desperaret: zona sua gutturi circumligata laqueo uitam finiuit. Et ut fabulæ ferunt in arborem Amigdalum sine foliis mutata est. postea reuersus Demophoon re cognita truncum eius amplexus est: qui ueluti sponsi sentiret aduentum folia emisit: unde etiam teste Ser. phylla graece folia dicta sunt a phyllide.[26] (sig. b.iii^r)

> Phyllis, impatient for love and feeling terrible pain, since she believed she had been abandoned and despaired of him ever returning, ended her life by hanging herself with her girdle tied around her throat. And, as the myths relate, she was transformed into an almond tree without leaves. Later, Demophoon returned and, realizing what had happened, embraced the trunk of the tree, which, as if it sensed the lover's arrival, sprouted leaves. This is also why, as Servius writes, leaves are called "phylla" in Greek, from "Phyllis."

---

24. Moss 1982, 11.

25. For a discussion of the relative importance of printers' house styles and contemporary norms of presentation in studies of early printed books, see Armstrong 2000, 13ff. Armstrong also highlights some of the difficulties inherent in defining the relationship between text and image.

26. Another (perhaps more fanciful) etymology appears in John Gower's *Confessio Amantis* 4.862–72: "And Demephon was so reproeved, / That of the goddes providence / Was schape such an evidence / Evere afterward ayein the slowe, / That Phillis in the same throwe / Was schape into a Notetre, / That alle men it mihte se, / And after Phillis Philliberd / This tre was cleped in the yerd, / And yit for Demephon to schame / Into this dai it berth the name." The filbert aetiology does not appear in any of the commentaries examined here.

The reference is to Servius's commentary on *Eclogues* 5.10: Clericus' account of the story matches Servius almost word for word.²⁷ Volscus tells it differently: in a version of the pathetic fallacy, the tree from which Phyllis hangs herself sheds its leaves, only to regrow them when Demophoon returns:

> ... inter tot leti genera fluctuans: demum se ex amigdala suspendit: exaruit arbor: qui in aduentum Demophoontis reuiruisse traditur.²⁸ (sig. c.iʳ)

> ... wavering between many different methods of suicide, finally she hanged herself from an almond tree; the tree shrivelled up, and is said to have grown leaves again on Demophoon's return.

The maker of the woodcut that heads the Phyllis poem in the 1528 Lyon edition (fol. viiiʳ) has chosen to follow Clericus' version rather than this one (Figure 2).²⁹ In the left panel of the triptych, we see Demophoon arriving in Thrace with a fellow Athenian; Phyllis is shown greeting them from a window. The central panel depicts Demophoon and Phyllis holding hands. In the third part we see, on the left, Phyllis half-metamorphosed into a tree and, on the right, Demophoon embracing a tree. This latter part is not at all relevant to Ovid's poem and only makes sense in the context of the commentaries: the Phyllis myth was not particularly well-known to a sixteenth-century audience.

The illustration in the 1543 Venice edition (p. 21) is more richly detailed (Figure 3). The scene it portrays has four main elements, set against the backdrop of a seashore. In the lower right-hand corner, Phyllis is shown, with a horse and a small boy, greeting Demophoon with open arms. In the upper right section, Demophoon's fleet can be seen departing from the shore. Roughly central we see Phyllis' lifeless corpse hanging from the branch of a tree. Lastly (in the chronological progression of the narrative if not in the visual arrangement of elements), Demophoon is shown in the background

---

27. The Berkeley commentary examined by Hexter has the same account of the Phyllis myth, also taken from Servius (Hexter 2002, 220). Hexter observes that the author of this commentary had a particular interest in narrative, and especially in stories relating to metamorphosis: this strand of the medieval *Heroides* commentary tradition evidently found its way into the humanist commentaries.

28. This in turn seems to be a variation on Ovid's own version, *Remedia Amoris* 606, where all the trees shed their leaves in sympathy for Phyllis. In the *Genealogia*, Boccaccio adds another explanation: when the Zephyr blows into Thrace from Athens, all the vegetation flourishes, representing the joy of Phyllis at Demophoon's return from Athens. Morillon quotes this version in his *argumentum* to the Sabinus reply epistle (sig. L1ᵛ).

29. To reassure the potential buyer that the illustrations are not taken from stock woodcuts, the front page of this edition boasts a text adorned with "aptissimis figuris."

Phyllis Demophoonti.   **Fo. VIII.**

Phyllis Demophoonti.

Ospita Demophoon tua te rho‑
dopeia Phyllis:
    Ultra pmissum tps abesse queror.
Cornua cum lune pleno semel orbe
coissent:
            *
Littoribus nostris anchora pacta tua est.
Luna quater latuit: toto quater orbe recreuit:
Nec vehit Acteas Scythonis vnda rates.
Tpa si numeres: bene q numeramus amantes:
Non venit ante tuum nostra querela diem.

Figure 2. *Epistolæ heroides Publij Ouidij Nasonis* (Lyon: J. David, 1528), fol. viii[r]. Cambridge University Library

DEMOPHOONTI

HVBER.
A

HOSPITA) Quidam interpretes in huius epistolæ argumento falsa quædam somniaue rût, Demophoontê ex Colchis cuz Argonautis reuertentem ad Phyllida Thraciã reginam diuertisse, cum Demophoon, eo tempore, aut nondum esset natus, aut certe nondum eius ætatis, vt ad talem expeditionem proficiscere

B

tur, verus ita res habet. Demophoon Thesei filius auxilium græcis, vt Iustinus libr. ij. scribit, aduersus Troianos tulit, qui ab eo bello rediens, tempestatibus maris, & longis erroribus actus in Thraciam delatus est, vbi a Phyllide, quæ per ea tempora regina Thracum erat, portu, hospitioqs exceptus & ab ea ardéter amat°, in coniugium rogatus est, qui ei coniugij fidem dedit, & ob beneficia accepta iurauit, se nunquam eam derelicturum vxorem, verus audita morte Mnesthei, qui post eiectum ex vrbe Thesea Demophoõtis patrem Atheniensium imperium occupauerat, Demophoon cupidus regnandi, dissimulata causa, petiuit a Phyllide aliquantum têporis, quo Athenas res suas ordinaturus accederet ad ea fide, se intra mensem reditum ad eam, verum cuz vltra iiij. mensem iam reditum suû distulisset: Phyllis amoris impatientia, & doloris impulsu, quod se spretam crederet, & eius reditû iam desperaret, zona sua gutturi circumligata, laqueo vitam finiuit, &, vt fabulæ ferunt, in arborem Amigdalum fine folijs mutata est. postea reuersus Demophoon, re cognita, truncum eius amplexus est, qui veluti sponsi sen-

C

tiret aduentum, folia emisit, vnde etiam teste Seruio, Phylla grece folia dicta sût a Phyllide. ante igitur hunc casum Phyllidis, cum Demophoon reditum suuq longe vltra promissum tardaret, Phyllis ad eum hanc epistolam scripsit, qua multis ex causis & rationibus eum reuocare nititur, cômemorans ei iusiurandû Demophoontis, & suorum erga se beneficiorum obligationes, postremo conatur eum mouere referens, quod nisi reuertatur, aliquo crudelissimæ mortis genere se interimet, in quo dicit fore, vt appareat ingratitudo, & crudelitas Demophoontis, vel per epitaphium eius inscriptum. (*Hospita*) ordo est, o Demophoon, ego Phyllis Rhodopeia. (*Hospita*) tua. (*Quæror te abesse &c.*) hospita dicitur foeminino genere, licet legatur hospes communis generis. Inhospita vero & foeminini generis reperitur, vt inhospita Syrtis, & neutri generis, vt Ouidius libro primo Metamorpho. & inhospita tecta tyranni. ingredior, (*Rhodopeia*) Threicia, nam Rhodope mons est

PVBLII OVIDII NASONIS
POETAE SVLMONENSIS
Heroidum Epistola secunda.

IN SECVNDAM EPIST. ARGVM.

DEMOPHOON, Thesei & Phædiæ filius, a bello Troiano in patriam rediens, maris tempestatibus in Thraciã delatus, a Phyllide Lycurgi & Crusthomeræ filia, quæ tûc Thraciæ imperabat, hospitio & lecto benigne susceptus est & cû aliquandiu secum fuisset, audita morte Mnesthei, qui post eiectum ex vrbe Athenarum patruu Thesea imperium occupauerat, regni cupidine captus, Phyllidi fide data se intra mensem reditu si, fi-gens se ad res suas côp: nendas se, refarciris nauibus, Athenas petijt, neqs de reditu curauit. Quatuor itaqs exactis mensibus Phyllis epistolam hanc scripsit, in qua suadet vt beneficiorû memor, seruatis sponsionibus, in fide persistat. Quod si negligat, violatum pudorem crudeli morte compensare minatur. Ferunt fabulæ Phyllidem zona sua laquei vicem supplente vi eam finijsse, in arboremq Amigdalu sine folijs mutatam esse, Demophoon te autem reuerso, redq cognita truncum eius amplexo, illum veluti sponsi sentientem aduentum folia emisisse.

HOSPITA Demophoon tua te Rhodopeia Phyllis
Vltra promissum tempus abesse queror.
Cornua cum lunæ pleno semel orbe coissent,
Littoribus nostris anchora pacta tua est.

deponentia omnia comunia fuerunt. (*Nostris littoribus*) id est vt adesset littoribus nostris, scilicet Thracijs, (supple tunc. (*Cum cornua lunæ coissent fimul pleno orbe*) idest vt, primum plenilunium esset, sed. (*Luna latuit quater*) scilicet in nouilunio, &. (*R recreuit quater toto orbe*) idest quater plenilunium rursus fuit, hoc est quatuor sunt transacti menses, nec vnda Sithonis, idest Thraciæ, hoc est mare Thracium

Thraciæ ita dictus a Rhodope muliere in eum conuersa, sicut & Hæmus, vt scripsit Ouidius libro sexto Metamorpho. Thraciam Rhodopen habet angulus alter & Hæmum, Nunc gelidos montes, mortalia corpora quondam. (*Promissum*) scilicet mihi a te. (*Cornua*) dicit spatium temporis sibi promissi, scilicet spatium vnius mensis, quod per lunam significauit. (*Cornua cum lunæ &c.*) idest cum luna semel esset facta plena, tunc enim extremitates lunæ, quæ ob similitudinem conua dicuntur, coeunt, idest côiunguntur, & se tangunt, & ideo dixit. (*Pleno orbe*) idest pleno circulo, ipsius lunæ. possumus tamen fortasse melius intelligere spatium medij mensis, quo luna crescit, & implet orbem. Inde & Iuuenalis dixit. Semestri vatum digitos circumligat auro, idest anulo rotundo, qualis est luna in medio mense. Licet Domitius Calderinus aliter interpretetur locum Iuuenalis non satis vere. (*Ancora*) idest nauis, instrumentum nauis pro ipsa naui posuit. (*Pacta*) promissa a te. (*Nostris*) Threicijs, vbi ego habito.

HOSPITA Demophoõ, ASCEN.
Argumentû enarrauit Prior commentarius, quod & Seruius recitat ad illud. Si quos aut Phyllidis ignes &c. Hospita per superabundantiãs dicitur, nam hic & hæc hospes reperitur, verum etiam in neutro genere inhospita saxa legimus, quasi ab hospitus hospita hospitum, & est hospes, tam qui recipit, quam qui recipitur hospitio, hic autem ho spita, quæ recipit. Videtur autem statim in primo verbo expostulare iniuriam, qp non nisi hospita sit eius, cuius secundum promissa coniunx esse deberet, sicut Dido Aeneidos quarto. Cui me moribundam deseris hospes? hoc solum, quoniam nomen de coniuge restat. Queror, idest conqueror. Cornua cum lunæ, &c. Ordo est. Anchora tua est pacta, idest in pacto tuo promissa, & ita potius passiue, quam actiue accipietur. Nec est tam dura Metaphora, quia

on the left-hand side, embracing a tree, though not the same one Phyllis is hanging from. Where the triptych shows a clear temporal progression, this woodcut condenses the entire narrative into one scene. The compression of several narrative temporalities into one illustration was fairly common in contemporary art. The technique known as "pluritemporalité" "consiste à représenter dans un même tableau divers moments d'une histoire, en y faisant figurer au besoin plusieurs fois les mêmes personnages."[30] It is a feature of medieval art; in the sixteenth century, it is combined with an understanding of perspective and is associated in particular with the Fontainebleau school. The Mannerists moved away from the linear depiction of narrative time favored in medieval religious art by introducing depth and perspective into the image space;[31] this made the "pluritemporalité" technique particularly well suited to illustrating the *Heroides*, in which perspective is the governing principle of composition. Ovid's heroines exist in a narrative in which past, present, and future events collapse together, subsumed by the immediacy of passion.[32]

The woodcut at the head of the Phyllis poem in Charles Fontaine's 1580 edition (p. 31) has a similarly detailed arrangement of elements (Figure 4). Once again, various points of the story are represented together. In the foreground Phyllis is shown sitting at the shore; she gazes into the distance and tears at her hair; she is in the process of writing the letter. Demophoon's ships are visible on the horizon. In the mid-background is a corpse hanging from a tree. Behind Phyllis, and in mirror-image, is just barely discernible a tree which bears some traces of human form. As we have seen, neither of the last two elements of the story is actually in Ovid's poem, but Fontaine mentions the method of suicide in his preface, referring the reader to the *Remedia Amoris* (see lines 55–58 and 591–608—where Ovid alludes to hanging). He does not, however, mention Phyllis' metamorphosis or Demophoon's return.

This illustration stands out from the others in that it represents Phyllis in the very act of writing, set within a visual narrative which unfolds around her with no regard for temporal progression. Here the author-narrator relationship is demarcated visually: the author and reader stand outside the frame of the representation and contemplate it; the narrator is within. The viewer, then, by virtue of the position he adopts, has a prior claim to inclusiveness and interpretive plenitude: one does not have to take account of the problematical and potentially dangerous discourse of the heroine if it can be

---

30. Rieu 1988, 297–310; 297.
31. Ibid., 298.
32. See Jacobson, ch.18, "The Role of Perspective."

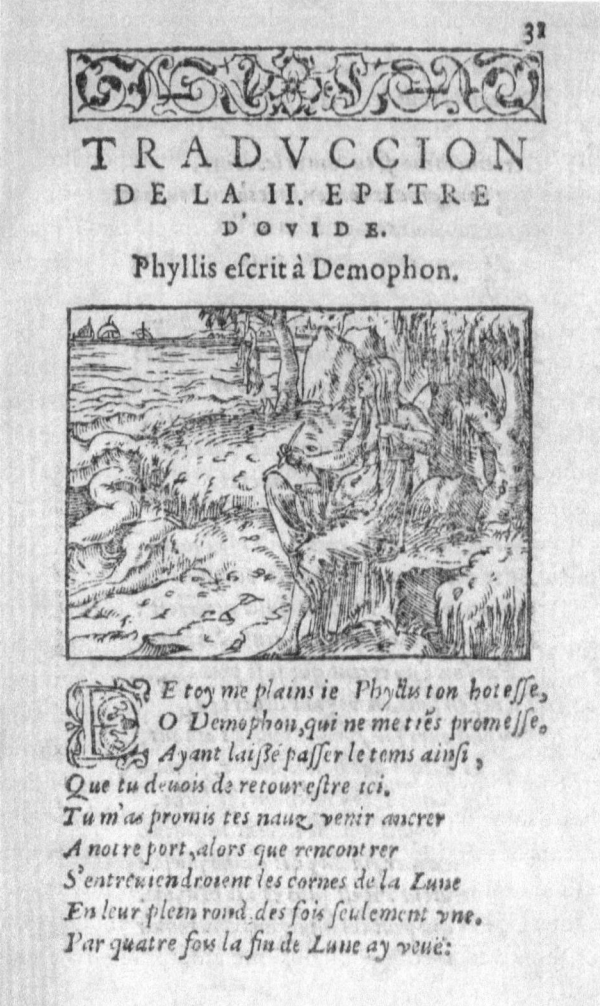

Figure 4. *Les XXI épitres d'Ovide* (Paris: H. de Marnef, 1580), p. 31. Bibliothèque nationale de France/Gallica

enclosed within a teleology which proves the truth of the dictum "exitus acta probat." The perspective of the narrator is shown to be limited by her own overwhelming passion: pen in hand, she gazes longingly at Demophoon's departing fleet, but fails to see the other elements of the picture. The natural outcome of her obsessive love is represented by the hanging corpse and the metamorphosed tree behind her back, neither of which Phyllis can see. But the viewer, retracing Phyllis' gaze toward the ships on the horizon, finds his eye arrested by the detail of the hanging corpse, which bisects the line of vision. The background detail becomes imposing, unavoidable. The detail short-circuits the eye's movement within the fictional space, disrupting the linearity of the narrative chronology: it is forever the inevitable outcome of Phyllis' desire. The illustration better allows the reader to impute a moral purpose to the author himself: like the reader, Ovid stands outside the frame of the narrative and is party to all of the evidence. Even before reading the poem, the sixteenth-century reader might draw the conclusion that the *intentio auctoris* is to condemn the excessive passion of the heroine, the natural outcome of which is her suicide and metamorphosis.

In common with the illustrations that accompany the Phyllis letter, the various woodcuts heading the commentaries and translations of *Heroides* 7 focus on different aspects of the narrative, not always relating directly to the text. The 1543 Venice edition simply depicts the shipwreck of the Trojan fleet (61); it seems more likely that this is a representation of the episode at *Aeneid* 1.81–123 than a realization of Dido's fears that Aeneas the perjurer will be punished by the sea (*Heroides* 7.45–60), or a reference to Dido's brief mention of the *Aeneid* episode (7.89). The 1528 Lyon edition has an illustration in triptych form which relates more closely to Dido's own story (fol. xxxiiii^r) (Figure 5): The first panel shows the Queen welcoming Aeneas with gifts (7.89–92); the second has Aeneas saying his farewells to Dido, with a departing ship in the background (7.139 and *passim*); the third shows Dido's suicide by the sword in front of a blazing funeral pyre (7.181ff). The woodcut heading Charles Fontaine's translation of *Heroides* 7 (117) is more detailed; once again various points in the chronology of the narrative are represented within a single frame (Figure 6). The composition of the Dido image is almost identical to the Phyllis illustration that preceded it in the same edition: it serves as a visual prompt to draw out the parallels between the two stories. Like Phyllis, Dido is depicted sitting on the shore, writing her letter; in the distance, a proleptic image, the Trojan fleet is shown departing over the horizon. On the left side, in the narrative 'present,' we see the Trojan fleet moored at the shore. Phyllis' suicide and Dido's suicide are both depicted in the same section of the background: Dido is shown atop a tower, falling on Aeneas' sword. However, the visual dynamic of the image is entirely different: whereas Phyllis is shown gazing into the distance, inviting the viewer's eye to fall upon the depiction of her suicide, Dido's gaze is fixed on the letter she is writing. Unlike Phyllis, Dido is not writing in order to persuade, having already resolved to die; she writes out of necessity, as the dying swan sings. The viewer's eye, moreover, is not guided by the heroine's gaze: it circulates freely within the image, but causal connections between details do not impose themselves so strongly. The viewer, in this case, is not in a position to read the narrative progression in simplistically moral terms.

Dido Enee   Fo. XXXIIII.

in lybiam cum sorore'anna celeriter adnauigauit vbi ab hiarba hammonis filio Numidarum rege empto solo
quatū circūdaret taurino corio:qūe in minutissima secuit lora:vrbē Carthagine codidit annos post captū iliū
c.lxiiij.vt rectius suppurarsit qui tēpoꝛa ratione tradiderūt. Constat ideo ad Didonē Eneā puenire non potuit
se:qui tertio anno post troie excidiū:vt Cassius Emina:Democrates:? alicarnasi* Dio.scri.in latio cōsedit:ini
to igit cum latino cōingio:messala l3 Eneā in aphrica delatū scribat. Dido .tn silētio pteritur. Sed latino:ū pt
mus hunc amorē Ennius cōmentatus est. Scipionis superioris gesta (no carmine cōplexus est:qnē deinde se
cuti latini poete nauibus ꝓfractis eneā naufragū ad Didonē delatū tradiderūt:susceptūqз ei*hospitio ? thala
mo demū mercurij iussu in italiā nauigasse:didoqз ardētissimo flagrabat amore de morte liberaū adꝫeneā scri
epi.hoc multū acrimonie h3 ? qrele:scri .em moribūda ad eū que nouerat mortis causam pubuisse.

⁊ Dido Enee.

Ic/vbi fata vocāt/ vdis abiectus
in herbis;
Ad vada Meandri concinit al
bus holoꝛ.

Nec quia te nostra spere prece posse moueri:

ANTO:
Situdo mag
gis oratoꝛi
poete con
gruit.
Canꝰ natu
ra.
Cygnoꝰ de
morte sabu
la.
Meander q
? vn fluat.
Ubi nas cy
gnoꝛū multi
tudo stabu
latur.
Que ꝓprie
alloq̄ dicāt.

Ic vbi fata vocant: vdis abie
ctus in herbis:de morte delibe
rasse situdine indicat:idꝙ poe
tis magis ꝙ oratoribus coueni
re Bristo.scribit:quāuis ? orato
res similitudine vtantur. Nom
Democrates nutricibus oratores contulit:
q̄ denorato cibo pueros salina inungūt Pla
to quoqз in republica canibus similes dixit
esse q̄ mortuos spoliant:canes em demoꝛso
lapide proijcientes nō ledunt. Albus ho
loꝛ: cocinit:cygnorum narratur in morte flebi
lis cantus: q̄d Plinio falsum esseuidetur. Ad
va.meandri:meander a celenis collib? effluēs
inter milerum et prienem:phrigiam cariam
Lydiāqз visteꝛginat:in quem influunt am
nes.marsias: orgas caper:vet lycus: flexus
sus est q̄d ei accidere scribit Strabo: quonis
multum limi accipiat: et modo in hanc mo
do in illam ripam deijciat:cygnorum multi
tudo traditur stabulari in ripis meādri. Ad
asiam paludē caicum amnē caistruꝫ et padū
propterea oloꝛigerūꝫ caistrū dixit. Elloquoꝛ
meos affectus aperio:ea enim alloquimur: q̄
aut summo affectu:aut extremo periculo nar
ramus:vnde Cergilianū illud extremū ꝙ te
alloq̄: hoc est in q̄ eꝑe ꝓpositū est. Meꝰ inde
vt moribūdꝰ cygnꝰ affeci* narro nō ꝙ te reno
care credā:sed cōpudicitis/violanerim:facile
est q̄ne ipudicitis argnāt pauca ꝫba iactare.

Ic vbi ilio troianoꝛ of a grecis euersa Eneas veneris ? Anchise filio patriam relinquens constructa
classe apud antandrum ciuitatem se mari credidit:cum patre et Ascanio filio dijs penatibus et mul
tis troianis qui se eius nauigationibus comites et socios prebuerunt et primam quidem in thracias
delatus,est vbi Abenum oppidum condidit:vt multi putant. Mox prodigijs territus ? voce polydo
ri crudelissime a polimnestoꝛe thracij rege interfecti indigne sugeret belū tenuit: illic
accepto ab Apolline responso errore patris male interpretantis responsum Cycladas insulas preternect* ad
Cretam venit:quas fatale terrā ? ab oraculo pdictā anchises crediderat:versꝰ cū ibi pestilētia laboraret a dijs
penatibꝰ in somniis monit* vt discederet ad strophadas delatus est insulas:inde preternecsus maritima gre
cie:apud Epirū suscept* est heleni hospitio q̄ troianus ? priami filij illi pyrrho successerat in regno inde profe
ctus Calabriā tenuit:vt qua statim discessit territus aduentu Diomedis:nauigauitqз vlqз ad Scyllā:? Caryb
dim ꝗ sunt in mari siculo Etne vicine:inde veto agitatus circuita maxima parte Sicilie Drepanū venit:vbi vt
Cer.volnit:parrē omisit:quo in Sicilia sepulto ? bonoribus prebitis: donatis qƀ aceste troiano qui in Sicilia
regnabat:qƀ mouet ceteris necessarijs:cū discessisset vt in Italiā veniret quas sibi satis dari ? a Crensa vxore ? ab
oraculo reperto in delo ? ab heleno intellexerat:tēpestate maris ? vi vētoꝛ agitatus i lybiam delatus est:ex.xx.
nauibꝰ vna dūtaxat submersa sorte p ea tpa:vt Cer.finxit. Dido q ex Tyro sugerat marito suo Sychoo a pygma
lione ipsius fratre interfecto metues et ipsa fratris senitis ? amaritijs:in terra libyca vrbē nouā Carthagine cō
debat:empto ab hyarba rege solo:qnātū posset taurino corio circūdare:quo secto in minutissimas corrigias in
tm id extendit:qd occupauit stadia vno ?.xx.quo spatio vrbem condidit. Ad hanc igit ur Didonem cū Eneas
venisset cū sociis ab ea ? viue ? hospitio exceptus est liberalissime: mox etiā ab ea amatus cum illa cōcubuisset:
qз ibi moratetur:admonitus ab Anchise patre in somnijs ? a Mercurio ab Ioue misso:vt inde discederet:? sata
lem terrā petere: nō ausus regine dicere:cū clā abire pararet regina Dido presentiens postqз srustra preciƀꝰ sa
tiganit Eneā singit ab Ouidio hanc epistolam ad eū scripsisse:in qua nititur renocare eū a proposito nauigan
di argneno ab honesto, ? tuto:ab honesto ꝙde:q: non deceat eā deserere:a qua hospitio sit:excepto ? oibus re
bus adiutus:cui fide dederit:a tuto quia mare procellosum ? tēpestuosum sit a quo sit tutum abstinere:? ha
beat terrā paratā:ignam relinquere ꝓuter incerta impudentio sit:cōmemoꝛat aūt sua in Enea bnficia: ? rogat:
vt si decrenit oino discedere:saltem differat ? expectet donec mare tranquillā sit. Nō sit nolnerit dicit* ꝙ seipsā
interimet:? inbebit inscribi epitaphiū in sepulchro quo eneas cognoscatur fuisse cans eius mortis. Sic vbi
dicit Dido se appropinquante sine sue vite effunderē flebiles voces ad Eneam:sicut cygnus vicinus morti so
let flebiliter cantare. Ferunt em appropinquantibus cygnis extremo vite pennam in capite nat*ꝫ paulatim in
cerebrum descendere:interea vero ipsos cygnos flebiliter cantare donec moriantur. Oui.li.q̄. fastoꝛ. Flebili*
munerio veluti canentia dura. Traiectus penna rpa cantat oloꝛ.Pli.li.x. oloꝛū morte narratur flebilis cantus
falso,vt arbitroꝛ:aliquot experimentis:ordo est. O loꝛ: albus. Abiectus positus. Ad vada.i.apud aquas:ⁱ
vada bicuntur aqne per quas pedibus vadere possumus:interdum simpliciter ꝓ omnibus aquis ponitur.
Meandri:fluuij lydie iuxta quā multi sunt cygni. Concinit cantat. Sic.s. flebiliter sicut ego ꝰ nūc canto. Ubi
i. quando, Fata vocaut:idest mors eum trahit. Moueri:idest flecti.

Huber.
Epistole ar
gumentum
hundum
ab humido
p syncopem
sactū nonnl
li volūt:qƀ3
ipm huidus
sigt ? id per
aspiratione
scribi ƀere
at meli* alij
sentiūt vdū
sine aspira
tione scribē
dū cē: dictū
a sudando
qīsudā.
Enee erro
res.
Spatiū v?=
bis cartha
ginis.

Cygnorum
fabula.

Cygnorum
fabula.

Uada que
sint.

Figure 5. *Epistolæ heroides Publij Ouidij Nasonis* (Lyon: J. David, 1528), fol. xxxiiiiʳ.
Cambridge University Library

Figure 6. *Les XXI épitres d'Ovide* (Paris: H. de Marnef, 1580), p. 117. Bibliothèque nationale de France/Gallica

Textual Criticism

Ann Moss (1982) observes that humanist commentators pay very little attention to matters of textual criticism until the latter part of the century.[33] The earlier commentaries do however make some attempt to establish the text and its orthography.[34] Ubertinus Clericus does so with relative diligence:

---

33. "The Gryphius edition of 1567 marks the transition from the rhetorical analysis of Morillon to the almost exclusive concern with textual problems which is characteristic of French editions of Ovid in the last thirty years of the century" (15).

34. Vinay has some general comments on Clericus's approach to textual issues: "Può interessare

often he gives alternative readings, making a judgment based on the priority of his "codex vetustissimus," on metrical demands, or on the sense of the line. For example, he prefers the present indicative "emo" over the imperative "emi" (7.118) because the tense fits the sequence better, and because "emi" has no evidence in earlier manuscripts. That anyone should prefer to read "emi," he continues, is "stultissimum"—and Badius agrees. At 2.6, Clericus explains why "Sythonis" is correct and not "Sithonis." He prefers "me" to "te" at 2.61 because it makes more sense, and because it is in the earlier manuscript. He occasionally prefers readings based on grammatical considerations (mood of verb): "portent: non ponitur portabunt ut quidam putant: sed modi est optatiui . . . " ("portent": not "portabunt," as some think: but it is in the subjunctive mood) (2.135). There are also variant readings based on metrical considerations: "Notandum est: quod ubi legitur ditis: legendum est: dei. Nam ditis primam naturaliter habet longam: et sic non staret hic uersus" (Note: where some read "ditis" we ought to read "dei." For "ditis" naturally has a long first syllable: and read thus the verse would not scan) (2.72). Clericus demonstrates an untypical sensitivity to the poet's individual style at one point when he uses it as a measure of the probability of interpolation (2.120–21). At 7.97, Clericus rejects the reading "Sichaeu," recognizing that Dido is apostrophizing "pudor" rather than her husband, and adding that "Sichaeus" is not disyllabic, like "Theseus," but trisyllabic, like "Antaeus." At 7.133 he prefers "relinquas" (present subjunctive) to "relinquis" or "relinques" (present or future indicative) because it matches the mood of the following verb in the sequence. On other occasions Clericus has no good reason to prefer one reading over another, so he chooses the one read in the majority of manuscripts he has seen ("nouere" over "mouere" in line 85).[35]

The base text of both poems varies slightly between editions. A pentameter and a hexameter are missing at 2.18–19 in the earliest editions; modern editions restore them. Volscus notes this in passing ("Absunt duo carmina: quæ in hunc locum falso contulerunt" [Two verses are left out, which had been erroneously inserted here]), but does not explain why he believes them to be false interpolations. The main differences between the texts of *Heroides*

---

una osservazione ove mostra di attenersi, nella scelta fra due lezioni, alla *ratio*, all'*historiae testimonium*, e al *verisimile*, il che, però, non toglie che, più innanzi, per rifiutare alcuni versi come apocrifi, si fondi, anzichè sul silenzio dei codici, su ragioni stilistiche" (146) (The observations may be of interest where they demonstrate that they are following, in the choice between two readings, reason, historical testimony, and probability; nevertheless, he might still base a later argument to exclude some lines as inauthentic on stylistic considerations rather than on the testimony of the manuscripts).

35. Some modern editions follow Housman in reading "sat me monuere" for "at me nouere"; Knox has "et me mouere."

7 are the inclusion or omission of two extra lines at the start of the poem, and lines 24–25. The 1543 Venice edition includes the epistolary salutation:

> Accipe, Dardanide, moriturae carmen Elissae
>   Quae legis a nobis ultima uerba legis. (61)

> Accept, Trojan, the song of Dido as she prepares to die:
> The words that you read are the final words you read from me,

although not as part of the main body of the text. Knox comments that these two lines had been added by a medieval reader as a more "suitable" epistolary opening: Dido's letter launches straight into the swan simile without a salutation. The lines appear in manuscripts from as early as the eleventh century.[36] Lines 7.24–25 are present in the 1543 edition (with the rather uninformative note "haec duo carmina in aliis non leguntur" [These two verses do not appear in other manuscripts]) but not in the earliest editions. Charles Fontaine has them in his translation, commenting in his notes: "I'ay lu en un exemplaire de Venise deux vers qui ne se lisent pas ordinairement" (130) (I read in a Venice copy two lines which are not usually included). Du Bellay does not follow Fontaine's example, leaving out the lines in his translation. Modern editions follow Housman in including them.[37]

Encyclopedic Content

The early humanist commentaries elaborate at length on the poems' mythological, geographical, and historical background. Volscus the antiquarian, in particular, has a professional interest in the details of classical culture. This proves a particularly rich seam in the case of the Phyllis story: Demophoon links Theseus and Athens with the Trojan War, and his family ties bring both Ariadne and Phaedra into play. Volscus gives extensive genealogy and sources in his *argumentum,* drawing attention to the confluence of myths here. On the subject of Theseus he cites Plutarch for background. Plutarch, indeed, seems to be his favored source (closely followed by Pliny and Cicero): later, at 2.103 ("altera coniunx"), to take one example, he comments: "uidetur

---

36. For a full treatment of the history and manuscript tradition of these lines, see Kirfel 1969, 61–64.
37. See the commentary by Knox (207–8); variant readings in the translations will be discussed further in chapter 4.

alludere ad Laodicen uirginem: quam Plut. tradit clam cognitam ex Demophoonte Minthium filium genuisse. Alii Calliopen fuisse scribunt" (this seems to allude to the virgin Laodice, who, Plutarch relates, was "known" secretly to Demophoon and gave birth to a son, Minthius, by him. Others write that it was Calliope). Alternative traditions are often mentioned. In his introduction to the Dido epistle, Volscus provides a wealth of background information not taken from the *Aeneid*. First, he gives a brief history of Thebes and Carthage (using Thucydides as his authority). Acknowledging the 'historical' version of the story adopted by Boccaccio, he mentions that Carthage was founded 164 years after the fall of Troy, and that Dido could not possibly have met Aeneas. Later in his commentary Volscus tells the story of Dido's flight from Tyre, following the version of the story found in Trogus. Dido's brother Pygmalion had killed her husband Sichaeus, a priest of Hercules, in order to steal his treasure; Dido had fled with a band of loyal subjects, stopping off at Cyprus along the way to pick up ninety virgins and a priest of Jupiter. Arriving in Libya, Dido had purchased a plot of land from King Iarbas, as much as an ox-hide would cover; cutting the hide into thin strips, she was able to surround enough land to found a city. Volscus adds the technical specifications of the city: it is on a peninsula measuring 450 stadia, surrounded by a wall measuring 60 stadia in length; the citadel was called "Byrsan"; at the top was a temple to Asclepius; the city was built on the site where a horse's head was found. Later Volscus also recounts in part the historical version recorded by Trogus and Justinus (note on 121ff): he mentions that Iarbas threatened war on Carthage when Dido refused his marriage proposal, but does not mention the version in which her suicide is connected with this. Ubertinus Clericus also mentions the Justinus version, placing emphasis on the "extraordinary love" Dido had for her dead husband.

The commentators provide a wide range of information on mythology, natural history, and ancient culture. Volscus in particular is diligent in his attempts to be as comprehensive as possible in collating useful factual information. For example, whereas the other commentators mention only examples taken from poetry in discussing the swan-song image at 7.1–2 (Clericus gives a reference to the *Fasti;* Badius refers to Martial), Volscus uses Pliny as his authority. He rejects as false the belief that swans sing before they die, and proceeds to give a detailed description of the river Maeander, its geographical location and its tributaries (referring here to Strabo). The information offered by Volscus is always supported by ancient authorities—usually prose authors but also some poets. His note on Triton (7.50), for example, refers to Pliny, Varro, and Statius. Sometimes two conflicting authorities are mentioned, as when Volscus annotates the line "parsque tui lateat corpore clausa meo" (and a part of you lies hidden in my body) with a discussion on medical theories of reproduction.

> Empedocles scribit fœtum a uiro & fœmina pariter concipi: quod negat Arist[oteles]. a uiroque tantum semen propagari in utero: nihilque conferre fœminam asseuerat.
> (sig. f.iv^r)

> Empedocles writes that the foetus is produced equally by male and female, which Aristotle denies: he claims that the seed grows in the womb by the sole agency of the male, and that the female contributes nothing.[38]

The commentators rarely miss an opportunity to furnish the reader with information on the network of associations between the gods, heroes, and heroines. In his introductory comments, Clericus engages with previous commentators—something which rarely happens—on the question of Demophoon's identity. He corrects the (unnamed) source that had assumed Demophoon to have been one of the Argonauts, demonstrating how that chronology cannot be made to fit. Clericus seldom indulges in elaboration of detail that has no narrative interest. At his most expansive, he releases the information that Hymenaeus is the Greek god of weddings and that the Romans call him "Thalassio"[39]; Phyllis invokes him in order to prove that their bond is legitimate and binding. Volscus adds that he is the son of Venus and Bacchus; Badius identifies the usage as metonymy "deum pro re." Morillon's note is concise: "Hymenaeus: Liberi siue Bacchi et Veneris filius nuptiarum deus" (Hymen: the son of Liber or Bacchus and Venus, god of weddings). Each commentator offers a slightly different piece of information; each has a slightly different emphasis.

In some cases the information offered is more comprehensive: where Morillon's marginal note to 2.69–70 briefly explains that "Scyron, Procrustes, Schynis latrones in Attica" (Scyron, Procrustes, Schynis were robbers

---

38. Aristotle makes this argument against Empedocles in the *De generatione animalium*, 1.18. Ian Maclean provides a useful account of medical theories of reproduction in the Renaissance (*Renaissance Notion of Woman*, chapter 3): the question of the existence of female semen was the subject of a debate between Galenists and neo-Aristotelians (35–38). Aristotle himself was not clear on this point, but in general terms the medical discourse denies agency to the female parent in the same way that the literary discourse denies agency to the female author. Kathryn L. McKinley has a brief discussion of the influence of these medical theories on literary representations of woman as irrational and excessively emotional (*Reading the Ovidian Heroine*, 6–9).

39. See, for example, Catullus 61.127.

in Greece), Volscus and Clericus go into much more detail. Volscus offers more than one account, citing Diodorus and Plutarch. Clericus, whose interest is in narrative and not gratuitous erudition, seeks references to the thieves in Ovid's other works (*Metamorphoses* 1 and the *Ibis*). Following this are notes by Volscus explaining the Minotaur, Centaur, and Hades allusions (71–72), and an extremely lengthy digression by Clericus which narrates the history of Thebes and the story of Theseus killing the centaurs. Mythological background is discussed in detail by Clericus only when it is of narrative interest: for example, he uses the reference to "tuum auum" at 2.37–38 as an excuse to give the story of Theseus' return from Crete and Aegeus' suicide on seeing the black sails. Clericus also likes to give the stories behind etymologies and aetiologies whenever they are of sufficient interest to a cultured audience: at 2.117, for example, he offers: "Tisiphone . . . dicta a Tisis quod græce significat ultionem: et phoni: quod significat cædem" ("Tisiphone" comes from "Tisis" which means vengeance in Greek; and "phoni" which means killing). At 2.121 he mentions the aetiology for the "Novem Viae" taken from the *Remedia Amoris* (55):[40]

> nam nouies iuisse dicitur: ut Ouidius in primo de remedio. Et per quod nouies saepius isset iter, & in eodem libro, Nona terebatur miseræ uia. (sig. b.vi^v)

> For she (Phyllis) is said to have gone down nine times, as Ovid puts it in the first part of the *Remedia Amoris:* "Nine times she went, and would have made the trip more often [had I been her teacher]"; and then again in the same book: "for the ninth time she, wretched, trod the path."

Geographical references abound in the text: each of the commentators is meticulous in his explanations of references to Athens, Thrace, and Thessaly, the mountains Haemus and Rhodope, the river Hebrus, Sithonia, and so on. Clericus avoids tedium by framing such information in narrative: in his note on 2.1 he supplies an aetion for Rhodope and Haemus, citing *Metamorphoses* 6 as his source.

Volscus the *magister* betrays no such concern to appeal to the reader's interest. Historical and factual detail is presented raw and unsugared. The legal language used by Phyllis at line 34 ("sponsor et obses"), for example, is explained at some length by Volscus, who refers to Livy to explain the workings of the Roman Senate. At 2.41–42, Volscus offers factual informa-

---

40. This is the reference given by Clericus; however it is in the *Ars Amatoria* (3.37–38) that Ovid specifically mentions this aetiology.

tion on Roman weddings, explaining the reference to Juno and the role of omens; Clericus, on the other hand, explains the significance of the secret rites of Ceres by offering the etymology of the word "mystica" and referring the reader to the *Ars Amatoria, Metamorphoses* 5, and Cicero, *In Verrem* 6. Where Volscus explains the portents at 2.115–20 with references to the solid authorities of Verrius, Pliny, and Plutarch, Clericus offers *Aeneid* 4 and *Metamorphoses* 6 (Tereus) in his commentary on the same passage.

The information provided by Volscus is not always dry or devoid of interest, however. At 2.137, he relates the fact (attributed to Pliny) that the only thing capable of eroding a diamond is goats' blood. But it is Clericus who works hardest to hold his reader's interest; and his emphasis is not always on edification. A titillating morsel of practical information is to be found in the brief overview of kissing techniques found at 2.94:

> Oscula pressa: presse infixa. qualia solent esse oscula amantium: quae non modo pressis labiis in faciem dantur: uerum etiam plærumque ex nimio affectu dentibus & morsu inferuntur. amatoria oscula dentibus impressa significat. (sig. b.vi^r)

> "Hard kisses": firmly pressed together, as lovers' kisses usually are: they are given not only with lips pressed to the face, but more often than not they introduce teeth and bites with excessive passion. The phrase "lovers' kisses" means kisses pressed together on teeth.

The swift citation of authorities (Ovid *Amores* 1 and Horace *Odes* 1) puts the information in a scholarly context.

References to other poets are found most often in Clericus and Badius. They are for the most part from Virgil or from Ovid's other works, and they usually serve to illustrate a piece of mythological or historical information. The references also point the student toward similar *loci:* those which might fit under a similar heading in a commonplace book. For instance, Clericus at 2.52 cites the *Ars* and *Aeneid* to show eloquence is useful in matters of love, and quotes Quintilian as saying that tears are the most effective way of persuading. Similarly, his explanation of 2.65 will send readers scurrying for their commonplace books: "nam ut ipse Ouidius inquit: credula res amor est" (For as Ovid himself says: "love is a credulous thing").[41] At 7.32 he offers: "nam ut inquit Ouidius in libro primo amorum: "militat omnis

---

41. Clericus does not identify the provenance of this quotation. In fact, he has a choice of two sources: *Heroides* 6.21 or *Metamorphoses* 7.826. Volscus, who quotes the phrase in a different context in his commentary (7.33), cites the latter: "amantes facile credunt: ideo in metamorphosi: *credula res amor est*" (Lovers are quick to believe: so in the *Metamorphoses:* "Love is a credulous thing").

amans et habet sua castra cupido" (For as Ovid says in the first book of *Amores:* "Every lover is a soldier, and Cupid has his own camp"); and at 7.130, Dido's "non bene cælestis inpia dextra colit" (It is not well for an impious hand to worship the heaven-dwellers) prompts Clericus to comment: "sententia est rhetorica" (this is a rhetorical expression); Morillon even goes so far as to call it a "catholica sententia" (universal idea). As well as suggesting related expressions taken from poetry, the commentators often compress Ovid's words into more user-friendly form, as proverbs. Clericus is always eager to supply the reader with related commonplaces: at lines 101–2 he turns Phyllis'

> et tamen exspecto; redeas modo serus amanti,
>   ut tua sit solo tempore lapsa fides.
>
> But I still await you; please return, though late, to your lover, and show that only for a time did you forget your pledge.

into the rather trite-sounding "melius est sero quam numquam" (better late than never).

Although Ovid's other works are frequently mentioned in the commentaries (the *Metamorphoses,* the *Ars Amatoria* and *Remedia Amoris,* and, less often, the *Amores*), other poems in the *Heroides* are not referred to as often as one might expect: surprisingly none of the commentators points out the parallels between *Heroides* 2 and 7. Clericus refers to Hypsipyle's letter on one occasion (commenting on 2.31–32), and later to Hypermnestra (40) and there is a brief mention of the Ariadne letter; in the Dido epistle, Volscus sees an allusion at line 166 ("virque paterque") to Hermione, whose father Menelaus and husband Pyrrhus fought in Troy; and Clericus observes that Dido's appeal to Anchises (162) recalls *Heroides* 3.135, where Briseis calls on Peleus. These are, however, isolated examples.

The commentators are clearly aware of Ovid's indebtedness to Virgil's Dido for his representation of Phyllis—*Aeneid* 4 is the reference cited most often throughout the commentaries.[42] Although there is little in-depth

---

42. Clericus: 2.9 ("spes quoque..."); 2.50: "idem probat Ver.iiii.aen" (Virgil shows the same in the fourth *Aeneid*); 2.81: "despecti: contempti a me, ut inquit Dido" ("scorned": despised by me, as Dido says); 2.109: "sic Dido obiicit Aeneæ" (Dido accuses Aeneas in this way); 2.118 (the owl). Badius: 2.40: "arcum et faces, ad quæ alludit Ver. in prin. IIII" (the bow and torches, to which Virgil alludes in book four); 2.63: "fallere credentem" (to deceive one who is trusting); 2.117: "ululauit" (shrieked): of the nymphs in *Aen.* 4.

discussion of the thematic continuities between *Heroides* 2 and *Heroides* 7,[43] the fact that the source text for Ovid's Dido is so prominent allows the commentators to focus more closely on the allusive strategies Ovid deploys in that epistle. This means that the notes on the text take a markedly different approach from the one used in the Phyllis letter, concentrating in particular on the literary antecedents to Ovid's text. The commentators are able to identify specific allusions to and departures from Virgil's version, and to show how Ovid is manipulating the original and why.

Language and Style

A broad range of scholarly techniques falls under the umbrella of stylistic analysis. At the most basic level it consists of glosses, prose paraphrases, vocabulary aids, grammatical notes, and parsing. This territory has been staked out early by Volscus; and the notes of the other commentators meet different needs for less advanced readerships. Badius, as with all his beginner-level commentaries (which he characterizes as "facilis explanatio" or "familiaris explanatio"), aims primarily to supply the student with aids to basic comprehension; most of his notes begin with the rubric "ordo est . . . " followed by a prose paraphrase. Clericus in particular among the earlier commentators, and Morillon later in the century, are preoccupied with the naming of poetic tropes and figures. At the next level belongs the more sophisticated rhetorical analysis that seeks to identify instances of technique—*amplificatio, ironia, pathos, commiseratio, metaphora,* and so on—as a guide to imitation and composition.

Volscus usually glosses vocabulary and expressions on a literal level; his notes serve as a linguistic crib for students. Occasionally, though, his definitions bring out implications in the author's choice of a particular word: for example at 2.1, Volscus shows how loaded with meaning the word "Hospita" is in the context of the poem: "Hospita: quæ te indigum et errantem hospitio acceptum tot beneficiis affeci" (Host: I who welcomed you and bestowed so many kindnesses upon you when you were in need and lost) (sig. b.iii^r). Clericus' commentary in this category mostly limits itself to grammatical

---

43. Jacobson (63ff.) discusses at some length the remodeling of Virgil's Dido in *Her.* 2, arguing that Ovid "approaches Virgil's Dido episode and adapts it two times in two different ways, once in the person of Dido herself, a second time in the guise of the Thracian heroine, Phyllis" (65). He further claims that few critics have noticed this influence (64 n. 13). While the fifteenth- and sixteenth-century commentators certainly do see the parallels, they generally do not speak in terms of influence but of similitude, using Virgil's text as an aid to understanding the concrete details of Ovid's poem.

notes: he sometimes explains grammatical peculiarities ("credimus: pluralis numerus pro singulari" [credimus: plural for singular]) and poetic locutions ("puppis: pars pro toto synegdoche" ["puppis" ("stern"): part for whole, synecdoche]). He also distinguishes between the different voices Phyllis introduces into her epistle: at line 99, for example, he points out that Phyllis ends her quotation of Demophoon's words and continues in the subjunctive. This difficulty is caused by the lack of punctuation in the text itself.

Volscus' attention to rhetorical figures is principally a matter of identification: poetic and rhetorical locutions are isolated, but not generally set in the context of the epistle as a whole. Indeed, the distinction between the rhetorical technique involved in the heroine's *suasoria*, and the poetic technique of Ovid more broadly conceived, is not made. Figures and tropes, rhetoric and poetics, *intentio auctoris* and *intentio mittentis*, are collapsed together: "pathos from repetition" (2.35ff); "*wounds:* this is used metaphorically" (2.48); "amplification" (2.55); "pathos from a commonplace" (2.61); "evoking sympathy by arguing from age and sex" (2.63); "she argues from duty" (7.31); "discouragement by arguing from experience" (7.53); "pathos from intention" (7.61); "pathos from age" (7.135); "the pathos is increased by adding names" (7.137); "she amplifies the argument with names" (7.166); "irony" (7.139,141); "she concludes the letter with a deprecation" (7.157); "apostrophe" (7.191).[44] Not all of Volscus' treatments are as cursory as the above, however: on occasion he elaborates on the suasive technique of the sender. At 2.81, "commiseratio est a comparatione: confert enim incommoda commodis" (sympathy is evoked by comparisons: for she compares disadvantages and advantages); at 2.91, "amplificatione utitur cum demonstratione sui officii et Demophoontis perfidiæ" (she uses amplification along with an explanation of her status and Demophoon's perfidy); at 2.99–100 "acclamatio est cum geminatione uerbi ad commouendam miserationem" (this is an interjection with doubling of the verb to elicit pity). Volscus also occasionally pays attention to the shifts and contrasts in Phyllis' use of rhetoric and their effects. At 2.27–30, he comments on her use of irony ("amoris simplicitatem pro ironia crimen apellat" [she ironically calls the candor of love a crime]) and the shift in tone that comes after ("post ironiam patheticæ sequuntur interrogatiunculæ et breues" [following the irony there is a sequence of short questions to elicit pathos]).

---

44. "pathos est a repetitione" (2.35ff); "uulnera: metaphora est" (2.48); "amplificatio" (2.55); "pathos a loco" (2.61); "commiseratio ab ætate et sexu" (2.63); "a pietate arguit" (7.31); "dissuasio ab experientia" (7.53); "παθοσ [*sic*] a uoluntate" (7.61); "παθοσ [*sic*] ab ætate" (7.135); "augetur παθοσ [*sic*] a nominibus" (7.137); "rem nominibus amplificat" (7.166); "ironia" (7.139,141); "colligit epistolam per deprecationem" (7.157); "apostropha" (7.191).

Clericus assumes a working knowledge of basic Latin, and does not incorporate paraphrases and glosses to the extent that others do. His interest is in poetic technique first and foremost. He is quick to identify features belonging to the poetic register of Ovid's Latin: "translatio" (i.e. metaphor, 7.27); "liptote" (litotes, 7.57); use of historical present "ut res nunc geri uideatur" (to make it seem that the action is taking place in the present) (7.115); and so on. Again, such features are not distinguished formally from rhetorical techniques attributable to the writing heroine: "[s]he dissuades by arguing from utility" (7.13); "[s]he begins to list her misfortunes" (7.113); "amplification of misery" (7.116); "[s]he elicits pity by arguing both from fortune and from her sex" (7.121); "[s]he gives consideration to any objections that Aeneas might have" (7.153).[45] Occasionally, though, Clericus explicitly attributes suasive strategies to the heroine herself: "ut maiorem captet commiserationem: et fraudem Demophoontis magis amplificet: multa commemorat de Demophoonte" (the better to gain sympathy and to amplify Demophoon's deception, she mentions several of Demophoon's attributes) (2.49–51).

Badius has a brief exposition of the rhetorical structure of Dido's letter:

principium uidetur tacitæ obiectioni per Antiphoram [*sic*][46] respondere. . . . Si certum, aut decretus est omnino tibi mori, teque interficere, cur scribis Dido? quid canis moritura? Respondet: Sic ubi fata uocant etc. (fol. xxxiiii^v)

The opening lines would seem to respond to a tacit accusation by "antipophora." . . . If it is certain, or finally decided that you are to die, and to kill yourself, why are you writing, Dido? Why sing when you are about to die? She replies: "Thus when the fates call, etc."

He acknowledges that, unlike the epistle of Phyllis, Dido's letter is not intended to persuade its recipient; rather it takes the form of an imagined conversation between the two actors, of which we are only presented with one side. Dido's language is meant to respond to the tacit objections made to her by the absent Aeneas, making use of the rhetorical figure of "antipophora." Because his concern is primarily with the elucidation of linguistic

---

45. "dissuadet ab utili" (7.13); "incipit enumerare infortunia" (7.113); "amplificatio infelicitatis" (7.116); "et a fortuna et a sexu mouet commiserationem" (7.121); "satisfacit obiectionibus quas Aeneas facere posset" (7.153).

46. This appears to be a printing error in the 1528 edition: the *editio princeps* of the Badius commentary (Paris: J. de Vingle for E. Gueynard, 1500) has the regular form "antipophora."

detail, and with supplying his audience of beginners with practical information about language, Badius focuses more than the other commentators on specific rhetorical techniques: he makes a point of naming figures such as anacoluthon (7.7), antiphrasis (7.96), and so on. Badius is also sensitive to the intertextual elements of Ovid's reworkings of myth. He constantly draws comparisons between Phyllis and Virgil's Dido. For instance, he brings out the irony of the dissonance between line 63 ("fallere credentem . . . ") and *Aeneid* 4.296: "quis fallere possit amantem?" (Who could deceive a lover?).

The vast majority of Morillon's marginal notes are concerned with rhetoric. The notes, aimed at an audience of schoolboys, identify rhetorical places for the purposes of composition. They are technical, concise, and stripped of context and anything but the most basic interpretation. 2.1 "synecdoche"; 2.29 "she ironically calls guilelessness a crime"; 2.55ff. "by means of a rhetorical defense her good deeds are brought to his charge"; 2.121–130 "she increases sympathy." As well as identifying linguistic effects such as hypallage (7.179), Morillon's notes describe the techniques used to persuade: "dissuasion arguing from utility" (7.13); "not without reverence she apostrophizes Venus" (7.31); "she dissuades by arguing from experience" (7.53); "she wins Aeneas over to her argument" (7.65); "artfully she mentions the fact that he will remember his guilty conscience in a time of great peril" (7.67); "pathos arguing from time" (7.91); "she apostrophizes modesty" (7.97); "justification on the basis of fate" (7.109); "irony" (7.139); "diminishing the significance of names" (7.167); "apostrophe to gain sympathy" (7.191).[47] Ann Moss comments that this attention to "sententiae" and the places of rhetoric ties in with contemporary theory: students would be expected to be able to use the "predicaments" enumerated here as the building-blocks of composition, a highly technical way of generating discourse through imitation. Moss also notes that Petrus Ramus made use of the *Heroides*, in his *Dialectique* of 1555, to demonstrate the processes of analysis and genesis.[48]

Moral Ethical Readings

In the medieval commentaries Phyllis is "the canonical example of *amor stul-*

---

47. "sinecdoche" (2.1); "ironice simplicitatem crimen uocat" (2.29); "per colorem rhetoricum beneficia obiecta" (2.55ff); "auget commiserationem" (2.121–30); "ab utili dissuasio" (7.13); "non sine pietate ad uenerem apostrophat" (7.31); "ab experientia dissuadet" (7.53); "Aeneam sibi conciliat" (7.65); "Artificiose conscientiæ recordationem in magnis periculis commemorat" (7.67); "a tempore pathos" (7.91); "ad pudorem apostrophat" (7.97); "a fatis excusatio" (7.109); "ironia" (7.139); "a nomine extenuatio" (7.167); "per commiserationem apostrophe" (7.191).

48. Moss 1982, 13–14.

tus."⁴⁹ Such categories, however, have more or less gone out of fashion by the time the humanist commentators are writing. In general they do not seem to be interested in relating the poem to any kind of absolute moral framework. That is not to say that ethical and moral issues are not discussed. Where they are, though, the commentators seem to adopt a relatively neutral tone.

The main point of interest in the Phyllis epistle is the treatment of the axiom "exitus acta probat"—an axiom that is made to measure for commonplace books—and the moral philosophy discussions that ensue. Hexter (176–77) comments on the popularity of lines 85–86 in medieval *florilegia,* which tended not to take account of the original context (i.e., the distinction between the two different speakers in the lines). In the twelfth-century commentary analyzed by Hexter, the moral discussion relies on the authority of Boethius. The humanist commentators are less interested in moral philosophy of this type.⁵⁰

"exitus acta probat" points up the way the *Heroides* were used in the schoolroom to furnish *exempla* and negative *exempla.* As we have seen, the humanist *Heroides* commentaries do not break entirely with the praise/blame framework provided by the medieval *accessus.* The fact that the heroines come to a bad end (misery, abandonment, suicide) proves the wrongness of excessive love. These accounts of the *Heroides* rely on teleological readings bolstered by notions of final cause, necessary outcomes, and clear intentions. However, this is not the whole story: in fact there is a basic discrepancy between the stated aims of the commentators (moral-ethical readings) and the form of the commentary itself. The line-by-line response to the language of the text does not apply this framework.

The humanist commentators do use "exitus acta probat" to illustrate a general ethical point, but this is rather exceptional in their commentaries on the *Heroides;* and the point is not applied to the examples presented by the stories of the heroines themselves. If there is a lesson to be learned from Phyllis' own "bad end," it is not stated by the commentators: the readings are becoming free from the reliance on intention and finality. In the medieval commentaries Phyllis more than any other heroine exemplifies "amor stultus," foolish, imprudent love. But by the mid-sixteenth century, the time Guy Morillon's commentary has become the one most often printed in northern Europe, commentary on the poems has been reduced to very brief

---

49. See Hexter 1986, 174. For the division of illegitimate love into three categories ("stultus," "incestus," "furiosus"), see Hexter, 160.

50. The humanist commentators are more likely to draw their moral distinctions from a passage in Cicero. The Italian humanist Parrhasius, for example, quotes from Cicero's *Epistulae ad Familiares* 1 in this connection: "if it all turns out as we want it to, and pray it will, everyone will say you acted wisely and bravely. But if anything goes wrong, those same people will say you acted ambitiously and rashly." There is a similar point at the beginning of Cicero's oration *Pro Rabiro Postumo.*

marginal notes on language and historicocultural detail, with no moralizing remarks at all.

Antonius Volscus glosses the lines as follows:

> ~Exitus acta probat~ per ironiam thracum uerba repetit: qui phyllidis consilia a fine damnabant. ~Careat successibus~ purgat se a fortuna. ~Successibus~ foelicitate. ~Ab euentu~ a casu: non a fine. (sig. b.v^v)

> ~The outcome is the measure of the deeds~ she ironically repeats the words of the Thracians who were condemning Phyllis' course of action by its end. ~May he come to a bad end~ she defends herself with an argument based on fortune. ~Successful outcomes~ good fortune. ~From the outcome~ from the [chance] outcome rather than from the [intended] end.

Volscus attributes the words to Phyllis, and remarks on their irony; and there is certainly a clever irony in Phyllis' wish that those who believe deeds should be judged on their outcome should come to a bad end themselves ("careat successibus"). For Volscus the explanation hinges on a distinction between "finis" (the ultimate end or objective) and "casus" (the circumstantial result); the "end" is the objective or aim that motivates an action (the "finalis causa" in the scholastic terminology), whereas the result ("euentus" or "casus") is the actual fortuitous or contingent events that follow an action. So "ends justify means" is surely not an accurate rendering of what Phyllis is saying here: she is focusing on the unforeseen results of an action, which, she maintains, cannot tell us anything about the rightness of the action in the first place.

Clericus elaborates on the distinction made by Volscus, and proposes an alternative reading.

> ~Exitus acta probat~ sensus est, a fine demonstrantur hominum facta, et est sententiae exornatio. ~Careat successibus etc.~ Sensus est, male illi eueniat, qui non a fine rerum, sed ab euentu facta hominum denominat, et notat. multa enim solent euenire ante finem, quae uidentur esse mala, quae postea ex fine cognoscuntur esse bona, ut exempli gratia, aliqua puella mediocris conditionis nupsit amatori diuiti clam, et nescentibus parentibus suis reprehenditur hoc factum ab his, qui hoc sciunt: at si ducatur uxor ab eo, omnes dicunt eam sapienter egisse, ita hic est intelligendum, sunt autem uerba Phyllidis dicentis, finis ostendit qualia sint facta q[uasi] d[icat] potes adhuc prouidere, ne uidear male fecisse cum te recepi in hospitio, & coniugio, ideo male illis eueniat, qui ante finem iudicant de his, quae feci per ea, quae euenerunt, quia non dum rediisti, nam adhuc redire potes. (ibid.)

~The outcome is the measure of her deeds~This means, the actions of men are defined by their ends; and there is a development of the idea~May he come to a bad end etc.~This means, may ill befall him who classifies and stigmatizes the deeds of men not by the end but by the result. For many things can happen before the end, which seem to be bad, but in the end turn out to be good. So, for example: some low-born girl contracted to marry a rich lover clandestinely and without the knowledge of her parents: this action is condemned by those who know about it. But if she is taken as his wife, everyone says that she has acted wisely. That is how this should be understood. These words are spoken by Phyllis; the end shows us the nature of the deeds—as she might say: "you may still see to it that I should not seem to have acted badly when I welcomed you as a guest and married you; therefore may ill befall them who judge, before the end, the things I did by the things that happened after, on the basis that you have not yet returned; for you may still return."

The application of this mercantile example to the situation depicted in *Heroides* 2 broadens the terms of the debate. The example is only tangentially related to the context of Phyllis' 'marriage' to Demophoon: Phyllis is a queen, not low-born. On the one hand Clericus reduces the heroine's plight to the status of a mundane dispute about marriageability; he recasts the tragic love affair in the context of mercantile negotiations over the ownership of women; he denies the heroine's own claim to judgment, showing that it is only the *force majeure* of social acceptance that can possibly give reason to a woman's choices. But on the other hand he implicitly reacts against the received reading of Phyllis as entirely irrational, a foolish lover: her actions may yet prove to have been pragmatic, to have political advantages.

The illustrative example Clericus uses here is perhaps something of particular interest to the audience of his commentary, which he wrote not for a schoolroom readership, but for the upper classes of Casale. The case described by Clericus would have been more likely a matter of concern to this readership than to the schoolboys or students the other commentators write for; and indeed the question of clandestine marriage was hotly debated in the sixteenth century. There is also a sense in which the example given is part of a wider ethical move, away from a "strong" moralizing reading in favor of a greater emphasis on the liberating potential of persuasive rhetoric: Warren Boutcher follows Lorna Hutson in observing that "the happy Terentian plot of clandestine courtship became a celebration of humanist man's transcendence of limiting moral and social conventions through the ingenious exercise of rhetorical plausibility."[51] It is also worth noting that

---

51. Boutcher, 21. In this connection it is worth noting Quintilian's assertion that rhetoric does

the word "exitus" was used in the legal context to mean "issue" in the sense of "offspring": with this in view, there might be hint of "a marriage is legitimated by offspring" to the aphorism.

Clericus then advances an alternative reading:

~ab euentu~ id est a casu, non a fine, qui potest uenire mihi melior: uel certe a fine, quem ego respexi, et propter quem feci nam finis mei facti fuit, prodesse mihi et meis, accipiendo te maritum, ergo ab hoc fine intentionis meae, et non ab eo, quod euenit iudicandum est id, quod feci, nam finis meae intentionis fuit bonus, licet euentus fuerit malus. Et hic sensus uidetur esse melior, et uerior, quam superior, licet uterque possit accommodari. (ibid.)

~from the result~ that is, from the chance outcome not from the end, which may turn out better for me; or else indeed from the end that I had in mind, and on account of which I acted; for the aim of my action was to benefit me and my people, by taking you as my husband. Therefore you should judge what I did from the end of my intention, and not from the end that actually happened; for the end of my intention was good, even if the result was bad. This reading seems better and more true than the one above, but both may be applicable.

The following lines, beginning "at si" would seem to support the "wait-and-see" reading Clericus considers the less convincing.

~at si~ sensus est: reprehendor, dicor male egisse, sed si ad nos reuersus fueris, omnes dicent me prudenter egisse, et ita exitus probabit acta mea non fuisse mala. (ibid.)

~but if~ this means: I am condemned, I am said to have acted badly, but if you return to us, everyone will say I acted prudently, and thus the outcome will prove that my actions were not wrong.

But Clericus leaves the question suspended between the two readings.

While Clericus takes "exitus acta probat" as descriptive of a general moral principle, which can be illustrated with examples, Badius remains close to the text: his particular commentary style does not accommodate

---

not aim at ends beyond itself: speaking well is an end in itself, and the art of rhetoric in realized in the act, not in the result (*Inst. Orat.* 2.17.25): "Ita oratori bene dixisse finis est. Nam est ars ea [. . .] in actu posita, non in effectu."

many digressions. He explains that the Thracian and Phyllis are talking only about this particular case, and that Phyllis is asserting the need to suspend judgment.

> aliquis (inquit) exitus probat acta, id est euentus rerum docet qualiter incoeptae sint, quasi prudenter incœpta non possint malum habere exitum. At quod respondet Phyllis, careat successibus opto, quisquis ab euentu facta notanda putat: quia sæpe prudentissime cœpta infœlicem sortiuntur exitum. unde qui eam damnabant, quia Demophoon non redibat, laudarent, si rediret. (fol. xi^r)

> Someone (says) "the outcome proves the deeds," which means, the outcome of something tells us about the nature of the undertaking—as if something sensibly undertaken could never have a bad outcome! But Phyllis replies, "may he come to a bad end, I pray, whoever thinks that deeds should be judged from their outcome" because things undertaken in all good conscience often happen to have an unfortunate outcome. So those who were condemning her because Demophoon did not return would praise her if he did return.

Though he hints at the Volscus reading ("the end doesn't matter, actions should be judged in absolute terms according to intention"), Badius follows the first Clericus interpretation: Phyllis is saying "the end may yet be good; Demophoon may yet return," and condemning the changeability of public opinion.

Charles Fontaine, too, considers these lines to be worthy of one of his lengthier notes; however, his reading is slightly different:

> Elle respond maintenant au propos precedent comme disant et confessant qu'il est bien vray que lon iuge des faits par la fin & issue mais toutesfois elle ne veut confesser que la fin & issue de son fait soit mauuaise, & qu'elle soit ia auenue, à savoir que Demophon l'ait du tout delaissee, & qu'il ne vueile plus retourner vers elle: ains au contraire elle presuppose que quelque cas, empeschement, ou infortune luy est auenue qui le retient & retarde de venir. (44)

> Here she responds to the preceding remark, as if to say and concede that it is certainly true that we judge actions by their end and outcome, but nevertheless she refuses to concede that the end and outcome of her action is bad, and even that it has yet come about—in other words, that Demophoon

has abandoned her at all, and no longer wishes to come back to her; but on the contrary she presumes that some accident, obstacle or misfortune has befallen him to detain him and delay his return.

He assumes that Phyllis is in agreement that deeds ought to be judged on their outcome, but that she is not yet ready to admit that the outcome is bad in this particular case. Here we can see the differences between the readings proposed by each commentator: while Clericus takes the "exitus acta probat" as descriptive of a general moral principle, which can be illustrated with examples, Badius' and Fontaine's comments speak more directly of attitudes to Ovid's text. Fontaine implies that it is Phyllis' delusions that make her incapable of clear moral judgment: instead of arguing that Phyllis rejects "exitus acta probat" either because (a) her intentions were good and the outcome was beyond her control or (b) the outcome has not yet been decided, he prefers to emphasize her lack of understanding of the situation. As a woman in the throes of passion, she is unable to grasp the truth of the Thracian countryman's words: "Voyez l'inconstance des propos d'vne femme amoureuse" (Observe the inconstancy of the intentions of a woman in love).[52] In contrast with the Latin commentaries, Charles Fontaine is quick to pronounce a negative moral judgment on the heroine. His preface to the Phyllis epistle alludes to the medieval treatment of Phyllis as the epitome of "amor stultus":

> Et pourtant toute femme doit bien ici prendre vn bel exemple, de ne mettre son amour trop ardemment & folement en vn homme, quel qu'il soit: car la fin de folle amour iamais n'en fut bonne. (29)

> And nevertheless all women ought to take a fine example from this, not to love any man, whoever he may be, too passionately and foolishly: because the end of foolish love never was good.

It is only because Fontaine is writing in the vernacular that such a retrogression is possible. He is far more concerned than the Latin commentators had

---

52. Elsewhere in his annotations, Fontaine claims that it is characteristic of women to want to trace events to their first causes, rather than to judge them from their outcome: "C'est vne coutume, & quasi vn fait de femme de ramener au deuant, & tousiours en ieu, les commencements, & premieres causes de leur malheur, comme appert quasi en chacune de ses [sic] Epistres" (It is a habit and practically a fact of female behavior to bring to the fore, and always bring into play the beginnings and first causes of their misfortune, as appears in almost all of these epistles). Fontaine is commenting here on Ariadne's "utinam" lament at 10.99ff.

been to impress moral lessons on his readership. Fontaine's translation was designed to reach a wider female audience than the Latin editions, which are primarily aimed at a more educated male audience.[53]

Expressions of moral censure might be expected to dominate discussion of the epitaph that ends the Phyllis epistle. But Volscus does not attempt to adopt a moral standpoint from which to judge the actions of Phyllis; instead he offers an interpretation of the epitaph from the point of view of Phyllis as the wronged woman: "In hoc maxime uituperari Demophoontem existimat, quod uiolato hospitii iure & hospitem & amantem ad mortem coegerit" (sig. c.i[r]) (She is of the opinion that Demophoon is most at fault in this respect: that he violated the law of hospitality, and drove her, both host and lover, to her death). There is no corrective judgment forthcoming. It is noteworthy, though, that Volscus has adopted the third person to describe Phyllis' state of mind where often his paraphrases are in the first person: that is, they rephrase from the point of view of the letter writer. Volscus chooses to end his commentary by distancing himself from the heroine, while avoiding an explicit condemnation of her.

Clericus' comments on the epitaph also fail to condemn Phyllis; instead, he admires the compactness of expression and rhetorical skill she displays in her writing:

> ecce carmen, quod paucis uerbis amplam complectitur materiam uidelicet beneficia Phyllidis in Demophoontem & eius ingratitudinem de his beneficiis: & mortem phyllidis ex causa Demophoontis. habent autem omnia uerba hic posita emphasim in uehementiam significationis. (sig. c.i[r-v])

> Behold this verse, which in few words encompasses a great wealth of meaning, namely Phyllis' services toward Demophoon, and his ingratitude about them: and the fact that her death was caused by him. To be sure, all of the words set down here are emphatic in their force of meaning.

Clericus commends Phyllis for her mastery of rhetoric, if not her mastery of passion. However there is an implicit sense of *moral* approval in the

---

53. The same concern with female morality dominates the liminary material in vernacular Italian editions of the *Heroides:* Patricia B. Phillippy (31–32, 37–38) discusses the overt didacticism directed toward a female readership in the translations of Remigio Fiorentino (1555) and Camillo Camilli (1587). On the ways in which Renaissance writers make famous women into exemplary models for female behavior, Ian Maclean remarks that "the heroic exploits of exceptional women are noted, but moralists do not advise emulation of them, but rather their translation into domestic and private terms" (Maclean, 58). If the *Heroides* are being used to provide models for female conduct, it is on these terms.

appreciation of her linguistic 'virtues.' This is present also, in a more obvious way, in Morillon's comment on lines 57ff: "Quam honestissimis uerbis rem ueneream exprimit" (how very decorously [s]he describes the sexual act).

In one medieval commentary on the *Heroides*,[54] Dido, like Phyllis, is identified as an example of "amor stultus," because hers was a love that could not be reciprocated. The Renaissance commentators have little use for such categories; indeed, Dido is rarely portrayed in a negative light. Sharing, it seems, the sympathy for Dido that caused Saint Augustine to weep tears of sorrow for her, the humanist commentators are more likely to rail against Virgil and Ovid for the injustice done to the heroine. Far from acknowledging the differences between Virgil's and Ovid's treatments of the myth, Fontaine sees both versions as supporting the Roman foundation narrative, and attempting to suppress the Carthaginian side of the story. He implies that Ovid's version does nothing to present Dido as the innocent party, unlike Boccaccio's version, which makes Dido an example of virtue and chastity:

> Nonobstant Bocace en son liure des nobles & vertueuses Dames, escrit de la mort de Dido autrement & à son honneur, la mettant au rang des vefves chastes: & la verité est aussi, qu'Eneas vint en Italie plus de cent ans auant que Dido fust: & aussi Ausonius ha escrit un epigramme à la louenge de la pudicité d'elle. Mais Virgile ha ainsi escrit de Dido, & apres luy Ouide, en faveur de Cesar Auguste & des Romeins, & en defaveur & deshonneur des Carthaginois, leurs anciens ennemis. (117)

> Nevertheless Boccaccio, in his book of noble and virtuous women, writes differently of the death of Dido, honoring her and placing her in the class of chaste widows: and the truth is indeed that Aeneas came to Italy over a century before Dido lived: and Ausonius also wrote an epigram in praise of her chastity. But Virgil wrote thus of Dido, and Ovid after him, to promote Caesar Augustus and the Romans, and to put down and dishonor the Carthaginians, their longstanding enemies.

Fontaine makes the case that we need not condemn Dido for her excessive passion toward Aeneas, since she never met Aeneas in the first place. By referring to the non-Virgilian historical tradition that makes Dido a model of queenly virtue, Fontaine encourages the reader to bear in mind the motivation behind such depictions of Dido: Virgil and Ovid present Dido in this way simply because their intention was to portray their enemies the

---

54. See Hexter 1986, 183–85.

Carthaginians in a negative light. The 'historical' countertradition, in which Dido never met Aeneas (this part of the narrative being Virgil's invention), is widely known in the Renaissance. According to Boccaccio in the *Genealogia deorum gentilium,* this version comes from Justinus and other ancient historians, and is the "historically accurate" version.[55] In his *De claris mulieribus,* Boccaccio leaves out the encounter with Aeneas entirely; instead he narrates Dido's flight from Tyre after the murder of her husband, Sichaeus (or Acerbas) by her brother, Pygmalion. After founding the city of Carthage, Dido is approached by Iarbas, king of Mauretania, who threatens war unless she agrees to marry him. Dido agrees to the marriage on the condition that she be given a fixed date to "go to her husband." On the appointed day, Dido climbs onto a pyre and stabs herself, saying: "Prout uultis ciues optimi, ad uirum uado" (Just as you wish, excellent citizens, I go to my husband). Boccaccio approves the actions of the historical Dido, making her into an example to be emulated by all Christian widows:

> O pudicitiae inuiolatum decus! O uiduitatis infractae uenerandum eternumque specimen, Dido! In te uelim ingerant oculos uiduae mulieres et potissime christianae tuum robur inspiciant.[56]

> O inviolate flower of modesty! O eternally admirable example of uncompromised widowhood, Dido! I would like all widowed women to fix their eyes on you, and especially for all Christian women to admire your strength.

The lesson to be learned from Dido's story is that it is far better for a widow to be faithful to her first husband than to marry again. Given that Boccaccio's readership could not fail to be aware of the better-known Virgilian version of the story, in which Dido does 'marry' again, it seems unusual that the author should propose her as an example of devoted widowhood.[57] As Craig Kallendorf comments, the emerging interest among humanists in rhetoric, and in particular its epideictic dimension, allowed Boccaccio to dispose of the moral ambiguities of the Dido story by showing how it functions either as a warning against improper desires (following Virgil's version) or as an exhortation to virtue and chastity (following Justinus).[58]

---

55. See Kallendorf, "Boccaccio's Dido."
56. Boccaccio, ed. by V. Brown, 2001, 174.
57. Especially since Boccaccio himself often portrayed Dido as the Dido of *Aeneid* 4 in his vernacular writings (see Kallendorf, 402–3).
58. Other "positive" accounts of Dido"s story include Chaucer's *The Legend of Good Women* (in which the author accepts the version where Dido meets Aeneas, but places the blame for the tragedy

In the humanist commentaries there is very little discussion of moral issues, still less condemnation of the heroine. Almost all references to negative moral qualities are to "impius" Aeneas—or rather to the rhetorical techniques used by Dido in her letter to cast Aeneas as the villain. Ubertinus Clericus describes Dido's attempt to persuade "ab honesto et tuto." Badius comments on line 65 ("nullum sit in omine pondus" [may there be nothing in the omen]) with approval:

> honesta, & amica parenthesis. Nam dum mala commemoramus, ne malorum omen in amicos conuertatur, auerti petimus ab eis, & in inimicos conuerti. (fol. xxxvi^r)

> A noble and gentle aside. For when we make mention of evil things, lest the evil omen be turned upon our friends, we seek to turn it away from them, and toward our enemies.

The only references made to the moral problems raised by Dido's actions are in the form of comments on her use of language, or clarification of the moral issues in their historical context. For example, Volscus comments on Dido's apostrophe to "laese pudor" (damaged honor) (7.97) thus:

> uiolatam pudicitiam secundo coniugio demonstrat. nam quæ semel nupserant tanquam uirgines coronabantur: quæ bis: inpudicitiæ nota arguebantur. (sig. f.iii^r)

> She shows that her honor was violated by taking a second husband. For women who had married once were still prized as virgins, but those who married twice were condemned with the mark of dishonor.

There is no effort to set this judgment within the context of the rhetoric of praise and blame, as Boccaccio had done with Virgil's Dido. Volscus does not make Dido into an *exemplum* for Christian women, a deterrent aimed at widows who remarry or love in excess. Rather, his comments are there to clarify the sense of Dido's lament.

Ubertinus Clericus also comments on the language used by Dido to describe her predicament (her "culpa," 7.191), without himself imposing a moral judgment:

> Culpae. amoris secundi mariti: quem culpam appellauit: ut Seruius uoluit:

---

squarely with Aeneas) and Christine de Pizan's *Livre de la Cité des Dames* (around 1407).

quia antiquo ritu bis nuptæ a sacerdotio repellebantur: sed melius placet culpam dici propter fidem non seruatam priori marito, ut apud Vergilium. (sig. f.v^r)

The fault: the love of a second husband, which she called a fault, according to Servius, because in ancient custom women twice married were banished by the priesthood; but it seems better to assume that the word fault is used because of the broken promise to her first husband, as in Virgil.

Unlike Boccaccio (and Servius), Clericus does not see Dido's remarriage as culpable in itself; it is only Dido's unusual devotion to Sichaeus, and the vow she had made to his ashes, that allow her action to be described as a fault.

Ovid's version of the Virgilian narrative makes little of the empire-building responsibilities of Aeneas. The point made by Knox is not explicitly acknowledged in the Renaissance commentaries:

> ... by refuting the arguments adduced by Virgil's Aeneas to justify his actions, O. poses a fundamental challenge to the heroic values of the *Aeneid*. What Lanham (1976) 60–61 has observed of the *Met.* is also true of this epistle: "Dido can be left behind [sc. in the *Aeneid*] because Virgil accepts Rome as an external sanction, the source of all legitimating explanations. There is no sanction in O.'s poem." (202)

Indeed, the commentators do not attempt to make a distinction between Ovid's and Virgil's treatments of the myth; if anything, the distinction is between Dido's side of the story here, and Aeneas's version in the *Aeneid*. Whilst acknowledging the line of influence from Virgil to Ovid, the commentators seems to treat both versions as belonging to a single continuous mythological narrative, rather than competing with or contradicting each other. That Ovid has created a sympathetic portrayal of Dido is not acknowledged; the truly sympathetic Dido would emerge later, in Du Bellay's translation of her epistle.

Analysis: *Heroides* 16–17

The so-called "double letters" have been neglected by scholars, even during the recent revival of critical interest in the *Heroides*.[59] Even setting aside problems to do with authorship, the time of composition, and the difficul-

---

59. With the notable exception of Rimell's 2006 study on *Ovid's Lovers*.

ties with the title "Heroides," we cannot help but recognize that the double letters function according to a different dynamic; that they are generically distinct from the main collection.⁶⁰ The hero writes first; the heroine replies. The man takes the dominant role; the woman, a passive, reactive one.⁶¹

It is, then, in the double letters that gender boundaries are most clearly demarcated: the male writers have available to them an entirely different lexicon of desire, a new set of rhetorical strategies and poses. Readings of the text in the humanist commentaries tend to divide modes of rhetoric along gender lines. Commentators treat the male- and female-authored epistles differently: a "strong," penetrating, suasive rhetoric belongs to the male authors; a "weak," prevaricating, evasive rhetoric is characteristic of the heroines' epistles. To the humanist commentators, it is Paris whose rhetoric meets with success; Helen is entirely "other"; her writing is incomprehensible except as a symptom of a specifically female condition. To modern readers, by contrast, Paris is more often seen as the self-regarding blowhard, an eloquent hypocrite, culpably short-sighted: "his rhetoric is that of one possessed by *ate,* divine infatuation" (Kenney, 5). Helen is a knowing, coquettish manipulator; schooled in the Arts of Love, she is willing to use every rhetorical ploy to turn the game to her advantage.⁶² Kenney sees Ovid's Helen as a "brilliant retrojection of Euripides' acid deconstruction": she is a younger version of the Helen of *Troades,* who is entirely *au fait* with the moral implications and rhetorical arguments of the case at hand; and who, in the words of the Chorus, "pleads well in spite of her villainy." Myth and literature have clothed Helen in many different guises: she has been by turns wicked, naïve, and morally ambivalent; she has even been the blameless victim of Homer's calumny (according to Stesichorus, Helen never went to Troy but was replaced by a phantom or *eidolon* made of clouds: this version was taken up by Plato in the *Phaedrus* and dramatized by Euripides in his play *Helen*). Helen's nature is ever-shifting, ontologically unstable, always elsewhere. She is already something of a ghostly presence in the *Iliad* and

---

60. For an account of these issues, see Kenney, introduction to *Heroides* XVI–XXI.

61. W. S. Anderson is no doubt correct to suggest that this scheme puts the heroines and not the heroes into the "dominating" position, in that their poems speak of responses to "new and exciting pressures" (71). However, they "dominate" only in terms of the poetic complexity and dynamism of Ovid's character studies; for the appraiser of suasive stratagems and rhetorical points scored, the dominant position is unarguably the male one.

62. This is, however, by no means the only reading of Ovid's Helen available to modern critics. Anderson, for example, suggests that this portrayal of Helen is "probably the most sympathetic to emerge out of antiquity"; she proves "a sensitive, clever, morally aware, sensual, responsive woman, one whom it is difficult not to like" (78).

Odyssey.⁶³ This elusiveness, the essential doubleness of the Helen figure, is what comes through when she is allowed to write *in propria persona* in Ovid's *Heroides*.

The *argumenta* to the Paris and Helen epistles betray certain early modern assumptions about the gendering of rhetoric. Volscus summarizes the Paris epistle thus: this letter is written while Menelaus is away; in it, he reveals how passionately he burns with love for Helen, and persuades her to flee; then he proves to her that she will be kept safe by the Trojans. Clericus focuses in more detail on the rhetorical strategies adopted by Paris: Paris, he writes, applies great skill ("utitur magno artificio") to commend himself above all other men—as lovers are meant to—in beauty, nobility, riches, and physical strength, as well as in the truth and sincerity of his love ("a pulchritudine, nobilitate, diuitiis & robore corporis: & a uero sinceroque amore"). He works hard to persuade Helen, arguing firstly "ab utili," then "ab honesto," that their love is unavoidable; he adds that her reputation will not suffer, and that Menelaus will not come after them; or if perchance he does come after them, that she will be protected from him easily (sig. k.vʳ). As we saw in chapter 2, the rhetorical scheme Clericus uses to summarize the letter follows closely the stages of composition recommended by Negri for writing an "epistola amatoria turpis." The emphasis of both commentators is on the rhetorical skill, strength, and dexterity of Paris; his composition is shown to conform to the classical model of strong suasive rhetoric.⁶⁴

Morillon's *argumentum* for the Paris epistle is clearly a précis version of the two described above; sections of both are reproduced word for word:

> Hæc autem artificiosa epistola detegit quanto amoris æstu ardeat, se ab omnibus commendando, quibus amatores laudari solent. Et quia nouerat muliebrum sexum esse fragilem, & gloriæ, & laudis a forma, atque genere cupidissimum, omnia affert Paris, quæ sibi Helenes animum conciliare possunt, & quæ odium mariti atque contemptum excitent. Fugam itaque suadet, quam Troianis uiribus tueri posse asserit. (sig. F8ᵛ)

---

63. See Austin 1994, 18–19 and chapter 1, *passim*. On the point of the ontological ambiguity of Helen, Austin quotes Karen Bassi: "The *Palinode* [of Stesichorus] is clearly drawing upon a tradition which figures women as imitations and substitutes and therefore as objects of incomplete and elusive reference" (10–11, n. 9). Italo Calvino remarks on Helen's two early appearances in the *Odyssey*, first as the accomplice of Odysseus in his disguise, second as the enemy who imitates the voices of the Achaeans' wives as they hide inside the horse: "Helen's role is thus contradictory, but it always involves deception" ("The Odysseys within the *Odyssey*," in Calvino 1999, 15).

64. It is worth remarking that the adjective most often used of the Paris letter is "artificiosa"; Badius describes it in the same way; Charles Fontaine, too, in the preface to his translation calls it an "artficielle epistre."

This artful epistle, then, reveals how passionately he burns with love, by commending himself on the basis of all those thing that lovers are usually praised for. And because he knows that the female sex is weak, and very eager for glory and praise of their beauty and nobility, Paris brings in all possible arguments to win Helen's heart and to elicit hatred and contempt for her husband. And then he persuades her to run off with him, and claims that the Trojan forces can protect them.

As well as modifying the language slightly, Morillon also alters the emphasis of Clericus' comments, attributing the success of Paris' rhetorical strategies to the weaknesses and vanity of the female sex. Paris' suasive rhetoric is bound to hit its mark, since it exploits the character defects of its addressee to great effect.

In the case of the Helen epistle, Morillon's *argumentum* is, again, a condensed version of the summaries written by the two earlier commentators. He repeats Volscus' comments word for word: Helen initially scolds Paris, pretending to be offended; then, in order to preserve her good name, she tries to refute Paris' *suasiones* with counterarguments of her own. However, at the same time, she sows the seeds of doubt, insinuating that she would not reject his advances outright. Morillon goes on to rephrase Clericus' introductory comments: Helen's rhetoric shows us clearly how various and changeable is a woman's nature. Like Clericus, he quotes *Ars Amatoria* 1.483–85 ("Forsitan et primo veniet tibi littera tristis, / Quaeque roget, ne se sollicitare velis. / Quod rogat illa, timet; quod non rogat, optat, ut instes"): what women want is not what they say they want.

Charles Fontaine follows the *argumenta* penned by Volscus and Clericus and rephrased by Morillon:

> Heleine . . . ayant receu l'Epitre du beau ieune amoureus Prince Paris, comme irritée lui respond, le tanse, & reprend de plein sault: puis (pour sauver son honneur & estimacion) s'efforce de rabatre ses raisons & persuasions: entremeslant ce pendant toutefois quelques petits traits de plume, descouurans aucunement son affeccion: à savoir qu'elle ne vouloit ne pouuoit despriser l'amitié que ce ieune Prince lui portoit: a quoy elle demontre bien quel est le naturel des femmes. (277–78)

> Helen . . . having received the epistle of the fine young suitor Prince Paris, replies to him as if annoyed, and straightaway reprimands and reproaches him: then (in order to save her honor and reputation) she endeavors to counter his arguments and persuasions: all the while, nonetheless, inter-

spersing her writing with several little hints and exposing little by little her real feelings: namely, that she neither would nor could scorn the love that this young Prince offered her: and in this she demonstrates well what women are really like.

Fontaine's comments describe a progression from the indignant reproachful Helen wishing to preserve her chastity to the vain, weak-willed, and flirtatious Helen. The revelatory moments in her letter (those "petits traits de plume") are defined either as evidence of some manipulative strategy on her part or as unintentional slips that prove her weakness and susceptibility to flattery. The commentators seem unable to decide whether Helen is wicked or foolish; and her inconsistency is explained away as the defining characteristic of a woman's natural character: "elle demontre bien quel est le naturel des femmes."

Ovid's Paris, then, is the seducer, the persuader, the skilful proponent of strong rhetoric; Helen is characterized as evasive and manipulative, but at the same time weak-willed and foolish. Her poem resists easy classification, and the humanist commentators have some difficulty in keeping track of the intention that underpins her rhetoric.

The initial reading of Paris and Helen as binary opposites does not tell the whole story, however. The illustrations in the 1580 edition, for example, suggest a different reading that tends to invert the masculine and feminine roles assigned to the two writers (257, 278) (Figures 7 and 8): Paris is feminized in this illustration, by analogy with the heroines in the first part of the collection: the composition of the image replicates that of the Dido illustration, with Paris replacing the abandoned heroine on the shore, intent on his task of writing and oblivious to the world of action. This is the typical pose of the epistolary heroine: the 1543 edition had depicted Helen in this pose (119)—and this same image had been reused for the epistles of Penelope, Laodamia and Sappho (Figure 9). Of course, Paris often takes the role of the effeminate, sensual weakling in readings of the myth: as we have seen, Erasmus described the Paris of the *Heroides* as more woman than man. However, the notion of a withdrawn, self-possessed Paris does not square with the image of the master of strong rhetoric advanced in the prefaces. Helen, on the other hand, is depicted not writing but in the action of transmitting her letter to an intermediary: her pose is more masculine; it is the pose of a *paterfamilias* conducting his business or a general marshalling his troops. The confusion over gender roles hinted at in these illustrations manifests itself also in the close readings of the masculine and feminine rhetorics and psychologies of *Heroides* 16–17.

Figure 7. *Les XXI épitres d'Ovide* (Paris: H. de Marnef, 1580), p. 257. Bibliothèque nationale de France/Gallica

EACH COMMENTATOR is at pains to highlight the suasive techniques used by Paris. He is shown to be more thoroughgoing than the female authors of letters 1–15 in his deployment of suasive rhetoric. This is a Paris who seems to be well versed in the seduction techniques advised by the *praeceptor amoris* in the first two books of the *Ars Amatoria*. Clericus, indeed, often comments on the similarities between Paris' techniques and the techniques recommended by Ovid in that work, as well as on Paris' understanding of female psychology. For example, at 16.14, he reminds the reader of the Ovidian *dictum* that when a girl reads the seal of a letter from her suitor,

278   HELEINE
quel est le naturel des fẽmes. En fin, quasi
se rendant veincuë, l'auise s'il ha quelque
chose à lui mander, de ne le faire par lettres, mais par ses deus Damoiselles bien
fiables, Climene & Etra : ce qu'il fit, aussi
elles deus suiuirent Heleine à Troye.

LA XVI. EPISTRE
D'OVIDE.

Heleine escrit à Paris.

A Pres que i'ay à mes yeux presentée
   La tienne lettre de diuers mots hantee,
Et que i'eu bien le faict tout pourpensé,

Figure 8. *Les XXI épitres d'Ovide* (Paris: H. de Marnef, 1580),
p. 278. Bibliothèque nationale de France/Gallica

the battle is half-won already. His notes are usually neutral in their moral stance, but at 16.232, he pointedly gives a counterauthority: although Ovid in the *Ars Amatoria* recommends the use of alcohol in seduction (the references seem to be to *Ars* 1.237 and 3.762; Morillon also quotes the latter), Saint Paul does not: Clericus quotes Ephesians 5:18: "Nolite inebriari uino in quo est luxuria" (And be not drunk with wine, wherein is excess).[65]

---

65. It should be noted that the adduction of Scriptural authorities in these humanist commentaries is a rare occurrence.

HELENA PARIDI

HVBER. VM Tua epistola) qua conatus es alienare me ab amore mariti, & ad tuũ soli citare. *Violarit*)leserit. *Nō referi.)sunt qui ita dicant: gloria nō rescribédi est visa mihi leuis.i.facilis.sf melius, Leuis, pro vili, & parua accipitur: vel certe sic verius: gloria rescribendi est visa mihi non leuis, ,i.non parua.i putaui magnaɜ gloriam mihi fore rescribere tibi, quia affecisti me magna iniuria. *Ausus*)obiicit ei ingratitudiné,& impietateɜ, qd̄ violauerit iura hospitii. *Temeratis*)violatis. *Sacris*)q̄, q̄n aliqs vir magn° excipiebaʳ hospitio: Ioui, & diis hospitalib°sacra fiebat: qd̄ Virg.ostédit lib.j.Aen.cũ Dido Aeneã excepit; Sic memorat, sic Aenean in regia ducit Tecta : simul dixit tẽplis indicit honorem. *Sollicitare*)cõmouere. *Scilicet*)dictio ē apta ad ironiã,& indignatione. *Taenaris*)Laconica. *Oppositas*)oclusas tibi. *A gẽte di.*)remota, & quẽ nobiscũ nō habuisseʳ p̄suetudine. *Idcirco*)pp hãc cãm. *Vt iniuria*)quaɜ paras mihi inferre. *Esset mer.*).i.re muneratio, & p̄miũ. *Tãti offi.*).i.beneficii accepti a nobis. *Sic*)ea intẽtione; vt mihi iniuriam faceres, & me abduceres. *Hostis*,an hospes)q.d.potius hostis. *Nec du.*).i.scio, q̄, licet iuste de te conquerar, iudicabis me tamen rusticam: quae conquerar de eo, qui me amet. *Sim*)concedentis est. *Dũ*)pro dũmodo. *Tenor*)perseuerantia. *Sine labe*)sine macula,& infamia. *Si non*)respondet ei parti: quaɜ dixit, Vultu non cætera duro Perlege, sed formæ cõueniẽte tuæ: dicit enim,quod si nõ est seuerí,& duri vultus,est tñ pudica, *Torua*)terribilis. *Supciliis*)qb° õdidit seueritas. Virg. Cõueniẽs Latio pone supcilia. *Vixi*)legit & lusi.i.fui læta, & iocata sum, salua tñ pudicitia mea. *Laudē de me*)vt possit se iactare de cõcubitu meo.

ASCEN. VNC Oculos &c.)epistola hæc r̄nsiua Helenę parũ qdē in rebus difficultatis h̄; eo q̄ argumentũ a Paridis epistola depedet, nec multum in verbis: est.n.facilior, & pedestrior, q̄ Ouidiana cõpositio: vñ ex sola phrasi Ouidianã ne

PVBLII OVIDII NASONIS
POETAE SVLMONENSIS
Heroidum Epistola decimasexta.

IN DECIMAMSEXTAM EPIST. ARG.

 VLTI Hanc epistolam nõ esse Ouidij contendunt, asserentes Sabinum omnes responsales literas confinxisse . Quod ipsius Ouidij testimonio comprobare nituntur, cũ in secundo Elegiarum ita ad Macrum scribat:

Quam cito de toto redije nixus oibe Sabinus,
Scriptaq̄ị diuersis retulit lik locis:
Candida Penel. pe signum cognouit Vlyssis.
Legit ab Hippolyto scripta nouerca suo .
Iam pius Aeneas miseræ rescripsit Elissæ ,
Quodq̄; legat P yllis, si modo viuit , habet :
Tristis ad H pliphylem ab Iasone litera venit .
Dat notam Phoebo Lesbis amica Lyram .
Quod quidem nihil ad rem facere videretur, cum nullam interim de Heleną mentionem faciat. Verum statim subiungit hos duos versus.

Et Paris est illic , & adultera nobile crimen ,
& comes extincto Laodameia vi o .
Quibus facile conuincuntur, nisi ad Sabinum referre malint.Sed cum Ouidianis epistolis respondent, quomodo possunt esse Sabini. Non enim Paris, nec Laodameia respondet, sed scribunt.Nõminum hæ quoq̄ Ouidianæ sunt, & codẽ penẽ stylo scriptæ, quo reliquæ. Helena autem, & ea Paridis epistola, quasi offensa, primum respondens obiurgat. Deinde vt pudorem tueatur, Paridis suasiones infringere conatur, quædam semina spargendo, nē omnino illius amorem negligere videatur. Et sic aperte ostendit, mulierē ẽ ingenium varium ẽē, atq̄ mutabil. Iuxta illud Ouidianum in Arte amandi.

Forsitan & primo veniet tibi littera tristis,
Quaq̄ị roget u e se solicitare velis :
Quod rogat illa timet , quod non rogat , optat vt instes :
Postremo Paridis voluntatem impletura, vt honestius, ita tutius visum est, si quid in desiderio erit,non literis mandare, sed vt Clymene, & Aethra comites fidissimæ exponerẽt, idq̄ cum fecissent, cum Paride, & Helena ad Troiam adductæ sunt .

HELENA PARIDI.

 Vnc oculos tua cũ uiolãrit epistola nr̄os:
Non rescribendi gloria uisa leuis.
Ausus es hospitii temeratis aduena sacris
Legitimam nuptæ sollicitare fidem?
Scilicet idcirco uentosa per æquora uectum
Excepit portu Tænaris ora suo?
Nec tibi,diuersa quamuis à gente uenires;
Oppositas habuit regia nostra fores?
Esset ut officii merces iniuria tanti?
Qui sic intrabas,hospes,an hostis eras?
Nec dubito,quin hæc,cum sit tam iusta:uocetur
Rustica iudicio nostra querela tuo.
Rustica sim sanè:dum non oblita pudoris;
Dumq̄ị tenor uitæ sit sine labe meæ.
Si non est ficto tristis mihi uultus in ore:
Nec sedeo duris torua superciliis:
Fama tamen clara est: & adhuc sine crimine uixi; *
Et laudem de me nullus adulter habet.

ges. In principiõaut alii nũc, alii tũc legũt, & vtriusq̄ị tolerari pōt.Ego autē legere potius nũc, sub hoc sensu.Cũ.Lita sit: q̄ epl̄a tua *Violarit*) p̄ violauerit:hoc est læserit. *Nũ c nr̄os oc.*) q̄ antehac nihil spu̶rcũ,aut lasciuũ viderat, aut legerāt(nã s oculi legũt) *Gloria nō reseri.).i.q̄ tēt eī nō rescribēdo. *Est mihi vi.le.*).i. modica.Presupponit ergo pecatũ eē in legēdis epl̄is amatoriis, & in rescribēdo,sed maius in legēdis: vsq̄; adeo, vt viola ta legēdo parũ gloriæ mereaʳ nō rescribēdo: & is certe aius ē mulierib°, vbi semel libata est pudicitia,nihil in eis post illã cõmedandũ est. Et Ioc vt monet Naso nr̄) Principiis obstadũ est.Nã qa ex visu,cuius prima est amoris linea, ad alios gradatim pueniẽt,qa ergo violatam se sensit legēdo: paruisa cit,ne amplius violeʳ rescribēdo. R escribit tñ criminãdo: sf ea quoqs est mulierũ natura, vt q̄ lubētissime factuæ sint, in principio negẽt, sic tñ, vt ni si insites, ipsæ se corrigãt, & placari posse significēt. *Dic ho spitalitatis aũt scias, q̄ id apud ãtiquos erat sctīssimũ, ita vt louē ei posse significēt. vñ.). Aen, Iuppiter (hospitib° nã te dare iura loquunt)&c.Erat aũt ho spiritũ amicitiæ non mercēdis ḡa,nã caupona dr̄ diuersoriũ mercenariũ, q̄ nũc nō tã frequẽs erat, & nũc, quapp̄ necesse erat hisi hospites cõparare, inter quos magna fides obseruabaʳ, quã Paris solicitãdo cõ iugē hospitis violasse crīmẽ tur. *Ora Tænaris*) pro Tænaria, nã Tænarius p̄montoriũ est Laconiæ, pro quo Imperiri. Tęnarius legit apud Alexādrũ. Tęnarus inferni &c. *Hospes,an ho.eras*) q̄.d.potius hositis: q̄ sic nō cũ rãta hospitalitate, sed iusta aio intrabas. *Nec du.*) callide iudicũdi illi laudat suãq̄; pudicitia cõmedat, in q̄ vɜ laborabat. *Vultus tri, siē uerus,& atrox.Et bene vultus potius,q̄ facies. Nã vultus q̄si a voledo dr̄,facies à faciēdo: & ita facies à factore fit, nec mutaʳ: Vultus à volutate alius, & alius fit. *Et laudē*)q̄si laudis sit habuisse pmerciũ cũ tã formosa: quo verbo audaciã Paridis potius pbat,q̄ dinet: sf mire ī se criuē cēset, q̄ in il lo laudē: quasi mulieri sit criminē, q̄ viro laudi datur: ita * a.l.Iuf enim mũdo videʳ, cũ eadē sit vtriusq̄; apud Deũ censura,

L ii

However, Clericus has nothing negative to say about Ovid's comments on the lover's licence to deceive: at 16.246 he quotes *Ars Amatoria* 1.569–70: "Hic tibi multa licet sermone latentia tecto / dicere, quae dici sentiat illa sibi" (Here you could say many things hidden under covert speech, for her to understand that they are addressed to her). Clericus is fairly slapdash when it comes to pinpointing the sources of his quotations: he is perhaps quoting from memory, since he locates 1.569 in Book 2 and 1.230 in Book 3. Morillon replicates the error in his note on 16.241 ("Hæc omnia ab amatore esse facienda ostendit Ouidius in 2 de Arte" (That all these things must be done by a lover is demonstrated by Ovid in the second book of the *Ars Amatoria*)—actually book 1).

The references to the *Ars* in commentaries on Helen's epistle are there primarily to reinforce readings of Paris' strong rhetoric; very little is made of the heroine's use of Ovid's advice to women in book 3. So Clericus in his introduction quotes *A.A.* 1.481 "quae uoluit legisse uolet rescribere amanti" (She who was willing to read, will be willing to write back to her lover) to show that it was Paris' rhetorical skill that motivated Helen's reply; she was unable to contain her guilty pleasure at his flattery:

> Helena igitur lecta epistola paridis cum ea delectata esset: licet ostendat se indignatam non potuit tamen non rescribere. Ita lenita est et demulsa blanditiis paridis: quos magno artificio contexuit. (sig.1.iii^v)

> So Helen, after reading Paris' letter, since it delighted her, however much she puts on a show of outrage, could not help replying all the same. So mollified and entranced was she by the blandishments of Paris, which he composed with great skill.

Although she initially adopts a tone of moral outrage, the fact remains that she was *unable to stop herself writing back:* Paris' words had weakened her will. Badius comments at length on this point: it is in a woman's nature, he writes, to try to act demure and aloof, but to be unable to suppress signs of their pleasure at flattery. Clericus recognizes a number of other references to the *Ars Amatoria* in Helen's epistle; but they promote Paris' seduction techniques rather than Helen's own strategies. For instance, he put into the context of the *Ars* the descriptions of Paris' technique of drinking from her cup (80), and his writing messages in wine on the table (87–88).

In the humanist commentaries the Paris epistle, which modern critics have judged less complex and interesting than Helen's reply, is prized for its systematic application of suasive techniques, for its eloquence and for its subtlety. Notes identifying rhetorical places and the parts of his argument feature heavily in all commentaries. Volscus is the most thorough in this regard; a sample of his notes on the technique of the Paris epistle follows: *captatio beneuolentiæ* (16.1); "he commends Helen on the basis of her reputation and fame" (16.36); "he commends himself on the basis of his nobility and power" (16.173); Volscus draws a comparison between Paris' assurance that Troy has the necessary manpower to protect Helen, and Cicero's rhetoric (16.179ff); attack on the character of Menelaus (16.205); "this deliberation elicits pity" (16.235); "he shows this love to be ordained by fate" (16.281); "he persuades her that it is easy" (16.299); "he persuades by the contrary" (16.313); "he refutes her fear of betrayal" (16.321); "he eases her fear with examples" (16.341); "he proves his bravery with an example" (16.359); "he concludes his epistle by dispelling whatever fears Helen might have had" (16.371). Volscus also brings to the reader's attention some of the rhetorical 'flavor' of Paris' words: e.g. 16.214, "this part should be spoken in a contemptuous tone"; 16.221, "this part should be spoken in irritation."[66]

Clericus also lists the stages of the argument in systematic fashion: "he begins by vaunting his nobility" (16.173); "he vaunts the nobility of the Trojans" (16.199); "he vaunts his beauty and bravery" (16.205); "he builds up hatred of the race of Menelaus" (16.211); "he pleads with her, and praises her at the same time" (16.273); "he subtly shows that sons and daughters derive their character from their parents" (16.293); "irony" (16.302); "he entices her with the promise of gifts" (16.337); "he exalts himself and diminishes Menelaus, showing that he does not have these claims to fame" (16.363). Morillon does likewise: "he entices Helen by praising her beauty" (16.147); "he praises her constancy" (16.163); "he vaunts his nobility and power" (16.175); "this deliberation elicits pity" (16.235); "he shows that sons derive their character from their fathers" (16.294); "by means of irony he shows that Menalaus is unworthy of such a beautiful wife. He brings contempt on Menelaus by censuring him" (16.301); "he takes the blame upon himself" (16.325); "he banishes her fear with examples" (16.343); "he concludes the letter by dispelling any fears Helen might have" (16.377–38).[67]

---

66. "Helenam a nomine et fama commendat" (16.36); "a genere et potentia se commendat" (16.173). "communicatio hæc miserationem mouet" (16.235); "arguit amorem hunc fore necessarium a fato" (16.281); "facilitatem suadet" (16.299); "a contrario suadet" (16.313); "fraudis timorem excludit" (16.321); "exemplis timorem soluit" (16.341); "exemplo suam fortiudinem probat" (16.359); "colligit epistolam abigens quicquid Helenam terrere potuisset" (16.371). "enunciandum cum contemptu est" (16.214); "cum stomacho hoc est enunciandum" (16.221).

67. "incipit se laudare a nobilitate" (16.173); "laudat phrygum nobilitatem" (16.199); "laudat se a pulchritudine et fortitudine" (16.205); "amplificat odium gentis Menelai" (16.211); "precatur eam: et laudat simul" (16.273); "latenter ostendit filios filiasue trahere mores a parentibus" (16.293);

The emphasis of the commentators is firmly on technique: the Paris epistle is a model of suasive rhetoric expertly targeted to achieve its aims. For the most part, Paris seems less concerned with justifying his actions than he is with allaying the cares of Helen and anticipating her reservations: he wishes to take on the burden of guilt for both of them (Volscus at 16.325: "purgat pudoris crimen transferens in se culpam" [he clears the charge against her modesty, taking the burden of blame on himself]); Clericus at 16.326: "uolo omnem culpam huius facti in me transferri" [I want to take all blame for this deed upon myself]); he assures her that she will not lose her reputation for chastity ("suadet facinus non modo non esse pudendum: sed summæ gloriæ futurum" [he persuades her that not only is the act without shame, but it will be most praiseworthy]—Volscus at 16.333). His rhetoric is at times direct, at times guileful; but it is always seen to hit its mark: for instance, at line 3 Volscus points out that Paris simulates doubt in order to manipulate Helen's response. The irony we intertextual readers find in Paris' positive attitude, and in his woefully inaccurate predictions for the happy outcome of their affair, is not often remarked upon by the commentators: they do not contrast Paris' narrative of future events either with the very different version predicted by Oenone in *Heroides* 5, or more generally with the Homeric-Virgilian account.

According to the commentators' reading of Helen's epistle, her intention mutates and develops in three stages: first, she attempts to refute the arguments of Paris and to vituperate him; second, she becomes Helen the chaste and rustic girl embarrassed and offended by Paris' advances; third, her deployment of veiled allusions, innuendoes, and asides betray her "true motivation" in writing the letter: to cede to Paris' immoral desires.

Examples of Helen's subtle manipulation of Paris' reactions are generally not seen as being part of Helen's rhetorical strategy as such; rather they are lapses that betray her feminine weakness and inconstancy. However, there is some inconsistency in the commentators' treatment of Helen's rhetoric: occasionally she is also seen as being perceptive, devious, and manipulative. Clericus notes the rhetorical links between Helen's reply and Paris' letter, identifying the specific parts of the letter to which Helen responds. For the

---

"ironia" (16.302); "allicit eam munerum pollicitatione" (16.337); "extollit se et Menelaum deprimit ostendens eum non habere hos titulos" (16.363); "a pulchritudinis laude Helenam allicit" (16.147); "constantiam suam laudat" (16.163); "a gente et potentia se laudat" (16.175); "communicatio hæc commiserationem excitat" (16.235); "natos a suis parentibus mores trahere ostendit" (16.294); "Per ironiam probat Menelaum indignum tam formosa coniuge. Menelaum ducit in contemptum eum taxando" (16.301); "pudoris culpam in se transfert" (16.325); "exemplis timorem eximit" (16.343); "colligit epistolam abigens quicquid Helenam terrere possit" (16.377–38).

most part, though, the commentators treat the subtext of the letter as a product of her vanity and inconstancy, rather than a calculated deployment of rhetorical skill. Paris is always the one in control: his letter came first; he proposed the elopement; and Helen only reacts to his persuasive flattery. The commentators deny that Helen stands equal to Paris in her mastery of rhetoric: it is Paris' letter that is *artificiosa;* Helen's is simply inconsistent and ill-considered.

The first Helen we encounter in the epistle is the indignant Helen. Volscus charts her efforts to deflect Paris' advances: "she brings hatred upon him by charging him with audacity and disrespect for religion" (17.3); "to increase contempt for him" (17.4); "in commending her own nobility she scorns the boasting of Paris" (17.51); "she shores her argument [that Paris should give up] by mentioning the difficulties that can arise when one is far away from home" (17.227). Clericus, too, approves Helen's technique: "she charges him with ingratitude and lack of respect" (17.3); and Morillon does likewise: "by this example [Theseus] she reproves Paris' (17.21); "she begins to condescend/to stoop to his argument" (17.33); "she scorns the boasting of Paris" (17.57). This Helen seems to be a woman fully in control of her rhetorical strategy, and firm in her moral stance. Clericus compliments Helen on her ability to marshal moral commonplaces: he clearly approves of the sentiment expressed at 17.191 ("With strangers love is never sure"): "this too is a statement of good sense." He singles out the *locus* at 17.234 "fair hope is often deceived in its own augury" for praise ("sententia est rhetorica"). Morillon explains the meaning of the adage: "she shows metaphorically that the greatest love can turn into hatred."[68]

The second Helen is the chaste, rustic Helen. She is less a master of rhetorical argument and more a plain-speaking girl embarrassed by Paris' advances; though her arguments remain commendable. Volscus: "she concedes that she is rustic, as Paris had charged; and she excuses her rusticity on the basis of modesty" (17.12); "persuasion by honor" (17.98); "she rebuffs him and tells him to stop bothering her with his words" (17.111); "she argues from like situations that such great love can turn to sorrow and hate" (17.235); "she discourages the abduction by adducing dreams: indeed this is a commonplace of persuasion or discouragement" (17.237). At 17.262

---

68. "ducit in odium ab audacia et temerata religione" (17.3); "ut augeat contemptum" (17.4); "sui generis commendatione Paridis iactantiam contemnit" (17.51); "propositum suum firmat ab incommodis: quæ possunt absentibus a patria exoriri" (17.227). "obiicit ei ingratitudinem et impietatem" (17.3); "hoc exemplo [Theseus] Paridem increpat" (17.21); "incipit condescendere" (17.33); "Paridis iactantiam contemnit" (17.57). "certus in hospitibus non est amor: et est sententia rationem continens" (17.191). "metaphorice ostendit maximum amorem in odium posse uerti" (17.234).

("Quid uoces colloquium") Volscus praises Helen's use of euphemism: "she has spoken more honorably than if she had said it outright"; Clericus is more blunt: "even though your 'conversation' means sex." Morillon, too, approves of Helen's moral stance at 17.213, calling it a "very true argument."[69]

The weak-willed, prevaricating, changeable Helen is the third term in the sequence. For Clericus it is in this role that Helen epitomizes the female sex: "ostenditur autem muliebre ingenium uarium et mutabile" (It is shown here that a woman's nature is various and chageable). This paraphrases *Aeneid* 4.569–70, Mercury's words to Aeneas: "varium et mutabile semper / femina." The *Heroides* commentators seem to be very fond of this commonplace: it is found in the texts of Clericus, Volscus, and Morillon. This misogynistic judgment is directed at Helen, though not at Ovid's Dido, Mercury's target in the original context. The glosses Volscus supplies at various points corroborate this reading: "Weak: womanish, and therefore changeable" (17.11); "see how, just like a woman, she already begins to be won over to Paris and flattered by him" (17.35); "she justifies her intention, though she appears weak" (17.109). At 17.136, Clericus judges Helen to have given in to her suitor's flattery: "She shows that women delight in praise of their beauty." Morillon, too, places emphasis on the signs of female weakness that come through in Helen's language: "She reviews the proofs of his love, so that she may argue with reason that she can be induced to love him" (17.73); "since woman is ever inconstant and changeful" (17.111); "having been convinced to love him she hopes that the deed itself will be easy" (17.141); "wavering in her trust of Paris she is at the point set against love" (17.189). Clericus comments that Helen's exclamation at 17.220 ("I'd rather be dead and buried!") is a "womanish" thing to say, quoting examples from *Aeneid* 4.24 (Dido) and *Heroides* 3.63 (Briseis) to prove it.[70]

In these examples, Helen is seen as exemplifying the weaknesses and vicissitudes characteristic of the female sex. This is a slightly different emphasis from the comments on Helen's deviousness and underhand rhetorical

---

69. "fatetur rusticitatem quam obiectauerat Paris: eamque a pudore excusat" (17.12); "suasio ab honesto" (17.98); "repellit eum a se ne amplius eam uerbis sollicitet (17.111); "a simili arguit posse in tristiciam et odium tantum amorem uerti" (17.235); "dissuadet rapinam hanc a somnis: nam locus est suadenti aut dissuadenti" (17.237). "Quid uoces colloquium: honestius locuta est quam si rem aperte dixisset" (17.262); "quamuis colloquium tuum esse concubitum." "uerissimum argumentum" (17.213).

70. "Molle: muliebre: et per consequens mutabile" (17.11); "ecce more muliebri iam incipit conciliari paridi et ei blandiri" (17.35); "excusat uoluntatem licet mollis uideatur" (17.109). "ostendit . . . mulieres laudibus suæ pulchritudinis delectari" (17.136). "Amoris signa recenset, ut a caussa arguat se allici posse ad amandum" (17.73); "Quoniam uarium et mutabile semper femina" (17.111); "in amorem adducta rei facultatem exoptat" (17.141); "anceps in Paridis fide adhuc amori repugnat" (17.189). "est imprecatio muliebris" (17.220).

strategies: in these examples, Helen is merely conforming to her natural disposition, as a woman unable to keep her language under control; her words betray her emotional fragility, not her manipulative skill. Helen wants to be taken in by Paris' rhetoric, because all women secretly want to be forced into sinning ("quia cupiunt puellae cogi"–Clericus, 17.185).

THE AMBIVALENCE of Helen's rhetoric leads the commentators into some confusion in their identification of rhetorical figures. Whereas in the other letters it is a relatively straightforward matter to identify instances of suasive rhetoric, arguments of self-justification based on the places of rhetoric, and so on, in Helen's letter it is not always clear what course of action she is trying to encourage. Nor do her efforts to establish the steadfastness of her moral character always mesh with the subtext of her words. This feature of Helen's discourse, which is often read by modern critics in terms of knowing irony,[71] is not recognized as such by the early modern readers. Volscus singles out instances of persuasive technique (e.g., line 98: "suasio ab honesto: ire contra appetitum fortitudo est" [persuasion by honor: to go against one's desires is steadfastness]), but does not comment on the underlying irony, or on the fact that Helen's aims in persuading are by no means consistent as her argument develops.

The commentators, however, are not always insensitive to the subtext of Helen's epistle. Indeed, they recognize the irony, if not the humor, in Helen's mock indignation and subsequent reversal. The crux of the argument is that it is not always clear whether Helen really intends to persuade or to dissuade: Volscus and Clericus both remark on examples of her rhetoric where the subtext diverges from the surface meaning ("latenter dicit . . . ").

Volscus' *argumentum* directs the reader's attention to the subtext:

> cui [Paridi] quasi offensa primum respondens obiurgat: deinde ut pudorem tutetur illius suasiones infringere conatur: sed *quædam spargit semina: unde non omnino illius amorem negligere uideatur.* (sig.1.iii^v; emphasis added)
>
> First she responds as if offended and chides him; then to preserve her honor she tries to undermine his arguments; but she scatters a few seeds, so she seems not to be completely unresponsive to his love.

Volscus recognizes the shift in tone between the indignant heroine, employing her best rhetorical skills to refute the arguments of Paris; and the flirta-

---

71. Following Belfiore, who views Helen's apparent self-contradictions as part of a conscious strategy of persuasion (Belfiore 1980–81, 136–48).

tious, devious Helen, delighted by the flattery and dropping hints that Paris' love will be reciprocated. At 17.35 ("Non tamen irascor"), she kindles hope in Paris even while rejecting his advances: it is not Paris' love itself that angers her, but the idea that his affection might be insincere: "dissimulata iracundia amantis spem suggerit. non nam inquit: queror quod a te amer" (With concealed resentment she gives hope to the suitor. For she does not say: I am angry because you love me).

Helen strategically brings up her previous experience of abduction by Theseus (17.22). Clericus comments that although this example seems to be intended to dissuade Paris, in fact it is a subtle way of encouraging him to carry out the abduction ("tamen latenter ad incitandum positum est": [but it is subtly expressed to be provocative]). Where Helen reproaches Paris, saying that where Theseus took only kisses from her, Paris would certainly demand more than that, Clericus sees a betrayal of Helen's true intentions: though she pretends to be indignant ("dum simulat . . . se dicere iniuriam paridi" [while she pretends that she is insulting Paris]), she is in fact leading him on ("eum magis incitat"). This is Helen the *fausse-naïve*. She wields a certain power over Paris: 17.152 ("sed cur desistas"): "latenter ostendit sibi gratum esse quia pergat" (But why should you cease?: subtly she shows that she is glad that he goes on). But she acts the wide-eyed innocent to spur Paris on to greater crimes: at 17.169 ("latenter innuit quod libenter peccaret: si auderet"), she secretly hints that she would gladly commit the sin if she dared.

Volscus sees line 131 as marking the point at which Helen finally reveals her hand ("hac diuisione quicquid insinuauerit detegit" [from this point she states openly what she has been insinuating]—Morillon also copies this note word for word). He does not comment further on how this revelation casts a different light on her rhetoric in the preceding arguments. After this point, Helen's rhetoric is shot through with ambiguity, which Volscus sees as intended on the part of Helen. At 17.138, Helen is seen as being deliberately ambiguous in order to entice Paris ("dubio sermone usa est ne omnino amantem excludere uideatur" [she has made use of ambiguous words so she would not seem to reject her suitor's advances completely]). She states her case in less ambiguous terms later, at 17.152, stating her immoral intentions without veiling them in rhetoric: Volscus comments (and Morillon repeats): "apertius extulit quod animi haberet" (she has exposed more openly what she had in mind). This interpretation of Helen's rhetoric differs from the readings of the weak-willed, misguided Helen; here, she is the one in control; her will reveals itself in the language she uses.

Volscus returns to the reading of Helen as weak-willed and swayed by flattery in his comments on lines 177ff. He sees Helen as ceding at this point to the *suasiones* of Paris, ready to commit the crime but for her inexperience in the protocols of unlawful love. She echoes the "commoditates" that Paris had listed, showing that she has now "gone over to his side." Her apparent reluctance is no longer to do with her moral principles, but with her fear of abandonment by her guest-lover, as her *exempla* drawn from *Heroides* 6, 10, and 5 demonstrate.

Although the commentators generally do not make consistent distinctions between the *intentio auctoris* and the *intentio mittentis,* such a distinction is perhaps implied in the rhetorical analysis of the Helen letter: it is used to accommodate contradictory readings of Helen as rhetorician. In this way, Helen can be dismissed as flittish and too weak to resist flattery and passion, at the same time as being called devious and manipulative. Helen's moral weakness is manifest in her language, which is distinctly 'female'; but her strength of character and ability to persuade are not really hers, but Ovid's.

The degree to which Helen is the agent of her actions is not fixed by the commentators. At one moment she is imagined to be calculating and manipulative; at the next she is merely ceding to the will of Paris, and not wanting to show it, but betrayed by lapses of her pen. Line 145, writes Volscus, is to be imagined as spoken "cum suspirio" (with a sigh), as if Helen has already been persuaded to elope, and wishes she had the wherewithal to make it happen (again the irony of Helen's claim to be a novice in the business of love is lost). The inconsistencies in the readings of Helen's rhetoric are put down to the "mutabilitas" of the female sex. As Clericus comments, the abrupt transition from compliance to resistance at 17.189 merely proves the inconstancy of women in general. It is not considered to be a rhetorical strategy on the part of the writer.

The Helen epistle isolates certain concerns that are common to all the heroines' epistles in the early modern readings; these concerns are set in relief because Helen's words must be read against the word of her male counterpart, Paris. The heroines in Ovid's collection oscillate wildly between roles they construct for themselves: alternately powerful and weak, active and passive, they resist systematized rhetorical analysis. In her study of the workings of desire in Ovid's text, Sara H. Lindheim draws on Lacan ("There is no such thing as Woman") to make the argument that in the *Heroides,* and especially in the Sappho poem, Ovid attempts to construct a representation of Woman, and that this construction proves to be illusory.[72] However, Ovid's heroines shift constantly, masquerade, play role after role; they

---

72. Lindheim, 183–84.

cannot be fixed in any one essence: the multiplicity of woman asserts itself "despite" Ovid's universalizing efforts. Lindheim is, in effect, "reading the heroines against Ovid": clearly there was no possibility for such an approach in sixteenth-century readings. As we have seen, in early modern treatments of the text, Ovid is often "read against the heroines," but the heroines may not be "read against Ovid."

THE METHODS and concerns of the humanist commentators of *Heroides* illustrate a wider point applicable to the practice of commentary as a whole, as it took on new forms and aims in humanist thought. At the same time as it is becoming more focused, more 'philological,' and more self-contained (in that it is explicitly 'authored'), commentary becomes more open-ended, more based on metonymy than metaphor, functioning by 'horizontal' connections designed to broaden understanding rather than 'vertical' connections bound to the established frameworks of interpretation. It breaks with finality. Poetry, especially Ovidian poetry, resists the imposition of ends; and the commentary form seems able to accommodate this. In their analyses of the line "exitus acta probat" none of the humanist commentators posits an authorial intention separate from that of the letter-writing heroine, no perspective from which to condemn or commend her speech. The ends of commentary are not so bound up with the need for moralizing, allegorizing readings that the study of literature cannot become an end in itself.

CHAPTER 4

The *Heroides* in Translation

Or, autre conséquence, "l'auteur de la lettre," lui aussi, "reste hors jeu." "Dès lors la responsabilité de l'auteur de la lettre passe au second rang auprès de celle qui la détient." Il y a détention mais non propriété de la lettre. Celle-ci ne serait jamais possédée, ni par son émetteur ni par son destinataire.

Jacques Derrida[1]

THE TRACE of a translation from one language into another is written into the heroines' discourse from the start: none of the mythological letter writers in the collection could be imagined to have composed her epistle in Latin. The question of translation is brought to the fore by Briseis, who makes specific reference to the fact that she writes in Greek, and by Sappho, who acknowledges that the reader might find it odd that her letter is written in (Latin) elegiac couplets. Briseis opens her letter with an explicit reference to the language in which it is written:

> Quam legis, a rapta Briseide littera uenit
>   uix bene barbarica Graeca notata manu. (*Her.* 3.1–2)

The letter you read, written in Greek only with difficulty by her barbarian hand, comes from captive Briseis.

This gesture toward verisimilitude only serves to draw attention to the artificiality of the conceit that is the basis of the whole collection, and to the distance between the fictive writer's 'original' text and the text the reader encounters. The reader is compelled to admit the intervention of a transla-

---

1. "Le Facteur de la vérité," in *La Carte postale*, 450. "Thus, second consequence, 'the author of the letter' too, 'remains out of play.' 'From then on, the responsibility of the author of the letter takes second place to that of its holder.' There is a holding, but not an appropriation, of the letter. The latter is never possessed, either by its sender or by its addressee" (trans. Alan Bass).

tor,² and such an intervention necessarily undermines any sense of psychological realism or emotional immediacy that might have been established. The self-conscious artistry of the poet asserts itself conspicuously: Ovid's own controlling 'hand' betrays its presence in the work.

Joseph Farrell remarks of *Heroides* 3 that "two putative translations occur, that of Briseis' thoughts and emotions from her native language into alien Greek, and the subsequent translation of her makeshift Greek into the Latin that we read."³ Briseis' words challenge the classical definition of a letter as a laying-bare of the soul, because she expresses herself in language only with great difficulty. The *Heroides* constantly draw attention to the implausibility of the conceit that the genesis of the heroines' writing is spontaneous and natural. Ovid, and in turn his first translators, must adopt the position of the orchestrator, the controlling hand that confers authenticity on the heroines' words and validates the ethical and rhetorical roles that they play.

In this way, Ovid's early modern translators intervene as the *de facto* addressees of his 'letters,' displacing the fictive addressees of the heroines' epistles. However, as they receive and in turn transmit the message conveyed to them across the centuries they nevertheless fail to 'possess' the discourse of Ovid's heroines. The story of the translation and retranslation of the text can be figured as the charting of an attempt to deal with the excessive element of the heroines' discourse.

THE EARLIEST extant translation of the *Heroides* is a Byzantine Greek 'metaphrasis' composed by a thirteenth-century monk, Maximus Planudes. This translation is included in full in Palmer's edition of the *Heroides*. The poems are rendered into Greek prose, with the occasional use of elegiac verse for epitaphs and inscriptions. Purser calls it "a flat and bald work, in a considerable number of places showing a very imperfect knowledge of Latin" (xlvii).⁴ The first complete translation of the text in any Western European vernacular language was the mid-fifteenth-century *Bursario o las Epístolas de Ovidio* of Juan Rodríguez. It is Marina S. Brownlee's contention that the

---

2. An editor must have intervened also; indeed, the *Heroides* can be said to thematize every stage of the editorial process. See Farrell, 329–38.

3. Page 334, n. 54. The seventeenth-century author of the *Lettres portugaises* also exploits the conceit that the letters he presents are translations (*ibid.*, with references).

4. On the transmission of this *Heroides* translation, see Papathomopoulos 1975, 107–18. For the dating of the translation in relation to Planudes' other Ovid translations, see Michalopoulos 2003, 359–74. Planudes also made a translation of the *Metamorphoses*, and the surviving fragments of a contemporary translation of the *Amores, Ars Amatoria,* and *Remedia Amoris* are probably by him. On the *Metamorphoses,* see Fisher 1990. On the amatory works, see Kenney 1963, 213–27.

translation by Rodríguez challenges the monologic authority of Alfonso's partial prose translation, on which it is based. Rodríguez included rubrics for each poem to indicate the edifying conclusions that ought to be drawn from the heroines' stories. According to Brownlee, the didacticism of these rubrics "is calculatedly counterfeit." The translator also included three epistles of his own composition, which he attributed to Ovid. Brownlee calls this "a blatant act of literary counterfeit."[5] Interestingly, the publication of Octavien de Saint-Gelais's French translation involves a similar case of literary imposture. In at least one edition of that translation, André de La Vigne's imitations are appended under the title "Quatre epistres dovyide nouvellement faictes & composees oultre les premieres."[6] The preceding page announces that these four poems have been "traduictes et composees par maistre Andre de la Vigne." The wording is pointedly ambiguous, and it is very unlikely that anybody would have mistaken these poems for actual works by Ovid, but this example demonstrates once again that Ovid's collection had never been fully and definitively bound or bounded. The text of the *Heroides* opens up an indeterminate space, a space of dramatic tension between voices gendered male and female, between primordial and civilized cultures, between languages. In its reception the *Heroides* continues to situate itself within a space of transition or mediation, in which there is a movement to efface difference and simultaneously to draw attention to it. The text comes to stand at the threshold dividing antiquity and modernity, Latin and the vernacular, Ovid and pseudo-Ovid. Daniela Dalla Valle suggests that the *Heroides* in their reception were always open to 'comparative' readings or adaptations; and that the production of *Heroides* translations and imitations is marked, from the start, by an attitude of antagonism, "une certaine attitude de contraste et d'opposition."[7] The epistolary fiction is itself ideally suited to explore the complications of cultural exchange and 'translation,' in all its forms. That the *Heroides* occupied a special transitional space, the space of "translatio studii et imperii," is suggested by "Sonnet acrostichic [*sic*] sur la transmigration des bonnes lettres d'Athenes et Rome à Paris, és personnes des Heroides d'Ovide," dated 1579.[8]

The first known translation of the *Heroides* into French dates from the thirteenth century. Translations of thirteen of the epistles, in prose, were inserted into a prose version of the *Roman de Troie,* which was in turn

---

5. "Hermeneutic Transgressions," 106, 112.
6. Saint-Gelais 1534. My references except where otherwise stated are to this edition.
7. Dalla Valle, 372, 378.
8. Inserted into the 1580 edition of Charles Fontaine's translation (441). The acrostic spells the name of the printer, HIEROME DE MARNEF.

included in the 'second redaction' of the *Histoire ancienne jusqu'à César*.[9] Prior to Octavien de Saint-Gelais's 1490s translation (first printed in 1500), only one other version is known, an anonymous fifteenth-century translation, translated for "la senechalle d'Armygnac," which is incomplete.[10] Saint-Gelais's translation is therefore the first complete translation of the *Heroides* into French.[11]

Les XXI Epistres d'Ovide by Octavien de Saint-Gelais went through at least nineteen editions between 1500 and 1550.[12] The appearance of this translation occasioned the rise in popularity of *Heroides* imitations during this period, and it was instrumental in shaping the *épître amoureuse* as a genre. It was a translation more influential on the French reception of the *Heroides* than George Turberville's was on Elizabethan culture.[13] Apart from an anonymous verse translation of five epistles printed sometime in the sixteenth century,[14] the only other major French version of the work was Charles Fontaine's retranslation of the first ten epistles, dating from 1551.[15] The translator included brief prefaces and annotations to each of the poems. Scollen (159) locates a further seven editions of this work, which was often printed in tandem with Saint-Gelais's versions of the other eleven (excluding Leander to Hero and Hero to Leander). A response of a different order, also of 1552, came from Joachim Du Bellay with a version of Dido's letter to Aeneas (*Heroides* 7), printed along with his translation of Virgil's *Aeneid*

---

9. See Constans 1914, 177–98. The translation is incomplete, omitting *Heroides* 7, 9, 12, 14, 15, 20, and 21. According to Constans, the translation is a loose one, though probably based on Ovid's text rather than prose paraphrases; it contains many errors (some of which he lists on pages 186–93); its literary value is "à peu près nulle." On the *Histoire ancienne* and *Roman de Troie*, see Meyer 1885, 1–81; Chesney 1942, 46–67. The epistles have recently been edited by Luca Barbieri, and published along with a detailed study of the translations (Barbieri 2005); a French translation of Barbieri's study is available (Barbieri 2007).

10. Lucas 1970, 225–53; 244.

11. Although Constans ("Une traduction française," "Appendice") speculates on the existence of an earlier complete French translation (excluding only the Sappho letter), which must have been the base text for an Italian translation of *Heroides* 1, 2, 3, and 5.

12. Composed in the earlier 1490s, and appearing in MSS from 1496, the earliest printing is c.1500: see Molinier 1910, 67; and Scollen, 20, 157–59. Scollen remarks its influence, 23–24. Joole (48) locates twenty-six editions up to 1568. Several manuscript editions are also extant.

13. On Turberville's translation and its influence, see: Greenhut 1988, ch. 2; and Moore 2000, 40–64.

14. Dalla Valle 2003, 374. For an account of seventeenth-century French translations of the *Heroides*, which were mostly in prose, see 374–76.

15. Fontaine's first preface is dated 1551, but the earliest printed edition seems to be *Les Epistres d'Ovide nouvellement mises en vers Françoys par M. Charles Fontaine Parisien* (Lyon: Jean Temporal, 1552). Fontaine composed the translation in the mid-1540s; in a preface dated May 1556, he mentions that the translation was done "il y a environ dix ans" (3). My references are to *Les XXI épitres d'Ovide* (Paris: H. de Marnef, 1580).

Book 4.[16] It seems as much provoked by Fontaine, whom he targeted in the *Deffence,* as by Saint-Gelais.[17] Saint-Gelais, Fontaine, and Du Bellay represent different possibilities for translation in mid-sixteenth-century France.

Charles Fontaine speaks of the success of the earlier translation in an "Avertissement aus lecteurs," rhetorically querying the necessity of his own new one:

> Mes bons signeurs, i'ay pensé qu'il seroit bon vous auertir en peu de paroles, que si d'auenture quelques gens peu entenduz me mettoient au deuant tels propos, de fait ou de pensée, Comment? ces Epistres d'Ouide n'auoient elle[s] pas, ia long tems ha, esté traduites par le signeur Octouian de Saint Gelais? quel besoin estoit il donq de la presente traduccion, et de faire vne chose ia faite? (438)

> Kind sirs, I thought it would be right to inform you in a few words, just in case some less than competent people put the following argument to me, in deed or in thought: What's this? Had not these Epistles of Ovid already been translated long ago by Octavien de Saint-Gelais? What need was there then for the present translation, and to do a thing already done?

Although Saint-Gelais's translation was well regarded and considered by many to be the definitive version, Fontaine in 1556 sees it more as a relic of the "bon vieux temps," a fine example of "bonne antique simplicité," but hardly able to fulfil the needs of a sophisticated audience (4). The reasons given by Fontaine to justify his undertaking are as follows: first, that Saint-Gelais's other translations have been reevaluated by other poets (most notably, his *Aeneid* has been redone by Louis des Masures); indeed there is a long tradition of multi-authored versions of the same work. Second, that the translation itself did not fully satisfy "aus bons esprits" because of its language:

> En quoy disant ie n'enten le blamer, ains plustot le vueil ie excuser, & prendre en bonne part ce qu'il ha fait lors que nostre langue Françoise n'estoit pas encor bien auant sortie de son enfance, ny n'estoient les arts & sciences tant esclarcies, ny les esprits si prompts, vifs & agus comme de present. (439)

---

16. Du Bellay 1552. My references are to Du Bellay, ed. by H. Chamard, 1931.
17. See Du Bellay, ed. by H. Chamard, 1948, II.11, 176.

In saying this I do not mean to blame him, but rather I wish to excuse him, and to take in good part what he did while our French language had still not yet advanced much beyond its childhood, when arts and sciences were not as brilliant, nor minds as quick, lively, and sharp as they are now.

Fontaine self-consciously places his work within the context of the transition from medieval to Renaissance poetry. He uses the tropes—very familiar in the contemporary critical discourse—of the 'childhood' of language and of clarity emerging from the shadowy obscurity of the past. This latter image persists in Fontaine's description of his specific approach to the text: the prefaces are there to clarify the reasons behind the stories and fables ("declarer les raisons des histoires & fables"); the notes fulfil the need for fuller clarification and understanding of obscure and difficult passages ("plus ample declaracion & intelligence des passages obscurs & dificiles") (440). He assumes a relatively sophisticated audience, and his prefaces and notes encourage the reader to compare versions, and even to read the translation critically alongside the Latin: in this respect his aims differ considerably from those of either Saint-Gelais or Du Bellay. Fontaine comments on the stylistic and sense choices he has made in his translation much more extensively than Saint-Gelais had done; indeed, the latter did not address the question of translation technique at all in his prologue.

The earliest editions of Fontaine's translation do not incorporate Saint-Gelais's versions of the remaining poems (*Heroides* 11–21). From 1556, Fontaine decided to include the extra poems to make the work complete. Still dissatisfied with the earlier translator's work, he undertook to review and correct it (in his words, to "pass[er] la main par dessus"), updating the language the better to harmonize with recent changes in the cultural and linguistic landscape. Specifically, Fontaine updated the orthography, corrected certain words or even entire lines where the sense seemed obscure, and at certain points made the line conform to the rules of prosody.[18] This, he claims, he did only where it could be accomplished easily, and without corrupting or diminishing Saint-Gelais's antique charm ("sans . . . corrompre ou perdre la grace de celle antiquité," 4).

Not all of the poems added in this edition are Saint-Gelais's translations: the letters from Leander to Hero and Hero to Leander come from a different

---

18. To take one or two examples of the sorts of changes made by Fontaine: the sixth line of Saint-Gelais's translation of *Heroides* 11, "De tescripre devant que ie me tue" (fol. lviii'), becomes "D'escripre à toy, devant que ie me tuë" (296); in *Her.* 16 "Point nest besoing soit a gaing ou a perte / Monstrer la flamme ia congnue et apperte" (fol. lxxxii') becomes "Quel besoin est, soit à gain ou à perte / Cacher la flamme ia connuë et aperte?" (257).

source. In the 1556 preface, Fontaine claims that these two versions are, as far as he knows, by a certain "Seigneur de Sainct Romat." They are followed in the 1556 and 1580 editions by Marot's translation of Musaeus' *Hero and Leander*.[19] Fontaine included them instead of Saint-Gelais's versions "because they are such fine examples of the high point of literary glory that we have now reached" ("par ce qu'elles sont trop mieus resentens la perfeccion de notre tems en l'honneur literaire"). He adds that if only "Sainct-Romat" or a poet of similar quality had translated the other poems too, there would be no need to settle for the inferior versions of "ce bon vieillart" (Saint-Gelais). Already in the 1552 "Petit avertissement," Fontaine had justified his choice to retranslate the poems on the grounds that "feu monsieur de saint Ambrois" and "monsieur de saint Romat" had been dissatisfied enough with Saint-Gelais's versions to undertake translations of their own, respectively, of the Paris and Helen letters, and of the Leander and Hero letters. Only the latter are included in Fontaine's edition however: he uses Saint-Gelais's versions of *Heroides* 16–17. I have been unable to find any other reference to the two translators named by Fontaine.[20]

In justifying his choice to translate the *Heroides*, Fontaine focuses in turn on its rhetorical virtues, its moral dimension, and its educative utility more broadly conceived. The material contained in the notes and prefaces consists partly in unfolding the moral and psychological implications of the poems and in explaining their historical setting (it being a mark of their supposed superiority over the *Metamorphoses* that they are not fabulous). The aspect that most interests Fontaine, however, is Ovid's art: he recommends Ovid as a "singular poet in invention, grace and ability" ("singulier poëte en invencion, grace et facilité"); and it is the *Heroides* that take the palm as his most 'artificial' work. Most of Fontaine's annexed "Translateur aus lecteurs" is taken up with how a sense of Ovid's art might be transmitted in French. Fontaine's interests conform with those evident in the commentary editions being printed at that time, which display, in Ann Moss's words, an "obsession with rhetoric which makes the mid-century editions read like manuals in the art of literary imitation."[21]

---

19. They had already been published alongside Marot's Musaeus translation in 1541; see Dalla Valle, 373–74. It appears that the only edition of this work that included the two epistles was the one printed in Paris by l'Angelier in 1541; this is one of the three editions disowned by Marot in his preface to the Gryphius edition printed later the same year. See Mayer 1954, 44.

20. Fontaine also addressed an epigram to Saint-Romat in his *Ruisseaux* of 1555: 'Vive la Muse docte humaine / Qu'en nostre Athene ie congnu, / Sur ce beau mont qui nous rameine / Tout l'honneur du Grec mont cornu" (200). Saint-Romat could be the "Saint-Roma*rd*" who penned an epitaph on the death of Marot.

21. Moss 1982, 15.

In common with the Latin commentaries, his notes focus on the work's sophisticated wit and richness of language; on its educative value in terms of myth and ancient culture; and on the ethical dimension (although, as with the humanist commentaries, they almost never attempt to moralize or allegorize the text along the lines of the medieval *accessus*). It is not only in the notes and prefaces that these concerns manifest themselves: they are woven into the text of the translations themselves.

The concerns of the translators shift emphasis as the century progresses and the intellectual climate changes. The late-medieval translator's concerns are with the morally edifying content of the letters; he focuses less on rhetoric and poetics, and not at all on 'encyclopedic content': the work is not treated as a source of mythological, historical and cultural information. The mid-century translator deals with moral issues in the paratext, but avoids them in the body of the translation itself. Fontaine is more concerned with rhetoric and poetics, and concentrates more on rendering the linguistic details and rhetorical effects into French. Accompanying this is a more prominent concern with textual accuracy. There is also a greater emphasis on the text's encyclopedic content: Fontaine is careful to include all mythological and historical detail, and often supplies explanations and glosses either within the translation or in the notes. With the translation of *Heroides* 7 by Du Bellay we observe a further shift in the role of the translator: the Pléiade poet is less concerned with exegesis of the moral and factual content of the text; his responsibility, as poet-translator, is to the *genius* of the source text, while remaining faithful to his own voice or "naturel." This shift in focus is not at the expense of scholarly erudition.

SAINT-GELAIS makes use of a familiar device in the introduction to his translation: he came across an edition of the *Heroides* by accident while browsing his library in search of something to offer his prince:

> Ie [*sic*] trouvay par my le nombre des autres volumes les epistres heroydes par le treseloquent & renomme poete Ouide, iadis compilees en forme latine doulce & melliflue. Et pource que la matiere & son art me sembla telle que langue de detracteur ne peult ferir ou attaindre contre lescu de sa value (ientens quant a reprouuer le merite de telle personne) cognoissant aussi que la louenge de luy auoit este perseuere en la bouche des hommes depuis les olimpiades lors nombres iusques aux modernes calendes. Cela toute autre cause regettee donna hardement & force de auguiser la pointe de ma plume a la pierre fine de son scavoir pour en tirer ce que pourroye. (fol. iᵛ)

> I found among a number of other volumes the *Epistulae heroidum* by the most eloquent and renowned poet Ovid, composed long ago in a smooth and flowing Latin style. And because the subject matter, and his art, seemed to me so great that no critical tongue could ever harm or taint the value of his currency (I mean by attacking the virtue of his character), knowing too that praise of him had been constantly on the lips of men throughout the "Olympiads," as they were then reckoned, and all through the "Calends" of the modern era. All other reasons apart, this alone gave me the confidence and assurance to whet the tip of my pen on the precious stone of his talent, to take from it what I could.

The qualities that commend the work are its fame, which has endured since ancient times and, above all, its eloquence. Saint-Gelais's attempts to do justice to Ovid's "sweet, mellifluous Latin" meet with varying degrees of success. His language is characteristic of his time: the features of his style that would strike Fontaine as deficient are generally features of the French language in the late fifteenth century, and not personal idiosyncrasies.[22] For instance, in his translation Saint-Gelais very often doubles verbs ("ie brusle et ars" for "uror" at 7.23), adjectives ("simple ou folle" for "stulta" at 7.28), and nouns ("par parolles ou escrptz" for "uerba" at 7.6) where the original Latin has a single word. This is occasionally used for emphasis of a particular idea ("oublier ou hair" for "odi" at 7.29) or verbal antithesis, but is more often the technique used to accommodate specific rhymes or to 'fill out' the couplet. This is certainly an aspect of contemporary poetic style, and is less conspicuous in the later translations. Fontaine also uses this technique, though far less frequently: "plena pudoris" (7.98) is expanded to "Pleine de honte et toute vergogneuse"; "tarda" (7.104) becomes "tardiue et variable"; and his translation of "hospes" (7.146) hints at the Ovidian play on hospes/hostis: "Et tu seras... hoste et estranger." Du Bellay seldom uses the technique.

Robert Griffin describes Du Bellay as "goaded" by the success of Saint-Gelais's *Aeneid* translation.[23] In the case of his *Heroides* translation, it is more

---

22. In the nineteenth century the translation was savagely criticized by Goujet on the grounds of its "barbarie de langage." In his *Essai biographique et littéraire,* Molinier is at pains to set the record straight, claiming that Saint-Gelais was in fact an outstanding poet in the context of the age in which he wrote. Saint-Gelais brought to this translation "sa grâce ordinaire, son élégance et sa facilité" (71); he respected out of a natural poetic instinct 'rules' that would only become established later—for example the 'alternance' of masculine and feminine rhymes (72). More recently, Anna Slerca (1997, 55–68) has shown that Saint-Gelais's translations, especially his *Aeneid,* made a significant contribution to the linguistic enrichment of French poetry. On the *Aeneid* translation, see also Brückner 1987.

23. Griffin 1969, 84.

likely that he was goaded by the endeavors of Fontaine, whose version met with a favorable reception, and went through several editions. Fontaine's is an only moderately foreignizing translation by the standard set in English by Turberville, who is often unintelligible without recourse to the Latin; but it makes few concessions to easy readability. Where Saint-Gelais endeavored to produce something "doulce & melliflue," Fontaine set out in his afterword his ambition to have reproduced Ovid's sense, and as closely as possible and as compactly ("le plus brief") as the French language allowed (186). The ideal of brevity, the avoidance of glossing interventions, the neglect of concessions of popular taste, is followed at the cost of labor to himself and difficulty for the reader. Occasionally the demands of French syntax force him to be more diffuse than he would like, but he strives always for brevity, and is sometimes even able to translate line for line. He criticizes those translators who turn one or two Latin lines into six or eight or ten lines and nonetheless skip over passages they do not understand. These vices, those of Saint-Gelais, are on the one hand to "weaken, mangle and mutilate" an author ("essoiner, detrancher, & mutiler"), and on the other to "confound and encroach upon him" ("trop le confondre, & entreprendre sur luy"): in the end, to "overturn and corrupt him, and to force him to conform to our meaning" ("le renuerser, corrompre & contreindre à notre sens," 188). An opposite set of vices threatens, but one to which he obviously feels more attracted: those associated with metaphrase. Word-for-word translation he declares impossible, for each language, he says, has its own diction, and its own particular character ("propre phrase, & proprieté particuliere") which makes it impossible to translate word for word or line for line. The cost is obscurity and confusion. He turns to those critics of translation—he must mean Du Bellay—who complain of translators' omission of expressions which have a grace and force of their own ("qui mesme ont grace & efficace," 189), and of others being imported as fillers or for the rhyme's sake. This he acknowledges; but he insists that the translator "se doit faire de si bonne grace, tant bien & proprement qu'ilz semblent estre comme de l'auteur, de sorte que si l'auteur eust escrit en la langue qu'on le traduit, seroit vray-semblable qu'il auroit ainsi escrit" (must do it so elegantly, so well and so precisely, that they seem almost to come from the author, so that if the author had written in the language into which he is translated, he would in all probability have written in this way) (190). That is, he insists that what is important is translatable, that Ovid will emerge looking like Ovid. The poetry is not what gets lost in the translation. It is in the domain of *elocutio,* it seems, that Saint-Gelais's translation is found wanting: Fontaine reevaluates the comments made by the earlier translator in his preface, specifying in his translator's note that the utility of the work is primarily in its rhetoric. He implies that his translation has done justice to this aspect of the work where Saint-Gelais's had failed. The specifically rhetorical virtues of an original are transferable:

> les propos bien deduits, les raisons & argumens de bonne inuencion, les motz bien couchez & apropriez, les belles comparaisons ou similitudes, les couuertes & douces insinuacions, les fortes & apparentes persuasions, les conclusions pleines de grandes & vehementes afeccions: à brief parler la grace & efficace[24] du Poëte. (192)

> well-turned phrases, well-sourced ideas and arguments, well-arranged and appropriate words, fine comparisons and similes, subtle and smooth insinuations, forceful and striking persuasions, conclusions full of great and powerful emotions; in short, the grace and effectiveness of the poet.

This description of the 'virtues' of Ovid's poetry bears a striking resemblance to Du Bellay's enumeration of the qualities that make poetry untranslatable in the sixth chapter of the *Deffence et illustration de la langue françoyse*. Fontaine's "grace & efficace du Poëte" seems to correspond to Du Bellay's notion of the poetic text's "énergie," "ne sais quel esprit," and *genius*.[25] For Fontaine, "efficace" is a measure of the clarity with which the poet sets forth his ideas in language; it can be replicated in the body of the translation by reconfiguration of surface elements within a different linguistic matrix. Fontaine goes on to affirm that when he rearranges words and makes alterations to the source text, it is always in the service of the original sense of the text, from which derive its particular "grace & efficace": it is exactly what Ovid would have done had he written in French. For Du Bellay, on the other hand, "énergie" is a measure of the poetic text's resistance to translation. Fontaine's optimistic conception of the *sine qua non* of the poetic text has less in common with Du Bellay's "énergie" than it does with Sebillet's "énargie": "a quality of verbal arrangement explicit in the source text and whose impact can be reconstituted in the visual patterns of the translative text."[26] This differs

---

24. The word "efficace" is related to the notions of *enargeia* and *energeia*. On the concept of the "efficace" of a text in the context of the poetic theory of Jacques Peletier, see Norton 1984, 299–302.

25. This is not to suggest that the theoretical position of Fontaine, an avowed follower of Sebillet and Marot's school, is in agreement with that of Du Bellay; but the two positions are closer than Du Bellay would have allowed. See, for example, Wiley 1972, 197–207.

26. Norton, 291. A similar distinction between *enargeia* and *energeia* is made by George Puttenham in his *Art of English Poesie* (1589), III: 3: *enargeia* is derived from "argos," "because it geueth

significantly from Du Bellay's notion of the "spirit" ("âme") expressing itself throughout the textual body: for Du Bellay, translation must begin with the energic core of the text and not with manipulation of the textual surface.

Fontaine uses the term "énergie" in his introductory comments to a later work, his 1555 translation of Ovid's *Remedia Amoris*.[27] There, it is one of many terms in an enumeration of the qualities that constitute the spirit of a text, qualities which may be successfully replicated in translation. "Energie," "vertu," and "force" combine with "grace," "elegance," and "doulceur" in defining the essence of the text. Just as Sebillet had imagined the "efficace" of a text to consist in the properties of words and expressions, Fontaine sees all these qualities as textual attributes which can effectively be expressed in translation; he conceives of "énergie" as something manifest in the text which can be recreated as long as the translator is not too slavishly bound to the idea of word-for-word translation, to the detriment of sense. This conception of "énergie" differs significantly from Du Bellay's notion of the resistant core or generative centre of a text.

It is clear from Fontaine's digression on the treatment of proper names (190–92) that he is engaging with Du Bellay's account of how they should be gallicized (*Deffence* II.6, 141–42). More generally, Fontaine's "Translateur aus lecteurs" seems to be a response to Du Bellay's attack in the *Deffence* on the possibility of usefully translating poetry (I: v–vi).[28] There, the virtues of "eloquution" "dont la vertu gist aux motz propres, usitez, & non aliénes du commun usaige de parler, aux methaphores, alegories, comparaisons, similitudes, energies" (35) (whose virtue resides in words that are fitting and familiar and appropriate to common usage, in metaphors, allegories, comparisons, similes, "energies") are beyond the translator, because every language has something uniquely its own ("je ne scay quoi propre seulement à elle"), and attempts to catch the 'naif' of another language will turn the translator's language into something constrained, cold and graceless ("contrainte, froide, & de mauvaise grace," 36). These "energies" are at this point identified with ornaments of speech, some at least of which will be transferable. They are "les motz bien couchez & apropriez" and so on, which make up "la grace & efficace du Poëte," and which Fontaine believes a good

---

a glorious lustre and light" and *energeia* derives from "ergon," "because it wrought with a strong and vertuous operation."

27. Fontaine 1555, 347–50.

28. Some have attributed to Fontaine the *Quintil Horatian*, a savage attack on the *Deffence*, now assumed to have been written by Barthélemy Aneau. However, it seems that the antipathy Du Bellay reserved for Fontaine was not reciprocated: in print, Fontaine showered the Pléiade poets with praise. See Roy 1897, 412–33. Roy argues that the attack on the unnamed literary parasite in *Deffence* II.2 is aimed at Fontaine.

translation can make evident to the Latinless reader of Ovid. Of course, Du Bellay changes his mind about translation in the couple of years that pass between his *Deffence* and the 1552 volume containing his Virgil and Ovid, and in the prefatory *Epistre à Morel,* declares that he feels no shame in bowing to contrary opinion—"je ne suis pas Stoique jusques là" (250–51). However, in saying that his naturalized Virgil still betrays his Roman origin, he says something different from Fontaine's saying he translates into such a French as Ovid would have written (190). In 1549 he wrote that no translator could command the grandeur, magnificence, boldness, variety of his originals, all that which made up "ceste energie, & ne scay quel esprit," which the Romans would call "genius" (40). But in 1552 he could write that the responsibility of the poet-translator was to the poetic *genius* of the source, while freed from the limiting invention of others ("les bornes de l'invention d'autruy"); and allowing for the constraint of rhyme, and the differences in character and structure from language to language ("la contraincte de la ryme, & la différence de la proprieté & structure d'une langue à l'autre"), he would not have failed in his duty if what he failed to render well in one place he endeavored to make good in another (249–50).[29]

J.-P. Néraudau remarks that Du Bellay's version of Ovid's poem says much more than does his version of Virgil about the Pléiade poet's thinking on translation,[30] and indeed, Du Bellay's translation of *Heroides* 7 must be read as an attempt to recreate the essence of the Ovidian *esprit* in French. It is clear from Du Bellay's description of his "compensation" technique that the translator values the poetic unity of the whole over a punctilious fidelity to superficial details; indeed, he does not even demand specifically equivalent effects. Significantly, Du Bellay does not label his *Complainte de Didon* a "translation": it is "immitée sur Ovide." His concern is with the *genius* of the text: the "ingénieuse facilité" of the poet which is in harmony with Du Bellay's own poetic voice. Fontaine describes a similar technique in his translator's note, but with a very different emphasis. The translator, he says, is sometimes forced to omit words or phrases from the text and to add elements of his own; this is allowed as long as the translator acts "de si bonne grace" that it is as if the original author were writing in French. The difference between the two authors is clear: for Du Bellay, "compensation" is a matter of give-and-take between translator and source author; the

---

29. Du Bellay, ed. H. Chamard, 1931, VI: 249–50.
30. Néraudau 1998, 369–86; 369. Du Bellay's poem is "at once the despairing cry of a woman about to die, and a stylistic manifesto, which is also the case of Ovid's poem" ("à la fois le cri de désespoir d'une femme qui va mourir et un manifeste stylistique, ce qu'est aussi l'Héroïde d'Ovide," 383).

distance between them is maintained, their separate identities preserved.[31] For Fontaine, it is simply a concession to the differences between structures of *phrasis,* a matter of balancing out verbal transactions in different linguistic economies. The translator merely does what the author would have done if he had written in another language: the effacement of the translator's identity is a matter of course.

Analysis: *Heroides* 2 and 7

The major differences between the translations are immediately apparent in a comparison of their formal characteristics. The 148 lines[32] of *Heroides* 2 are rendered in 294 lines of decasyllabic French verse in Saint-Gelais's version, and just 252 lines in Fontaine.[33] In the case of *Heroides* 7, Ovid's 196 lines (or 194 if lines 24–25 are omitted, as they are by both Saint-Gelais and Du Bellay) become 432 lines in Saint-Gelais's translation and 360 lines in Fontaine's version. Du Bellay's translation has 96 six-line stanzas but is effectively shorter than Fontaine's, comprising just 3264 syllables. Saint-Gelais is a prolix translator, whose interpretation of the text shades into commentary on occasion; Fontaine is more concise and methodical, rendering textual detail as closely as possible, elaborating his original only to avoid obscurity or to make obvious a rhetorical point; Du Bellay has done something else altogether.

The poetic form adopted by Du Bellay merits closer examination. Avoiding the conventional *rimes plates,* the Pléiade poet has chosen to translate Ovid's elegiac couplets into a lyric meter comprising six-line stanzas with rhyme-scheme aabccb. Seven-syllable lines alternating with trisyllabic lines sound out a syncopated rhythm. Du Bellay uses this stanza elsewhere, in "Les Louanges d'Amour," again, as it happens, adapting Ovid's elegiac couplets—the praise of Venus in *Fasti* IV, 91.[34] The proposal implicit here, in defiance of Fontaine's principles, is a much more thorough gallicization of the original. He has apparently abandoned his preference for no rhyme at all

---

31. As Norton comments, Du Bellay seems to believe in "a double space in which reciprocity is only occasional, often a compensatory donation of translator to author, and always grounded in an impossibility, a sense that never the twain shall meet" (256).

32. Or 146 lines, depending on the text used. Fontaine includes lines 18–19 in his translation, whereas Saint-Gelais does not. Similarly, in the case of *Heroides* 7, lines 24–25 are omitted by Saint-Gelais and Du Bellay, but included by Fontaine.

33. Fontaine has been as brief as he could be, though not as brief as Turberville's English, translated couplet for couplet.

34. *Œuvres poétiques,* III: 11.

to constraining and artificial rhyme (*Deffence* II.7, 147). It seems also that he has reconsidered his criticism of Marot, since the stanza form is borrowed from that poet, who used it in his version of Psalm 38 ("Domine ne in furore tuo arguas me"), designed for singing. Some see a mismatch between Marot's matter and his stanza, "a prayer set to a dance tune" or "le *Dies Irae* sur le mirloton."[35] But it was already popular in religious complaint, and its use continued in both Huguenot psalms and Catholic carols, expressive, says Vianey in the same place, of liveliness, movement, urgency, dynamic continuity ("l'élan, le mouvement, l'instance, la continuité du mouvement"). The liveliness and urgency do not seem obviously suited to Dido's complaint;[36] but heterometric schemes appealed to the Pléiade poets, and they did adopt this form in a wide variety of their compositions. Ronsard used it in his ode to the hawthorn ("Bel aubepin, fleurissant") of 1550, and in his *Voyage d'Hercueil* ("Debout! J'enten la brigade") of 1552. Baïf was to employ it widely in his imitations of the *Basia* of Johannes Secundus, and Belleau would use it in his poem "Avril."

Du Bellay's strong emphasis on rhyme contrasts sharply with Fontaine's opinions on the subject. Fontaine admits to having paid little attention in his translation to the exigencies of rhyme, "estimant la rime estre la ministre & chambriere du sens, & non au contraire" (187) (considering rhyme to be the servant and handmaid of sense, and not the other way around). Du Bellay, by contrast, shows in his version that rhyme must be integral to sense; it can even be dynamic and liberating. The multiplication of rhymes is what drives Du Bellay's composition: it is his major compensatory strategy.

These peculiarities grant the poet full license to stamp Ovid's original with his own stylistic flourishes, musicality, word-play, and linguistic ingenuity. The translator will grant himself a greater liberty with the source text, as long as it contributes to the emotive effect, and to the music of his version. For instance, he collapses the syntax of "nec quia te nostra sperem prece posse moueri / alloquor" (Not because I hope you can be moved by my pleas do I address you) (3–4):

Sans espoir de te pouvoir
Emouvoir
Mes complaintes je reveille. (307)

---

35. Emile Faguet, quoted in Vianey 1936, 44–57; 52–53.
36. Néraudau suggests that it is in the very dissonance between form and matter that Du Bellay is closest to Ovid's poetic vision: the "déséquilibre rythmique" of Du Bellay's chosen stanza form does to the decasyllabic couplet exactly what Ovid's limping elegiacs had done to the epic hexameter (379–80).

Fontaine had translated this literally (and prosaically): "Ie ne te parle esperant te mouuoir" (118). Du Bellay's lyric meter operates differently than Ovidian elegiacs, but it is capable of evoking a comparable psychological complexity.

Ovid's Dido, uncertain what she is going to write next, produces the syntactically broken "aut ego, quae coepi (neque enim dedignor), amorem, / materiam curae praebeat ille meae!" (Or I who commenced—and I do not scorn it now—this love—let him supply the substance of my affection!) (33–34). Fontaine gives the almost literal "Ou moi, qui ay l'amour encommencee: / (Car ne desdaigne amour en ma pensee) / Que lui aussi mon amour ne desprise" (119–20). Du Bellay's Dido balances the equation of love and pain through the ironic rhymes "amer / aymer" and "amante / tourmente," which have no counterpart in Ovid's version:

> Ou moy, qui ne trouve amer
> L'art d'aymer:
> Celuy qui me faict amante,
> Qu'il me donne seulement
> Argument
> D'aymer ce qui me tourmente. (p. 310)

The overall structure of Du Bellay's translation closely follows the structure of Ovid's composition. For the most part Du Bellay respects the semantic divisions of Ovid's couplets: 96 stanzas render 97 elegiac couplets, excluding lines 24–25 in both cases. The only occasion where Du Bellay's translation collapses two couplets into one stanza is at lines 181–84, perhaps because these lines contain some redundant repetition; the reference to the "Troicus ensis" in line 184 is transposed to the next stanza. The first couplet is abridged to half a stanza simply by deflating its rhetoric: "si minus, est animus nobis effundere uitam; / in me crudelis non potes esse diu" (If not, it is my intention to force an end to my life; you cannot be cruel to me much longer) (7.181–82) becomes "Si non, tuër je me veux. / Tu ne peus / M'estre longuement rebelle" (p. 328). Du Bellay does not always render Ovid's 'rising' hexameters and 'falling' pentameters accurately, often preferring to collapse the sense units together. Where Ovid's couplets usually form two distinct semantic units, introducing an idea in the hexameter and repeating, amplifying or resolving it in the pentameter, Du Bellay may collapse the parallel sense units together, blurring the transition from the longer to the shorter line. For example, when Ovid's Dido, reflecting how the harshness of the storm gives way to calm, wishes her lover would change like the winds (7.51–52):

> tu quoque cum uentis utinam mutabilis esses!
>   et, nisi duritia robora uincis, eris.

> Would that you too were changeable with the winds! And, if you are not harder than oak, you will be.

Du Bellay expands the idea contained in the pentameter to fill the whole stanza and reduces the hexameter to a single word, "ainsi":

> O que ton cœur endurci
> Peust ainsi
> Adoucir un peu son marbre!
> Je croy qu'il s'adoucira,
> Ou sera
> Plus dur que le cœur d'ung arbre. (312)

In Fontaine: "Que fusses tu comme les vents divers / Ores muable, et le seras ainsi / Si tu n'es dur plus qu'arbre et pierre aussi" (121). Du Bellay leaves implicit the comparison to the mutability of the winds, preferring instead to expand the image of the hard oak, introducing the parallel metaphor of marble. The second three lines of the stanza do little more than repeat the sense of the first three. The constraints imposed by metre and rhyme force the translator into unusual turns of phrase and word-order: although he does not often introduce new ideas or images not present in Ovid's version, he does make full use of poetic licence in the domain of syntax, often manipulating the grammatical structure of the Latin couplets. For example, in his translation of 7.143–44, Du Bellay reverses the apodosis-protasis order of Ovid's conditional clause:

> Pergama uix tanto tibi erant repetenda labore,
>   Hectore si uiuo quanta fuere forent.

> Troy itself would hardly cost you this much effort to regain—if it were now what it was when Hector was alive.

> Si telz que du temps d'Hector,
> Restoient or'
> Les fiers Pergames de Troye,
> Si ne devrois tu pourtant
> Voguer tant,
> Pour en retrouver la voye. (323)

In Ovid the impossibility of reaching lost Troy comes as an afterthought; in Du Bellay it dominates the stanza. The sense in the translation, even were it not complicated by the quibble on "si," is even more elusive than in the original.

Fontaine translates what in modern editions and his preferred one are two couplets (lines 23–26) in *Heroides* 7:

> Ie brule, ainsi comme torche de cire
> Auec le soufre, ou comme on pourroit dire
> L'encens qu'on gette au feu des mortuaires:
> Et à mes yeus, à tout repos contraires,
> Tousiours vn seul Eneas se presente:
> Le iour, la nuict Eneas represente
> Dedans mon cœur continuellement. (119)

Du Bellay prefers in this case a text which omits the central lines. This choice gives a couplet that is uncharacteristic of Ovid, since the idea introduced in the pentameter bears no obvious relation to the image evoked in the hexameter.[37] Du Bellay manages to conjure a certain continuity, however, through rhyme: "Comme le tizon gommeux / Tout fumeux / Du soufre et de cire ardente, / Je me consume: et l'amour / Nuit et jour / Mon Enée me presente" (309).

DU BELLAY deliberately transforms Ovid's epistolary manner into a singing one: "Ou fuy'-tu? voicy l'hyver / Arriver, / L'hyver me soit favorable, / Oy le bruit, que les vens font / Jusq'au fond / De la mer inexorable" (311). Du Bellay's composition, indeed, is not presented as a letter: the title implies that it is an oral *complainte* and there is no epistolary superscription or valediction. Ovid's poem itself—unlike many of the *Heroides*—does not immediately announce itself as a letter, opening, as it does, with the swan simile. Ovid generally lets us know his heroines are writing: "Hanc tua Penelope . . . tibi mittit . . . nil mihi rescribas" (This letter your Penelope sends to you: do not write back) (1.1–2); "Quam legis, a rapta Briseide littera uenit" (The letter you read comes from captive Briseis) (3.1); "Perlege quodcumque est" (Read on, whatever is here) (4.3). Occasionally he does not: Phyllis, for example, says "te . . . ultra promissum tempus abesse queror" (I complain that you are still not here now the promised time is past) (2.2), but Saint-Gelais thinks it appropriate to remind us that Phyllis is a letter-writer, introducing herself

---

37. See Knox, 207–8.

bizarrely as one "Dont a present son epistre tu lis" (fol. vi^v). Although *Heroides* 7 does not announce itself as a letter from the outset, Ovid's Dido later defines herself explicitly as a writing subject. She writes: "aspicias utinam quae sit scribentis imago! / scribimus, et gremio Troicus ensis adest" (Would that you could see what a spectacle I make as I write! I am writing, and a Trojan sword is on my lap) (7.183–84). Saint-Gelais translates, a little less emphatically: "regarde vng pou lymage / De celle la qui escript le langaige" (fol. xlii^r); Fontaine has her call on the gods to grant "Que ton œil vist le trespoure meintien / De l'escriuante" (129). Dido's allusions to the written word are suppressed or made ambiguous in Du Bellay's translation. For example, at 183–84 the reference to letter writing is suppressed:

O qu'eusse' tu le pouvoir
De me voir
Faisant ma plainte mortelle! (328)

Here, the comment directed at the letter's addressee becomes an apostrophe to the absent Aeneas; Dido is no longer writing but lamenting. Interestingly, this stanza of Du Bellay's translation is the only one that compresses two couplets into one stanza: the translator suppresses the reference to the Trojan sword on Dido's lap, transferring it to the next stanza. Moreover, Dido's "plainte mortelle" recalls the comparison to the dying swan's lament with which Dido began her letter. The unusual opening to Dido's epistle, which had caused Ovid's commentators some confusion, is given new force by Du Bellay's promotion of the bird to the first line of the poem, and his creation of a tableau the more vivid for the bird's not being identified until the final line of the stanza, and then only implicitly: "Comme l'oizeau blanchissant ... Chante l'hymne de sa mort, / Qui au bort / Du doux Mëandre l'appelle" (307). Néraudau (372–73) observes that Du Bellay paints the setting in more sensual, melancholy tones: the suggestion that Dido sings her complaint transforms Ovid's swan song image, and imbues the poem as a whole with a heightened pathos. In recasting *Heroides* 7 as an oral complaint, Du Bellay contrives to achieve a greater continuity between *Aeneid* 4 and *Heroides* 7.

This choice might be said to undermine the artistic autonomy of the heroine. Now Dido is no longer a writing subject exercising full control over her words but a speaking subject whose words are necessarily only available to us through a (male) intermediary. In the Latin text, Ovid pointedly absents himself from the text in adopting the conceit of the epistolary form: we read the words "as the heroine wrote them." In Du Bellay's version, the heroine does not write. A poet mediates her words. It is significant that where Fontaine makes specific reference to the notion of Ovid *writing* in French—"si l'auteur eust escrit en la langue qu'on le traduit" (190), Du Bellay's ideal is to make the ancients *speak* French.[38] This attitude is suggestive of a striving for spontaneity and the expression of natural *genius*. But the result of the imposition of orality on the heroine tends in opposite direction. The striking stanza form adopted by Du Bellay reinforces the impression that we are distanced from the heroine's "authentic" words. Du Bellay's translation of Dido's letter into an oral lament, far from bringing us closer to the emotional "truth" uttered by the heroine, in fact diminishes the effect of immediacy and spontaneity that had been the basis for Ovid's text.

Reading the *Heroides* Morally

Much of the paratextual material in editions of Saint-Gelais's translation in the first half of the century exhibits a concern with moral utility, and with setting the parameters for correct readings of the text. For example, a 1546 edition includes a preface by one François de Villiers.[39] In it, Villiers seems to be confused about the identity of the translator: his note names "reverend pere en dieu maistre André de la Vigne" as the one responsible for the translation—a hybrid of the bishop Octavien de Saint-Gelais and the poet André de la Vigne, whose Ovidian imitations are printed alongside the translation in this edition. Villiers stresses the importance of the "sens moral" lying behind the fables, suggesting that the narratives should be understood parabolically: "morallement, comme les parabolles, lesquelles nous trouuons souuentesfois alleguees en la saincte escripture" (morally, like the parables we often find set down in Holy Scripture). The first letter, for example, instructs the reader on the ways in which a Christian wife ought to comport herself in the absence of her husband. The Canace-Macareus epistle, obviously, is a warning against "disorderly" and incestuous love. The moral had not been left implicit by Saint-Gelais, who was more or less constantly intervening in his text to encourage moral reactions.[40]

---

38. In the *Deffence* (I.5, 37), he despairs of his contemporaries' attempts to make Petrarch "parler Francoys." Du Bellay often frames his comments about translation in terms of speech rather than writing.
39. Saint-Gelais 1546, 181.
40. Similar interventions can be found in Saint-Gelais's earlier translation of Aeneas Silvius' *Eurialus and Lucretia;* there, the translator had felt the need to interject two concluding "huitains" to instruct readers on how to interpret the story as a warning against "fole amour." See Molinier, 65.

Less emphatically perhaps, Charles Fontaine's prefaces to his own translation call the reader's attention to the morally edifying content of the work. In the "Translateur aus lecteurs" he addresses the question directly:

> Or meintenant je vueil declarer quel bien & vtilité lon peut tirer de ma traduccion. Le proufit donq qui en vient est double. Premierement, quant à la Rhetorique. [Fontaine lists the rhetorical virtues of the text.] Secondement, l'vtilité est quant aus meurs pource qu'il n'y ha personne tant adonnée & eschaufée en l'amour voluptueuse, qui ne soit bien refroidie & destournée, apres qu'elle aura bien leu ici dedans. (192)

> But now I wish to declare what benefit and utility can be drawn from my translation. The profit that it offers, then, is double: firstly, in the domain of rhetoric. Secondly, its utility is in the domain of morals, because there is nobody so abandoned to and inflamed by the pleasures of love that they would not be cooled and turned away from them after having read through this work.

Fontaine follows the early commentators in dividing the heroines' stories into examples of behavior to be emulated (Deianira, Penelope) or avoided. He contends that, even though the poems have love as their subject, there is "rien de vilein ou deshonneste"; in this respect they are unlike Ovid's *Amores* or his *Ars Amatoria*. The only real bad example is Phaedra: but Fontaine hopes that readers will more readily emulate Hippolytus's chastity than Phaedra's incestuous passion. The prefaces to both translations focus much more sharply on this aspect of the work than the Latin commentaries had done. The intended audience of those earlier editions consisted of students and educated men; the translators' concerns with moral utility stem from an awareness that a vernacular version of the work is more likely to reach a female readership. The prefaces prescribe a certain way of reading the text that does not overstep the bounds of acceptability. Such prescriptive readings are also to be found elsewhere in the body of paratext, in the notes accompanying individual letters. Whereas Saint-Gelais's translation incorporates moral readings into the text of the translation itself, in Fontaine's version, moral concerns are edged out of the translation and into the peripheries.

In his notes to the Phyllis letter, Fontaine sets out to unfold the moral implications of the narrative, reading the text as a warning against *amor stultus*. Ovid's version of the Dido narrative is not so easy to categorize. Despite the fact that *Heroides* 7 clearly follows *Aeneid* 4, it is by no means certain that Ovid shares the values that form the basis of Virgil's narrative. As we saw in the previous chapter, Fontaine attempts to resolve the ambiguities of this version of the story by directing the reader toward the historically accurate version of events found in Boccaccio's *De claris mulieribus,* insisting on the truth of the "other" Dido—the virtuous, virginal Dido. Although Du Bellay expresses no interest in the moral implications of Dido's history, he contextualizes his translation by offering the reader a variety of "sources" to compare different versions of Dido. He favors the "historical" version of the heroine, as represented in an epigram of Ausonius, which he also translates.[41] This piece is in the form of an inscription for a statue. It is composed in the person of Dido, who reproaches Virgil for having misrepresented her as revelling in "incestis . . . cupidinibus," when she in fact lived and died "sine crimine," a paragon of "pudicitia." Du Bellay claims that he is including this piece in the interests of balance:

> J'ay encore adiousté ung epigramme d'Ausone, déclarant la vérité de l'hystoire de Didon, pour ce qu'il me sembloit inique de renouveler l'injure qu'elle a receu par Vergile, sans luy reparer son honneur par ce qu'autres ont escrit à sa louange. (253)

> I have also added an epigram by Ausonius, declaring the truth of Dido's story, because it seems wrong to me to revive the insult that she received from Virgil, without making amends to her honor with what others have written in praise of her.

Though he, like Fontaine, condemns Virgil's (and, implicitly by the same token, Ovid's) characterization of Dido, he acknowledges the force of Virgil's description of Dido's passion. Néraudau suggests that it was an interest in the psychological complexity of the Dido figure, as much as the literary challenge, that spurred Du Bellay to undertake his translation (371). This is at least partly true: Dido remains a figure who excites pity, and the machinery of pathos is of great interest to both Du Bellay and Fontaine.

In Saint-Gelais's translation, moral judgments are subsumed into the translation itself. Often the translator is at pains to bring out the moral message of Ovid's text, to make explicit a point that was just implied, or to bring to the fore the supposed *intentio auctoris*. As we have seen, Fontaine's preface makes it clear to the reader what is the moral to be drawn from Phyllis' story: it is a warning to all women not to love in excess. Nevertheless Fontaine does not make this message explicit in his translation. Saint-Gelais's

---

41. This epigram is already itself a translation, from Greek into Latin.

translation accommodates more easily the emphasis on moral exemplarity which was troublingly absent from Ovid's text. Fontaine extracts an edifying moral message from the poem and sets it as a disclaimer in his introductory comments. This strategy frees him from the obligation to insert moralizing emphasis into his translation: with the moral out of the way, he is able to present the reader with the Phyllis that Ovid depicted. Saint-Gelais's version, which stands alone without prefatory comments to instruct the reader on how the poem should be read, must incorporate the moral readings into the poem itself.[42]

For example, Demophoon's "epitaph" at line 74 ("HIC EST CVIVS AMANS HOSPITA CAPTA DOLO EST" [Here lies one by whose deception a loving hostess was taken in]) is expanded by Saint-Gelais:

Cy gist celluy tresfaulx et deceuant
qui abusa iadis en son viuant
Par sa cautelle vne lealle amante
Trop prompte a croire en amour vehemente. (fol. ix^r)

Saint-Gelais makes Phyllis' condemnation of her faithless lover into a bitter self-reproach. The charge levelled at Demophoon, violator of the sacred bond of hospitality and deceiver of his naïve lover, is mitigated: it is Phyllis, "Trop prompte a croire en amour vehemente," who deserves condemnation. This final line shifts the burden of blame back to Phyllis: it is she who fell victim to a foolish love. Ovid's text carries no such implication: Saint-Gelais is possibly incorporating marginal notes from his manuscript source into the body of the translation.

A second example of Saint-Gelais's manipulation of the text comes at a point which, we have seen, binds together several different strands of our

---

42. An interesting exception to this: there is at least one edition that does incorporate a large amount of prefatory material; however, this material is not geared toward a moral reading of the text. These prose prefaces, composed by somebody other than the translator, appear in one manuscript edition dating from after Saint-Gelais's death (1502). See the article by Brückner (1989, 93–101). Here is an excerpt from the preface to the Phyllis letter, transcribed by Brückner, 96: "Et dit Ovide que ce fut une des femmes du monde qui, pour avoir veu ung homme si peu de temps, ayma de la meilleure amour [. . .]. La royne Philis vit Demophon qui estoit honneste et bien parlant, et l'escouta par tant de foys qu'elle en fut amoureuse en telle sorte qu'ilz coucherent ensemble. Et quant cela fut fait, la dicte Philis luy donna force argent et luy fist reffaire ses navires toutes neufves [. . .]. Mais si tost qu'il fut en Espaigne, il fut amoureux d'une aultre dame et oublia Philis qui l'avoit secouru a son grant besoing et qui tant de bien luy avoit fait. Et quant Philis ouyt dire qu'il amoyt une aultre femme qu'elle, elle fut si marrie que, avec l'amour et regret qu'elle avoit en luy, elle se pendit." The *préfacier* appears to have no interest in making strong moral judgment against any of the heroines: he suggests that Ovid's purpose in writing the *Heroides* was simply to show that there is nothing greater in the world than love ("Car en ce monde n'y a chose qui vaille tant que amour," 95).

inquiry: lines 85–86, where the words of the Thracian countryman—"exitus acta probat"—elicit a bitter reply from the heroine. Saint-Gelais's translation does not take account of the change in speaker in line 85, with Phyllis' "careat successibus" being a refutation of "exitus acta probat"; Fontaine's version does. This reading results in a translation that is much more critical of Phyllis' actions than Ovid's text had been:

> Maint en ya qui aussi dit et compte
> Ores voyes que la fin faict le compte
> Certes philis trop a vng se tenoit
> Cest a bon droit si pis luy aduenoit
> Ainsi de moy chacun la fin regarde. . . . (fol. ix^v)

This moralizing voice is completely absent from Fontaine's translation of the same passage:

> On dit bien vray, la fin approuue l'œuure:
> Aussi ie pry que celuy ne recœuure
> Issue à gré, qui maintient en effect
> Que par vn cas il faut iuger du faict. (36)

As we saw in the previous chapter, Fontaine judged that these lines required one of his lengthier notes, in which he drew out the implications of the ethical question at issue. I suggested in the introduction that the *locus* "exitus acta probat" speaks of many issues relating to the reception and interpretation of the *Heroides;* it is perhaps the place at which the text "opens up" to appropriative readings at the most fundamental level.

Heroides 7 presents the translators with a more problematical representation of female weakness. In his translation, Saint-Gelais attempts to resolve the moral problems of Ovid's Dido by presenting her unambiguously as the wronged woman; this strategy also enables him to show that her tragedy comes as a result of feminine weakness.[43] He departs somewhat from Ovid's version of the narrative in placing more emphasis on the physical beauty of Aeneas: this Dido was first ensnared by the deceptive appearance of the stranger, rather than by his moral qualities. This seems to stem from a misreading of line 35 ("fallor, et ista mihi falsae iactatur imago" [I am mistaken, and this is an illusion that shimmers before my lying eyes]), which Saint-Gelais paraphrases as:

---

43. Saint-Gelais also makes moralizing interventions in his translation of book IV of the *Aeneid,* but with a different emphasis; there his concern is to justify the departure of Aeneas and to condemn the foolishness of the love affair with Dido. See Slerca, 568, n. 16.

> Ha que moult fut cause de mon dommage,
> Quant me fiay a son plaisant ymage,
> Et trop pour vray a lheure decue fus,
> Quant sa beaulte me gaigna sans refus. (fol. xxxvii^r)

The translator goes on to establish a contrast between the physical beauty of Aeneas and his moral ugliness, a point not made by Ovid's Dido. To some extent this strategy resolves the ambivalence that complicates Ovid's Dido, whose Aeneas is neither fully immoral nor the "pius Aeneas" of Virgil. Saint-Gelais abandons the subtlety of Ovid's portrayal of this ambivalence with his unusually full expansion of the line "matris ab ingenio dissidet ille suae":

> Certes en meurs, en doulceur & en grace
> A sa mere est difforme en toute place,
> Car elle est doulce, & il est inhumain,
> De loyaulte ne tient goutte en sa main. (ibid.)

At line 64 Saint-Gelais alters Dido's bitterly ironic wish for Aeneas to live so that he may be reputed as the cause of her death to a more noble sentiment:

> Viure t'est mieulx, si bon sens te remord,
> I'ayme plus cher ta vie que ta mort,
> Et plus desire que par toy mort me vienne,
> Que nul peril en me suiuant t'aduienne.[44]

And at line 105 the translation provides Dido with an extenuating justification which is not in the original:

> Donne et octroye a ma coulpe pardon,
> Ce nay ie fait par argent ne par don. (fol. xxxix^v)

Where Saint-Gelais softens the underlying anger of Dido's invectives, Fontaine sometimes inserts phrases or rhetorical touches that emphasize the wronged woman's bitterness. The ironic tone of the rhetorical questions in lines 19–22 is brought out in the sarcastic addition: "Mais, ie te pri, respon moy sans mentir," prefiguring lines 81ff. At line 85, Ovid's "haec mihi narraras" is translated by Fontaine with the bitterly ironic "Tant de beaux cas de toy me racontois."

---

44. Here I follow the 1546 text (fol. 44^v) because the 1534 version has multiple errors.

Saint-Gelais occasionally shifts the emphasis of Ovid's text from the particular to the universal. Where Ovid's Dido justifies her actions with reference to the singularity of her situation ("adde fidem, nulla parte pigendus erit" [If he proves faithful, in no way will I be wronged]), Saint-Gelais's Dido draws upon the discourse of exemplarity, making the justification into a comment on the universality of female weakness:

> Ie ne scay femme, tant fust bonne ou apprise
> Que de l'amour dung tel neust este prise
> Car en luy na tant peu soit de deffault
> Sinon que foy et pitie luy deffault. (fol. xxxix^v)

Often Saint-Gelais places emphasis on a moral judgment which is underplayed in Ovid's text: line 92 "concubitus fama" (the public knowledge of our affair) becomes "De mon peché la femme et renommée." The apostrophe to "laese pudor" (damaged honor) at line 97 is not closely translated by Saint-Gelais, who chooses to emphasize more fully the note of moral self-reproach:

> En la roche malheureuse et prochaine
> Ou ie perdy ma bonte primeraine.
> Bien se deust plaindre mon mary trespasse
> Dit sicheus veu quay oultre passe
> De loyaulte et chastete la bourne,
> Plus ne me doy desormais nommer bonne
> Ains requerir aux dieux punicion
> De ma mauuaise et faulse intencion. (fol. xxxix)

Dido's resolution to commit suicide in line 181 ("est animus nobis effundere uitam") is altered slightly by Saint-Gelais. His translation softens the implication of the threat, implying that suicide is not Dido's intention, but that the actions of Aeneas might bring about her death by some unspecified means: "Sil ne te plaist & que ton vueil pourchasse / Que tost la mort me tue & me defface."

The translator's moral judgment intrudes into the narrative again at line 190; Saint-Gelais seems to be relying on the medieval commentators' use of the category of *amor stultus* to censure Dido:

> Ce ne sera le premier glaiue ou dart
> Qui a perce mon cueur de part en part

> Car autresfois amour qui tout affolle
> Le me naura, dont ie fus simple & folle. (fol. xlii^v)

A similar addition is found in Fontaine's translation, where the line "unde tibi, quae te sic amet, uxor erit?" (Where will you find a wife to love you this much?) is expanded to:

> Ou prendras tu vne femme qui t'ayme
> Ainsi que moy d'ardente amour extreme? (119)

In the description of Dido's love as "ardente" and "extreme" there is an implicit moral judgment which does not appear in the original. This type of addition is, however, uncharacteristic of Fontaine's translation technique.

Approaches to the Text

The three translators deal very differently with the mythological, geographical, historical, and cultural detail encountered in Ovid's text. Both Fontaine and Du Bellay are concerned to render effects. They are both as a matter of professional duty concerned with rhetorical and linguistic detail. Saint-Gelais is a moralist with a conventional interest in fluency. As we have seen, he recommends Ovid's Latin, rather oddly, as "doulce & melliflue" (fol. i^v), and in consequence he reproduces nothing that would interrupt the easy flow. The difference between the three poets is well illustrated in their treatment of proper names.

Saint-Gelais often leaves out proper names, choosing to render geographical and mythological detail with vague circumlocutions. Fontaine almost always includes proper names in their original form; he explains in his annexed "Translateur aus lecteurs" that he has done so partly at least "pour la reuerence de l'antiquité" (190). Occasionally he updates them: the mention of the Hebrus at 2.15 is translated as "Marissa" (the Maritsa river in modern Bulgaria). Sometimes he seems even to enjoy their resistance. "aspice, ut euersas concitet Eurus aquas" (See how Eurus churns the stormy waters) (7.42) becomes "O Eneas, voy comme Eurus tourmente / Les flots de mer" (120). "Mater Amorum / nuda Cytheriacis edita fertur aquis" (It is said that the mother of the Loves emerged naked from Cytherian waters) (7.60) becomes the virtuoso "Car des amours la mere / Nue fut née en la mer de Cythere" (121).

Du Bellay had thought and written at length about the naturalization of

Latin proper names (*Deffence* II.8). Where Saint-Gelais had suppressed references to gods and mythological figures in his translation, Du Bellay does the opposite: on several occasions he adds proper names not present in Ovid's original. He is so free with his newly gallicized deities that he can forgo them altogether or import them to supply the place of expressions from his point of view inadequately figured. So on the one hand he translates 7.42, the line Fontaine so enjoyed that he introduced another proper name into it, as "ceste mer, que souvent / Par le vent / Ores tu vois agitée" (311), and on the other "pelago suadente" (when the sea encourages travel) (55) as "Et quand Neptune apaizé"; "in rabido freto" (on the raging sea) (7.142) as "A la mercy de Neptune" (323) or "pro spe coniugii" (by the hope of marriage) (7.178) as "Pour l'espoir, qui m'estoit né / D'Hymené" (328).

At 2.113–14, Ovid's Phyllis claims to have surrendered to Demophoon the wide realms of Lycurgus "qua patet umbrosum Rhodope glacialis ad Haemum, / et sacer admissas exigit Hebrus aquas" (where icy Rhodope extends to shady Haemus, and sacred Hebrus drives on his free-flowing waters). Saint-Gelais chooses to omit all of these references, offering simply:

> Car du royaulme dont ie suis heritiere
> Teusse fait part & portion entiere. (fol. x^r)

Fontaine, on the other hand, translates them all, and incorporates exegetic description into the translation: the reader easily understands what kind of geographical features are meant, without having to refer to explanatory notes:

> (Rhodope glacialis)   . . . Rodopé, le mont plein de froidure
> (umbrosum ad Haemum)   . . . Aemus, plein d'ombre et de verdure
> (sacer Hebrus)   . . . Heber, sacré fleuue. (38)

In the Dido epistle too, Saint-Gelais usually prefers the general to the particular: the references to Phthia and Mycenae in line 165 are left out: "Ie ne suis pas . . . / Naye de terre qui te fust ennemie." Fontaine includes them, clarifying the allusion in a marginal note:

> Ie ne suis pas de Thessalique terre,
> Dond fut celuy qui ce liura la guerre: (Achilles)
> Aussi ne suis de Mycene la grande
> Encontre toy n'as eu vne grand'bande. (128)

Du Bellay in his translation chooses not to explain the allusion, instead relying on the erudition of his readership: "Pour mien je ne recongnoy / Le terroy / De Mycenes ou de Phthie" (326).

It is not only geographical detail that Saint-Gelais omits. The references to Tisiphone and Allecto at lines 115–20 of the Phyllis epistle are lost in the anonymity of Saint-Gelais's "les dieux d'enfer" (fol. x^r); Fontaine restores the references. The gaping omission of detail at lines 67–73, in particular, leads us to suppose that Saint-Gelais was deliberately leaving out detail to allow the verse to flow, or because the mythological content was considered too difficult. The mentions of Sciron, Procrustes, Sinis, the Minotaur, the Centaurs, Thebes, and the Underworld are all omitted. Fontaine, by contrast, manages to accommodate them all without difficulty.

In the opening lines of the Dido letter, Saint-Gelais suppresses the allusion to the legend of the swan on the banks of the Maeander. His version of Dido's opening lines differs from Fontaine's in emphasis: where Saint-Gelais's swan sings "doulcement . . . et à voix tresseraine," Fontaine's is "triste et seul." Du Bellay's translation has "languissant" (for "abiectus"), and uses simply "oiseau" for "olor": evidently he expected his intended audience to know the legend.

At line 50 Saint-Gelais leaves out the reference to Triton driving his horses across the sea, and omits lines 51–52 completely. Fontaine's translation of this section shows the influence of the commentary notes, making "Tritons" plural rather than singular. Du Bellay's version alters the sense slightly, having Triton metonymically "galloping," rather than driving his horses.

Saint-Gelais excises 7.157–62 from his translation, giving only a brief approximation of 161–62. References to the mythological narrative are for the most part suppressed, avoiding the need for exegesis: here, the translator mentions Anchises and Ascanius, but makes no mention of Venus, Cupid, the Trojan penates, or Mars. Fontaine's translation of these lines is fuller, though he apparently reads "patrem" for "matrem" in line 157 (as does Du Bellay).

Saint-Gelais occasionally suppresses references to the gods in favor of a more anthropocentric emphasis: the adverbial phrase "aduerso deo"—which is, in fact, an easy metaphor in Ovid's version, and hardly a reference to a "god" at all—in line 4 is rendered as "Bien sçay pourtant que ma malheuereté / Empeschera toute ma volunté" (fol. xxxvi^v). Here the "external" barrier to Dido's will is translated into an internal barrier. Fontaine does this too: "Ains à malheur et sans aucun espoir" (118). Du Bellay restores the reference to the adversity of the gods, changing the emphasis of the complaint: "Car aux ingrates douleurs / De mes pleurs / Les Dieux font la sourde oreille" (307). The addition of the image of the gods "turning a deaf ear" to Dido's lament (which, once again, hints that Dido's complaint is spoken, not written) prefigures the reference at line 27 to Aeneas "ad mea munera surdus." This metaphor is retained by Saint-Gelais in his translation, and by Fontaine. Interestingly, Du Bellay does not translate "surdus" at that point, having already transferred the image to the gods at the start of the poem, an example perhaps of his "compensation" technique.

Saint-Gelais omits any detail that he does not expect his audience to be familiar with; an exegetic translation would disrupt the flow of the verse. The translator has no way of accommodating the Latin forms of Ovid's proper names to his "smooth" couplets. At lines 33–34 of the Phyllis epistle, he omits "Hymenaeus," a name which is explained in the commentaries and was clearly not as well known to the early sixteenth-century audience as the major gods. He also leaves out the—hardly obscure—allusion to Ceres at line 42. Fontaine is usually able to include proper names because his notes deal with the more salient difficulties. However his notes do not explain every mythological detail, and it seems clear that Fontaine had more of a learned audience in mind than Saint-Gelais did—as his *Avertissement aus lecteurs* attests.

Saint-Gelais misses the pun on the etymology of "Carthage" (which the commentaries do not fail to point out). "[N]ova Carthago" is translated as "Carthage la gentille"; Fontaine restores the reference (an allusion to *Aeneid* 1.366) "la neuve Carthage," Du Bellay does not. Saint-Gelais ignores the *militia amoris* topos at line 32 ("castris militet ille tuis" [he will serve in your camp]); Fontaine retains the military metaphor, but renders it slightly differently ("ô frere Amour, ton frere, / Tant rigoureus, vien cherir, embracer, / Et à ton camp reduire et auancer," 119), as does Du Bellay ("Et toy aussi, ieune archer, / Fai' marcher / Ton frere sou' ton enseigne"). There are one or two occasions where both translators of the Phyllis epistle omit proper names: at 2.6 neither attempts "Acteas" or "Sithonis"; at 2.90 "Bistonia" becomes an anonymous "lac."

Saint-Gelais's frequent departures from the source text cannot all be explained as textual variants and misreadings. It is possible that he is incorporating manuscript glosses into his translation, whether because they were not distinguishable from the text in his manuscript, or because he wished to resolve (moral) ambiguities. For example, at lines 113–14 of Ovid's text, Saint-Gelais interpolates several lines explaining the mythological background in detail: he makes it clear that Pygmalion, Dido's brother, killed Sichaeus to satisfy his greed. Later, Saint-Gelais fleshes out the characterization of Pygmalion, transforming the reference to the brother's "manus inpia" (evil hand) (127) into the striking image "Pygmalion . . . trop plus fier qu'un lion." Although Fontaine's translation of lines 113–16 requires ten lines to convey accurately the sense of Ovid's four lines, he does not include the background information in the main body of the text, but adds a marginal note explaining the reference, and gives the whole back-story in the endnotes. Later at line 150, Fontaine adds a line to his translation of "aduectas Pygmalionis opes" (the wealth of Pygmalion, which we brought here) explaining the moral cause of the crime:

> Et les tresors lesquels Pygmalion
> Ha pourchassez par grande ambicion. (127)

Occasionally, Saint-Gelais also expands on details relating to ancient culture: at 7.57–58 there is an allusion to the belief that the sea punishes those who have broken vows. Saint-Gelais's translation explains the allusion at some length. He also has a tendency to "naturalize" cultural references. At 2.116 "zona" (the bridal belt) refers to a Roman practice that Saint-Gelais perhaps did not expect his readers to be familiar with. In his translation, the ungirdling of the "chaste zone" is altered slightly: "Tu deschiras ma pudique chemise." Fontaine prefers to keep his translation faithful to the original: "chaste ceinture."

Saint-Gelais often omits elements of the pagan culture which might seem alien to a Christian readership. His translation of Dido's description of the shrine dedicated to Sichaeus leaves out certain details of pagan customs. The references to the green fronds and wool fillets hanging about the marble walls are omitted, and the "sacred" image of Sichaeus ("sacratus . . . Sychaeus") becomes an "ymage paincte." Fontaine's translation meticulously restores this detail, and adds a note explaining the custom, remarking on the similar description of the shrine in Virgil.

Fontaine's Dido, for the most part, remains a distinctly pagan heroine in his translation. However on certain occasions she has something of the courtly princess about her, a characterization which it is difficult to square with her more pagan sensibilities. The translation of line 123 "mille procis placui" (I attracted a thousand suitors) modernizes the situation, and eliminates any hint of impropriety:

> Certeine suis mes meurs sont agreables
> A plus de cent bons Chevaliers notables. (125)

THERE ARE numerous occasions when the translators are clearly using different manuscript readings; sometimes, too, the lack of punctuation in manuscript and early printed editions leads the translators into different interpretations of the text. When confronted with difficulties, Saint-Gelais often omits parts of the text or resorts to vagueness; this is entirely characteristic of translation practice in Saint-Gelais's time. Fontaine is more thorough: the notes that he appends to his translation show evidence of his having used commentaries to clarify certain readings of the text. Saint-Gelais clearly had more limited access to commentaries or was using the late-medieval commentaries which are less focused on textual matters.

In the case of *Heroides* 2, lines 18–19 stand as the most obvious point of difference in the translations. Saint-Gelais does not include them; Fontaine does. In his commentary, Peter Knox (116–17) notes that most early manuscripts did not have the lines, but that four later ones and the first Aldine edition of 1502 have them; the omission of the lines leaves the sentence without a verb. They are left out of Badius' edition (which, as we have seen, was the most popular of the commentary editions printed in France in the first half of the century); Antonius Volscus comments briefly on the omission. The problem was evidently known to the sixteenth-century editors. Fontaine clearly had access to multiple editions and used them to establish a text that was to his liking. There is certainly evidence that he used his own judgment in choosing one reading over another. Lines 7.24–25 tell a similar story: Saint-Gelais does not have them, Fontaine does, Du Bellay chooses to leave them out.

Lines 2.61–62 also present some textual difficulties. Where modern editions have "speraui melius, quia me meruisse putaui" (I hoped for better, because I thought I deserved it), the sixteenth-century editions have "quia *te* meruisse putaui." Ubertinus Clericus in his Latin commentary disagrees with this reading, preferring "me" to "te" (" . . . ut sensus exigit. et codex meus uetustissimus habet" [as the sense requires, and as it appears in a very old manuscript of mine]); however the reading remains intact in the text itself. Fontaine uses the "te" reading, but his translation does not cause too many problems:

I'esperois mieux, car ie pourpensois bien
Que tu valois tant d'honneur, et de bien.
Bien esperer doit cil qui bien merite. (35)

He even adds a note to make it clear that the reading "te" is merely his own preference, and supplies a translation for the alternative reading ("Que ie valois tant d'honneur et de bien").

Saint-Gelais has a completely different reading. The marginal notes show that he is reading "quia te *metuisse* putaui" (because I thought you were in danger), a one-letter variable that sets his translation on a wildly different course:

> Ie mieulx cuide quil ne mest aduenu
> Car bien pensoye que fusses retenu
> Pourtant iamais sans faire de partie
> Mais esperance est de moy tost partie. (fol. viii^v)

It is difficult to see how this could be right, especially since the last part directly contradicts line 9 ("spes quoque lenta fuit" [hope too was slow to leave me]). This is not the only point where Fontaine intended his translation to serve as a corrective to Saint-Gelais's.

The parenthesis at 7.45, "numquid censeris inique?" (or are you being hard done by?) is read in three different ways by the three translators. Saint-Gelais reads a second person active verb: "Ne scay pourtant si tu crois le contraire." Fontaine's translation obviously uses a different verb, and is more expansive: "Combien pourtant que ta grande lascheté / L'ayt desserui, et tresbien merité." Du Bellay's version is different again: "Ce mespris / Plus superbe ne te face." Fontaine is very probably working from a text that uses the reading "quamuis merearis" (although you deserve it), transmitted in a very small number of manuscripts. Saint-Gelais must be basing his translation on the more commonly attested reading "quod non meditaris" (you do not think so) (an active form, since "meditor" is a deponent verb). It is more difficult to see what reading Du Bellay is using; indeed, his translation of the entire couplet 45–46 departs significantly from the Latin text.

Either the text Saint-Gelais is working from in translating the Dido epistle does not have lines 95–96, or the translator chose to omit the references to the Eumenides. Both Fontaine and Du Bellay restore the reference; Du Bellay's translation effectively brings out the sense of "nymphas ululasse putaui" (I thought the nymphs were shrieking) (an allusion to *Aeneid* 4.168), where the wedding-song of the nymphs is also a presage of doom:

> Des Nymphes les longues vois
> Celle fois
> Sembloyent huller l'Hymenée:
> Les Furies l'ont sonné,

Et donné
Le signe à ma destinée. (317–18)

There is some confusion, arising from the lack of punctuation in the manuscripts, about the sense of 7.139, "sed iubet ire deus" (but the god commands you to go). Whereas Saint-Gelais reads it as a concession made by Dido, Fontaine's translation preserves its ambiguity: "Mais de partir le Dieu t'a commandé" might well be read as an ironic echo of Aeneas' own words. Du Bellay's reading is slightly different; the comment becomes a conditional clause: "Si ton partir de ce lieu / Vient de Dieu. . . " Modern editions enclose the phrase in quotation marks, implying that the comment is a sarcastic repetition of Aeneas' own words.

IN GENERAL Fontaine seems to be more sensitive than Saint-Gelais to the allusiveness of Ovid's poetry. Often the verbal echoes, prolepses, and self-referential markers that characterize Ovid's style risk being drowned out in translation. At 2.9, for example, an attuned ear might hear a faint echo of the first line of the collection. "spes quoque lenta fuit" (hope too was slow to leave me) recalls Penelope's first line ("Haec tua Penelope lento tibi mittit, Vlixe" [Your wife Penelope sends you this letter, Ulysses, slow in coming]) and so gives sense of thematic continuity to the collection as a whole. Saint-Gelais's translation of Phyllis' line uses a very Latinate vocabulary, but does not translate the verbal echo: "Mon esperance a este tarde et lente" has nothing in common with Penelope's "Puis que tu es de retour paresseux" (a whole line translating the single word "lento"). Fontaine's translation is more expressive, despite seeming to depart further from the Latin:

Mesme l'espoir que i'ay eu en ta foy
N'a point esté que bien tardif en moy (p. 32),

and the verbal echo remains intact: "O Ulysses que trop tardif i'atten."

Although Dido is perhaps the most influential model for Ovid's Phyllis, the Ariadne of Catullus 64 and *Heroides* 10 is a definite presence in the text. The mention of Demophoon's white sails ("alba . . . vela") in line 12 is an oblique allusion to the crime of his father, Theseus, and its causes and consequences. Phyllis imagines Demophoon's returning sails to be white, a vain hope that history will not repeat itself, that he will not abandon her as Theseus abandoned Ariadne. Saint-Gelais omits this reference entirely, neglecting to translate the detail that the sails were imagined to be white. Fontaine's version restores the detail: "tes blancs voiles."

Although the narration of the death of Phyllis is beyond the scope of Ovid's poem, he includes in line 93 a proleptic allusion to her eventual fate:

> ausus es amplecti colloque infusus amantis
>   oscula per longas iungere pressa moras.

> You dared to embrace me, and, clinging around the neck of your lover, to press long kisses to my lips.

This allusion to hanging (Demophoon's arms around his lover's neck) has all the more resonance later in the poem as Phyllis imagines possible methods of suicide, and herself mentions hanging (141–42). Once again, Saint-Gelais's translation misses the significance of this description:

> Mais dy moy comment osas tu lors
> Tant membracer et estraindre le corps. (fol. ix^v)

Fontaine, on the other hand, captures the foreboding tone nicely:

> Lors tout ton corps dessus mon col pendoit. (37)

Dido's invective based on the parentage of Aeneas has its literary precedents, as the humanist commentators point out, in *Aeneid* 4.365ff after *Iliad* 16.33ff, as well as Ariadne's complaint in Catullus 64. The translators seem to be aware of these models. Fontaine's translation of lines 37–40 includes the references to rocks, mountains, trees and the sea, and expands on the mention of "saevae . . . ferae" by making the wild beasts into "Tygres cruelz, pleins d'outrage et nuisance." This shows a certain influence from *Aeneid* 4.367, where Virgil's Dido speaks of Hyrcanian tigresses. Saint-Gelais's translation has greater variation on the theme: his Dido accuses Aeneas of having been born "parmi monstres, serpents et lavers,"[45] adding the explanatory line "Car sans merci tu es de leur nature."

Making Ovid Speak French

Ovid is a difficult poet to translate; the greatest barrier to translation consists

---

45. The meaning of the word 'laver' is unclear: it appears in that form uncorrected in several different editions. The word does not seem to be in any French dictionaries of the period. Cotgrave has two possibilities: '*lave:* a (wild) Sow that hath young ones,' and '*larve:* 'A Hag, Spirit, Goblin, Nightghost.' Alternatively, the word may refer to a type of seaweed (cf. Latin *laver-eris*).

in those features of his poetry that define the Ovidian *esprit:* his virtuoso manipulation of rhetorical figures and tropes, his intricate word play, his delicately balanced antitheses and syllepses. Our translators propose a variety of solutions in dealing with these difficulties.

Saint-Gelais often seems reluctant to translate poetic images. The periphrasis at 2.3–5 (Phyllis counting the months by the phases of the moon—hardly an unusual trope to use in poetry) is left out by Saint-Gelais. Instead we have the relatively prosaic:

> Dedans vng moys ta nef deuoit reprendre
> Chemin vers moy et seure terre prendre
> Par foy promise en mes prochains quartiers
> Mais ia escheuz sont quatre moys entiers. (fol. vii^r)

Fontaine, on the other hand, translates the periphrasis in full, remaining as close as possible to the text. The result is somewhat awkward: "alors que rencontrer / S'entreuiendroient les cornes de la Lune / En leur plein rond, des fois seulement vne," and "Par quatre foys la fin de Lune ay veuë: / Par quatre fois en sa rondeur est creuë" (31). The same contrast can be seen in the two versions of lines 123–24. Phyllis' periphrases for night and day ("siue die laxatur humus, seu frigida lucent / sidera, prospicio" [whether the earth softens by day, or the cold stars shine, I gaze out]) are translated eloquently, if not entirely accurately, by Fontaine:

> Soit que de iour se relache la terre,
> Soit que la nuit par froidure la reserre. (38)

Saint-Gelais's version is more streamlined and workmanlike: " . . . et iour et nuyt . . " (fol. x^v). Du Bellay, famously, is keen on periphrastic figures.[46] A fine example in Dido's letter—"nunc leuis eiectam continet alga ratem" (now the light seaweed holds your ship aground) (172)—disappears altogether in Saint-Gelais. It is given by Fontaine as "Ores au port ton nauire enserré / Est lié d'herbe" (128); Du Bellay has "La nef au port attendant' / Ce pendant / Parmy les alges demeure" (327).[47]

There are several instances of anaphora in the Phyllis epistle, which the two translators deal with in different ways. The repetition of "ubi nunc" in

---

46. Du Bellay has a particular liking for "antonomasia." He cites in the *Deffence* (II.9, 162) an elaborate way of saying "from East to West": "Depuis ceux qui voyent premiers rougir l'Aurore jusques la ou Thetis recoit en ses undes le filz d'Hyperion." It is, he says, a figure unused in French, though it is hard to see why.

47. Chamard reads "Parmy la glage demeure," but suggests the emendation adopted above.

lines 31–34 is expanded in Fontaine's translation into a six-line construction, with "Ou est" / "Ou sont" repeated four times. Saint-Gelais makes the repetition less emphatic, and is in this respect untypically closer to Ovid's text. The following lines (35–42) emphasize Demophoon's treachery with the anaphora "per . . . per . . . per . . .": Demophoon had sworn, writes Phyllis, "per mare . . . per quod saepe ieras, per quod iturus eras, / perque tuum . . . auum, / per Venerem . . . per mystica sacra" (by the sea . . . over which you had often sailed, and were about to sail again, by your grandfather, by Venus . . . by the mystical rites) (lines 35–42). Saint-Gelais drastically compresses the series and misses a lot of detail; Fontaine endeavors to translate it as fully as possible: "par la mer . . . Sur qui . . . nauigué tu auois, / Sur qui . . . nauiguer tu deuois / Par ton ayeul . . . Et par Venus . . . Et par Iuno . . . Et par Ceres . . . Par sacres siens."

The tricolon crescendo at lines 49–51 ("credidimus blandis . . . uerbis / credidimus generi . . . credidimus lacrimis" [I trusted your flattering words, I trusted in your nobility . . . I trusted your tears]) causes some difficulties. Saint-Gelais make the word "trop" the focus of the construction:

> Las *trop* ie creu a tes doulces parolles
> Dont tu es plain qui ne sont que friuolles
> *Trop* ay donne dasseurance et de foy
> A ta noblesse dont deceue me voy
> *Trop* tay chery tes plaintes et tes larmes
> Tes grans soupirs & tes douloureux termes. (fol. viii^r; emphasis added)

Fontaine's version does not emphasize the repetition to such a degree, but it conveys well the escalating tone of Phyllis' accusations:

> En tes propos abondans, plains d'attraits
> Me suis fiee, en ta race, en tes Dieux,
> Pareillement aux larmes de tes yeux:
> Mais peut on bien les feindres? [*sic*] . . . (34)

Saint-Gelais is, for the most part, averse to schematic repetition: in even so simple a case as Dido's appeal to her sister, "Anna soror, soror Anna" (7.191), he leaves out the chiasmus altogether. Fontaine rearranges it slightly: "Anne ma seur, qui scez ma forfaiture, / O ma seur Anne" (129). Du Bellay sticks to the Latin: "Ma sœur Anne, Anne ma sœur" (329).

The intricate word play and compactness of expression of Ovid's Latin is always difficult to translate effectively. The opening lines of *Heroides* 2 exemplify this resistance to translation. The noun-adjective interplay ("Hospita, *Demophoon,* tua *te* Rhodopeia Phyllis") binds Phyllis to Demophoon while simultaneously denying the possibility of union: she is Thracian, he a foreign guest. The first word brings out Demophoon's dereliction of duty as the main theme of the poem. The juxtaposition of "tua" and "te" encapsulates Demophoon's ambivalence and duplicity. Saint-Gelais's effort at putting this into French is rather diffuse, inserting as it does an extra line for sense ("Dont a present son epistre tu lis"), and making two lines into six. Fontaine deals with the interplay of adjectives and nouns and pronouns better, and in a much more concise way. The first line gives:

> De toy me plains ie Phyllis ton hostesse
> O Demophon . . . (31),

which fashions a neat chiasmus from the semantic units you—I—I—you. Where Ovid's Phyllis had been able to embrace Demophoon grammatically if not in reality, Fontaine's version projects Demophoon as embracing Phyllis.

Syllepsis, a figure whereby "literal and figurative are joined in syntactical wedlock," is one that Ovid "made his own."[48] A famous case occurs in *Heroides* 2.25–26:

> Demophoon, uentis et uerba et uela dedisti;
>   uela queror reditu, uerba carere fide.

C. S. Lewis isolates Turberville's "Demophoon to the windes ingagde his promise with his saile" as the single good line in his version.[49] Turberville's succeeding line is more awkward, however: "I sorrow that the ones returne, and th' others faith doth fayle." French, too, has difficulty accommodating such constructions, and the effect of the double syllepsis is particularly hard to convey. Saint-Gelais has:

> O demophon tu as doresnauant
> Tes promesses et voilles mises au vent.
> Tes voilles blasme pour leur grande absence
> Et tes promesses pour leur grant deceuance (fol. vii^v),

---

48. The expressions are from Kenney 2002, 27–90; 45–47. Kenney is anxious to distinguish "syllepsis" and "zeugma," its "grammatically licentious" relation. But few rhetoricians (and no ancient ones) distinguish them, and some invert the distinction.

49. Lewis 1954, 252 n. 21.

which is not the most elegant solution, not least in his inattention to syllable quantity. Fontaine's version inserts a detail not in the original, but reads all the better because of it:

> Toy, Demophon, plus leger que tes toiles,
> As mis au vent tes propos, et tes voiles.
> I'acuse à droit tes voiles qui ne viennent
> Et tes propos qui point de foy ne tiennent. (33)

The resonating rhymes "tes toiles" / "tes voiles" and "ne viennent" / "ne tiennent" come close to conveying the sylleptic effect which would usually sound unnatural in French. The links, or alternative links, are supplied by the rhymes.

This particular configuration of sails and promises evidently appealed to Ovid. He used it first of Ariadne who lamented the "periuri promissaque velaque Thesei" (*Amores* 1.7.15—"Her perjured Theseus" flying vows and sails" in Marlowe's version). He uses it again of Dido's sad plea to Aeneas: "atque idem uenti uela fidemque ferent?" (*Heroides* 7.8). Turberville gives "And with the selfe same windes thy sayles and fickle faith shall go" (much less good than his effort with 2.25). Fontaine has "Les mesmes ventz, soufflans dedans tes toiles, / Emporteront et ta foy et tes voiles" (118), which does not avoid redundancy in the first line. Du Bellay's version is astonishingly economical: "Les vens, qui t"emporteront, / Souffleront / Tes voiles et ta parole" (308). The winds carry off not only the sails and the promises, but the promise breaker. Dryden despaired of the line as untranslatable: "for the Latin (a most severe and compendious language) often expresses in one word which either the barbarity or the narrowness of modern tongues cannot supply in more. . . . What poet of our nation is so happy as to express this thought literally in English, and to strike wit, or almost sense, out of it?"[50] In the event his own effort was "with loosen'd sails and vows."

In the case of *Heroides* 7, all three of the French translators avoid the syllepsis at line 179 "dum freta mitescunt et amor," a conjunction of the stormy sea and Dido's love. Saint-Gelais ignores it completely. Fontaine's translation has a neat solution to the difficulty of translating the expression into French, splitting the syllepsis into two verbs and linking them together through rhyme:

> En attendant que la mer se tempere
> Et que l'amour par le tems s'amodere. (129)[51]

---

50. Preface to *Ovid's Epistles* (1680), in Dryden, ed. by G. Watson, 1962, I: 269.
51. Indeed, Turberville, whose idiom is quite tolerant of foreignism, adapts it in much the same

Du Bellay's version of the same lines does not translate the syllepsis, but renders the couplet with a more symmetrical structure and a greater sense of balance than the Latin. The translator disentangles Ovids lines "dum freta mitescunt et amor, dum tempore et usu / fortiter edisco tristia posse pati" (until the sea and my love abate, until time and experience teach me how to bear sorrows resolutely), and weaves them into a stanza in which rhymes provide the links, with Dido's sorrow echoing, responding to the sea:

> En ce pendant, que la mer
> Au ramer
> Fera ses eaux mieux traitables,
> La douleur de jour, & jour
> Et l'amour
> Me seront plus equitables. (328)

The binary oppositions which are thematically so important in Phyllis' complaint are frequently brought out in Ovid"s antithetical verbal structures. Lines 83–84, for example, posit the opposition between Athenian erudition and the uncivilized belligerence of Thrace:

> atque aliquis "iam nunc doctas eat," inquit, "Athenas;
>   armiferam Thracen qui regat, alter erit . . . "

> And somebody says: "Let her go now to learned Athens; another will reign over warlike Thrace in her stead . . . "

Fontaine captures the sense of this well, setting up an opposition between "Cethine sauante" (with a marginal note to inform the reader that this refers to Athens)[52] and "Thrace la belliqueuse." Saint-Gelais misses the point of this antithesis and seems to misread the lines:

> Maintz en ya disans à voix haultaines,
> S'en voise or [sic] Phyllis droict à Athenes,
> La trouuera Demophon son amant
> Qui d'elle aura tout le gouuernement. (1546 ed., fol. 11ʳ)

The translator interprets "alter" to mean Demophoon, and "Thracen" as referring to Phyllis rather than Thrace itself.

Both Phyllis' letter and Dido's end with epitaphs, which take Ovidian

---

way: "Till surge of seas doe cease and love doe temper trade."
    52. "Cethine," or "Satines," appears to be simply a corruption of the word "Athens."

compactness to the last point of refinement. Phyllis' epitaph at lines 147–48 combines ironic juxtapositions with syllepsis and intertextual allusion (a window reference to Virgil's Dido via *Heroides* 7):

> PHYLLIDA DEMOPHOON LETO DEDIT HOSPES AMANTEM
>   ILLE NECIS CAVSAM PRAEBVIT, IPSA MANVM.

> DEMOPHOON, A GUEST, BROUGHT DEATH TO HIS LOVER
>   PHYLLIS.
> HE FURNISHED THE CAUSE, SHE THE HAND BY WHICH DEATH
>   CAME.

The two translators deal with this difficult couplet in different ways; neither is entirely satisfactory. Saint-Gelais's translation juxtaposes the names ("Cy gist phillis laquelle demophon . . . "), but fails to convey the sense of Ovid's ironic "hospes amantem." The syllepsis in the final line is dealt with well: "Il bailla l'heure, et el lexecuta." Fontaine in his translation does convey the sense of Phyllis as lover and Demophoon as guest:

> Phyllis amante icy git morte à tort
> Que Demophon, son hoste, ha mise à mort (40),

but adds a superfluous line ("Luy desloyal, et de cœur inhumain") in order to accommodate the conclusion: "Y mit la cause, elle y ha mis la main."

Saint-Gelais has an untypically concise translation of Dido's epitaph (7.195–96); but he misses the entire second line, leaving the couplet unbalanced:

> PRAEBVIT AENEAS ET CAVSAM MORTIS ET ENSEM
>   IPSA SVA DIDO CONCIDIT VSA MANV.

> AENEAS FURNISHED BOTH THE CAUSE OF DEATH AND THE SWORD;
> IT WAS BY HER OWN HAND THAT DIDO MET HER DEATH.

> Cy gist Dido, a qui le faulx Aenee
> Cause de mort et l'espee a donnee. (fol. xlii^v)

Fontaine's translation forfeits the compactness of Ovid's version in favor of a fuller rendering of the sense:

> Ci git Dido, qui d'Eneas à tort
> Reçeut la cause, & lespée de mort:
> Puis tot apres de celle mesme espée
> S'est par sa main d'un mortel coup frapée. (130)

This version alters the oppositional structure somewhat, making Dido the subject of both verbs. Fontaine reproduces all the semantic elements of Ovid's couplet, but misses the pathos. Du Bellay's translation, by contrast, retains the grammatical structure of the original, filling in the gaps with adverbial phrases and adjectives. His "A grand tort" and "miserable" perhaps strike a tone different from Ovid's couplet; but once again, it is the rhyme that does most to elicit irony and pathos:

> Enée a de ceste mort
> A grand tort
> Donné la cause et l'espée:
> La miserable Didon
> De ce don
> A sa poictrine frapée. (330)

IN THE SPACES between the two treatments of Ovid's Phyllis, we discern the progression from medieval to Renaissance ideas about rhetoric, poetics, and ethics. Saint-Gelais's translation has the standards of accuracy of a late-medieval text, often omitting details or allusions for reasons of clarity or because of formal constraints. The translator often adds elements not present in the source text, either incorporating manuscript glosses in order to clarify certain references or adopting a moralizing stance. More frequently he suppresses difficult allusions and simplifies the mythological narrative. The text Saint-Gelais is working from is corrupt, with many variants not to be found in the later printed editions or in the later translations.

Fontaine in his translation rarely departs from the source text and strives to be comprehensive as possible: where a reference is not clear from the translation, notes are provided for background. The prefaces and notes serve also to harbor moral interpretations of the poems' edifying content that generally do not find their way into the text. Fontaine's translation was motivated by the significant changes in the cultural climate and in the French language itself between the time Saint-Gelais was writing in the late fifteenth century and the time of the later translations in the 1550s. The French language is no longer in its infancy; it is in a better position to accommodate the demands of Ovid's language. Although Fontaine perhaps disagrees with Pléiade poet about methodology, he shares with Du Bellay the belief that once the French language has been furnished with the requisite *thesaurus* of expressiveness, "effective" versions of ancient texts can be constructed within an authentically copious discourse.

Although Du Bellay's translation is in some respects an exceptional case, it certainly illustrates the impact of the innovations of the Pléiade on the poet's art. Du Bellay's translation is not intended as a complete rendering of Ovid's text; instead he offers an interesting poetic *remaniement*. The unusual metre offers much scope for word-play and textual games, and Du Bellay exploits these without departing too far from the source text. Instead of suppressing or explaining difficult allusions, Du Bellay expects his ideal reader to recognize them; he even adds erudite touches of his own. Whereas Fontaine's translation is perhaps intended to be read in parallel with the Latin text, Du Bellay's version stands alone as a poetic composition in its own right. Du Bellay is not so impudent as to pretend to have "contrefaict au naturel les vrays linëaments de Vergile" (250), but against his "divine magesté" he stands a better chance of catching the "ingenieuse facilité" of Ovid (252). Elsewhere in his poetry, Du Bellay shows a particular affinity for Ovid; in his *Complainte de Didon,* the poet-translator's voice harmonizes with the *genius* of the text.

Ovid's hand in the transmission of the heroines' complaint had been prominent in early modern readings of the text. The controlling presence of Ovid is ultimately responsible for the orchestration of the heroines' epistolary discourse. Phyllis and Dido, in writing their own epitaphs, assert the influence of their own hand ("ipsa manus") in their stories. The translators literally efface the heroines' "hand" in the work. Theirs is a work of "remaniement" of Ovid"s text. Ovid"s hand betrays its presence in the text still; but the hand of the translator, especially in Du Bellay's text, disrupts that dynamic or dialectic of intentions "auctoris et mittentis." This tendency to exclude the voice of the heroine from her own story comes to its natural conclusion with the writing of reply epistles.

CHAPTER 5

Replying to the *Heroides*

Comme désir, la lettre d'amour attend sa réponse; elle enjoint implicitement à l'autre de répondre, faute de quoi son image s'altère, devient autre.

Roland Barthes[1]

Oh happy state! when souls each other draw,
When love is liberty, and nature, law:
All then is full, possessing, and possess'd,
No craving void left aching in the breast:
Ev'n thought meets thought, ere from the lips it part,
And each warm wish springs mutual from the heart.

Pope, *Eloisa to Abelard*

O WRITE A REPLY to the *Heroides* is to open up a space of exchange, to engage in dialogue with Ovid's text; but it is also to set a limit. It is to undertake to reanimate a dead letter; but it is also to offer closure, to hope to resolve an inner conflict, to put an end, finally, to the life of the *lettre en souffrance*. Once the hero has received and replied to the heroine's letter, the letter can no longer circulate: the possibility of any further interception by an intermediary is denied. The letter rests in the hands of its addressee.

This is why all attempts to write the heroes' responses must fail. The heroine's letter can never be possessed by its reader: it continues to circulate, despite its having been taken out of circulation. The epistolary discourse of Ovid's heroines stubbornly resists closure. The state of grace Eloisa longs to restore will be possible only in the timeless fixity of heaven: it is not available to Eloisa as long as she hopes to lose the sin, yet keep the sense; nor is it to Ovid's heroines as long as they remain inhabitants of language.

In their letters Ovid's heroines reinvent their own myths. Between the painful subjectivity of the lover's discourse and the allusive re-readings of

---

1. *Fragments d'un discours amoureux,* 189. "Like desire, a love letter expects a response; it implicitly enjoins the other to reply, failing which their image changes, becomes 'other.'"

their own textual realities, the heroines "unravel . . . the phenomenology of myth itself."[2] The prefaces and commentaries attempt to define and contain the heroines' texts within a scholarly framework, to re-endow myth with interpretative plenitude. They represent the need to rehabilitate the ambiguous subjectivities of Ovid's heroines into an objective universal structure. The processes at work here are also central to those texts which form a kind of intradiegetic protective shell around the problem of the heroines' discourse: the heroes' responses to them. The notion of writing replies to the heroines' epistles must have seemed an attractive prospect to imitators of Ovid's elegiac poetry. The reply as a mode of imitation seems to be an obvious choice, generated—invited, even—by the very form of the *Heroides*: the absence of the addressee suggests a void waiting to be filled, the implied reaction furnished by the imagination of the reader-imitator. However, the absence of the addressee is also a principle central to the composition and reception of the *Heroides,* in which the absence or distance that conventionally define the epistolary genre as a whole are made prominent as integral structural features. None of the heroines, moreover (with the exception of Sappho), actively asks for a response; indeed, the first letter in the collection begins with an injunction: "nil mihi rescribas." The psychological complexity of Ovid's studies in abandonment reveals itself in the fragmented discourse they generate; for the most part the rhetorical devices which Ovid uses to elicit pathos, irony, and dramatic tension rely on the knowledge that these complaints will not be heeded, that a tragic end is in sight, that the lover's discourse flails onward unchecked, aleatory, unanswered. As Marina S. Brownlee observes of the seventh epistle:

> Unlike Virgil's heroic, despairing Dido, Ovid's heroine is still hopeful, clinging to the illusion that her words may be convincing. We as readers of Ovidian mythology, of course, know otherwise—that the letters will actually have no effect on the men they are intended to persuade.[3]

---

2. M. S. Brownlee, *The Severed Word,* 8.

3. Pp. 28–29. Brownlee's observation holds true as long as we posit a single version of the mythological narrative against which the heroines' stories must be read, in this case, Virgil's *Aeneid.* In many cases, though, Ovid's intertextual heroines can be read as playing on multiple versions of their narratives. Renaissance interpreters found it relatively unproblematical to switch between different versions depending on what aspect of the heroine's narrative they wished to emphasize. In her study of *The Ovidian Heroine as Author,* Laurel Fulkerson nuances the conventional reading somewhat with her argument that even though the letters have no discernable effect on the men to whom they are addressed, they may have an effect on the female "community" of readers and writers within the *Heroides.*

Once we have in front of us the reply to Dido's complaint, though, a large part of this rhetorical effect is lost. This is not to say that the genre of the heroic reply is entirely restrictive or reductive. To what extent does the writing of counter-epistles dismantle or undermine or endorse the rhetorical scheme of the *Heroides*? To what extent does the notion of replying lay bare the mechanisms of response to the literary text in general?

The elegiac scheme underpinning the heroines' complaints in the *Heroides* always figures the object of desire as absent. Each of the letters can thus be read as a variation on the *paraclausithyron,* the elegiac lover's lament to the locked door. Philip Hardie develops this reading: "The locked door is the most basic instrument of elegiac absence, and one that Ovid develops into a metaphor for the almost but not quite permeable barrier between what lies inside and outside a text. . . . "[4] The possibility of fulfilment (the overcoming of the elegiac obstacle) is always held out as a lure; presence turns out to be an illusion. Epistolary presence seems to be less problematical in the double letters, as if the reply itself guarantees some sort of alignment between subject and object, a connection between words and things. This functions most obviously in the Acontius-Cydippe myth, where Acontius' words have illocutionary success.[5] Problems remain, however: even if the aim of letter writing is to make absent people present to us (as Seneca, Turpilius, and Cicero affirm),[6] the writing subjects in the *Heroides* always remain aware of the uneasy relation between epistolary presence and 'real' presence. This leads to the fetishization of the letter: Leander personifies his letter and hopes that Hero will sleep with it (18.217–18). The letter is all the more a presence in the real world if it is acknowledged by its recipient: in this case the words of the letter, like those written on Acontius' apple, will have achieved their desired effect. However, the exact content of the message from Acontius to Cydippe is never made explicit in *Heroides* 20–21. The apple as a figure for the letter points up its function as a circulating signifier, whose meaning is only determined by its place in the structure: by who reads it, when, and where. The single pieces in the *Heroides,* much more obviously than the double letters, play on the shifting ambivalent relation of the subject to an essentially absent object. That is why the reply poem must fail in its attempt to 'complete' the text by supplying the desired object; indeed, often the attempts at resolution create ambiguities of their own as well as bringing to the fore the complexities of Ovid's text.

---

4. Hardie 2002, 109–10.

5. Hardie, 110–21: "*Heroides* 20 and 21 conclude the book with an apotheosis of writing, a demonstration of the power of the poet's own craft."

6. See Hardie, 106–8.

The necessary failure of the heroes' attempts to reply speaks of Renaissance anxieties surrounding the possibility of engaging with the literature of antiquity. The perceived need to fill the vacuum left by the absent addressee may be related more broadly to Renaissance obsessions with dialogue. The dialogue genre, remarks Eva Kushner, was "so widespread during the Renaissance that it seems to represent a fundamental and innovative aspect of its intellectual life."[7] Moreover, one of the most convincing aspects of Mireille Huchon's recent study of the authorship of the works of Louise Labé is its account of the extent and nature of collaborative literary communities in sixteenth-century France: coteries of poets wrote prefatory material for each other's publications, engaged in projects of mutual praise, and opened up poetic dialogues with one another by means of allusive literary games. The circulation of texts was driven by a ludic spirit of poetic invention. This is not to say that such dialogues were never adversarial in tone. To take one example: the catalyst for the extended poetic dialogue known as the "querelle des amyes" was Charles Fontaine's response (as "La Contre amye de Court") to La Borderie's provocative "Amye de Court." Raphael Lyne argues that the writing of *Heroides* replies illustrates a feature of literary networks in Tudor England: poets operated within a "culture of response." Humanist culture favored in particular the dialogue form and the writing of poetic responses and counterresponses; and these forms, even as they sought to justify the terms of their own existence, often betrayed anxieties about the possibility of engagement with the culture of antiquity.[8] In an essay published in the *Printed Voices* volume, François Rigolot relates the "inward turn" of the dialogue form to what he has elsewhere called the Renaissance crisis of exemplarity.[9] As we shall see, the writers of the reply epistles experience particular difficulties with the application of schemes of exemplarity.

The form of the reply epistle only enables responsiveness in a limited way; it does not allow for the sort "open-ended" dialogue that was the ideal of Renaissance humanism. At the same time as they open a dialogue with the Ovidian text and within the contemporary poetic community, Ovid's respondents close off possibilities for a free-flowing exchange with the literature of the past. Ovid's work had fundamentally questioned the validity of conventional reading practices. As Raphael Lyne points out, the "monologic" autonomy of the *Heroides*, their refusal of the possibility of reply "ironically

---

7. Kushner 2004, 229. Kushner has worked extensively on the Renaissance dialogue genre and has published several articles on the development of the dialogue in sixteenth-century France (see bibliography in *Printed Voices*).
8. Lyne, Autumn 2004, 149.
9. Rigolot 2004, 3–24.

challenges later writers' capacity to engage with the past and thereby validate their own project" (161). Ovid himself looks askance with gentle irony at the undertaking of his friend Sabinus in *Amores* 2.16. Can a limiting response to the Ovidian text ever be a valid one?

The Sabinus Epistles

As we saw in the previous chapter, the publication of *Heroides* translations and imitations was often bound up with questions of authorship and authenticity. Such problems were part of the reply-poem tradition from the very start. The earliest instance of composition by a second hand of replies to Ovid's *Heroides* occurred almost as soon as the first part of the collection was written. As Ovid writes in the *Amores,* one Sabinus[10] was quick to compose replies to the early *Heroides:*

> Quam cito de toto rediit meus orbe Sabinus
> scriptaque diuersis rettulit ille locis!
> candida Penelope signum cognouit Vlixis;
> legit ab Hippolyto scripta nouerca suo.
> iam pius Aeneas miserae rescripsit Elissae,
> quodque legat Phyllis, si modo uiuit, adest.
> tristis ad Hypsipylen ab Iasone littera uenit;
> det uotam Phoebo Lesbis amata lyram. (2.18.27–34)

How quickly has my friend Sabinus returned from his travels all over the world, and brought back with him writings from various places! Fair Penelope has recognized the seal of Ulysses; the stepmother has read a message from her Hippolytus. Dutiful Aeneas has now written back to wretched Dido, and a message for Phyllis to read, if she is still alive, is here too. A sad letter from Jason has reached Hypsipyle; the poetess from Lesbos, now loved, may dedicate her lyre to Phoebus.

Further information about Sabinus is supplied by Ovid in the *Epistulae ex Ponto:*

> et qui Penelopae rescribere iussit Vlixem

---

10. It is far from clear who Sabinus was. Ronald Syme concludes only that "the *cognomen* Sabinus is too common to lead anywhere," though he does mention three Augustan *rhetores* of that name: Asellius, Clodius, Gavius (Syme 1978, 75).

> errantem saeuo per duo lustra mari,
> quique suam Troezena inperfectumque dierum
> deseruit celeri morte Sabinus opus. (4.16.13–16)

And he who made Ulysses reply to Penelope as he wandered the wild seas for ten years, Sabinus, has abandoned to swift death his Troezen and an unfinished work of days.

This is generally not believed to be the same Sabinus whose three replies to Ovid's *Heroides* are extant, although the debate on this question remains unresolved. The convoluted history of the Sabinus epistles is dealt with in an article by B. Geise on the attribution of the work to Angelus Sabinus de Curibus (whose birth name is often given as Angelo Sabino of Corese; the name Angelo Sani di Curi has also been suggested).[11] A 1486 Venice edition was long thought to be the *editio princeps* of the text (on the authority of Nicolas Heinsius), but Geise, following Häuptli, points out that a 1477 edition put out by Domitius Calderinus is the first to have contained the letters. The involvement of Domitius Calderinus in the publication of the letters is perplexing, since it is known that Angelus Sabinus was embroiled in an acrimonious dispute with Calderinus, with mutual accusations of plagiarism: each scholar had accused the other of copying his notes on Juvenal.[12]

The only mention that Angelus Sabinus makes of his replies to the *Heroides* comes in the dedication of his 1474 edition of that commentary on Juvenal, entitled *Paradoxa in Iuvenalem*. In an epistle addressed to Perotti, Angelus Sabinus claims to have composed replies to the *Heroides* in the summer of 1467: "cum [. . .] heroidibus Nasonis poetae inclyti heroas respondentes facerem, uenit ad me uir quidam. . . . "[13] (while I was composing the heroes' responses to the heroines of the famous poet Ovid, a certain man visited me. . .)." This evidence is inconclusive, however. It is possible that Angelus Sabinus meant to discredit his enemy Calderinus. Perhaps he knew that Calderinus meant to publish a manuscript of the Sabinus letters, and intended to lay down a 'spoiler' in advance, by falsely claiming to have written them. Indeed, Bruno Häuptli sees the Calderinus connection as

---

11. Geise 2001. See also Dörrie, *Der heroische Brief*, 104–6.
12. On the dispute between Domitius Calderinus and Angelus Sabinus, see Eva M. Sanford's article on Juvenal editions in the first volume of the *Catalogus Translationum et Commentariorum: Medieval and Renaissance Latin Translations and Commentaries*, ed. by P. O. Kristeller (Washington: Catholic University of America Press, 1960); see also Sanford 1948, 102–5 and Grafton and Jardine, 63–64.
13. Quoted by Pendergast 1969, 248; and more fully by Geise, 8.

proof that the letters were not composed by Angelus Sabinus, reasoning that there is no possible way a scholar of Calderinus' stature would have printed the letters if they were not genuine, especially given his animosity toward Angelus Sabinus. Alternatively, perhaps Angelus Sabinus had intended to pass off the letters as works by the ancient Sabinus and saw Calderinus as the ideal stooge for such a hoax, given their history. Both of these possibilities seem unlikely, however, and there is no definitive evidence to suggest that we are dealing with a hoax. Further confusion is caused by a different text of the Ulysses letter, also attributed to Angelus Sabinus, which might be by a different author, or a first draft of the later poem.[14]

Renaissance editors were eager to believe that the poems were genuine works of antiquity. Sixteenth-century editors did not concern themselves for long with the question of authorship: it seems that the authority of *Amores* 2.18, coupled with the name "Sabinus" were evidence enough to confirm authenticity. Humanists were, in general, keen to give works of uncertain vintage the benefit of the doubt: many pseudo-Virgilian works, for example, were readily granted authenticity, as were the pseudo-Ovidian *Nux, Pulex,* and *Philomela,* among others. Several sixteenth-century editions, including the 1545 Guy Morillon edition of Ovid's *Poemata amatoria,* print the three compositions attributed to the ancient Sabinus.

However, the early reception of the Sabinus epistles was shrouded in misunderstanding and uncertainty. The fact that there are three reply poems in Ovid's own text, making up the six "double letters," no doubt contributed to this confusion.[15] Antonius Volscus dismissively attributes these three compositions to (the ancient) Sabinus, citing the above passage as evidence:

> Qui contendunt paridis, leandri & aconcii epistolas non esse Ouidii non recte opiniari existimo [. . .] Eas uero quæ illis respondent, ut ostendemus, non esse Ouidii sed Sabini crediderim. (sig. k.iv^v)

> I think that those who argue that the epistles of Paris, Leander, and Acontius are not by Ovid are not correct. But the epistles that reply to them, as we shall demonstrate, I might attribute not to Ovid but to Sabinus.

Volscus, writing around 1481, is clearly not aware of the "new" Sabinus replies (he says that they have all been lost), but is quite happy to attribute

---

14. The text of this poem survives only in manuscript. See Butrica 2002.
15. Letters 16–21 were probably written at a different time (possibly A.D. 7 or 8 rather than the first year B.C.) and form a separate work, but are generally thought to be Ovidian by modern critics (see, for example, Rand 1925, 27; Wilkinson 1955, 85; Jacobson, ix).

the replies to the "double-letters" (Helen, Hero, and Cydippe) to Sabinus rather than Ovid.

> Nullam quæ respondeat epistolam fecisse Ouidium aperte constat: cum suis omnibus Sabinum poetam respondisse in amoribus ipse testatur cum dicit: [Volscus quotes *Amores* 2.18.27–29]. Reliqua curiosis illic legenda relinquimus. Satis est admonuisse. Sabinus imperante Octauio uixit. ad Trisenam amicam elegiarum librum dedit. Fastorum inchoatos reliquit. epistolis Ouidii respondit, cuius helenam & hero Cydipeique legimus fragmentum.[16] Cæteras, ut multa alia, sæculorum ignauia desideramus. sunt qui has epistolas nec Ouidii nec Sabini esse animo coniiciant: quibus satis responsum esse existimo: cum nulla habeant argumenta quibus propositum firmare possint. Nos autem Sabini Helenam legendam contendimus. (sig.1.iii^v)

> It is definitely the case that Ovid composed no reply epistles, while he himself affirms in the *Amores* that the poet Sabinus replied to all of his epistles. [. . .] We leave out the rest, which interested parties can read there. It suffices to have raised the point. Sabinus lived when Octavian was emperor. He gave a book of elegies to his girlfriend Trisena. He left a collection of "Fasti" unfinished. He replied to Ovid's epistles; of these, we can still read his Helen, his Hero, and a fragment of his Cydippe. The others, as so much else, we are missing owing to the neglect of ages. There are some who conjecture that these epistles are not by Ovid or Sabinus. To them I think this response is sufficient, that they have no arguments to support the hypothesis. We contend, then, that the Helen should be read as the work of Sabinus.

Interestingly, he claims that Sabinus wrote a book of elegies to his mistress Trisena. This is based on a variant reading of *Pontics* 4.16.15, where other editions have Troezena (that is, an epic on Troezen). The mistake is replicated by the annotators of many later editions.[17] The evidence given by Volscus later on is simply that Ovid never mentions that he wrote replies, but he does mention that Sabinus did. The question is explored in no further detail ("satis est admonuisse"), but the Helen epistle is headed: "Sabini poetæ epistola qua Alexandro Helena respondet" (The epistle by the poet Sabinus

---

16. The Cydippe epistle lacks lines 15–250 in many early editions. The commentary of Volscus covers the first twelve lines only.

17. For example, Morillon has the note: "Aulus Sabinus, imperante Octauio, atque Ouidii temporibus claruit. Ad Trisenam amicam Elegiarum librum dedit, Fastorum inchoatos reliquit" (sig. K7^r) (Aulus Sabinus flourished during the reign of Octavian, in Ovid's time. He gave a book of elegies to his girlfriend Trisena, and left a collection of "Fasti" unfinished).

in which Helen replies to Alexander [Paris]). Despite the denial that these poems are by Ovid, they are not treated as lesser works by the commentators: their antiquity and *latinitas* were never in doubt.

Conversely, Morillon in his *argumentum* to the Helen epistle suggests that there is no reason to attribute the Paris-Helen exchange to Sabinus, since *Amores* 2.18 makes no mention of Helen, Hero, or Leander, and the letters are written in the same style as the others in the collection ("nimirum hæ Ouidianæ sunt, et eodem pene stylo scriptæ quo reliquæ," sig. G7ʳ [without doubt these are by Ovid, and they are written in almost the same style as the others]). Confusingly, he goes on to acknowledge that the final four epistles might not be by either Ovid or Sabinus, and that Ovid would surely have laid claim to the letters if they were by him.[18] Badius, for his part, doubts that the Helen and Hero epistles are by Ovid, but the reasons he gives are different: the style is too easy and straightforward to be Ovid's ("facilior et pedestrior"). In any case, the question of authorship generally does not detain any of the commentators for long: Morillon echoes Volscus in his noncommittal conclusion: "Reliqua studiosis illic legenda relinquimus: satis est admonuisse" (We leave the rest for interested parties to read there: it suffices to have raised the point).

The commentary of Ubertinus Clericus exacerbates the confusion by introducing yet another element. Clericus seems to think that Ovid himself composed a reply from Ulysses to Penelope, among others:

> Sicut Ouidius exercendi ingenii gratia hanc epistolam a penelope ad Vlyssen scriptam fixit: ita & responsiuam ab Vlysse remissam se scripsisse fatetur in secundo amorum ad Macrum: ubi conmemorat, ut supradiximus, aliquot epistolas responsiuas a se scriptas, quæ hodie non extant. (sig. b.iiᵛ)

> Just as Ovid composed the letter written by Penelope to Ulysses for the sake of exercising his talent, so he states that he wrote a reply sent by Ulysses—in the second book of *Amores,* to Macer [i.e. *Amores* 2.18]: where he records, as we said above, that several reply letters were written by him, which today do not survive.

Such misreadings of *Amores* 2.18 undoubtedly contributed to the integration

---

18. "... cum nusquam constet, ut iam diximus, Ouidium neque Sabinum scripsisse Epistolas Leandri, Herus, Acontii, Cydippes. Quas si Ouidius composuisset, ne suo labore priuaretur, certe meminisset, sicut de reliquis. Si de Sabino contendas, uideas quæso, si bene cum Sabini stylo conueniat" (sig. I7ʳ) (... since it is nowhere established, as we have already said, that either Ovid or Sabinus wrote the epistles of Leander, Hero, Acontius, and Cydippe. If Ovid had written them, he would surely have recorded the fact (as he did for the others), to ensure he would get credit for the work. If you contend they are by Sabinus, please go and see whether they are consistent with Sabinus' style).

of the Sabinus replies into the Ovidian corpus: the very idea that Ovid himself wrote replies adds an extra element of confusion to the authenticity issue.

The name of Angelus Sabinus was first proposed by Otto Jahn in 1837. All critical judgments before then are based on the attribution of the reply epistles 1, 2, and 5 to Ovid's friend Aulus Sabinus. Ovid nowhere mentions the *praenomen* Aulus. The origin of this is in the prefatory note that accompanies the text in many editions from 1486: "A. Sabinus, eques Romanus celeberrimus uatesque, Nasonis temporibus floruit. Qui has omnes responsorias et alias edidit, quæ non reperiuntur" (A. Sabinus, a very famous Roman knight and poet, flourished in the time of Ovid. He published all these reply epistles, and some others which are lost). The "Sabinus" of *Amores* 2.18 has somehow acquired an initial, "A," which was later assumed to stand for Aulus, in accordance with convention. The note also mentions that his rank was "eques," another fact that is not mentioned by Ovid. It is unclear whether the editors got this note from the MSS or inserted it themselves. There is also a brief summary of the life of "Aulus" Sabinus, recycled in many editions of the poems in the sixteenth century, which is based on the information given at *Pontics* 4.16.13–16.

The first critic to deal with the question of the Sabinus epistles is Aldus Manutius. In the notes to the 1515–16 edition of Ovid's works, Aldus disputes the attribution of the three poems to the ancient Sabinus. This is the first suggestion that the letters might not be authentic: Aldus states unequivocally that the Sabinus letters have not survived, and that the three letters published in his edition are not by Sabinus, nor even by a particularly good poet:

> Sabinus poeta Ouidii temporibus scripsit Epistolas, quibus Ulysses Penelopae, Hippolytus Phaedrae, Aeneas Didoni, Demophoon Phyllidi, Iason Hypsipylae, Phaon Sapphoni respondent. Sed non exstant. Nam tres hae quae habentur, mihi non modo non uidentur Sabini, sed ne excellentis quidem cuiusquam poetae.

> The poet Sabinus, a contemporary of Ovid's, wrote epistles in which Ulysses replies to Penelope, Hippolytus to Phaedra, Aeneas to Dido, Demophoon to Phyllis, Jason to Hipsipyle, and Phaon to Sappho. But they have not survived. The three that are held to be his, not only seem to me not to be his, but not even by any remarkable poet.

and later:

> Diximus superius Sabini Epistolas, de quibus in Amoribus Ouidius memi-
> nit, non exstare: tum quae Sabino inscribuntur, non modo uideri mihi
> non fuisse Sabini, sed ne egregii cuiusquam poetae. Idem et hic confirma-
> mus.[19]

> I said above that the Epistles of Sabinus, which Ovid mentions in the
> *Amores,* have not survived: and that those poems attributed to Sabinus not
> only seem to me not to have been written by him, but not by any outstand-
> ing poet. I here reiterate this opinion.

However, the opinion of Aldus is by no means representative of sixteenth-century views. Many editions printed the three epistles as genuine works of the ancient Sabinus, and it is rare for editors to express reservations. Julius Caesar Scaliger's response to the argument of Aldus is that it is wrong to refute the authenticity of the letters on the basis of their poor quality, since we do not know if Sabinus was any good as a poet anyway. He reminds the critics that the Augustan age had its fair share of terrible poets, and that Sabinus might well have been one of them.[20]

The next prominent scholar to enter the fray is Daniel Heinsius, who agrees with Aldus that the letters are so poor that they could not have been written in the Augustan age. He adds that the language is all but unintelligible in places, and that the text is full of errors.[21] The first editor to deal thoroughly with the textual problem was Nicolas Heinsius, who added dozens of emendations to those proposed by his father. N. Heinsius believed the poems to be authentic, but the lack of a manuscript tradition meant that his corrections were based more on stylistic considerations than on evidence. The view of a certain Mr. Salusbury, English translator of the Sabinus epistles in a 1688 edition, provides a stark contrast to the opinions of Daniel Heinsius: Salusbury follows Nicolas Heinsius in calling the poems "A Treasure," and judges that they show evidence of "A true Poetick genius" that is sustained and consistent. It is hard to believe that he is talking about

---

19. Quoted by Jahn 1826, 24.
20. "Tres Epistolae Ulyssis, Demophoontis, Paridis sane parui sunt momenti; quas propterea qui negant Sabini esse, si Sabinus quantus fuerit nesciunt, quonam pactoculo exstitisse Marsos, Suffenos, Volusios, Bauios, Maeuios, Anseres" (The three epistles of Ulysses, Demophoon, Paris are of little importance; but those who deny on that account that they are by Sabinus, do not know if Sabinus was good enough to have outdone somehow the likes of Marsus, Suffenus, Volusius, Bavius, Maevius, and Anser) (*Poetices libri septem,* 1561). See Jahn, 27.
21. "Sabino quae adscribuntur [epistolae], ita languent, ut ne hac aetate quidem scriptas ferre possem" (The epistles that are attributed to Sabinus are so weak that I could not even allow that their composition dates from that age) (1629). Jahn, 24.

the same poems roundly condemned by such luminaries as the elder Heinsius, the German critic G. J. Vossius, and the Dutchman Pieter Burman.

Later critics, such as J.-C. Jahn himself, suggested that Nicolas Heinsius was overzealous in his emendations, and frequently altered the text to suit his own taste even when the meaning was fairly clear (32). The nineteenth-century editor J. A. Amar, while approving of the corrections of Heinsius, acknowledged that the text had become almost unrecognizable: it would be better to call the letters "Heinsianae" than "Sabinianae." Amar was also of the opinion that the letters are authentic. He concedes that the style is somewhat weak and unpoetic; but there are certain turns of phrase that are worthy of Ovid himself, and he is confident that anyone who reads the poems will find much of merit.[22] Siding with the argument for authenticity is J.-C. Jahn, who concludes his study of the reception of the Sabinus poems by saying that there is nothing in the language to suggest they are by a late author.[23] The German critic Loers agreed with Jahn in the notes to his 1830 edition. Cabaret-Dupaty, a nineteenth-century French translator of the three epistles, does not even mention the possibility that they were not by an ancient author.[24] Despite some reservations about the quality of the poems, he finds in their author more to praise than to reproach ("plus à louer qu'à reprendre"). Listed among the admirable qualities of the poetry are its "vers . . . doux et coulants," an "esprit . . . des contes de Bocace et de La Fontaine," and "une vive imagination et une sensibilité délicate" ("smooth and flowing verses"; "the spirit of Boccaccio's tales and of La Fontaine"; "a lively imagination and delicate sensibility"). Modern critics generally attribute the letters to Angelus Sabinus. With the argument for inauthenticity comes a decline in critical interest.[25]

---

22. J. A. Amar's 1825 edition of Ovid's *opera omnia* includes the Sabinus replies with extensive notes, as well as the Sidronius Hosschius reply to the Phaedra epistle. My references to the text of the Sabinus epistles will be to this edition: *Publii Ovidii Nasonis Quæ Extant Opera Omnia*, ed. by J. A. Amar, Bibliothèque Classique Latine (Paris: N. E. Lemaire, 1825), I: 17–25, 43–49, 115–21.

23. "In Epistolis praeter aliquot apertas librariorum corrupteles nihil reperitur, quod ab Augusteo aeuo abhorreat, aut Sabinum carminum auctorem esse redarguat. Neque orationis tenuitas et obscuritas et sententiarum languor et defectus, si qui est, huic auctori aduersatur. Quare nihil obstare uidetur, quo minus Ouidii testimonio et editionis principis auctoritati obedientes has Epistolas Sabino suo reddamus, aduersariorumque sententias iustis argumentis non probatas, sine haesitatione reiiciamus" (In these epistles, other than a few glaring errors introduced by the copyists, nothing can be found that is inconsistent with the Augustan age, nor anything that proves Sabinus is not the author of the poems. Nor do the slightness and obscurity of the language, and the weakness and deficiency of the ideas, if such is the case, argue against this author. Therefore there seems to be nothing to prevent us—when we take into account the testimony of Ovid himself and the authority of the *editio princeps*—attributing these epistles to his friend Sabinus, and rejecting without hesitation the opinions of the opposing camp, which are not supported by convincing arguments) (33).

24. Cabaret-Dupaty 1842, 2–5.

25. One exception is the 1969 article by Pendergast, cited above. Pendergast undertakes a

The Sabinus poems were first translated into French in the early seventeenth century. Pierre de Deimier included prose translations of the first two letters, along with another of his own composition, in his 1612 edition of his prose translation of Ovid's collection. The first full translation of all three letters, by Michel de Marolles, did not appear until 1661.[26] In England they had already been translated by George Turberville as early as 1567.

The *Heroides* reply tradition, then, can trace its lineage back to Ovid's own time: not only does it possess the authority of antiquity, but it is also endorsed by the poet himself. The ur-text for this tradition would be the ancient Sabinus poems. Given that Sabinus' three replies are printed alongside Ovid's poems in many of the most prominent sixteenth-century editions, it seems unlikely that any imitator of Ovid would have been unfamiliar with these works, which had fast become 'classics.' Heinrich Dörrie gives an account of the works' success, suggesting that the poems had been absorbed into the Ovidian corpus almost as soon as they were published.[27]

There existed, then, a precedent for composing replies to the *Heroides*. The 'discovery' of the Sabinus letters seems to have prompted a handful of authors to compose their own reply letters. Such compositions, though, were less common than one might think. The sixteenth century, when the Sabinus replies were still "new," seems to represent a "Golden Age" in the history of the tradition. Heinrich Dörrie, in his chronological bibliography (536–70), lists only eleven texts which include "Antwortgedichte zu den *epistulae Heroidum* Ovids." Six of these are sixteenth-century texts; before 1500 there are just two (including Angelus Sabinus in 1468); between 1600 and the twentieth century there are three. The sixteenth century, then, represents a particularly productive time for *Heroides* replies, albeit on a limited scale. The fact that such an obvious mode of imitation never really caught on might be explained in part by examining the textual problems posed by the form itself.

Michel d'Amboise: *Les Contrepistres d'Ovide* (1541)

Michel d'Amboise's *Contrepistres d'Ovide* enjoyed some success in their time, although modern critical judgments of the work have not been favorable.[28]

---

metrical analysis of the Sabinus poems and shows that the imitator has indeed been responsive to Ovid's particular style. Although he judges that Sabinus "treats his topics in a jejune way," he concludes that the Latinity of the poems is in no way faulty (253).
 26. Dalla Valle, 379.
 27. Dörrie, *Der heroische Brief,* 105–6.
 28. My references are to *[Les] Contrepistres d'Ovide* (Paris: Maurice de la Porte, 1546). On the *Contrepistres,* see for example Morisset (158–70); Scollen (28–29); and LeBlanc (178). For critical

D'Amboise produced a large number of poetic works, among them several collections of *épîtres* written under the name of "l'Esclave fortuné." Many of these poems bear a strong similarity to the *Contrepistres*, being themselves partial imitations of the *Heroides*. For example, in *Les Complaintes de l'Esclave fortuné*, the "Lettre envoyee par une dame a son mary estant sur la mer lieutenant general pour le roy" opens with a typically Ovidian salutation: the writer wishes to send her husband the "salut" that she herself does not possess.[29]

D'Amboise's mythological heroes in the *Contrepistres*, moreover, in lamenting the injustices meted out to them by adverse Fortune, in their lyrical flights of amorous devotion, and in their indignant self-justifications, borrow heavily from the language and style of the author's own "Esclave fortuné" persona. Just as in his translation of Mantuan's *Adolescentia* (1530), d'Amboise had been less concerned with fidelity to the complexities of the source text than with adapting the language to suit his own poetic temperament,[30] so in the *Contrepistres*, the poet's style is characterized less by strict imitation of Ovid than by "elements borrowed from his own experience, and from his erotic poems."[31]

Richard Cooper notes the connection between d'Amboise's framing of an exchange of letters between separated lovers in the *Penthaire* and *Epistres veneriennes*, and the genesis of the *Contrepistres* (454–55). Those letters had an autobiographical basis, in the poet's relationship with his wife, Isabeau de Bois. Elsewhere, d'Amboise was to write a touching tribute to her:

> Cest la rayson pourquoy tant la regrette
> Entre aultres choses elle est femme secrette [sic]
> Les unes changent: mais ceste est plus que stable [sic]
> Nestant ung brain en ses faicts variable
> En ung propos est tousiours permanente
> Jamais nen feut une plus amyable
> Une plus doulce: une plus charitable
> De mieulx apprinse nya entre cinquante
> Elle est iolye et tant bien advenante

---

judgments of d'Amboise's *œuvre* more generally, see Cooper 1997, 445–46, with references.

29. D'Amboise 1529, fol. lxxviii^v. This *épître* is in fact written in the person of Michel's cousin, Antoinette d'Amboise; in the closing *rondeau*, Michel writes her name into the poem by means of an acrostic.

30. See Hulubei 1938, 83–86.

31. "des touches empruntées à son expérience, et à ses poèmes érotiques": Hulubei, 84. The author is commenting here not on the *Contrepistres* but on d'Amboise's Mantuan translation.

Que se nature leust voullu faire mieulx
Elle neust sceu: sans le conseil des dieux.³²

This is the reason why I miss her so; among other things she is my confidante. Other women change: but she is more than constant, and not at all fickle in her deeds, ever unwavering in her convictions. Never was there any woman more lovely or more gentle, or more charitable. You will not find one in fifty better brought up; she is so pretty and so very comely that if Nature had wished to improve on her, she would have failed, without the help of the gods.

D'Amboise strikes a profoundly personal note in the midst of the strictly conventional expressions of Isabeau's singularity. The contrast between the character of this idealized woman and the heroines against whom Michel's heroes rail in the *Contrepistres* is obvious: Isabeau is the "femme secrette," hardly likely to display an immoral eloquence like Ovid's letter writers; she is "stable," "permanente," never "variable," the exact opposite of the pagan heroines, if we believe the charges brought against them by the Latin commentators and the heroes of the *Contrepistres* alike.

D'Amboise's works paint a picture of a lively literary circle centered on his aunt and sometime patroness Catherine d'Amboise, to whom he dedicated a number of poems, for example in his *Penthaire* (1530) and *Epistres veneriennes* (1532). This cultural network seems to have been particularly interested in imitation of the *Heroides*. Catherine d'Amboise herself penned a short collection of devotional poems influenced by the *Heroides*, entitled *Les Devotes epistres*.³³ Her uncle Georges d'Amboise had been involved in the propagation of Saint-Gelais's translation. He was an important patron of the arts, and in Rouen he established a workshop of scribes and miniaturists producing handsomely illustrated manuscripts. Of the five illuminated manuscripts of Saint-Gelais's *Heroides* translation known to Durrieu and Marquet de Vasselot, authors of an 1894 study, at least two originated from the Rouen workshop established by Georges d'Amboise.³⁴ Although

---

32. *Complaintes*, fol. xxvi.
33. The date of composition was after 1542. The *Devotes epistres*, which circulated only in manuscript, were published in an 1861 edition by J-J. Bourassé, and more recently, by Yves Giraud (2002).
34. P. Durrieu and J.-J. Marquet de Vasselot, offprint from: *L'Artiste* (1894), *Les Manuscrits à miniatures des "Héroïdes" d'Ovide, traduites par Saint-Gelais et un grand miniaturiste français du 16e siècle*. The illustrations from both manuscripts have been made available online by the Bibliothèque nationale: MS. 873 at <http://gallica.bnf.fr/Catalogue/noticesInd/MAN01079.htm> and MS. 874 at <http://gallica.bnf.fr/Catalogue/noticesInd/MAN01080.htm> (accessed 25 June, 2005).

the *Heroides* manuscripts were made for Louis XII, as the authors comment, the artists of the Rouen workshop were producing manuscripts to the taste of their patron, Georges d'Amboise; this accounts for the Italianate style of the text and the Botticelli-influenced nature of the illustrations. The manuscript illustrations no doubt influenced trends in the making of woodcuts for the printed editions. The d'Amboise family had a significant influence on the mode of presentation of the text of the *Heroides* reaching beyond the first years of the century.

Michel's interest in the *Heroides* might well have been prompted by this family connection, and in particular by the writings of his aunt and patroness.[35] Indeed, among the circle of poets that Catherine had gathered around her in the 1540s, we find more than one whose works figure prominently in the story of the vernacular reception of the *Heroides*. D'Amboise's friend François Habert, whose many poetic works throughout a long and prolific career show a particular affinity for Ovid, published a collection of Christian *héroïdes*. Habert was influenced by d'Amboise's "fantaisies" in his *Visions fantastiques;* and he singles out d'Amboise for praise in his *épître* "sur l'immortalité des poètes français." Habert took his poetic pseudonym "le Banny de liesse" from a verse in d'Amboise's *Epistres veneriennes*.[36] Habert's religious *Epistres heroides*, published a decade after Catherine's own *Devotes epistres* were written, must have been influenced by the work of Michel's aunt. Another poem attributed to him, *L'amant infortuné*, displays many thematic and stylistic similarities with Catherine's work *La complainte de la dame pasmee contre Fortune*. It seems that many of the most important vernacular imitations of the *Heroides* came from poets somehow associated with the figure of Catherine d'Amboise. Raphael Lyne's discussion of the importance of cultural networks in the evolution of the reply poem in Tudor England is equally applicable to the cultural climate of mid-century France. Humanist literary culture was built on ideals on community and exchange; Ovid's *Heroides* flourished in such an environment precisely because it opened up possibilities for a responsive engagement with antiquity.

In the preface to the *Contrepistres*, d'Amboise acknowledges an ancient model:

> . . . en chascune de ces epistres ie respondz, comme anciennement auoit

---

35. On Catherine's patronage see Souchal 1976, 485–526, 567–612; 598ff.

36. Cooper 1997, 447, 467. On the affinities between the two poets, see also: Hulubei, 83–86, 222–44. It is worth noting, too, that Pierre Habert, brother of François, wrote—or rather plagiarized—a letter-writing manual in 1559: *Sur le style de composer toutes sortes de lettres*. See Bray, *L'Art de la lettre amoureuse*, 8 n. 5.

faict le poete Quintianus en ses vers latins, lesquelz nous a osté le temps dissipateur des œuures humaines. (sig. Aii')

... in each of these epistles I reply, as in times past did the poet Quintianus in Latin verses, which have been taken from us by time which brings human endeavors to naught.

The identity of the "Quintianus" named by d'Amboise is uncertain. D'Amboise is probably referring to the lost poems of Sabinus, mistaken in his attribution of them to "Quintianus";[37] there are no references to reply poems by any other poet of antiquity in Ovid, nor in the humanist commentaries. Dalla Valle suggests that this Quintianus is Quintianus Stoa, who had supplied notes to commentary editions of the *Heroides* (378). This cannot possibly be the case, since d'Amboise's description is clearly of an ancient poet whose works have been lost in the mists of time, and not of a near-contemporary. Quintianus Stoa's main period of literary production coincided with d'Amboise's own lifetime, and he was, indeed, still alive at the time d'Amboise wrote these words.

D'Amboise goes on to give his reasons for undertaking the task of replying to Ovid's heroines:

Qui pour donner quelque allegement de l'espoir tant entendu, aux cendres des Dames royalles, qui par cy deuant ont escript à leurs amys, a suscité & emeu aucunement ma plume a respondre, tant pour leurs [*sic*] satisfaire que pour effacer le blasme de tant de vaillans hommes, sans cause charge d'ingratitude & desloyaulté enuers elles. (ibid.)

The idea of giving some relief from their famous hopes, to the ashes of these royal Ladies, who prior to this wrote to their companions, stirred and moved my pen, so to speak, to reply, as much to satisfy them as to clear the name of so many worthy men, baselessly accused of ingratitude and disloyalty toward the women.

As if to approve this explanation formally, an anonymously penned "epigramme" (in both Latin and French), addressed to d'Amboise, is included in the back matter of the 1546 edition:

O esperitz des femmes Heroides

---

37. Lyne comes to the same conclusion, 150.

Qui demourez pres des undes humides
Du fleuue Stix, uueillez à moy entendre.
Ne nourrissez plus d'espoir uostre cendre,
Voicy le iour, uoicy l'heure uenue
Ou uous aurez response bien congneue
De uos escriptz, non en latin, Aincoys
Vous la lirez en langaige Francoys
Car ung d'Amboyse ayant de uous pitié
Pour satisfaire à si grande amitié,
N'a point uoulu si long temps estre uains
Voz espoirs, ny les labeurs de uoz mains.

Ne me uantez uostre Poete Ouide
S'il a pour uous bien escript: Car ie cuyde
Que s'il en a louange, que d'Amboyse
Ne l'aura moindre en sa langue Francoise,
Et comme fut Ouide le bruyt, uoire
Le seul honneur de Salmo, & la gloire:
Ainsi sera d'Amboyse la uantance
De Cheuillon, en la langue de France.

O spirits of heroical women who dwell by the flowing waters of the river Styx, please hear my voice. Cease nursing your ashes on hope: now the day, the time has come, when you will hear a worthy response to your writings, not in Latin, but instead you will read it in French, because one d'Amboise, taking pity on you, to fulfil such a great love, did not want your hopes, or the work of your hands, to be in vain for so long.

Do not boast that your poet Ovid wrote well for you: because I believe that if he gets praise for that, then d'Amboise will get no less in his own language, French, and just as Ovid was the fame of Sulmo, and indeed its sole renown and glory: so will d'Amboise be the pride of Chevillon, in the language of France.

Quæ colitis stygias (sanctæ ô Heroides) undas,
    Spes cineres uestros non alat ulterius.
Illa dies hæc est in qua rescripta legetis
    Carmina pro uestris Gallica quæque modis,
Hoc etenim Ambasius uestras miseratus amantum
    Tempore spes uanas noluit esse diu

> Non hic Nasonem mihi uos iactate poëtam
>   Non minus ambasii Gallica musa ualet.
> Ut fuit ille suæ Pelignæ gloria gentis,
>   Ambasius nostræ gloria gentis erit. (sig. Oiiii^v)[38]

This paratextual or "liminary" poem, which places the heroines in a liminal space between hope and fulfilment, between life and death, figures the afterlife of the heroines as the *Nachleben* of their text. The poem suggests that d'Amboise is in some sense "writing against Ovid": Ovid is the poet that belongs to the heroines ("uostre Poete Ouide"); he takes their part. D'Amboise writes for the heroes, as an additional poem by Gilles Corrozet affirms (sig. Ovii^r). This opposition merges into the opposition between Latin and French, and between Sulmo and Chevillon. The Latin expression "rescripta legetis / Carmina pro uestris Gallica quæque modis" is ambiguous, playing on the double meaning of "rescribere." Are the heroines to read *replies* to their letters in French verse instead of Latin; or are they to read their own verses *rewritten* in French?

The heroines of Ovid's work are figured as spirits in limbo, caught in the same type of non-space their letters occupy, unanswered. The trace they leave is both physical—ash—and textual—the fundamentally incomplete speech-act. D'Amboise's replies will therefore resurrect the heroines—confer upon them full presence in the scheme of d'Amboise's work—and at the same time lay their souls to rest, resolving the excess of desire. The emphasis here is on completion, satisfaction of desire, and the sort of linguistic plenitude entailed in the *translatio studii:* the complementarity of Latin and French versions completes the circle.[39] The act of replying to the *Heroides* is shown to be bound up with issues of cultural exchange: the variously authored "responses" to the text included in editions of both Fontaine's translation and d'Amboise's *Contrepistres* are a testament to the humanist ideal of dialogue and response within poetic communities.

The idea that d'Amboise's *Contrepistres* function as a corrective to the heroines' epistles is expressed in the *rondeau* which stands as a sort of epilogue to the work:

---

38. I offer here an English translation of the Latin text, since it does not correspond on all points with the French version: "You who haunt Stygian waters, o blessed Heroines, may hope nourish your ashes no longer. Now the day has come when you will read poems in reply, each one in French instead of in your own strains; for indeed d'Amboise, taking pity on your situation, did not want the hopes you had in your lovers to go long unanswered. Do not boast to me of your poet Ovid: d'Amboise's French Muse is no less worthy. Just as your man was the glory of his Paelignian people, so d'Amboise will be the glory of our people."

39. Cf. the acrostic sonnet on this theme included in Fontaine's later editions. See above, chapter 4.

De folle amour, ô mes seigneurs & dames,
Qui desirez oster uoz corps & ames,
Lisez ces uers & escriptz Marotiques,
Et euitez tous escriptz impudiques:
Escript lascif lasciueté enseigne.
Honneste escript de uertu porte enseigne
Faict les lisans a honneur attirer,
Et leurs espritz & leurs cueurs retirer
    De folle amour.
Or qui se ueult par uraye amour unir,
Tresgrand honneur il luy en peult uenir:
Ainsi qu'on dit assez communement,
Qui ueult aymer doibt aymer loyaulment.
Mais grand honneur ne peult iamais uenir
    De folle amour. (sig. Ovii^v)

Of foolish love, my lords and ladies who wish to divest body and soul, read these verses and writings in Marot's style, and avoid all shameless writing: lustful writing teaches lust. Moral writing bears the standard of virtue, turns its readers onto good morals, and turns their souls and hearts away from foolish love.

And so whoever wishes to come together in true love, the greatest honor may come to him: just as it is generally said, he who chooses to love, should love faithfully. But great honor can never come from foolish love.

The author of the *rondeau* reads the *Contrepistres* as a continuation of the tradition that situates the *Heroides* within a discourse of exemplarity. It is no doubt the case that, whereas in the *Heroides* the role of perspective is all important—there exists only the subjective, emotional interpretation of the myth—in d'Amboise's replies the heroes usually attempt to impose a more conventional objective structure onto the heroines' narratives. Their stories are reintegrated into the various mythological and literary traditions that had been fractured by Ovid's heroines: Ulysses narrates his heroic exploits, recuperated from Homer's epics, and Aeneas explains his empire-building responsibilities. But d'Amboise has chosen for himself a Sisyphean task: his text can no more circumscribe Ovid's than his heroes' letters can reciprocate or satisfy the desire of Ovid's heroines. Nevertheless the failure of d'Amboise's work (and of the reply-letters in general) is a necessary and interesting one: in attempting to bolster the moral framework of Ovid's text, the heroes' letters betray the instability of their own discourse.

Dalla Valle argues that d'Amboise takes a direction that runs counter to Ovid's attitude in the *Heroides* because "he does not accept Ovid's bias in favor of the women, but claims to re-evaluate positively the role of the hero" ("il n'accepte pas son orientation favorable aux femmes, mais il prétend remettre en valeur le rôle du héros," 378). Are the *Contrepistres* to be understood as a "débat" text? Is d'Amboise to be taken entirely seriously in the anti-feminist position he pointedly adopts? Is he really straight-facedly rejecting Ovid's favorable viewpoint on women? Or does the humor of the poems in some sense denounce the absurdities of such a position? I would suggest that d'Amboise's intention, and in particular his comments in the preface, must be read as essentially ironic or parodic, and that the work is entirely in tune with the spirit of Ovid's text. The playful manipulation of poetic traditions, the updating of classical myth to the concerns of a sophisticated, urbane poet's audience, the liberties taken with verisimilitude: all these are already features of the *Heroides*; they are simply taken to their extreme, often absurd, conclusions in the *Contrepistres*.

Gilbert de Golefer, in his *Epîtres des héros, ou réponce aux Epîtres d'Ovide*, published in 1620, takes a fundamentally different approach from d'Amboise in the *Contrepistres*. The differences are primarily to do with the literary culture of the period in which the work was written: Golefer was writing to a different set of concerns and demands, and, as Dalla Valle observes, he is basically "rationaliste et moraliste" in the choices he makes (380). He comments in his preface that he felt compelled to omit to write responses by Hercules to Deianira (on the grounds of *invraisemblance*) and by Phaon to Sappho (on moral grounds, and because Phaon is not 'heroic' enough). No such scruples prevent d'Amboise from composing replies by both Hercules and Phaon in his collection. This is partly to do with the different expectations of the literary climate in which he wrote, and partly to do with the fact that he does not take entirely seriously his proclaimed undertaking to "effacer le blasme de tant de vaillans hommes, sans cause charge d'ingratitude & desloyaulté."

Mark Alexander Boyd: *Epistulae Quindecim* (1590)

The chief source for information concerning the life and works of Mark Alexander Boyd (1563–1601), other than personal testimony to be found in manuscripts held at the National Library of Scotland,[40] is a work by

---

40. MS. 20759 (which contains the text of the 1590 *Epistulæ quindecim*) and Adv. MS. 15.1.7

the seventeenth-century geographer and natural historian Sir Robert Sibbald.[41] The inclusion of the study of Boyd's life and works in a volume principally dedicated to the natural history of Scotland strikes the reader as slightly unusual, especially given the rather conspicuous absence of many other famous Scots in the section entitled "De singularibus quibusdam hominibus" (On certain remarkable men). The author's interest in Boyd is explained by his personal involvement with the fortunes of that family, to which he was related.[42] Sibbald was also responsible for the conservation and transmission of manuscripts belonging to the Boyd family, containing many works penned by Mark Alexander himself.

The biographical information found in Sibbald's study is reproduced, in greatly embellished form, in a *Sketch* by Lord Hailes, published in English in the eighteenth century.[43] Hailes is certainly less generous than Sibbald had been in his assessment of the quality of Boyd's literary achievements, and rather more censorious of the young Scotsman's lifestyle. For example, where Sibbald had somewhat indulgently reported Boyd's substantial gambling losses on his arrival in Paris as "unfortunate" ("occulti ueluti fato, quicquid peculii habuit, perdidit Alea" [by the mysterious workings of fate, as it were, he lost all the money he had to gambling]), Hailes corrects him thus: "*This*, the author of his memoirs ascribes to 'some secret fate.' But we may absolve *fate;* for, when the raw and self-sufficient go amongst harpers, they ought to ascribe their ruin to *folly*" (2). According to Sibbald, Boyd was something of a miracle baby, born with a set of teeth he never lost. This prodigious occurrence, it seems, was not inconsistent with Boyd's character, his "impetuous and unruly temper,"[44] which saw the young man renounce his studies to take up the military profession. Indeed, an amusing—not to say bizarre—anecdote is to be found in the diary of Mr. James Melville, who in 1578 taught Boyd at the University of Glasgow. Boyd is described as "a youth of grait spirit and ingyne, bot verie commersom and refractar." When the master took him to task for "absenting him selff from the kirk, and pleying the loun on the Sabbathe," Boyd reacted by stabbing himself in the face with his pen, tearing his books to shreds, and using the pages to smear blood over his face. Having been suspended from the college for a month, he plotted to take revenge on the master; which he did by ambushing him outside the castle and attacking him with a sword.[45]

(which has some of the material printed in the 1592 edition).
    41. Sibbald 1684, pt. 2, bk. 3, ch. 2.
    42. See Cunningham 2000, 161–62.
    43. Dalrymple 1787.
    44. Dalrymple 1787, 1.
    45. Melville 1842, 69–70.

Boyd left for France soon after this. Throughout the 1580s he led the life of an itinerant scholar and soldier of fortune. In Paris from 1581, he attended lectures given by Jean Passerat, and by a certain J. Marius d'Amboise, Professor of Philosophy.[46] He went on to study Civil Law at the University of Orléans, and then under Cujas at Bourges. When the plague broke out there, Boyd fled to Lyon, and then to Italy, where he made the acquaintance of Cornelius Varus. He maintained a correspondence with Varus, and several of his letters are printed in the 1592 volume; in one of them Boyd holds forth at some length on the subject of poetry, and passes judgment on contemporary poets (whom he largely holds in contempt) and on the ancients. Boyd returned to Lyon around 1585, and in 1587 fought on the side of Henri III against the German and Swiss troops invading France under Henri de Navarre. He resumed his study of civil law in 1588 at Toulouse, but was arrested in the midst of an insurgency, and subsequently fled the city. His itinerary took him from there to Bordeaux, La Rochelle, and finally to Fontenay in Poitou.[47] He returned to Scotland around 1595, and died in 1601.

Boyd made the acquaintance of several prominent figures of the period, both French and Scottish. The 1592 book is dedicated to James VI; the dedicatees of his *Hymni* include Peter Young (tutor to James VI), Jean de Sponde (with whom he was acquainted from his time in La Rochelle), and a certain P. C. Dantonet.[48]

In the preface to the printed edition of his *Epistulæ quindecim*,[49] Boyd claims that the work was prompted by his reading of the extant Sabinus letters. Unlike d'Amboise, however, Boyd undertook to compose his own responses not in imitation of the poems of the *soi-disant* friend of Ovid, but as a corrective to the Sabinus work, which Boyd judged to fall well short of the original. Boyd is the only Latin poet other than Sabinus to have composed replies to *Heroides* 1, 2, and 5; this work therefore appears to be the only complete collection of reply epistles in Latin.[50] The poetry that results from Boyd's challenge to the 'canonical' reply poems is of uneven quality,

---

46. It is unclear from the *Dictionnaire de biographie française* entry for Jacques-Marius (or Jacques-Marie) d'Amboise whether he was closely related to the Amboise family that interests us. Nevertheless, it is pleasing to note the recurrence of the name: a member of this family seems to have been involved in some capacity at every stage of our study.

47. On Boyd's connections in southwest France, including his association with Nicolas Rapin, with a certain Louis Blouin, and with members of the Tiraqueau family, see Brunel 1974, 59–75. I am grateful to Carolin Ritter for having drawn my attention to this article.

48. On whom see Dalrymple 1787, 4 (where he is called Danconet) and Cunningham, 164. Robert Donaldson describes Claude Dantonet as the "author of 'une Paraphrase poétique des Lamentations de Jérémie, La Rochelle, 1602'" (Donaldson 1994, 353–54).

49. Boyd 1590.

50. See Dörrie1968, 108.

to say the least. Lord Hailes was especially scathing in his assessment of the work:

> His first work, *Heroes,* in answer to the *Heroides* of Ovid, was a juvenile performance; but on which, if we believe him, he bestowed the intense application of *five* years . . . (12; emphasis in original)

Boyd himself judged his second attempt (the *Epistulæ Heroides* of 1592) to be a great improvement on the first; Hailes disagrees:

> To me, they [Boyd's 1592 *Heroides*] seem puerile, flimsy and incorrect. Most of the lines might have been written by lads in the *fifth* form of Eton school; and some of them would not have passed in the *fourth* without animadversion. (12; emphasis in original)

Sir Robert Sibbald's judgment of the same work provides an interesting contrast: although, he admits, the 1590 work was hastily published by Boyd "inemendatum," the 1592 elegies proved "delicate" and "properly Latin" ("Felix hæc, tenuis, *Latina* et legitima Elegia"). The same work is spoken of by Lord Hailes in terms of "base Latin" and "abominable false qualities."

The 1590 work includes alongside the fifteen reply epistles a single epistle penned by a heroine, from Thisbe to Pyramus. The story of Pyramus and Thisbe was a popular one among *Heroides* imitators, as we saw in chapter 2. Boyd's Thisbe epistle was reprinted in a slightly different version in his second *Heroides*-inspired work, the *Epistulæ heroides, et hymni* (Antwerp, 1592).[51] This collection brings together imitations of Ovid's single epistles using situations from Greco-Roman mythology and Roman history. A certain "P. C. D." is named as the author of two "Imitations" in French printed alongside Boyd's *Heroides* in the 1592 edition; this must be the P. Claude Dantonet whom Boyd tutored in Lyon, and fought alongside in 1587. These "imitations," of the letters from Atalanta to Meleager and from Callionira to Diomedes, which are in part close translations of Boyd's Latin, are in some respects an improvement on the originals. Boyd's elegiac couplets are translated into French alexandrines. The longer lines offer the poet a greater flexibility and expressivity than had the decasyllabic forms in favor in the earlier part of the century.

---

51. Robert Donaldson (364–65) argues that this is a false imprint: the types and ornaments used are consistent with the Haultin printing house, based in La Rochelle. Simon Millanges, the Bordeaux-based printer who published Boyd's 1590 work, was known to use material cut by Haultin. The true place of publication is likely to be either La Rochelle or Bordeaux.

BOYD'S PREFACE to the 1590 collection of reply poems leads the reader to believe that he is unfamiliar with d'Amboise's *Contrepistres* (or that he holds vernacular poetry before Ronsard in such low esteem that it does not merit a mention). He claims to have been amazed, when studying the *Heroides*, that no poet of his age had attempted to write replies to a work which seems to demand them. He goes on to explain why the task of imitating Ovid is not to be undertaken lightly: anyone can imitate a Propertius, but only poets of a certain genius can imitate Ovid. The three letters of Sabinus he does not consider to be up to the required standard ("Sabini Epistolas tres retexui, quod mihi non placerent" [I have composed new versions of the three epistles by Sabinus, because I did not like them]).

Boyd makes it clear that the only possible way to "write back" to Ovid is by trying to write like Ovid:

Esse necesse qui Nasoni respondet, Nasonem ut referat quoque; & quoad fieri licuerit eodem fuco, eodemque foco exprimat. (6)

I saw too that it was essential that whoever would reply to Ovid should imitate him also; and as far as possible should reproduce him in his same colors and on his home ground.

"Writing back" to Ovid is the equivalent of "bringing back" Ovid: in order to "Nasoni respondere" it is necessary to "Nasonem referre." "referre" here means restore, repeat, reproduce, resemble: in short, to imitate.[52]

---

52. A concern with imitation and paternal resemblance also informs the language used by Boyd's heroes. They return again and again to the idea of paternity and inheritance as they struggle with the heroines' rhetoric of blame. In the third epistle, the reply of Achilles to Briseis, Achilles insists on the exemplarity of his own heritage—Thetis, Peleus, or Aeacus would never allow such a crime to be suffered—and contrasts it with the negative example of Agamemnon's paternity:

Utque ego iam uires refero genitoris, & arma,
    Atrei labes exprimit ille sui:
Utque ego uirtutem generis, sic ille parentum
    Omnia si referat crimina, diues erit. (21)

Just as I take after my father's strength, and arms, he replicates the faults of his father Atreus. Just as I [take after] the virtues of my ancestry, so he, if he reproduces all the crimes of his forefathers, will be rich.

The language used here, with the emphasis on the tragic predestination or fatedness of sons of fathers—Atreus, Agamemnon's father, repeated the sins of Tantalus and Pelops—prompts a poetological reading of the text. Boyd, indeed, uses exactly the same vocabulary of repetition and expression ("referre" and "exprimere") to speak of his technique in imitating Ovid as Achilles uses to speak of the heroic or tragic destiny of sons. *Exempla* in the discourse of epistolary heroism are very often markers of intertextuality, influence, and imitation of models. The deployment of the paternal *exemplum* in

Boyd, like Morillon in the preface to his edition of the *Heroides,* suggests that once one has been exposed to Ovid, one cannot help but imitate him. Even if he (Boyd) has failed in his attempt to "referre" Ovid, his own poetic nature was such that he could not have written the work in any other way.

> Nam quis a Propertio suauitatem, connexionem, decursum, tenuitatem expectabit? Quis a ceteris decorum in personis, uim uatis in principio, in fine impetum, perspicuitatem integram, & aequabilem eloquentiam extorquebit? Longe leuiore opera defuncti istos exprimimus, quorum artem mediocres ingenio non mediocri studio, & labore interdum assequuntur; at Nasonis natiuum impetum arti simul, & huic maximae praenitentem, nemo in se esse putabit, qui non eodem cum illo quasi redeunte sydere se natum censet. Nam quae artis sunt ex aequo pene omnes, qui huic inhaerent sibi uendicant; quae ingenii uero frustra reposcet is, cui deus magnum mentis impetum pernegauit.

> For who will hope for smoothness, unity, rhythm, fineness from Propertius? Who will wrest from those others appropriate characterization, poetic force in beginnings, strong endings, total sharpness of vision, and uniform eloquence? We can easily expend much less effort and imitate those whose art mediocre talents have on occasion equalled, by the application of uncommon zeal and effort; but Ovid's natural force outshines art, even the greatest art, and nobody will think he possesses *that* unless he believes himself born under the same star. For almost everybody who sticks at it has one equal claim on the things that are proper to art; in vain, though, are things proper to genius claimed by him to whom god has denied this great force of mind.

The unavoidable implication is that it is he, Mark Alexander Boyd, who is the true heir to Ovid's poetic legacy: his poetry flows forth freely with the natural force of his genius, checked by nothing so vulgar as "effort" or "art." Boyd goes on to demand the reader's indulgence, defending himself, it seems, against charges of incorrect Latinity: he appeals to the reader to indulge a pure, unpedantic mode of speech, the only mode in which an

---

heroic mythological narrative comes to stand for the complex relations involved in poetic imitation. There is a simultaneous *denial* and *affirmation* of paternal influence. Later in the Achilles epistle, the hero rhetorically asks "An soboles genitore prior?" (meaning: will Agamemnon outdo his father Atreus in the worst of his crimes?)—and equally, we might ask whether the imitator might precede his precursor, might prove the undoing of his model text, just as the heroes strive to undermine and preempt their accusers.

imitator of Ovid could possibly write. As a kindred spirit with Ovid, Boyd's achievement (he suggests) is to have reproduced Ovid's genius "in rebus," a rare kind of glory, if not "in verbis," which would have been but a vulgar achievement in any case: "nec in verbis vulgarem huius saeculi laudem, sed in rebus ipsis perraram ingenii gloriam venari" (not to seek after the vulgar renown of this age in words alone, but after the most rare glory due to genius, in the matter itself).

Boyd uses various techniques in service of his stated aim first to "revive," then to "compete with" Ovid. He recasts poetic formulations; he overturns Ovid's delicately balanced couplets; he reconceptualizes the "symbolic register" of the *Heroides* by redefining the key terms (*fides, hospitium, memoria*) that make up the conceptual framework of the heroines' narratives; he inverts rhetorical figures and sets them to work against the flow of the heroines' discourse. His text oscillates between a *compliance with* and a *resistance to* the Ovidian poetic dynamic.

The prefatory epigram, penned by P. Claude Dantonet, is strikingly similar to the one that introduces d'Amboise's *Contrepistres*. It frames the praise of Boyd's undertaking in terms of completion, reincarnation, inheritance, and paternity.

In hoc opus Epigramma

Nobilis Elysium Nasonis uenit imago;
    Hanc uidit passis Icariana comis,
Uidit & Hypsipyle, uiolentaque Phillidis umbra,
    Et memor admissi tristis Elisa sui,
Hippodamia gemens, & quam despexit Iason,
    Et depictarum caetera turba deûm.
O te foelicem nimium dixêre Poetam
    Si quod coepisti perficeretur opus,
Ac ita respondere leues potuêre mariti,
    Et patrocinio subdere colla tuo.
Hic Naso erubuit: nec fas ait, ite puellae,
    Defuncto ueneris continuare iocos:
Sed Bodius nascetur amans Nasonis imago:
    (Hunc edes graemio Scotica terra tuo,)
Qui procul a patria, dum Celtica percolit arua,
    Et par Aeneidi dum meditatur opus,
Peligni admittet sub amico pectore formam,
    Et tendet uento uela secunda meo.
Ergo nascentem Bodium perquirite: namque
    Hic mihi qui finget pectora, solus erit. (9)

Ovid's noble ghost came to Elysium; there it was seen by Penelope, her hair in disarray, and by Hypsipyle, and the furious shade of Phyllis, and sad Dido, still mindful of her crime, and sighing Hippodamia, whom Jason abandoned, and the rest of the band of gods he depicted. "Oh how blessed a poet you would be," they said, "if the work you began could be finished, and if our fickle husbands could have replied, and bowed down to your influence." Now Ovid blushed, and said: "Away, maids, it is wrong to bring silly matters of love to the dead: but Boyd, the loving likeness of Naso, will be born: (you, Scotland, bring him forth from your womb) who, far from home, gracing the land of the Gauls, and contemplating a work to equal the *Aeneid*, will accept into his favorable heart the image of the Paelignian, and will spread his sails to my wind. Seek, then, this Boyd when he is born: for he alone will form a soul like mine.

Ovid encounters the shades of the dead heroines in Elysium;[53] they plead with Ovid to finish the work he had begun. The Roman poet delegates the task to Boyd, an exiled Scot wandering through Gallic lands. Epistolary heroinism crosses borders: both in the sense that it is inscribed with imposture (literary transvestism, forgery, travesty) and in the sense that it is a dialogue between antiquity and the Renaissance world, or between Ovid's Rome and Boyd's Scotland, set within the international community of letters. Dantonet's poem situates the Scot Boyd in a relation of dialogue/emulation with Ovid, as the sole inheritor of his "genius."

As we saw with the liminary epigram to d'Amboise's work, the spirit of dialogue underwriting treatments of the *Heroides,* insofar as replying is associated with regeneration and the revitalization of the poetic word, operates also at the level of literary communities, setting the present in a relation of dynamism with the past. However, where d'Amboise's versions of the heroes' replies are characterized by a certain lightness of touch and humor, Boyd

---

53. The motif of the visit to the underworld bridges into the first poem of the collection proper, the reply of Ulysses to Penelope. Boyd's Ulysses narrates his descent to the Underworld (modified somewhat from the account in the eleventh book of the *Odyssey*), where he, like Ovid himself, encounters characters from the mythological world of the *Heroides*. Where Ovid had met Penelope, Hypsipyle, Phyllis, and Dido, Ulysses meets Achilles (*Heroides* 3) Protesilaus (*Heroides* 11), and Priam, who relates the story of the crimes of Pyrrhus, which is the narrative basis of *Heroides* 8, the exchange between Orestes and Hermione. These are the respondents to the heroine's epistles: the hero is aligned with the poet-imitator, and the shades of the dead lovers with the poetry, the "flebile carmen" to be revived. Meetings with the ghosts of literary heroes and heroines closely resemble the poetic device of the "exemplary catalogue": lists of *exempla* that gesture toward sources. The alignment of poets with examples from the world of heroes and their heroic predecessors is replayed elsewhere in the collection. *Exempla* cause problems for the respondents to the heroines' epistles. A large part of the rhetorical strategy of the "reply epistle" consists in the systematic analysis and refutation of the poetic figures that are the very rhetorical substance of the *Heroides*.

takes a different approach. His compositions are perhaps closer to Ovid's original poems in diction and setting and the avoidance of anachronism; but they fall short as a match for Ovid's wit and sense of irony.

Comparing Versions: Sabinus, d'Amboise, and Boyd

Assuming that the original work by Ovid's friend Sabinus is not extant, we can find a relatively substantial body of criticism on a work which, effectively, does not exist. It is interesting to look at the views of modern classicists on what the replies by Sabinus might have looked like.[54] These range from the unpromising (Duncan Kennedy suggests that Sabinus did not really "catch on"; he "seems to have been oblivious to, or to have been prepared to overlook, the implausibility that any of Ovid's heroines should receive replies from their absent menfolk") to the more generous. Gianpiero Rosati thinks Sabinus was on to something: a "clever idea"; "the generally witty, provocative character of Sabinus' ploy is evident, above all, in the very notion of writing replies to letters which do not envision them." Alessandro Barchiesi agrees:

> The initiative taken by Ovid's friend Sabinus . . . might have been a lighthearted and intentional violation, something a prankster would do (but still in the Ovidian spirit, given Ovid's passion for unmasking literary conventions in all their arbitrariness). At *Am.* 2.18.32 (*quodque legat Phyllis, si modo vivit, adest*) one almost perceives a playful distinction on Ovid's part, based on the strict temporal set-up typical of epistles 1–15. The situation in which Phyllis is writing does not allow any time for response. (168–69, n. 1)

If Sabinus' replies were worth reading, they must have had an element of humor to them: in short they must have functioned as parody: a literary in-joke, a very Ovidian critique of genre and convention.[55] The three

---

54. Kennedy, 418; Rosati, 1996, 209–10; Barchiesi, 168–69, n. 1. See also Jolivet's discussion of the point (255–57): "Les réponses de Sabinus aux *Héroïdes* ont vraisemblablement été inspirées par la claire perception de la fiction ovidienne et notamment par cette capacité à imaginer, grâce à une exacte connaissance des œuvres de référence, la réception des *Héroïdes* par les destinataires; elles sont le signe de la réussite du jeu littéraire ovidien."

55. Ronald A. Knox's Latin reply epistle to Penelope takes the humor of the epistolary conceit to absurd extremes: the twentieth-century poem is a parody of some of the absurdities of the genre. His Ulysses writes home from inside the Trojan horse; he tells his wife not to worry that the letter is written in blood: it is someone else's, not his. He complains that it is particularly difficult to write neatly when there is no elbow room; the Greeks, he says, are packed together like "Sardinii pisces in finibus ollae" (like sardines in a tin); the rocking of the horse is giving him seasickness, and as Penelope

Renaissance treatments of the heroes' replies meet these criteria with varying degrees of success.

In d'Amboise's collection, the Theseus reply seems unusual in that it does not partake of any prominent mythological tradition in its explanation for the hero's motivation.[56] A large section of his letter is the transcription of a speech by Ariadne telling him to flee; Theseus claims he did not want to go but was compelled because Minos was after him, and Ariadne was suffering from seasickness. He goes on to reproach Ariadne for taking a new lover even though he had promised to return in three months. At work here is a *contaminatio* of different traditions of the myth; and indeed of elements from separate mythological narratives. D'Amboise appears to have borrowed the span of three months from the Phyllis-Demophoon narrative. Read within the context of d'Amboise's preface, the letter seems consistent with the author's declared intention to "effacer le blasme de tant de vaillans hommes, sans cause charge d'ingratitude et desloyaulté." This is done by imposing a totalizing masculine discourse onto a deceptive and unreasonable female discourse. Theseus reverses Ariadne's scheme of guilt and innocence: now it is she who is faithless, a traitor, an amnesiac. However, it is tempting to see this as parody, a comic travesty of the "facts" of the myth. The fact that the Ariadne of the *Contrepistres* is said to have been suffering from seasickness suggests that d'Amboise is in some sense following this version of events given in Plutarch.[57] Plutarch relates the story that the women of Cyprus forged letters from Theseus to console Ariadne in her distress. This casts some doubt on the identity of the author who writes under the name of Theseus. Could this epistle be a forgery, a counterfeit letter composed by the women of Cyprus? It is hardly likely to "console and alleviate" Ariadne's distress, since it presents a Theseus preoccupied with his own self-righteous

---

knows, he never was much of a sailor.

56. Theseus is usually motivated either by another girl, a sense of patriotism, amnesia, or by Athene herself (see Jacobson, 227, n. 35).

57. "In Pæon, however, the Amathusian, there is a story given, differing from the rest. For he writes that Theseus, being driven by a storm upon the isle of Cyprus, and having aboard with him Ariadne, big with child, and extremely discomposed with the rolling of the sea, set her on shore, and left her there alone, to return himself and help the ship, when, on a sudden, a violent wind carried him again out to sea. That the women of the island received Ariadne very kindly, and did all they could to console and alleviate her distress at being left behind. That they counterfeited kind letters, and delivered them to her, as sent from Theseus, and, when she fell in labor, were diligent in performing to her every needful service; but that she died before she could be delivered, and was honorably interred. That soon after Theseus returned, and was greatly afflicted for her loss, and at his departure left a sum of money among the people of the island, ordering them to do sacrifice to Ariadne; and caused two little images to be made and dedicated to her, one of silver and the other of brass" (Plutarch, *The Lives of the Noble Grecians and Romans,* trans. by John Dryden [Chicago: W. Benton, 1952], 7).

concerns and unyielding to the complaints of Ariadne. But it might furnish Ariadne with enough material to justify her lament against the faithlessness of men at Catullus 64.132–201.

Volscus notes that some writers of glosses claim that there were two Ariadnes, the one that married Bacchus and the one Theseus abandoned; others claim that Ariadne committed suicide on Naxos or Dia. He adds that Ovid's version is in agreement with that of Diodorus Siculus: that Theseus was warned by Bacchus in a dream to leave Ariadne on Naxos (sig. g.vi^v). Morillon also gives this account of Theseus' motivation in his *argumentum*; as does Fontaine: Theseus acted "out of fear of going against the will of Bacchus" ("pour cause de creinte d'aller contre la volonté de Bacchus," 174). Boyd's Theseus uses this as his justification: he was commanded to leave, against his will, by Bacchus in a dream. "[Theseus] non potuit Bromio fortior esse deo" (Theseus could not be stronger than Bromius, a god) (37). Boyd's solution to Ariadne's problem with the postal service at Naxos is to have her letter conveyed by carrier pigeon, or rather, by the more appropriately heroic equivalent, the eagle ("Dictæi uolucris deliciosa Iouis" [the bird beloved of Cretan Jove]). His Theseus does not follow d'Amboise's example in blaming Ariadne. Instead he accuses Bacchus of orchestrating the entire episode. What chance did he have against the will of the gods? He takes his argument of diminished responsibility to its logical conclusion, claiming that it is hardly "uerisimile" to suppose that he would prefer to wed Phaedra instead of her more beautiful and noble sister Ariadne: therefore he cannot have done it deliberately.

Boyd takes the plight of the hero seriously; his heroes are more distinctively elegiac than his precursors' versions. Typically their language is peppered with interjections ("heu!"), lamenting apostrophes to the gods, and weeping. In Boyd's versions, the heroes weep as much as the heroines: Theseus describes the moment he was forced to leave the sleeping Ariadne: "Sæpe ubi discessi uictus mærore redibam, / Udaque sunt lachrymis uestra labella meis" (Often when I left I would return overwhelmed by sorrow, and your lips are wet with my tears) (40). When forced to set sail from Naxos, Theseus seeks time alone away from the crew of his ship, weeping and lamenting in elegiac solitude. The heroes reclaim their share of tears from the heroines: where in the *Heroides* tears had been multivalent symbols,[58] in Boyd's poetry tears are reduced to mere tokens of sincere suffering on the part of the hero-lover, a fundamentally un-Ovidian move.[59]

---

58. Tears can deceive (Jason's fake tears at 12.91) as well as guarantee faith (like blood, an actual part of the beloved imbued in the letter); they flow like words and they blot words.

59. As Rimell observes, in the *Ars Amatoria* men only use tears as tools of rhetorical persuasion

Not all of Boyd's heroes take on the role of the elegiac lover: his Protesilaus, for example, is more straightforwardly militaristic, scorning Laodamia's pleas to return. Laodamia's epistle was a profound exploration of elegiac absence; she played out obsessive fantasies of presence and fulfilment by conjuring up *imagines* and *simulacra* to compensate for the absence of her husband.[60] D'Amboise's Protesilaus fuels Laodamia's obsession. He imagines Laodamia constantly present at his side; but imagination is not the same as reality, he acknowledges, so a *letter* must be sent to supplement the work of fantasy. The letter, writes Protesilaus, can repair the deficiencies of imagination by imbuing it with solid reality. Like Ovid's Hero, Protesilaus eroticizes and fetishizes his lover's letter: he sleeps with it in place of her body, showering it with kisses. However, having indulged Laodamia's fantasies of presence, Protesilaus goes on to undermine them radically. Her vision of the first Greek death at Troy, he argues, is illusory. There are three kinds of dreams: realistic daydreams, such as the fantasy of being with an absent lover; dreams between sleep and waking, which convey only confused sensations and vague impressions; and true visions, as when a sacred figure or prophet appears to us. Had Laodamia's vision been of this third kind, she would have seen the death itself, rather than merely hearing an unspecific prediction. In any case, he goes on, dreams are untrustworthy, being simply repetitions of our daily thoughts. Protesilaus is no longer writing the language of amatory devotion: he is arguing for the need to accept the reality principle. The irony is striking: by the end of his letter, Protesilaus has comprehensively dismantled the very workings of Laodamia's coping mechanism.

Supporting the reading of d'Amboise's poems in a spirit of mockery, the two replies penned by Jason are brazenly contradictory. In his letter to Hypsipyle, Jason, protesting his undying love for her, gives an account of his exploits. He pointedly omits to mention Medea's help in his conquering of the fleece. Medea is first mentioned afterwards. He maintains that he did his best to resist her advances; however she used her magic to enchant him and to make him forget his vow to Hypsipyle. The whole of this defense is prefaced by a lengthy oath: Jason swears that he is telling the truth, under pain of death, dishonor, and destitution. Having sworn to tell the truth, he does nothing but lie. Parts of his letter to Medea directly contradict the version of events he gave in the earlier letter. There, he acknowledges Medea's help in the yoking of the bulls, the slaying of the band of warriors,

---

(2006, 135, n. 39).
60. See Hardie 2002, 132–37.

and the winning of the fleece. He admits that he married Medea because he was indebted to her. He has retained only a selective memory of his vow to Hypsipyle, since he tells of his marriage to Creusa soon after; Hypsipyle is never mentioned. His decision to leave Medea he justifies by blaming her for the cruel murder of his uncle Pelias. He omits to mention that Pelias was his enemy. Boyd's two Jasons are more honest, and less extravagant: in his letter to Hypsipyle he acknowledges Medea's help, and begs Hypsipyle's indulgence. In his second letter, Jason does his best to reason with Medea, but is interrupted while writing by a messenger, who brings news of the deaths of his sons, and of Creon and Creusa.

Jason's claim that he will "always remember" Hypsipyle ("beneficii hypsiphyles semper esse memorem") is a typical strategy of Boyd's heroes; Aeneas follows suit, reassuring Dido that he will never forget her ("Didonis . . . nunquam fore immemorem"). Virgil supplies much of the justificatory rhetoric of Aeneas: the speech Aeneas gives to Dido at *Aeneid* 4.333–61 is the starting point for all versions of the reply. D'Amboise combines it with a slightly modified account of events as described in books 1 and 5; Nicolas Heinsius composed a Latin version in 1646 which is really an extended adaptation for an elegiac meter of Virgil's parting scene. It is different from d'Amboise's version of the same letter in its setting: Aeneas has not left Carthage; he writes to Dido from the shore as his men prepare the ships for departure.[61]

The ending to Ovid's Deianira epistle (in which the heroine is informed of the death of the addressee) poses some difficulties for the composer of a response. Deianira continues to write even after she knows of Hercules' death. Few modern critics have been willing to forgive Ovid the absurdity of this conceit.[62] Golefer was to reject the idea of a response entirely on the grounds of *invraisemblance*. D'Amboise's Hercules, indeed, is perhaps the most absurd respondent in the collection. His epistle is by far the most misogynistic of d'Amboise's compositions: Deianira is made into a universal example of female cruelty and vanity. But the invective against women's deceptiveness and foolishness is framed by passages which paint Hercules as a Stoical "homme prudent" facing death with all the equanimity of a Socrates; and at the end, Hercules as a Christian Prince *avant la lettre*,

---

61. Raphael Lyne remarks that an English vernacular version of the Aeneas reply attributed to Isabella Whitney is different from every other version, in that it mobilizes a misogynistic "stereotypically male rhetoric" to attack Dido's character (156–57).

62. However, Jolivet, who deploys an intertextual reading which sets the epistle in the context of Sophocles' *Trachiniae*, argues that the addressee of the letter changes at this point: Deianira writes for her son Hyllus, who will be the first reader of her letter (184–85).

graciously forgiving Deianira because, he says, merciful clemency pleases the gods. Hercules even invokes Scriptural *exempla,* using Samson and David as examples of men whom women have deceived. Biblical references abound elsewhere in the *Contrepistres:* Hippolytus condemns Lot for his incestuous relationship with his daughters; an unrepentant Macareus cites Absalom and Thamar as an example of the strong bond between siblings in support of his own incestuous relationship with Canace. Unlike the versions of Sabinus or Boyd, d'Amboise's *Contrepistres,* by virtue of their sheer exuberance, easily accommodate *jeux d'esprit* of this kind.

Boyd is for the most part more straight-faced: his Hippolytus (fittingly enough, it must be said)[63] is a humorless prude. He tries to persuade Phaedra first by taking her to task on moral grounds, comparing her to her loathsome mother Pasiphae, and finally by putting forward legal arguments ("quod ne faciat metu legum Athenensium deterret" [he discourages her by saying she should not do it, for fear of the laws of Athens]). The rest of the letter is taken up with a self-righteous defense of his own virginity and dedication to the cult of Diana.

Boyd's Achilles proves to be more concerned with his own reputation than with love for Briseis ("sic totum scelus in Agamemnon retorquet, et se potius dignitatis suæ memorem quam amoris præbet" [So he deflects the whole blame on Agamemnon, and shows that he is more concerned with his own honor than with love]). This Achilles has little in common with the version portrayed in d'Amboise's *Contrepistres,* whose Achilles is a flatterer, prefiguring the Achilles of Racine as the "parfait galant."[64] Elegiac complaints about the pain of absence soon give way to the emotion most associated with Achilles, anger. In this regard Boyd's Achilles seems most responsive to Briseis's desire, if we follow Fulkerson's reading that Ovid's Briseis "places Achilles in the role of elegiac lover, but would clearly prefer him to be an epic warrior" (96). Most of the epistle of Boyd's Achilles is taken up with an attack on Agamemnon and his family. Achilles refuses to cede to the requests of Briseis, and orders her not to write again in support of the tyrant Agamemnon, slandering his own reputation. This Achilles is

---

63. Perhaps the most successful example of the *Heroides* reply poem in Latin was a response to the Phaedra epistle. Sidronius Hosschius, a seventeenth-century Jesuit author, composed a response in the person of a morally outraged Hippolytus. His Hippolytus is by turns pious, indignant, and bitterly sarcastic. J. A. Amar comments that the substance and style of the letter owe more to Seneca's *Phaedra* than to Ovid; Hosschius certainly relies more on moralistic aphorisms than witty word-play. This poem seems to have been the most successful of all the attempts to write replies to Ovid's heroines, excepting the Sabinus letters. At least four authors wrote vernacular imitations of the Hosschius poem (Dutch and French); it was printed in Amar's 1825 edition of the *Heroides* alongside the Sabinus replies, and Pieter Burman considered it the best of all efforts to write replies.

64. Cooper, 457.

hardly concerned at all with love; the Achilles of the *Contrepistres* could not be more lovelorn. That Achilles is effusive in his expressions of love for Briseis; he craves her "amitié loyalle"; she has stolen his heart; he longs to hear her voice, which soothes his soul like sweet music. There, too, Achilles attacks Agamemnon; but in comical terms. He imagines his "dame" Briseis sleeping alongside Agamemnon, a stinking, snoring "vieillart," "who does nothing but shiver and shake, cough, spit, and snore and sleep" ("Qui ne faict rien que trembler et fremir, / Tousser, cracher, et ronfler et dormir," sig. Ci^r).

Orestes and Lynceus both promise vengeance and assure their heroines that wrongs will be righted at the earliest opportunity. These heroes are not at fault, so there is less dramatic potential in their letters. Nevertheless, both of these stories proved popular among imitators of the *Heroides*. The German neo-Latin poet Jacobus Philomusus Locher penned a reply in the person of Orestes (1512). Locher's Orestes puts on an impressive display of bravado. Fresh from killing Aegisthus and Clytemnestra, he promises to avenge the wrongs done to Hermione by slaughtering Pyrrhus. As with Boyd's Orestes, the burning love he feels for Hermione is soon replaced by a burning desire to take revenge on Pyrrhus. The Dutch scholar and poet Janus Douza wrote a Latin reply from Lynceus to Hypermnestra (1569). Like Locher's poem, this one is based on a situation where the sanctity of the marriage bond is at stake. Lynceus briefly narrates the story of his escape from death, after Hypermnestra warned him of the plot her father and sisters were preparing. He laments the fact that he is impotent to avenge the deaths of his brothers and rescue his wife, wishing that he had died along with them. Finally he steels himself and swears that he will return to avenge the crime. Boyd's treatment of the Lynceus epistle is broadly similar. D'Amboise's version is entirely different, focusing as it does on the wifely loyalty and quasi-Christian virtues of Hypermnestra. It incorporates a lengthy mock-epic recapitulation of the Io story (the reason for Juno's wrath). Borrowing from the first book of the *Metamorphoses*, d'Amboise's Lynceus paints a burlesque portrait of Jupiter, the self-obsessed dandy, and Juno, the wily and manipulative wife. This digression is meant to demonstrate the importance of prudence in tempering the crazy impulses of desire; but the bizarre humor is entirely at odds with the stated message.

Boyd's Latin style in these letters is at times somewhat inconsistent with the subject matter; on occasion it might even have been judged unseemly by his contemporaries (as it surely was by Lord Hailes, two centuries later). Moreover, Boyd does not seem to have the same lightness of touch and sense of humor that d'Amboise had brought to his version. An example of Boyd's stylistic excesses comes in the Macareus letter:

> O soror ô coniunx ô impia iussa parentis.
> Quo feror? Ut ualeo! torqueor, uror, amo. (55)

> O sister, o wife, o unjust commands of a father! Whither I am I carried?
> Strong though I am! I writhe, I burn, I love.

Expressions such as this have much in common with contemporary French vernacular tragedies; the merging of the Ovidian epistle with the language of drama seems to prepare the way for what the *héroïde* was to become in the seventeenth and eighteenth centuries: essentially a tragic monologue.

Nevertheless, Boyd's poems do occasionally engage directly with Ovid's text. For example, in response to the epitaphs penned by Ovid's heroines, Boyd incorporates two epitaphs into his collection. The first closes the letter from Hercules to Deianira, and is suitably damning (Hercules writes the letter on his deathbed, as the poison seeps into his veins):

> Et cane dum memor es, Argiua per oppida tantum,
> Hæc duo de fato carmina scripta meo:
> Nec labor Alcidem, neque uis furiosa, nec ensis
> Uicit; at indigno fœmina ficta dolo. (55)

> Only sing, as long as you remember, through all the towns of Greece, these two verses written on my death: "Nor toil, nor frenzied violence, nor steel defeated Alcides; but a deceitful woman with a shameful ruse."

The epitaph convention is turned on its head in Phaon's letter: instead of writing his own epitaph, he rewrites Sappho's history, penning an alternative epitaph for her:

> Efficiam, Sappho, post impia funera tandem,
> Hæc pateant tumulo carmina bina tuo:
> Dum Phaon accelerans Sappho succurrit amanti
> Illa suo fato Parca Phaonis erat. (74)

> I shall see to it, Sappho, finally after your blasphemous death, that these two verses be on display on your tomb: "While Phaon hurried to come to his lover Sappho's aid, she by her death became Phaon's Fate."

In this, the final poem of the collection, Boyd's Phaon attempts to silence definitively the female voice. He denies the right of speech and self-determination to Sappho, Ovid's preeminent "lettered woman."[65]

In order to get a fuller sense of the relationship between the three texts, let us now compare the replies by Sabinus, d'Amboise and Boyd from a stylistic and thematic point of view. Unlike d'Amboise, Boyd does his best to avoid treating these subjects in the same way as the 'canonical' reply poems.

Ulysses to Penelope

In comparing the Latin reply poems with d'Amboise's *Contrepistres* we must take account of the role played by Saint-Gelais's translation in shaping the style of d'Amboise's compositions. Whereas Sabinus and Boyd are able to imitate Ovidian poetic expression closely within a linguistic and metrical scheme that matches Ovid's, the rhythms of d'Amboise's poem are very much in tune with Saint-Gelais's translation. The Sabinus composition opens with a point-by-point response to Penelope's arguments, a sequence of verbal echoes of the Ovidian original, with subtle modifications. Sabinus' Ulysses begins by breaking down the first couplet of Penelope's letter into its constituent units: "arguis ut lentum" (line 5); "nil tibi rescribam curae est" (11). Having answered these points he continues to dismantle Penelope's rhetoric: the accusatory "Troia iacet certe, Danais inuisa puellis" (*Heroides*.1.3) (Troy surely lies fallen, hated by Argive girls) takes on a slightly different emphasis in the reply: "Non me Troia tenet, Graiis odiosa puellis" (18) (Troy does not detain me, Troy detested by Greek girls), but echoes Penelope's poetic style. Ulysses even seems to suggest to Penelope some possible improvements in her poetic technique: he reduces her:

> iam seges est ubi Troia fuit, resecandaque falce
>   luxuriat Phrygio sanguine pinguis humus (1.53–54)

> Now there are cornfields where Troy once was, and the soil, made fertile by Phrygian blood, is overgrown with crops ready for the sickle

---

65. It is interesting to note that elsewhere in his writings Boyd would adopt a different position, arguing that women had a prior claim to literature. In his letter to Marie Tiraqueau, which is published in the 1592 volume, Boyd writes in praise of Marie's learning; he claims that in the past he had refused to recognize the achievements of the female sex, and had imagined that all the works attributed to learned women by the ancients were really composed by men; but now he sees that the right to compose poetry justly belongs to women, and that men have unfairly snatched it from them (163–67). Jean Brunel ("Un Ecossais") supplies a French translation of this letter.

to the more compact "iam cinis, et tantum flebile, Troia, solum" (18) (Now Troy is ash, and nothing but tear-soaked soil).

D'Amboise's opening is similar but more diffuse: it has none of the concision and density of the Latin. Obviously this is partly due to formal constraints: d'Amboise is not writing Latin elegiac couplets but French decasyllables, so when his Ulysses writes:

> Pareillement que ma longue demeure
> Te faict gemir et plourer a toute heure,
> Te faict mauldire et Paris et Heleine
> Ores par qui tu portes tant de peine
> Par qui tu es sans auoir les deduictz
> Qu'auecques moy eusses eu tant de nuictz . . . (sig. Aiii^r)

Likewise my long absence makes you sigh and weep constantly, makes you curse Paris and Helen both, who now cause you so much suffering, who deprive you of the delights you should have had with me for so many nights,

we inevitably hear the voice of Saint-Gelais's Penelope, rather than Ovid's, in the background:

> O pleust a dieu que le tresbeau paris
> Luy et ses gens fussent mors et peris
> Quant il passa la mer par grant alaine
> Pour entailler la gracieuse helaine
> Car sainsi fust froide dedans mon lict
> Ne fusse pas et seulle sans delict. (fol. ii^v)

Would to god that handsome Paris had perished and died along with all his kind when he crossed the sea at full sail to take away the beautiful Helen: because if that had happened, I would not be cold and alone and loveless in my bed.

The opening lines of Penelope's epistle set up an opposition between the "full presence" of physical proximity and the "absent presence" of the letter:

> Haec tua Penelope lento tibi mittit, Vlixe;
>   nil mihi rescribas attinet: ipse ueni! (1.1–2)[66]

---

[66]. Sixteenth-century editions generally read: "nil mihi rescribas: attamen ipse veni."

> Your wife Penelope sends you this letter, Ulysses, slow in coming; there is
> no need to write back to me: come in person!

The imperative "ipse ueni" is ironic,[67] since Ulysses might have already returned to Ithaca, but in disguise: present, but not "as himself." In the reply poems we get another Ulysses who is perhaps not present "as himself": here is a devoted husband who has never deceived his wife; this is not the devious Odysseus skilled in verbose dissimulation, but a model of reciprocal conjugal devotion. In ignoring Penelope's warning not to write back, Ulysses attempts to construct a coherent and morally sound representation of himself, a self contained within the boundaries of his text.

Boyd's Ulysses does not suspect or accuse Penelope of any wrongdoing in his absence. This Penelope is the exemplary faithful wife. In the very first line Penelope is "fida":

> Quæ tibi Dulichius fidæ rescribit amanti,
>   Ipse licet uenio, tu tamen illa lege. (11)

> This reply Dulichius [Ulysses] writes to you his faithful companion; though
> I am coming in person, read it nevertheless.

This is a straight inversion of *Heroides* 1.1–2: Ovid's Penelope had told Ulysses "Don't write back: come in person"; Boyd's Ulysses responds "Even though I am coming in person, read this letter all the same." The following lines respond directly to the fears Penelope had expressed in her letter: Ulysses denies that he has settled in a new homeland, and that a new bride makes him forgetful of his old life. He then proceeds to apostrophize the adverse winds, seas and gods for the next thirty lines, bemoaning the anger of Neptune and appealing to Thetis to remember his good service to her son, Achilles. At line 38 he addresses Penelope once again ("o pia Penelope") and goes on to claim that he alone deserves the credit for the fall of Troy, and so he alone has borne the brunt of the gods' wrath. Boyd's Ulysses is alternately the self-aggrandizing, crafty Ulysses, and a self-pitying autoflagellating Ulysses. He laments the consequences of the war in a tone better suited to the elegiac lover than to the epic hero: this Ulysses bemoans the cruelty of the gods and the fates in the same way that the subject of elegy bemoans the cruelty of Amor.

The Ulysses replies match Penelope's model of wifely devotion with the model of a devoted husband, whose prime concern is with "the love that a

---

67. Hardie (107, n.4) makes this point, further commenting that "in Ovid the word *ipse* often signals a problematization of selfhood."

man owes his wife" ("l'amytié qu'homme doibt à sa femme"). Howard Jacobson (243–76) proposes a reading of Ovid's poem according to which Ovid's Penelope is not the straightforward paradigm she is in Homer; the Ovidian creation is possessed of a greater psychological complexity.[68] The Sabinus poem takes account of this other side to Ovid's Penelope:[69] his Ulysses does not seem entirely confident that his wife will be able to rebuff the suitors, asking himself where her eye wanders when she looks up from her tapestry. D'Amboise, on the other hand, makes Ulysses correct Penelope's deviations from the paradigm. In the scheme of d'Amboise's poem, the ambiguities of Ovid's Penelope are resolved into the dominant tradition of the "faithful, chaste, and good" Penelope.

The purpose of the Ulysses letter is to satisfy Penelope's desire, to create the illusion of presence. Thus for d'Amboise's and Sabinus' Ulysses all the obstacles exist only in the natural world (seas, winds, monsters, etc.); there is no psychological barrier. The suggestion throughout is that physical obstacles will be overcome: here we are not in the realm of elegy, and Ulysses is not the *exclusus amator*. Desire *can* be fulfilled. We see this in Ulysses' fantasy of return, a narrative shift into the future tense:

> Et s'il aduient, que par trop d'ans passez
> En ton visaige y ayt rides assez,
> Tu pourras voir aussi et sans faintise
> Toute ma barbe estre maintenant grise
> [. . .]
> Mais toutesfois que ie soys deuenu
> Caducque, vieil, et de mon poil chenu,
> Si esse bien que l'amour que te porte
> Autant ou plus est en cest aage forte,
> Qu'en ma ieunesse elle estoit et sans faille
> Quoy que vieillesse a present me travaille,
> Penelopé dame tant bien famee
> Est de Vlixes autant, et plus aymee
> Qu'elle fut onc . . . (sig. Avii^v)

And if after so many years your face is all wrinkled, you'll see too, and no lie,

---

68. According to Jacobson, this departure from the *Odyssey*-based Penelope partakes of a counter-tradition which makes Penelope into a sluttish adulteress, and the mother of Pan (see 246–49).

69. Sabinus borrows much of his material from Homer; but he evidently also uses other sources, for example, for the allusion to the feigned madness of Ulysses, which is not mentioned in Homer. As Pendergast points out, many detractors of the Sabinus poems have condemned them for their excessive use of obscure mythology, though he himself denies this criticism (253).

that my beard is now completely grey . . . But even though I have become
frail and old and hoary-haired, still that love I have for you is as strong or
stronger at this time in my life, as it was in my youth, and assuredly, even
though old age now plagues me, my lady Penelope, who is so celebrated, is
loved by Ulysses as much as, or more than she ever was . . .

D'Amboise's Ulysses holds the conviction that it is enough for husband
and wife to look each other in the face with a reciprocal desiring gaze for
the idealized love of their youth to be restored in its fullness.[70] For Ovid's
heroines, such satisfaction of desire is never possible.

In lines 75ff of Boyd's epistle, Ulysses recounts his descent to the Underworld, and his encounters with various heroes. He meets with Agamemnon, a fresh victim of wifely infidelity:

> Et memini frendens dextram mihi dixit in aurem,
>   'Si sapis a Stygia doctior ibis aqua.
> Nec cadat incauto, neque lethi exsorbeat unda,
>   Desertæ nullam coniugis esse fidem.'
> Sed cito respondi: 'tua si mihi Tyndaris esset:
>   At iacet in stratis Icariana meis.' (14; punctuation mine)

> And, I recall, gnashing his teeth he said in my right ear: "If you are wise
> you will go away from the waters of the Styx forewarned: let it not befall
> you unawares, and let not the Lethe's wave swallow it up: an abandoned
> wife has no fidelity." But quickly I replied: "If your wife Clytemnestra were
> mine: but it is Penelope who lies in my bed."

Agamemnon's warning, that no wife left alone will remain faithful, is countered by Ulysses: he is not married to Clytemnestra, but to Penelope.[71] This is an appeal to *ethos:* how could Penelope possibly deviate from her role as the epitome of wifely devotion? That, after all, is her role in the discourse of exemplarity. Boyd's Ulysses is anxious to assert the certainty of this fact: that Penelope will always remain *that* Penelope, and never the other Penelope.

---

70. D'Amboise's Ulysses has obviously read his own story in the *Odyssey:* in Book 23 (lines 174–78), Athene restores Odysseus' youth on his return to Ithaca. However, the cunning hero has turned a blind eye to the less convenient details (Penelope will not recognize him at first sight; he will have to depart from Ithaca once more to fulfill the prophecy of Tiresias).

71. Boyd's account is based on Agamemnon's words to Odysseus at *Odyssey* 11.499–518. There, however, Agamemnon himself assures Odysseus that Penelope would never behave as Clytemnestra did. Nevertheless, his advice to Odysseus to return to Ithaca incognito since a woman can never be trusted suggests that even Penelope is not above reproach.

In lines 82ff, Ulysses responds to the news that the suitors have taken over in his absence. Entertaining only briefly some doubts about the fidelity of Penelope, he quickly reassures himself that Penelope will resist their advances, making use of an elegiac—or perhaps more specifically Catullan—lexicon:

> O decor, ô facies, ô sole tepentior annus,
>   O data furtiuo tempora tuta toro.
> Cur tamen hæc timeo? (subiit quoque) pono timorem:
>   Penelope fueras, non leuis uxor eras. (14)

> O beauty, o charm, o year warmer than the sun, O time granted to indulge a secret love. But why do I fear these things? (this too has occurred to me) I put aside my fear: you had been Penelope, you were not a fickle wife.

Such thoughts prompt a crisis of self-doubt in this Ulysses. He recalls his own infidelities, and offers himself up to be punished by Penelope. He imagines his return to Ithaca and the moment when husband and wife will be reunited. He asks that she strike him with physical violence when he returns. There is a certain erotic undertone:

> Tunc reus Aeolides noxæ dedetur inermis,
>   Et si conueniat corpore nudus erit:
> Et licet insultes, & tela minantia sumas,
>   Non metuet bilem dura puella tuam.
> Carcer erit thalamus, fient tua brachia casses,
>   Ac eris in poenas ingeniosa meas.

> Then Ulysses, stripped of his arms, will give himself up to be tried for his crime, and if it please the court, his body will be naked. And though you kick at him, and take up threatening weapons, he will not fear, hard-hearted girl, your anger. My prison cell will be a bed, your arms will become my fetters, and you will be ingenious in devising my punishments.

In Ulysses' fantasy, torture and sex become indistinguishable. He will present himself, naked, to be punished by the "dura puella." Her embrace will ensnare him in the prison of the marriage bed, where she will devise all manner of "punishments" for him.[72] The tone recalls Ovid's pleading with

---

72. At this point in the manuscript (NLS MS. 20759) the bottom section of the page has been torn out, perhaps by some censorious individual disapproving of this overtly erotic section of the

Corinna to punish him for a transgression in *Amores* 1.7: though the violence is all the more sexually charged.[73] Boyd's Ulysses goes on to end his letter on a more threatening, militaristic note, where Sabinus and d'Amboise had ended on an affirmation of Ulysses' love for his wife.

Demophoon to Phyllis

Treatments of the Demophoon epistle differ in narrative setting and in the motivation attributed to the writer. Although titled as a reply, Sabinus' second letter seems to have been written by Demophoon before he received Phyllis' communication. This device immediately solves the narrative problems to which Ovid himself alludes at *Amores* 2.18.32, where the suggestion is that Phyllis would not have lived long enough to receive a reply. Here, Demophoon remains unaware of Phyllis' suicide, and is able to construct his self-justification around elements of the myth which are "off-screen" in Phyllis' version. Raphael Lyne notes that Demophoon comes to understand as he writes that Phyllis is to commit suicide, and eventually decides that he will not return: "This poem questions the validity of its own presence in the story" (148). Moreover, Sabinus' Demophoon displays a remarkable familiarity with the content of a letter he has not read.

The other versions are indeed replies, and this difference has far-reaching consequences: where d'Amboise's and Boyd's Demophoons must focus their rhetorical energies on rewriting Phyllis' words to correct her perspective, Sabinus' Demophoon can be concerned primarily with his own rehabilitation.

Sabinus' epistle resounds with verbal echoes of Ovid. These are inexplicable at the level of narrative, since Demophoon has not read Phyllis' letter; he seems, though, to have read his Ovid. He insidiously appropriates Phyllis' rhetoric, and gives his own bias to the moral concepts that formed the basis of her lament. Now it is Demophoon whose "patria" takes precedence; his dalliance ("mora") with Phyllis was the cause of strife in Athens; now it is time for him to forget his past weaknesses and fulfill manly responsibilities. He reproaches himself for his effeminate behavior in remaining silent and passive when duty called.

---

poem. The first page of the Ulysses poem is also missing from the MS, so readers of this version will enter the letter's narrative *in medias res,* as it were.

73. As Duncan Kennedy comments (on *Amores* 1.7): "The elegiac lover's self-styled 'enslavement' to his mistress needs to be seen in the light of this pleasure in sexual aggression and domination" (Kennedy 1993, 56).

The closing lines of the poem contain the most striking verbal echo: Demophoon sends his letter on its way with the words:

> Nunc uenti mea uerba ferant, qui uela tulerunt.
>   Est animus reditus; sed pia causa tenet. (49)

> Now let the winds that bore my sails bear my words. My intention is to return; but a righteous cause detains me,

which dismantle Phyllis' rhetoric:

> Demophoon, uentis et uerba et uela dedisti;
>   uela queror reditu, uerba carere fide. (2.25–26)

As we saw in the previous chapter, the wordplay and precision of the Latin phrase posed problems for the French translators; and d'Amboise does not tackle it. But his Demophoon ends his letter with a similar rhetorical trick. His closing lines echo *Heroides* 2.147–48 rather than 25–26, but the rhetorical procedure is unmistakably the same. Moreover, the closing lines:

> Phyllis d'aymer le moyen inuenta
> Et Demophoon apres l'executa (sig. Bvi^r)

> Phyllis discovered the means to love, and then Demophoon acted on it

perhaps owe more to Saint-Gelais's:

> Cy gist Phyllis [. . .]
> Dont de ce crime et mal quelle porta
> Il bailla lheure, et el lexecuta (fol. xi^r)

> Here lies Phyllis: for the crime and the wrong she bore, he supplied the cause and she acted on it

than they do to the Latin original.

In d'Amboise's version, Demophoon's task in writing back is rather more pressing than Ulysses', in that he has to contend with a particularly tricky obstacle to desire: the death of his lover. Phyllis' own letter is shot through with the knowledge of her own death, from the conviction that Demophoon has forgotten her name and therefore obliterated her (2.105), to the writing of her own epitaph (2.147–48). Demophoon's words are meant to confer presence, to "ressurect" her, through affirmation of his promise to return. But Demophoon seems to have the same concerns as Ovid's Penelope about the insubstantial presence afforded by a letter: he admits that the writing of a letter is a poor substitute for his actual arrival and the completion of their marriage vows:

> Que pleust à dieu que i'eusse le loysir,
> Le temps propice et le vent a plaisir
> Ie ne ferois n'y epistre ny [*sic*] lettre
> Ains au chemin ie me vouldrois tost mettre
> Pour t'aller voir, et les nopces parfaire
> Que i'ay promis auecques toi de faire. (sig. Aviii^v)

> Would that it were god's will to grant me the time, favorable weather, and a following wind: I would not write an epistle or letter, but would immediately set out to come and find you and complete our marriage vows, as I promised you I would do.

Later, he expands on this idea, imagining a situation in which his bodily presence would take the place of his letter: if it were possible,

> Tu me verrois plustost en ta maison
> Que mon epistre, affin qu'eusse achoison,
> De rappaiser le tien cueur mal content
> Et d'esiouyr le mien qu'il est autent
> A celle fin que ton desir aduint
> Et que le mien pareil au tien deuint. (sig. Biii^r)

> You would see me in your house and not my letter, so that I might have the opportunity to relieve your heart of its distress, and to bring joy to my own heart in its distress, in order that your desire be fulfilled, and that my own be mutual with yours.

This fantasy posits the fulfilment of desire through parity, the perfect alignment of subject and object.

D'Amboise's Demophoon is mainly concerned with offering Phyllis a model for proper behavior: effectively showing her how a Christian woman ought to comport herself. This is done through reference to other exemplary myths which stand adjacent to his own, and which appear in the

Heroides: Theseus, Demophoon's father, is defended against the charges Phyllis had leveled; Phaedra, Demophoon's stepmother, lurks in the background as an admonition against female lust. Here the treatment of the *Heroides* in education as moral example and negative example is introduced into the fictional space itself: Demophoon is made to speak the words of the moralizing exegete. Answering Phyllis' jibe at *Heroides* 2.75–80, Demophoon asserts:

> Puis que de vice ores mon pere accuse
> C'est bien raison Phylis que ie l'excuse
> [...]
> Or maintenant que iugement soit faict
> Si Theseus mon pere a rien meffaict,
> Abandonner une femme yurongnesse
> Sans luy tenir loyaulté ou promesse,
> Certes ie croy que les femmes de bien
> Diront que non, car en femme n'est rien,
> Plus vicieulx et plus a vergonger,
> Qu'est le trop boire, et le trop yurongner. (Bii^{r-v})

Since you now accuse my father of wrongdoing, it is only right, Phyllis, for me to defend him [...] and so let it be judged whether my father Theseus did anything wrong in abandoning a drunken woman and failing to keep faith and his promise: I strongly believe that good women will say not, because there is nothing more sinful or more shameful in a woman than drinking too much, and excessive drunkenness.

Ariadne is characterized as a drunken slattern (presumably because of her association with Bacchus), and Theseus' responsibility toward her is therefore absolved. Demophoon's defense, couched in terms that relate it to universal law, is intended to render Phyllis a docile, compliant subject.

Demophoon manipulates and reshapes Phyllis' words to serve the ends of a masculine rhetoric. This is most evident in the final lines of the poem, in which Phyllis' epitaph—words which attest the ultimate absence, Phyllis' own desire for death—is recast by d'Amboise's Demophoon as an expression of reciprocal, fulfilled desire (quoted above). The act of writing her own epitaph had been a *prise de parole,* a paradoxical mastery of her destiny through the claim to be the active player, to seize the "upper hand":

> PHYLLIDA DEMOPHOON LETO DEDIT HOSPES AMANTEM
> ILLE NECIS CAVSAM PRAEBVIT IPSA MANVM. (2.147–48)

DEMOPHOON, A GUEST, BROUGHT DEATH TO HIS LOVER
PHYLLIS.
HE FURNISHED THE CAUSE, SHE THE HAND BY WHICH DEATH
CAME.

Demophoon's version of the epitaph denies the words their performative power: it imposes a structure which affirms, rather than denies, the possibility of fulfilment. Moreover, Demophoon has reappropriated the role of active doer, relegating Phyllis to the secondary role: in this scheme, she supplied the "means" for him to love by being the passive object of desire; it was he who "executed" the act of loving.

Boyd's Demophoon is, by contrast, caught up in the conventions of elegy. He characterizes Phyllis as the "dura puella"; her letter as "tua callida littera." But Phyllis is both "callida" and "stulta" at the same time: Boyd's Demophoon clearly anticipates that Phyllis is to become "the canonical example of *amor stultus*" when he makes her murderous hands "foolish," by hypallage: "A gemina stultas subtrahe cæde manus" (16) (Stay your foolish hand from a double murder). And Phyllis herself, like the elegiac *puella*, embodies a contradiction:

> Eheu quam duros sub amico pectore mores,
>   Et non detectos fœmina mollis habet. (16)

> Alas, how hard the nature that woman, weak though she appears, keeps hidden behind a friendly disposition.

The incompatibility of the gender-specific epithets "durus" and "mollis" speaks of female duplicity: a "soft," feminine exterior masks a "hard," masculine inner nature. Phyllis, like Penelope in the previous letter, is repeatedly addressed as "dura puella" and "immitis": Demophoon accuses her of being cold to his grief for his father, Theseus (although of course Ovid's Phyllis knows nothing of Theseus' death). Demophoon, now the elegiac lover to Phyllis' "dura puella," reclaims his share of tears: he imagines himself weeping profusely as he returns to prove his faith to Phyllis ("Demophoon quando lachrymans descendet ab alto, / Et curres teneram læta datura manum . . . " [When Demophoon will sail back from across the sea, and you will run, overjoyed, to offer him your tender hand . . .], 17); and relates how his family and friends in Athens had ridiculed the tears he wept for her ("Cum mea ridebant spirantia uota parentes, / Cum frater lachrymas luderet ipse meas" [When my parents were mocking my sighing prayers, when even my brother ridiculed my tears], 19).

In Phyllis' letter, Demophoon had been "perfidus"; in his reply he constructs himself, again and again, as "fidus": "percipies fidum Demophoonta tuum" (you will possess your faithful Demophoon). Where Phyllis had complained that Demophoon's words and sails lacked faith, Demophoon reshapes the figure, resolving to sail into port a metonymical "faithful ship" ("fida carina").

Boyd has Demophoon pleading diminished responsibility, and using various rhetorical ploys to persuade Phyllis not to commit suicide. He argues that his own tardiness, though irritating, is hardly grounds for such drastic action on her part, and that he ought not to be judged the "author of her death": the phrase "Si pereat Phyllis [Demophoon] funeris autor erit?" (If Phyllis dies, will Demophoon be the author of her death?) answers Phyllis' epitaph, but also echoes Dido's "funeris auctor eris" (you will be the author of my death) at 7.136. His rhetoric mirrors the rhetoric used by Phyllis to condemn him: she had used the anaphora figure to emphasize the falseness of his vows (2.35ff.); now he uses the same language to plead with her and to dissuade her from suicide:

> Per superos, mea lux. per patria numina, quæso
>   Per modo quæ celerem prouehit aura ratem,
> Perque opus exactum, per lecti uincula, Phylli . . . (16)

By the gods above, my darling, my my ancestral spirits, I pray, by the ship which the wind bears along swiftly, by the task I have completed, by the bonds of the marriage bed, Phyllis . . .

His failure to return is to be blamed on adverse fate; he did not have the power to change the wind's direction. Demophoon's conclusion to the letter is threatening rather than comforting: "When I return as your faithful husband," he writes, "let's hope you'll have repented of your mistake":

> Et sic mansueta, ut fido ueniente marito,
>   Te uideat culpæ penituisse tuæ. (19)

And [you will be] so tamed, that when your faithful husband returns, he may see that you have repented of your sin.

Earlier, he had answered Phyllis' character attack based on paternal heritage by pointing out its logical inconsistencies:

Finge, quod ingenuam linquebat in aequore Theseus,
    Quid tamen ad mores efficit ille meos?
Non ubi peccarunt sequimur uestigia patrum
    Pignora, sed puris facta probata diis.
Undique si patrem retulissent semina, quare
    Non meretrix Pallas? Cressus adulter erat.
Sed neque faemineo comperta in crimine Pallas,
    Nec pater ad uetitos desinit ire toros.
Desine plura queri; quicquid tibi suaserit alter,
    Percipies fidum Demophoonta tuum;
Quicquid & extincti dederint mihi semina Thesei,
    Et quicquid genitrix Cressa puella dedit.
Si tibi pollicitum, iurataque numina fallam,
    Edicar culpa perfidus esse mea:
Nec pater ex nostro plectetur crimine: patris
    Cur ego delicto percutiendus ero? (lines 35–50)

Imagine, just because Theseus abandoned an innocent girl at sea, what does he have to do with my own conduct? We offspring follow not the footsteps of our ancestors when they have sinned, but only deeds that have been approved by the faultless gods. If offspring always take after the father, why is Pallas not a harlot? Cretan Jove was an adulterer. But Pallas was never convicted of a woman's crimes, nor does her father cease from visiting forbidden beds. Cease complaining further: whatever another might have advised you, you will realize that your Demophoon is faithful, whatever the seed of my dead father Theseus might have given me, and whatever the Cretan girl, my mother, gave. If I should betray my promise, and the gods I swore by, let me be called "treacherous" through my own fault: and let not my father be punished for a crime that is mine: why must I be flogged for a fault that is my father's?

He uses counter *exempla* to undermine the role of *exempla* in demonstrative rhetoric: he seems to be saying that *exempla* cannot persuade, and that the argument from race is false. The paternal heritage attack, a staple of invective in heroic discourse from Homer onwards, had become an intrinsic part of the abandoned woman complaint which had developed, with its origins in the *Heroides*, into a literary genre all of its own.[74] Boyd's heroes dismantle

---

74. Such is the standard use of the paternal influence argument by Ovid heroines. One varia-

this structure and reconfigure the relations invoked by the heroines in their accusations. They undermine the very viability of the technique itself by deploying a wholly different reading of the paternal *exemplum*. It seems that in order for the heroes to reply to the heroines' letters, the poet-imitator must pull apart the very substance of the genre into which they are placed; must unpick the standard strategies of rhetorically aware writing. The imitator must deploy an essentially *unpoetic* reading of poetic text. The reply epistle is anti-poetry.

Paris to Oenone

D'Amboise's treatment of the Paris epistle proves that the French poet did indeed have the Sabinus poems in mind when composing his *Contrepistres*. The opening lines of Sabinus' version are translated fairly closely (with some expansion) by d'Amboise:

> Quæ satis apta tibi tam juste, Nympha, querenti
>   Rescribam, fateor quærere uerba manum;
> Quærit, nec subeunt; sentit sua crimina tantum;
>   Soluere quæ sentit non sinit alter amor. (115)

I confess, my hand seeks the right words to answer your fully justified complaint, Nymph; it seeks them, but they do not come; it knows the crimes it commited; but another love does not allow it to express what it feels.

> Lors que i'euz veu propos, termes & tiltre
> De ta tant iuste, & raisonnable epistre,
> Pour te respondre, ainsi que ton espoux
> Ma main cerchoit conuenables propos,

---

tion on the paternal heritage attack—particularly prominent in the discourse of the abandoned woman—is the claim that the hero was spawned by wild beasts, monsters, the sea, or rocks: see for example *Heroides* 10.131–32. This goes back to Virgil's Dido (*Aen.* 4.365–67), Catullus's Ariadne (64.154–57), and ultimately to Homer (*Iliad* 16.34). Phaedra even turns the argument on herself, explaining her own fatal character in terms of the unlawful or bizarre sexual practices associated with her ancestors (*Heroides* 4.53–66). It seems that the heroes, however, have a different set of arguments available to them. In one of Ovid's own reply epistles, Paris deploys the argument in trying to persuade Helen to cede to his advances: "uix fieri, si sunt uires in semine morum, / et Iouis et Ledae filia casta potes" (16.293). This is not without irony, as in the following lines Paris hopes that Helen *will* fail to take after her parents—but not before she is with him in Troy. See also Fulkerson, *The Ovidian Heroine as Author*, on the importance of familial relationships in the heroines' community of readers and writers: family ties often point up allusive structures.

En les cerchant trouuer ne les pouuoye
Tant de tristesse, et de douleur i'auoye,
[. . .]
Selon laquelle or t'eusse respondu
Si autre amour ne me l'eust deffendu. (sig. Dv^{r-v})

When I saw the subject, terms and theme of your most fair and reasonable letter, to reply to you, even as your husband, my hand sought fitting words, and seeking them could not find any, so much sorrow and pain did I have. . . . Accordingly still I would have replied, if another love had not prevented me.

Paris concedes from the very start that his actions were indefensible and that Oenone's letter is unanswerable. Boyd's Paris differs in that he does not admit the justness of Oenone's charges so readily. He takes a predictable line, arguing that Amor is to blame for the whole episode, not he. Dispensing with the formal salutation, he opens his letter on a note of indignation:

Quid facis Oenone? Paridi sua crimina prodis?
   An licet in causis arbiter esse meis? (29)

What are you doing, Oenone? You charge Paris with his crimes? Is my case not to be allowed a judge?

The reference to a "judgment of Paris" wittily alludes to the episode that set the whole tragedy in motion. Paris goes on to describe at some length his suffering at the hands of a merciless Cupid and as a slave to Fate. To justify his actions he supplies *exempla* of other gods and heroes who failed to stick with their first girlfriend: Jupiter and Hercules in particular. Paris concludes the letter by laying the blame squarely at the feet of Cupid, the "puer Gnydius, tenerum moderator amorum" (The boy of Cnidos, master of tender love) (33). We might read this as an allusion to Ovid, the self-described "tenerorum lusor amorum" (one who trifled with tender love) (*Tristia* 4.10.1). It would be a neatly "Ovidian" touch were Boyd's Paris to blame Ovid—the poet and architect of his situation—for his plight.

Given the tone of Paris's love-letter to Helen in the second part of Ovid's *Heroides,* it would seem that Paris finds himself in a uniquely difficult position, condemned in advance by his own words. Might we expect a humorous replay of *Amores* 2.7 and 2.8, in which the elegist protests his innocence in convincing terms and promptly reveals his deception in the following letter?

There is a further difficulty in that Ovid sets aside certain aspects of the myth that make Oenone the violently jealous vengeful lover.[75] D'Amboise's Paris is not in a comfortable position; as it turns out, his self-justification generally works along the lines of the old standard: "The gods compelled me to it, despite myself" ("Les dieux m'y ont maulgré moy efforcé"). Like Demophoon he has recourse to universal law of heroic destiny in his defense:

> O Oenone ie congnois seurement
> Que l'homme est fol qui promet largement
> Et mesmement de la chose future
> Car si la tient, ce n'est que d'aduenture,
> Par dessus nous sont les dieux qui nous voient
> Qui noz desirs, & volontez foruoient,
> Et nous conduisent contre nostre desir [*sic*]
> Ou il leur plaist à leur vueil et plaisir. (sig. Dvi^r)

O Oenone, I know for certain that the man who makes promises too freely is a fool, especially about the future, because if he grasps it, it is only fleetingly. Above us are the gods who look down on us: they make our desires and wishes go astray, and lead us against our will wherever they please, for their own amusement.

Ovid's Oenone remembered Paris' vow to love her until the river Xanthus flowed backwards. In this account Paris carved the Xanthus *adynaton* into a tree, an act which in her eyes made the vow binding. But d'Amboise's Paris, unlike Acontius, is oblivious to the binding force of oaths: he claims that since he made the vow orally, he can modify or retract it, and combines this claim with an implicit condemnation of Oenone. In an inversion of the Acontius-Cydippe exchange, here it is Paris who reproves Oenone for twisting language to her own ends. Even if Oenone's magic charms have the same power to effect change in the world as Acontius' apple-message, her words are deemed to have no legitimacy in the masculine discourse. Paris concludes his argument with a neat twist on the Xanthus figure, borrowed from Sabinus:[76]

---

75. See Jacobson (176–77) for an account of this tradition.

76. The majority of d'Amboise's closing lines are imitated from Sabinus, including the section on Oenone's magical powers (with minor alterations: bulls become sheep and wolves stand in for lions) and the witticism based on the "split-divinity":

> Quid retro Xanthum, retro Simoenta uocatum
>   Adjiciam cursus non tenuisse suos?

Tu faiz tourner Xanthus contre ses sources
Toutes les fois qu'à luy tu te courrouces,
Tu faiz ton pere en son cours retarder
Quand il te plaist, et puis retrograder. (sig. Eiiii^v)
You make Xanthus reverse his flow whenever you get angry with him; you make your father halt in his tracks whenever you wish, and then go back.

Here Oenone is characterized as a spoiled girl who has her father (the river-god Cebren) twisted around her little finger. Paris is unwilling to grant the possibility that Oenone's words can connect with and influence "the way things really are."[77] Instead of offering—as Ulysses and Demophoon do—a corrective discourse which guarantees presence, Paris mobilizes a masculine discourse which denies Oenone access to reality: effectively he pushes her out of the mythic narrative.

One rhetorical effect of which Boyd seems particularly fond is anacoluthon: very often the flow of the hero's speech hesitates, falters, begins again. For example, Boyd has his Paris write: "Sed nunc deficio sed nunc mea funera cerno . . ."[78] (29) (But now I am fading, but now my death is in sight . . .) Ovid himself had put this kind of effect to use in conveying a sense of the heroines' indecision. Boyd's heroes are clearly not writing responses to reassure or mollify the heroines, the role d'Amboise had claimed for his heroes. Their language reflects their faltering resolve; perhaps even subverts their heroic stories in much the same way that Ovid's work had subverted the heroines' mythological narratives. Paris' uncertainty in his self-interrogation suggests a lack of control over his own words, and the nagging suspicion that he has bitten off more than he can chew (very unlike the over-confident Paris of *Heroides* 16): "Ast ego quid meditor? quid opus mihi talibus armis? / An Paris in tanto crimine solus erit?" (But what am I

Ipse pater Cebren, natæ male tutus ab ore
    Cantatas quoties restitit inter aquas! (120–21)

Why should I add that you called Xanthus and Simois backward from their normal course? How many times did your father Cebren, himself not immune to his daughter's words, halt spellbound in the midst of his waters!

The third line is Amar's reading. Sixteenth-century editions have the line "Ipse pater, seu rem natæ male tutus haberet," which makes little sense.

77. But Oenone's words at *Heroides* 5.31 ("Xanthe, retro propera, uersaeque recurrite lymphae" [Xanthus, rush backwards, turn your waters and reverse their flow]) can be seen to affect the real world: Achilles will cause the waters of the Xanthus to flow backwards at *Iliad* 21.305–84 (see Fulkerson, 58).

78. A similar line appears in the manuscript version of Demophoon's letter, though not in the printed text: "Sed nunc decipior sed nunc mea funera cerno / Nunc uideo uitæ tela parata meæ" (But now I am deceived, but now my death is in sight; now I see the weapons that will end my life).

thinking? Why should I have need of such weapons? Will Paris be the only one charged with such a great offence?) (32). Paris expects the answer to that question to be in the negative, and he goes on invoke the infidelities of Jove and other divinities as justification for his own. His allusion to Hercules spinning for Omphale suggests that he himself is unashamed to be called effeminate, and it is his powerlessness that is emphasized throughout: unable to resist the will of the gods or to control his own destiny, he is entirely unlike the rhetorically assured Paris that emerges from most sixteenth-century readings of *Heroides* 16.

Conclusions

Michel d'Amboise's *Contrepistres d'Ovide*, far from being straightforward imitations of Ovid's *Heroides*, are situated within a complex tradition of reply-poems. The text by Sabinus had been absorbed into the Ovidian *corpus:* in the sixteenth century, Sabinus' replies had almost the same authority and influence as Ovid's own works. D'Amboise clearly had the Sabinus replies in mind when composing his *Contrepistres*, even though the two versions are on the whole very different structurally. Moreover, Saint-Gelais's popular 1500 translation of the *Heroides*—itself instrumental in the creation of the *épître* and *élégie* genres in the first half of the century—influenced d'Amboise's style as much as Ovid's original text. The *Contrepistres* themselves are of indeterminate status: literary parody or failed attempt to "write like Ovid"? Witty *divertissement* or serious *débat* text? The problems posed by Ovid's original letters are never resolved, despite the respondents' best attempts. A reply text might attempt to "short-circuit" the workings of desire by superimposing a discourse which resolves the ambiguities of the Ovidian subject and fixes the receding object of desire within a definitive system of moral absolutes. In so doing, however, the author succeeds only in conveying a sense of the singularity of subjective experience, and opening out the play of presence and absence which forms the basis for the Ovidian text.

D'Amboise's and Boyd's versions represent fundamentally different approaches to the text. D'Amboise privileges the parodic, humorous aspect: his stated intent to restore order to the fragmented narratives of the heroines and to make possible the mutual satisfaction of desire is played out in the *Contrepistres* in tongue-in-cheek style. Boyd's heroes generally write in a more distinctively elegiac mode: their emphasis is on the impossibility of satisfaction of desire. Subject to forces beyond their control, the heroes weep tears of despair as they lament their lost loves. On the other hand, Boyd's heroes can also be anti-elegiac: his militaristic Achilles is unconcerned with love; Orestes burns with the thirst for revenge. Anger replaces love as the driving emotion; but the tone remains largely the same. Their epistles move toward identification with the tragic monologue, but they are deprived of universal significance: as is the case with Ovid's *Heroides,* their basis is the reduction of the mythological narrative to the emotional reality of a certain character at a certain moment in time.

These two approaches to imitation of the *Heroides* mirror the two sides of epistolary elegy as practiced by Ovid: on the one hand the playful, parodic deflation of the language of epic and tragedy; and on the other the serious, realistic representation of the emotions and of the psychopathology of love.

A major feature of the heroes' epistles is that they must be for the most part *wrong*—wrong in their optimism, wrong about how things will turn out, wrong in their protestations of innocence, wrong in their denials that the heroines are right. Since Ovid's epistles rely in large part on devices of dramatic irony and foreshadowing—on a foreknowledge on the part of the reader about how the story will turn out—the heroines' fears and threats are usually fully aligned with the outcome of the story that is familiar.[79] The heroes, however, must deny all this, must effectively deny the truth of the mythological narrative itself—they must make themselves look foolish, or deceitful. Therefore the overturning of the structures upon which the *Heroides* are predicated cannot take place *within* the framework of the mythological narrative Ovid constructed; it must be at one remove, at the level of the secondary author—Boyd the poet engaging in *aemulatio* with Ovid, rather than the letter-writing hero engaging with the heroine's argument. The poet who replies confronts his model, his text is set against the source text in a relation of antagonism, and the mechanisms of its functioning (already quite exposed by design in Ovid's text) are laid bare.

The poetic strategies which the reply epistles "write against" are bound up with what the heroines and their stories *had become* over the course of their integration into Renaissance scholarship and pedagogy—they had become *exempla* themselves, and their letters had become objects of scholarship; much as they themselves (in the hands of Ovid) had seemed to be engaged in writing exercises, in tracing and playing out the rhetorical and poetic conventions that defined them. Hence the bind, the impenetrability of the text, which no poetic imitation can supplement.

---

79. Notwithstanding Laurel Fulkerson's argument that we do not have to read the heroines' self-constructions as constrained by the master narrative of their myths.

The reply letter as a "supplement" to the Ovidian text necessarily displaces the original text, in the sense that the writing heroes edge out the heroines' discourse, sabotage their rhetoric of blame and exemplarity. But as we observed in chapter 1, there can be no privileged position outside of the text from which to contain it. Even the deployment of ironic self-reference is framed itself by textuality. Barbara Johnson's account of Derrida's reading of "The Purloined Letter" is once again pertinent, in its exploration of "the effects of the frame and of the paradoxes in the parergonal logic": "the structure of the framing effects is such that no totalization of the border is even possible. Frames are always framed, thus, by part of their content."[80]

Boyd claims to have rewritten ("retexui") the Sabinus epistles because he judged that they might be improved. The reply epistles are themselves always open to rewriting, to being endlessly rewoven or retextualized. Responses to the *Heroides* are, as it were, all on the same interpretive plane: they cannot stand outside of the circulation; they merely add to the sequence; they do not put an end to it. The poet-imitator, unable to supply closure to the open-ended laments of Ovid's heroines, intrudes to collapse the delicate balance of the source text, encroaches upon that space where Ovid's games with genre, intertextual subtleties, and metatextual ironies are played out.

Check list of *Heroides* Replies

1430?	Anonymous	Phaon to Sappho	Latin
1467-8	Angelus Sabinus	Ulysses to Penelope Demophoon to Phyllis Paris to Oenone	Latin
1512	Jacobus Locher Philomusus	Orestes to Hermione	Latin
1541	Michel d'Amboise	*Les Contrepistres d'Ovide* (15 replies)	French
1542	John Shepreve	Hippolytus to Phaedra	Latin
1559	Cornelis van Ghistele	12 nieuwe responsieve epistelen (12 replies)	Dutch
1560s or 1570s	?Isabella Whitney	Aeneas to Dido	English

---

80. Johnson 1980, 128.

1569	Janus Douza	Lynceus to Hypermnestra	Latin
1590	Mark Alexander Boyd (Bodius)	*Epistulæ quindecim quibus totidem Ovidii respondet* (15 replies)	Latin
1595	Jacobus Eyndius	Phaon to Sappho	Latin
1620	Gilbert de Golefer	Epîtres des héros	French
1646	Nicolas Heinsius	Aeneas to Dido	Latin
1653	Sidronius Hosschius	Hippolytus to Phaedra	Latin
1658	Christoffel Pierson	(12 replies)	Dutch
1671	Joost van den Vondel	Hippolytus to Phaedra	Dutch
1704	Francesco Dyni	(12 replies)	Latin
1716	Joan de Haes	Hippolytus to Phaedra	Dutch
1720	Elijah Fenton	Phaon to Sappho	English
1723	Henri Richer	Hippolytus to Phaedra ('imitée de Sidronius')	French
1727	Simon Tyssot de Patot	Hippolytus to Phaedra	Dutch
1741	Janus van den Broucke	Aeneas to Dido / Protesilaus to Laodamia	Latin
1921	Ronald A. Knox	Ulysses to Penelope	Latin

Sources: Heinrich Dörrie, *Der heroische Brief* (Berlin: Walter de Gruyter, 1968). http://www.let.leidenuniv.nl/Dutch/Heroides.html [accessed 7 July 2005] (Dutch *Heroides* Research Project, Olga van Marion). http://www.english.cam.ac.uk/ceres/AIhome.htm [accessed 7 July 2005] ("Aeneas and Isabella Project," Raphael Lyne).

Conclusion

Long before your letter reached me I had formed an intention of writing to you, and I should really have done it if it had not been for the lack of a common language.

Petrarch, Letter to Homer[1]

HE PROHIBITION written into the first lines of the collection, "nil mihi rescribas," has been violated again and again by readers of the *Heroides*. The Latin verb "rescribere" encompasses a range of perspectives on responses to a literary text. Its primary meaning is "to write back"; but it can also mean "to write against." Taking a direct object, it can mean "to rewrite" or "to revise." In the context of business it can be used in the sense of repayment of a debt.

The *Heroides* that a sixteenth-century readership had access to is not the same *Heroides* we read today. In the first place, the text was materially different; its content varied significantly from edition to edition, lacking the uniformity of modern editions. The Sappho epistle was not numbered fifteenth but located at the end of the collection; the Paris and Cydippe epistles in many editions lacked a large number of lines; the text was not yet accurately established. But there is another sense in which the text is not the same: it is constantly "rewritten" by editors, commentators, translators, and imitators. Its content is never fixed but shaped anew with each generation of readers. Editors and adapters of the text are concerned with framing it in such a way as to make it "readable" to a sixteenth-century audience. The text had to be reworked, accommodated to the expectations and requirements of

---

1. "Dudum te scripto alloqui mens fuerat, et fecissem, nisi quia linguæ commercium non erat." *Epistolæ de rebus familiaribus et variæ / studio et cura Iosephi Fracassetti*, 3 vols. (Florence: F. Le Monnier, 1863), 3: 293. The translation is James Harvey Robinson's: *Petrarch: The First Modern Scholar and Man of Letters*, ed. by J. H. Robinson (New York: Haskell House, 1970), 253.

a humanist readership. A more extreme case of forceful reappropriation is presented by the *Metamorphoses,* a text that underwent a constant process of transformation, appearing in multiple guises as partial editions, paraphrases, illustrated works, encyclopedic textbooks, and so on. The *Heroides* lent itself more easily to publication in full; but it was never fully established as a bounded work: its peripheries were always permeable.

In early modern conceptions of writing and eloquence, receptiveness is a feminine characteristic. But the text of the *Heroides* complicates the scheme. The heroines write. It is the extradiegetic reader that "receives." Reception becomes active; reflection comes into play: reading is recast as an active making of the text. "Rescribere" comes to mean "writing against." Writers undertake to contest the charges of the heroines, to give the lie to the heroines' ethical positions by outmaneuvering them rhetorically. In this process they also come to contest Ovid: this is *aemulatio,* in Quintilian's sense of a simultaneous challenge to and endorsement of one's model. A response to the *Heroides* functions at once as a challenge to the ethical heroine that emerges from the text, an entity which may or may not coincide with Ovid's 'intention'; and as an endorsement of the heroine's discourse insofar as it is a product of the canonical poet's genius.

Such negotiations take place at two levels of comprehension, the doubled *intentio auctoris et mittentis;* but the levels of this tangled hierarchy are not easily separable. The third meaning of "rescribere" brings into play notions of exchange within textual economies. Respondents to the text are to be seen as "paying back" a debt owed to the text, or to its proprietor. They must negotiate a place for their texts within the symbolic circuit of letter and response. Difficulties arise for respondents: the circulation of the letter is always already in motion: the circuit denies the respondent a point of intervention.

The text is not generated *ex nihilo* in the matrix of sixteenth-century literary culture. In a certain sense, the future of the text's reception is predetermined, written into the text from the very start. The epistolary elegy in its Ovidian manifestation in particular is a mode of writing that depends on the reader's awareness of a certain literary and cultural background. It is very much rooted in a culture of Augustan Rome: Ovid, it has become a critical commonplace to point out, transposes his heroines from Greek myth to a very Roman setting. Moreover, the *Heroides,* like all epistolary literature, rely on the reader's awareness of the moment, and of the way in which the letter-writers "write to the moment." The heroines write their own stories from a singular perspective; but that perspective is not limited, since the heroines, read as intertextual creatures, have access proleptically and analeptically to an accumulation of literary and mythological traditions that determine their story. Furthermore, the *Heroides* seem to predict and enact their own destinies as letters and as literary texts. The extradiegetic addressee stands in place of the hero. The heroines write the reader into the process of literary production and reception; the text preempts all possible responses in its deployment of an allusive reflexivity that functions as metapoetic commentary on its own publication and reception. The text's potential for meaning is actualized at the moment of its reception; the reading is the realization of the act of writing ("exitus acta probat"), as interpretation enacts the dialectic whereby the contingent becomes the necessary reading.

Is Ovid's text, then, distinctly "anti-pédagogique," as Hélène Cazes argues?[2] The very fact that the pieces that comprise the *Heroides* are often identified with *progymnasmata* exercises suggests otherwise. In the sixteenth century, the text occupied a prominent place at every stage of education, as well as at the level of learned humanist culture. However, as we saw in chapter 2, the text's universal appeal, its versatility and the broad range of applications it had in education also posed problems: it became difficult for humanists to categorize the work definitively. Erasmus was unable to fix the text within his scheme of epistolary genres and subcategories; critics were unable to establish a *mode d'emploi* for the application of the discourse of exemplarity to the text; its deployment of "female eloquence" complicated notions of gendered rhetoric. The heroines' volubility (in the full sense of the word) poses a problem that attracts and frustrates the attempts of humanist readers to encode it, to make it fully 'readable.'

The encoding of the text takes place at several different 'levels' of reception: in the contexts of the systematized procedures of humanist thought; of translation from Latin into the vernacular; and of literary adaptation and imitation. It is in the vernacular treatments of the text that difficulties with the generic identity of the text are at their most acute. The epistolary elegy straddles genres in Latin literature: Ovid himself claimed to have invented it. In the vernacular, too, it is not easily categorizable, as we saw in the very different treatments of the text in translation; and especially in the slippery,

---

2. Of the *Metamorphoses* in particular: "[L]e texte en soi, continu, ambigu, facétieux, est antipédagogique et se prête fort mal aux manipulations humanistes et morales des fervents lecteurs du XVIe siècle. Ainsi, la poésie d'Ovide, si peu propice aux découpages et aux exercises pédagogiques de la Renaissance, devient un enjeu de lecture et de culture" (The text itself, continuous, ambiguous, playful, is anti-pedagogical and lends itself particularly poorly to the humanistic and moral manipulations of eager sixteenth-century readers. Thus Ovid's poetry, so unsuitable for the excerpting and pedagogical exercises of the Renaissance, becomes a major issue of reading and culture). Cazes suggests that the canonicity of Ovid's works in the sixteenth century is atypical or even paradoxical. See Cazes 2003, 240.

Conclusion

elusive versions by Du Bellay and Michel d'Amboise. The literary translations and imitations of the *Heroides* often call attention to an underlying anxiety. Their publication is often plagued by troublesome questions about authenticity and authorship; the texts themselves are often marked by indeterminacy, or disowned by a treatment characterized by authorial distance and a self-ironizing stance; they often cross genres and fail to sit well in any given category. The heroical epistle continues to evolve in later centuries: it is never a self-contained literary genre. It is by turns associated with the epistolary genre (in various guises); with love elegy, with serious interventions in the *querelle des femmes;* with comic parody of epic or tragedy; with Christian devotional poetry; and finally, in the eighteenth century, it attains its apotheosis as a literary mode, the *héroïde,* identified principally with the tragic monologue. The text of Ovid's *Heroides* is a multiplicity of texts; just as the *heroides* of Ovid's text are never readable as fixed representations of 'Woman.'

The anxiety that underwrites attempts to integrate and accommodate the heroines' discourse through institutionalized readings is also an anxiety about the fundamental *otherness* of the feminine voice. There is a suspicion that there is something in the heroines' speech that is more than their speech, that exceeds the grasp of the reader, that resists symbolization. This ineffable element is necessarily unable to be contained by the disciplines of rhetoric and moral philosophy. It can only be dealt with in a literary mode, and then only by a certain bias; it is never approached directly.

A concept that might help to illustrate the problems confronted by humanist readers engaging with the text is that of the "Alexandrian footnote." This is the technique, characteristic of Ovid, whereby the "poet turns scholiast," as it were, signposting an allusion by means of an appropriation of the commentator's idiom. As Stephen Hinds explains,[3] the poet adopts a scholarly stance (introducing pieces of information with verbs such as "dicitur" or "ferunt," for example) to flag up allusions as if by an 'external' editorial intervention. Hinds goes on to suggest that signposting of allusions is "more deeply encoded, more fully integrated into its narrative contexts" when it is the fictional character herself whose words draw attention to an allusion (Ariadne's "memini" at *Fasti* 3.473).

This functions slightly differently in the *Heroides:* there too, allusion is figured in the metaphor of the heroines' 'remembering' of events in their own stories; but they also have access to the language of 'literary response'

---

3. Hinds 1998, 1–5.

as they interpret those events—as readers of literature.[4] Future scholarly interventions are in some sense gainsaid by the heroines' discourse. Ovid's heroines already figure themselves as readers and annotators of their own literature. This procedure has the effect of blurring the boundary between poem and commentary, between text and paratext, work and *parergon*. In the *Heroides*, the impersonal "dicitur"—the characteristic marker of the "Alexandrian footnote"—is often replaced by the first- and second-person forms "dicor," "dicar," and "diceris." The effect is one of heightened immediacy and, at the same time, of distancing: the heroines reduce every aspect of a complex mythological narrative to their own immediate concerns; but their use of the passive voice ("You are said to have . . . "), particularly in the future tense ("Shall I be called . . . ?"), allows them to jump outside of their own narratives to comment on them. Sometimes they emerge as impassive readers of mythology: "they say you accomplished this or that heroic exploit"; more often the effect is an ironic distortion of what the scholarly material *really* says (Phaedra: "dicar . . . fida nouerca" [I shall be called a dutiful stepmother]).

This highly self-referential technique carries though into the reply-poem imitations, which are effectively running commentaries on the heroines' epistles, complete with scholarly explanations of references and tendentious glosses on the more obscure parts of the text. However the mode shifts from "they say" or "the story goes . . . " to "I saw" and "I did": the heroes present themselves as primary actors in their stories. As we saw, this is readable also at the level of poetic *aemulatio*. As Hinds remarks of Ovid's own engagement with his poetic precursors, "A competition for mythological primacy thus shades into a competition of poetological primacy."[5] The reply poems remain allusive in the extreme; but they necessarily fail to maintain the conceit that the information is reported from other sources, and the "Alexandrian footnote" effect is diminished.

If scholarly readings of mythology are second-guessed or gainsaid in the original text, this would seem to make the work of commentators and annotators difficult, if not redundant. The terms for negotiation are fixed in advance. If the pieces that make up the *Heroides* had their origins in school-

---

4. This emerges, too, in the habitual practice of the heroines' conflating two or more (sometimes mutually exclusive) versions of their own myth. See, for example, Hinds, "Medea in Ovid," 14. Laurel Fulkerson (*The Ovidian Heroine as Author*, 48) remarks on the deployment of the Alexandrian footnote device in the *Heroides* to indicate that the heroines have read each other's stories as well as different versions of their own stories. This supports Fulkerson's wider "intratextual" argument that the heroines constitute a community of readers/authors.

5. Hinds 1999, 128.

room rhetorical exercises, the text finally challenges the viability of such modes of reading. It emerges as an ironic commentary on the procedures of scholarship, and reductive modes of reading literary texts. The *Heroides* is a literary text that internalizes and plays out the process of its own reception. It predicts the ways in which institutionalized readings will attempt to appropriate it. It figuratively teases out the complications involved in translation from one language or culture into another. It questions the very basis of the assumption that it is possible to articulate an authentic response to a literary text.

Hinds's readings of what he terms "reflexive self-annotation" allow for an inversion of the hierarchy of "tenor" and "vehicle," of metapoetic "ground" and "figure." Similarly, our readings of the ways in which ideas written into the text of the *Heroides* prefigure and illustrate the process of a literary text's reception can also be taken as readings of the ways that the process of the text's reception reveals and illustrates ideas written into the text. As well as reading the influence of the *Heroides* forwards into the Renaissance, we can also "read backwards," in the manner of Barchiesi's "future reflexive" readings of allusive techniques in the *Heroides:* the process of reading may "reverse the original direction of the stream of literary creation."[6] If the *Heroides* preempt scholarly interventions, how do respondents negotiate a place for their texts? Is our concern to offer readings of the *Heroides* in order to "find a way into" Renaissance literary culture; or to offer readings of Renaissance culture in order to "find a way into" the text of the *Heroides* itself? The answer must be: we read in both directions simultaneously. The letter always arrives at its destination because its trajectory is not linear, but circular.

---

6. Barchiesi, 105.

BIBLIOGRAPHY

(I) Primary Sources: Editions

(A) PRINTED

The Jesuit Ratio Studiorum of 1599. trans. by A. B. Farrell (Washington, D.C.: Conference of Major Superiors of Jesuits, 1970)

Amboise, C. d,' *Les Devotes Epistres de Katherine d'Amboise,* ed. by J.-J. Bourassé (Tours: Imprimerie A. Mame, 1861)

———. *Les Devotes Epistres, présentées et éditées par Yves Giraud,* ed. by Yves Giraud (Fribourg: Éditions Universitaires Fribourg, 2002)

Amboise, M. d,' *Les Complaintes de L'Esclave Fortuné* (Paris: Jehan Sainct Denis, 1529)

———. *[Les] Contrepistres d'Ovide* (Paris: Maurice de la Porte, 1546)

Boccaccio, G., *Famous Women,* ed. by V. Brown (Cambridge, MA: Harvard University Press, 2001)

Bouchet, J. *Epistres morales et familieres du Traverseur* (Poitiers: Jean et Enguilbert de Marnef, 1545)

Boyd, M. A. *Epistolæ Heroides, et Hymni* (Antwerp [sic]: 1592)

———. *Epistolæ Quindecim, Quibus Totidem Ovidii Respondet* (Bordeaux: S. Millanges, 1590)

Clericus Crescentinas, U. *Hubertini Clerici Crescentinatis in Nasonis heroidas commentum* (Casale: Antonius de Corsino, 1481)

Dryden, John. *The Poetical Works of Dryden,* ed. by G. R. Noyes (Cambridge, MA: The Riverside Press, 1950)

———. *Of Dramatic Poesy and Other Critical Essays,* ed. by G. Watson, 2 vols (London: Dent, 1962)

Du Bellay, J. *Le Quatriesme livre de l'Eneide de Vergile, traduict en vers francoys; La Complaincte de Didon à Enée, prinse d'Ovide* (Paris: V. Certenas, 1552)

———. *La Deffence et illustration de la langue françoyse*, ed. by H. Chamard (Paris: M. Didier, 1948)

———. *Oeuvres poétiques III: Recueils lyriques*, ed. By H. Chamard (Paris: Droz 1912)

———. *Œuvres poétiques VI: Discours et traductions*, ed. by H. Chamard (Paris: Droz, 1931)

Eobanus Hessus. *Operum farragines duae* (Schwäbisch Hall, 1539).

———. *Heroidum libri tres, nuper ab auctore recogniti* (Paris, 1546)

Erasmus. *Brevissima maximeque compendiaria conficiendarum epistolarum formula* (Paris: N. de Pratis, 1521)

———. "De conscribendis epistolis," in *Opera omnia Desiderii Erasmi Roterodami* I–II (Amsterdam: North Holland Publishing Company, 1971)

———. *Opus epistolarum Des. Erasmi Roterodami / denuo recognitum et auctum per P. S. Allen*, 12 vols (Oxford: Clarendon, 1906–1958), II

Espence, Claude d'. *Sacrarum Heroidum liber* (Paris: Frédéric Morel, 1564)

Fabri, P. *Le Grand et vrai art de pleine rhétorique*, ed. by A. Héron (Geneva: Slatkine Reprints, 1969)

Fabricius, G. *De re poetica libri VII* (Leipzig: J. Steinman, 1589)

Filelfo, G. M. *Novum Epistolarium* (Basel: Bacilerium de Bacileriis, 1489)

Fontaine, C. *Les Epistres d'Ovide nouvellement mises en vers Françoys par M. Charles Fontaine Parisien* (Lyon: Jean Temporal, 1552)

———. *Les Ruisseaux de Fontaine* (Lyon: T. Payan, 1555)

———. *[Les] XXI épitres d'Ovide* (Paris: H. de Marnef et la Vve G. Cavellat, 1580)

Habert, F. *Les Epistres heroides pour servir d'exemple aux Chrestiens* (Paris: Michel Fezandat, 1560)

———. *La Jeunesse du Banny du lyesse* (Paris: D. Janot, 1541)

Labé, L. *Œuvres complètes* (Paris: Flammarion, 1986)

Lemaire de Belges, J. *La concorde des deux langages, et Les épîtres de l'amant vert* (Cambridge, MA: Schoenhof's, 1964)

Marot, C. *Les Epîtres*, ed. by C. E. Mayer (London: Athlone, 1958)

———. *Œuvres complètes de Clément Marot: 6, Les Traductions*, ed. by C. E. Mayer (Geneva: Slatkine, 1980)

Nannius, P. *Dialogismi heroinarum* (Paris: Chrétien Wechel, 1541)

———. *Cinq dialogismes, ou Délibérations de 5 nobles Dames, à sçavoir Lucrèce, Susanne, Judith, Agnès, Camma Galathienne; traduits du Latin de Petrus Nannius par Jean Millet* (Paris: Araroul l'Angellier, 1550)

Negri, F. *Opusculum Epistolarum Familiarum* (Paris: D. Roce, 1500)

Ovid. *P. Ovidii Nasonis Epistolæ heroides, una cum expositionibus eximiorum virorum Antonii Volsci, Ubertinique clerici Cresentinatis* (Venice: B. Locatellus, 1492)

———. *P. Ovidii Nasonis Heroidum Epistolae / cum triplici explatione* (Paris: J. de Vingle for E. Gueynard, 1500)

———. *Epistolæ heroides Ovidii / cum commentariis Antonii Volci et Ubertini Crescentinatis* (Paris: N. Depratis, 1509)

———. *Heroides; Ibis* (Lyon: N. Wolff, 1511)

———. *Epistolæ heroides Publij Ouidij Nasonis / commentantibus Antonio Volsco [et al.]* (Lyon: J. David, 1528)

———. *Heroides epistolæ / cum omnibus commentariis ubiq[ue] locorum hactenus impressis* (Venice: Hieronymus Scotus, 1543)

———. *P. Ovidii Nasonis Poetæ Sulmonensis Poemata Amatoria,* ed. by Egnatius Morillon (Antwerp: Michael Hillenius, 1545)
———. *Epistolarum Heroidum Liber: Interpretatione & Notis Illustravit D. Crisp. Helvetius* (London: C. Rivington, 1775)
———. *Publii Ovidii Nasonis Quæ Extant Opera Omnia,* ed. by J. A. Amar, Bibliothèque Classique Latine, 1 (Paris: N. E. Lemaire, 1825)
———. *Heroides,* ed. by A. Palmer (Oxford: Clarendon, 1898)
———. *P. Ovidii Nasonis Epistulae Heroidum,* ed. by H. Dörrie (Berlin: de Gruyter, 1971)
———. *Heroides: Select Epistles,* ed. by P. E. Knox, Cambridge Greek and Latin Texts (Cambridge: Cambridge University Press, 1995)
———. *Heroides XVI–XXI,* ed. by E. J. Kenney, Cambridge Greek and Latin Texts (Cambridge: Cambridge University Press, 1996)
Perotti, N. *Rudimenta Grammatices* (Paris: U. Gering, 1479)
Petrarch, F. *Epistolæ de rebus familiaribus et variæ / studio et cura Iosephi Fracassetti,* 3 vols (Florence: F. Le Monnier, 1863)
———. *Petrarch: The First Modern Scholar and Man of Letters,* trans. by J. H. Robinson (New York: Haskell House, 1970)
Piccolomini, Aeneas Silvius *The Tale of Two Lovers: Eurialus and Lucretia,* ed. by E. J. Morrall (Amsterdam: Rodopi B. V., 1988)
Plutarch. *The Lives of the Noble Grecians and Romans,* trans. by John Dryden (Chicago: W. Benton, 1952)
Poliziano, A. *Commento Inedito all'Epistola Ovidiana di Saffo a Faone,* ed. by Lazzeri, E. Studi e testi (Istituto Nazionale di Studi sul Rinascimento); 2 (Sansoni, 1971)
Pontanus. J. *Jacobi Pontani de Societate Iesu In P. Ovidii Nasonis, poetarum ingeniosissimi, Tristium, et De Ponto libros novi commentarii; Item Hortuli Ovidiani, id est sententiae et proverbia, ex quotquot poetae monumentis ab eodem conquisita, in locos communes redacta, et commentationibus explicata. Cum indice rerum & verborum copiosissimo* (Ingolstadt: Adam Sartorius, 1610)
Ronsard. P. de. *Oeuvres complètes XV* (Paris: Société des textes français modernes, 1953)
Saint-Gelais, O. de. *Les XXI epistres d'Ovide* (Paris: Jean Trepperel, 1512)
———. *Les XXI Epistres D'Ovide Translatées de Latin en Francoys / Par Reverend Pere en Dieu Monseigneur Levesque Danguulesme* (Paris: G. de Bossozel, 1534)
———. *Les Vingt et Une Epistre* [sic] *d'Ovide Translatée de Latin en Francoys / Par Reverend Pere en Dieu Monseigneur l'Evesque d'Angoulesme* (Paris: Nicolas du Chemin, 1546)
Sebillet, Aneau, Peletier, Fouquelin, and Ronsard. *Traités de poétique et de rhétorique de la Renaissance,* ed. by F. Goyet (Paris: Livre de Poche Classique, 1990)
Shakespeare, W. *The Riverside Shakespeare,* ed. By G. B. Evans (Boston: Houghton Mifflin, 1974)
Turberville, G. *The Heroycall Epistles of the Learned Poet Publius Ouidius Naso, in English Verse Set Out and Translated by George Turberuile Gent. With Aulus Sabinus Aunsweres to Certaine of the Same* (London: H. Denham, 1567)
Vives, J. L. *De conscribendis epistolis,* ed. by C. Fantazzi (Leiden: E. J. Brill, 1989)
———. *De institutione feminae christianae: liber primus,* ed. by C. Fantazzi and C. Matheeussen (Leiden: E. J. Brill, 1996)

(B) Manuscripts

Amboise, C. d'. Bibliothèque nationale, Ancien fonds français, 8033
Boyd, M. A.
———. National Library of Scotland, Adv. MS 15.1.7
———. National Library of Scotland, 20759
Saint-Gelais, O. de. Manuscript illuminations, *Cote BNF Richelieu Manuscrits Français 873. Ovidius, Heroides (Traduction de Octovien de Saint-Gelais), France, Paris, XVe–XVIe Siècles* (http://gallica.bnf.fr/Catalogue/noticesInd/MAN01079.htm: Gallica, bibliothèque numérique de la Bibliothèque nationale de France)
———. Manuscript illuminations, *Cote BNF Richelieu Manuscrits Français 874. Ovidius, Heroides (Traduction de Octovien de Saint-Gelais), France, Paris, XVIe Siècle* (http://gallica.bnf.fr/Catalogue/noticesInd/MAN01080.htm: Gallica, bibliothèque numérique de la Bibliothèque nationale de France)

(II) Secondary Literature

Allen, D. C. *Mysteriously Meant: The Rediscovery of Pagan Symbolism and Allegorical Interpretation in the Renaissance* (Baltimore: Johns Hopkins University Press, 1970)
Altman, J. G. *Epistolarity: Approaches to a Form* (Columbus: The Ohio State University Press, 1982)
———. "The Letter Book as a Literary Institution 1539–1789: Towards a Cultural History of Published Correspondences in France," *Yale French Studies* 71 (1986): 17–62
Alton, E. H. "Ovid in the Mediæval Schoolroom," *Hermathena* 95 (1961): 70–82
Anderson, W. S. "The *Heroides*," in *Ovid*, ed. by J. W. Binns (London: Routledge & Kegan Paul, 1973), 49–83
Armstrong, A. *Technique and Technology: Script, Print and Poetics in France 1470–1550* (Oxford: Clarendon, 2000)
Armstrong, R. *Cretan Women: Pasiphae, Ariadne, and Phaedra in Latin Poetry* (Oxford: Oxford University Press, 2006)
Austin, N. *Helen of Troy and Her Shameless Phantom* (Ithaca: Cornell University Press, 1994)
Baldwin, T. W. *William Shakespere's Small Latine and Lesse Greek*, 2 vols (Urbana: University of Illinois Press, 1944)
Barbieri, L. *Le "epistole delle dame di Grecia" nel Roman de Troie in prosa: la prima traduzione francese delle Eroidi di Ovidio* (Tübingen: Francke, 2005)
———. *Les Epistres des dames de Grèce: une version médiévale en prose française des "Héroïdes" d'Ovide* (Paris: Champion, 2007)
Barchiesi, A. *Speaking Volumes: Narrative and Intertext in Ovid and Other Latin Poets* (London: Duckworth, 2001)
Barthes, R. *Fragments d'un discours amoureux* (Paris: Seuil, 1977)
Bate, J. *Shakespeare and Ovid* (Oxford: Clarendon, 1993)
Beebee, T. O. *Epistolary Fiction in Europe, 1500–1850* (Cambridge: Cambridge University Press, 1999)
Belfiore, E. "Ovid's Encomium of Helen," *The Classical Journal* 76.2 (1995): 136–148

Bergeron-Foote, A. Thesis abstract, "Les œuvres en prose de Catherine d'Amboise, dame de Lignières (1481–1550)" (http://theses.enc.sorbonne.fr/document1.html: 2002)

Besomi, O., and C. Caruso (eds.). *Il Commento ai testi (Atti del Seminario di Ascona, 2–9 ottobre 1989)* (Basel: Birkhäuser Verlag, 1992)

Bizer, M. *Les Lettres romaines de Du Bellay: les "Regrets" et la tradition épistolaire* (Montreal: Presses de l'Université de Montréal, 2001)

Boutcher, W. "'Who Taught Thee Rhetoricke to Deceive a Maid?': Christopher Marlowe's *Hero and Leander*, Juan Boscán's *Leandro*, and Renaissance Vernacular Humanism," *Comparative Literature* 52.1 (Winter 2000): 11–52

Bray, B. *L'Art de la lettre amoureuse: des manuels aux romans (1550–1700)* (The Hague: Mouton, 1967)

———. "Les *Lettres amoureuses* d'Etienne Pasquier, premier roman épistolaire français?," *Cahiers de l'Association Internationale des Études Françaises*, 29 (1977): 133–45

Brownlee, M. S. "Hermeneutic Transgressions in the *Heroides* and *Bursario*," *Stanford French Review* 14 (1990): 95–115

———. *The Severed Word: Ovid's "Heroides" and the "Novela Sentimental"* (Princeton: Princeton University Press, 1990)

Brückner, T. *Die erste französische Aeneis: Untersuchungen zu Octavien de Saint-Gelais' Übersetzung. Mit einer kritischen Edition des VI. Buches* (Düsseldorf: 1987)

———. "'Octovien de Saint-Gelais' Ovide-Übersetzung: Der Pariser Codex fr. 874 (B.N.)," *Wolfenbütteler Renaissance Mitteilungen* 13 (1989): 93–101

Brunel, J. "Un Ecossais en Bas-Poitou et en Aunis vers 1590: Marc-Alexandre Boyd (1562–1601)," *Société d'Emulation de la Vendée. Revue d'études historiques et archéologiques* 121 (1974): 59–75

Buisson, F. E. *Répertoire des ouvrages pédagogiques du XVIe Siècle: bibliothèques de Paris et des départements* (Paris: Imprimerie Nationale, 1886)

Butrica, J. L. Review, "Christina Meckelnborg, Bernd Schneider, *Odyssea: Responsio Ulixis ad Penelopen. Die humanistiche Odyssea decurtata der Berliner Handschrift Diez. B Sant. 41. Beiträge zur Altertumskunde 166*. Munich and Leipzig: K. G. Saur, 2002." English (http://ccat.sas.upenn.edu/bmcr/2002/2002-10-21.html: Bryn Mawr Classical Review, 21 December 2002)

Cabaret-Dupaty, M. *Poetae minores,* Bibliothèque latine-française: traductions nouvelles des auteurs latins depuis Adrien jusqu'à Grégoire de Tours (Paris: C. L. F. Panckoucke, 1842)

Calvino, I. *Why Read the Classics?* trans. by M. McLaughlin (London: Jonathan Cape, 1999)

Carocci, R. *Les Héroïdes dans la seconde moitié du XVIIIe siècle, 1758–1788* (Paris: Nizet, 1988)

Cazes, H. "Les Bonnes Fortunes d'Ovide au XVIe Siècle," in *Lectures d'Ovide, publiées à la mémoire de Jean-Pierre Néraudau*, ed. by E. Bury and M. Néraudau (Paris: Les Belles Lettres, 2003), 239–64

Chesney, K. "A Neglected Prose Version of the *Roman de Troie*," *Medium Aevum* 11 (1942): 46–67

Clark, J. E. *Elégie: the Fortunes of a Classical Genre in Sixteenth-Century France* (The Hague: Mouton, 1975)

Clément, M. "Louise Labé et les arts poétiques," *Méthode* 7 (December 2004): 65–77

Constans, L. "Une Traduction française des *Héroïdes* d'Ovide au XIIIe siècle," *Romania* 43 (1914): 177–98

Cooper, R. "Michel d'Amboise, poète maudit?" in *La génération Marot: poètes français et néo-latins (1515–1550): Actes du colloque international de Baltimore, 5–7 décembre 1996*, ed. by Gérard Defaux (Paris: Champion, 1997), 443–70

Cosenza, M. E. *Biographical and Bibliographical Dictionary of the Italian Humanists and of the World of Classical Scholarship in Italy, 1300–1800*, 6 vols (Boston: G. K. Hall, 1962–1967)

Coulson, F. T. "Hitherto Unedited Medieval and Renaissance Lives of Ovid (I)," *Mediaeval Studies* 49 (1987): 152–207

———. "Hitherto Unedited Medieval and Renaissance Lives of Ovid (II): Humanistic Lives," *Mediaeval Studies* 59 (1997): 111–53

Cunningham, I. C. "Marcus Alexander Bodius, Scotus," in *A Palace in the Wild: Essays on Vernacular Culture and Humanism in Late-Medieval and Renaissance Scotland*, ed. by L. A. J. R. Houwen, A. A. MacDonald, and S. L. Mapstone (Leuven: Peeters, 2000), 161–74

Dainville, F. *L'Éducation des Jésuites (XVIe–XVIIIe siècles)* (Paris: Editions de Minuit, 1978)

Dalrymple, D. (Lord Hailes). *Sketch of the Life of Mark Alexander Boyd* (London: 1787)

Dalla Valle, D. "Les *Héroïdes* en France et les lettres héroïques au XVIe et au XVIIe siècle," in *Lectures d'Ovide, publiées à la mémoire de Jean-Pierre Néraudau*, ed. by E. Bury and M. Néraudau (Paris: Les Belles Lettres, 2003), 371–84

Dauvois, N. *Le Sujet lyrique à la Renaissance* (Paris: Presses Universitaires de France, 2000)

DeJean. J. *Fictions of Sappho, 1546–1937* (Chicago: University of Chicago Press, 1989)

Derrida, J. *La Carte postale: de Socrate à Freud et au-delà* (Paris: Flammarion, 1980)

Desgraves, L., *Les Haultin, 1571–1623* (Geneva: Droz, 1960)

Desmond, M. "When Dido Reads Vergil: Gender and Intertextuality in Ovid's *Heroides* 7," *Helios* 20.1 (1993): 56–88

Donaldson, R. "'M. Alex: Boyde.' The Authorship of 'Fra Banc to Banc,'" in *The Renaissance in Scotland: Studies in Literature, Religion, History and Culture*, ed. by A. A. MacDonald, M. Lynch, and Ian. B. Cowan (Leiden: Brill, 1994), 344–66

Donnini, M. "La 'Lectura Ovidii Epistularum' nel cod. Asis. lat. 302," *Giornale italiano di filologia* 31 (1979): 209–29

Doran, M. "Some Renaissance 'Ovids,'" in: *Literature and Society, by Germaine Brée, and Others. A Selection of Papers Delivered at the Joint Meeting of the Midwest Modern Language Association and the Central Renaissance Conference, 1963*, ed. by Bernice Slote (Lincoln: University of Nebraska Press, 1964), 44–62

Dörrie, H. "L'Épître héroïque dans les littératures modernes: recherches sur la postérité des *Epistulae heroidum* d'Ovide," *Revue de Littérature Comparée* 40 (1966): 48–64

———. *Der heroische Brief* (Berlin: Walter de Gruyter, 1968)

Durrieu, P., and Marquet de J.-J. Vasselot. Offprint from: *L'Artiste* 1894, *Les manuscrits à miniatures des "Héroïdes" d'Ovide, traduites par Saint-Gelais et un grand miniaturiste français du 16e siècle* (1894)

Fantazzi, C. "Vives versus Erasmus on the Art of Letter Writing," in *Self-Presentation and Social Identification: The Rhetoric and Pragmatics of Letter Writing in Early Modern Times*, ed. by T. Van Houdt, J. Papy, G. Tournoy, and C. Matheeussen (Leuven: Leuven University Press, 2002), 39–56

Farrell, J. "Reading and Writing the *Heroides*," *Harvard Studies in Classical Philology* 98 (1998): 307–38

Féret, P. "Claude d'Espence," in *La Faculté de théologie de Paris au moyen âge et ses docteurs les plus célèbres* (Paris: Alph. Picard et fils, 1901), 101–18

Ferguson, G. "Introduction," in: Anne de Marquets, *Sonets spirituels* (Geneva: Droz, 1997)

Fisher, E. A. *Planudes' Greek Translation of Ovid's "Metamorphoses"* (New York: Garland, 1990)

Franchet, H. "Introduction," in: *Le Philosophe parfaict et Le Temple de vertu de François Habert nouvellement remis en lumière avec notice et notes, par Henri Franchet*, Bibliothèque littéraire de la renaissance 8 (Paris: Champion, 1923)

Fritsen, A. "The Renaissance Afterlife of *Heroides* 15: Two Humanist Responses to Sappho (*Commendatio Marci Siculae poetae* and *Epistula Phaonis ad Sappho*)," *Manuscripta* 49 (2005): 41–58

Fulkerson, L. *The Ovidian Heroine as Author: Reading, Writing, and Community in the "Heroides"* (Cambridge: Cambridge University Press, 2005)

Fumaroli, M. "Genèse de l'épistolographie classique: rhétorique humaniste de la lettre, de Pétrarque à Juste Lipse," *Revue d'histoire littéraire de la France* 6.6 (November–December 1978): 886–900

Galand-Hallyn, P. "Corinne et Sappho: *elocutio* et *inventio* dans les *Amours* et les *Héroïdes* d'Ovide," *Bulletin de l'Association Guillaume Budé* (1991): 336–58

Geise, B. Online article, "Die Tres Epistulae A. Sabini - antik oder humanistisch?," *Osnabrücker Online-Beiträge zu den Altertumswissenschaften*, German (http://www.geschichte.uni-osnabrueck.de/projekt/online_beitraege_pdf/tres_epistulae.pdf: Osnabrücker Online-Beiträge zu den Altertumswissenschaften, May 2001)

Genette, G. *Seuils* (Paris: Seuil, 1987)

Ghisalberti, F. "Mediaeval Biographies of Ovid," *Journal of the Warburg and Courtauld Institutes* 9 (1946): 10–59

Gibson, R. K., and C. Shuttleworth Kraus (eds.). *The Classical Commentary: Histories, Practices, Theory* (Leiden: Brill, 2002)

Giraud, Y. and A.-M. Clin-Lalande. *Nouvelle bibliographie du roman épistolaire en France, des origines à 1842* (Fribourg: Editions Universitaires Fribourg Suisse, 1995)

Glendinning, R. "Pyramus and Thisbe in the Medieval Classroom," *Speculum* 61 (1986): 51–78

Goulet-Cazé, M.-O. (ed.). *Le Commentaire entre tradition et innovation* (Paris: Vrin, 2000)

Grafton, A. "On the Scholarship of Politian and Its Context," *Journal of the Warburg and Courtauld Institutes* 40 (1977): 150–88

———, and L. Jardine. *From Humanism to the Humanities: Education and the Liberal Arts in Fifteenth- and Sixteenth-Century Europe* (London: Duckworth, 1986)

———. *Defenders of the Text: The Traditions of Scholarship in an Age of Science, 1450–1800* (Cambridge, MA; London: Harvard University Press, 1991)

Green, L. D., and J. J. Murphy. *Renaissance Rhetoric Short-Title Catalogue 1460–1700* (Aldershot: Ashgate, 2006)

Greenhut, D. S. *Feminine Rhetorical Culture: Tudor Adaptations of Ovid's Heroides* (New York: Peter Lang, 1988)

Griffin, R. *Coronation of the Poet: Joachim Du Bellay's Debt to the Trivium* (Berkeley: University of California Press, 1969)

Gross, N. P. "Rhetorical Wit and Amatory Persuasion in Ovid," *Classical Journal* 74 (1978–79): 305–18

Hagedorn, S. C. *Abandoned Women: Rewriting the Classics in Dante, Boccaccio, & Chaucer* (Ann Arbor: University of Michigan Press, 2004)

Hanisch, G. *Love Elegies of the Renaissance: Marot, Louise Labé and Ronsard* (Saratoga: Anma Libri, 1979)

Hardie, P. *Ovid's Poetics of Illusion* (Cambridge: Cambridge University Press, 2002)

Häuptli, B. (ed.), *Ibis, Fragmente, Ovidiana* (Zürich: Artemis & Winkler, 1996)

Hexter, R. J. *Ovid and Medieval Schooling: Studies in Medieval School Commentaries on Ovid's "Ars Amatoria," "Epistulae ex Ponto" and "Epistulae Heroidum"* (Munich: Arbeo-Gesellschaft, 1986)

———. "Narrative and an Absolutely Fabulous Commentary on Ovid's *Heroides*," in: *Latin Grammar and Rhetoric: Classical Theory and Medieval Practice*, ed. by C. Lanham (London and New York: Continuum, 2002), 212–38

Higham, T. F. "Ovid: Some Aspects of his Character and Aims," *Classical Review* 48 (1934): 105–16

Hinds, S. "Booking the Return Trip: Ovid and Tristia 1," *Proceedings of the Cambridge Philological Society* 31 (1985): 13–32

———. "Medea in Ovid: Scenes from the Life of an Intertextual Heroine," *Materiali e discussioni per l'analisi dei testi classici* 30 (1993): 9–47

———. *Allusion and Intertext: Dynamics of Appropriation in Roman Poetry* (Cambridge: Cambridge University Press, 1998)

———. "First among Women: Ovid, *Tristia* 1.6 and the Traditions of "Exemplary" Catalogue," in *Amor: Roma. Love and Latin Literature*, ed. by S. Morton Braund and R. Mayer (Cambridge: 1999), 123–42

Huchon, M. *Louise Labé: une créature de papier* (Geneva: Droz, 2006)

Hulubei, A. *L'Eglogue en France au XVIe siècle: époque des Valois (1515–1589)* (Paris: Droz, 1938)

Huppert, G. *Public Schools in Renaissance France* (Urbana and Chicago: University of Illinois Press, 1984)

Jacobson, H. *Ovid's "Heroides"* (Princeton: Princeton University Press, 1974)

Jahn, J.-C. *De P. Ovidii Nasonis et A. Sabini Epistolis Disputatio* (Leipzig: B. G. Teubner, 1826)

Jauss, H. R. "Theses on the Transition from the Aesthetics of Literary Works to a Theory of Aesthetic Experience," in *Interpretation of Narrative*, ed. by M. J. Valdés and O. J. Miller (Toronto: University of Toronto Press, 1978), 137–47

———. "The Theory of Reception: A Retrospective of its Unrecognized Prehistory," in *Literary Theory Today*, ed. by P. Collier and H. Geyer-Ryan (Cambridge: Polity Press, 1990), 53–73

Jensen, K. A. *Writing Love: Letters, Women and the Novel in France, 1605–1776* (Carbondale: Southern Illinois University Press, 1995)

Johnson, B. *The Critical Difference: Essays in the Contemporary Rhetoric of Reading* (Baltimore; London: Johns Hopkins University Press, 1980)

Jolivet, J.-C. *Allusion et fiction épistolaire dans les Héroïdes: recherches sur l'intertextualité ovidienne* (Rome: Ecole française de Rome, 2001)

Joole, P. "Les Héroïdes d'Ovide et les épistoliers de la grande rhétorique," in *Regards sur le passé dans l'Europe des XVIe et XVIIe siècles*, ed. by Francine Wild (Berlin: Peter Lang, 1997), 47–53

Kallendorf, C. "Boccaccio's Dido and the Rhetorical Criticism of Virgil's Aeneid," *Studies in Philology* 82.4 (Fall 1985): 401–15
———. "Ascensius, Landino, and Virgil: Continuity and Transformation in Renaissance Commentary," in *Acta Conventus Neo-Latini Bariensis: Proceedings of the Ninth International Congress of Neo-Latin Studies* (Medieval and Renaissance Texts and Studies, 1998)
Kany, C. E. "The Beginnings of the Epistolary Novel in France, Italy and Spain," *University of California Publications in Modern Philology* 27 (1937): 1–158
Kauffman, L. S. *Discourses of Desire: Gender, Genre, and Epistolary Fictions* (Ithaca: Cornell University Press, 1986)
Kennedy, D. F. "The Epistolary Mode and the First of Ovid's *Heroides*," *The Classical Quarterly, New Series* 34.2 (1984): 413–22
———. *The Arts of Love: Five Studies in the Discourse of Roman Love Elegy* (Cambridge: Cambridge University Press, 1993)
———. "Epistolarity: the *Heroides*," in *The Cambridge Companion to Ovid*, ed. by P. Hardie (Cambridge: Cambridge University Press, 2002), 217–32
Kenney, E. J. "A Byzantine Version of Ovid," *Hermes* 91 (1963): 213–27
———. "Two Disputed Passages in the *Heroides*," *Classical Quarterly* 29.2 (1979): 394–431
———. "Ovid's Language and Style," in *Brill's Companion to Ovid* (Leiden: E. J. Brill, 2002), 27–90
Kirfel, E.-A. *Untersuchungen zur Briefform der Heroides Ovids* (Bern and Stuttgart: Verlag Paul Haupt, 1969)
Kristeller, P. O. editor in chief, *Catalogus Translationum et Commentariorum: Mediæval and Renaissance Latin Translations and Commentaries,* 7 vols. (Washington: Catholic University of America Press, 1960–2003)
Kushner E. "Renaissance Dialogue and Subjectivity," in *Printed Voices: The Renaissance Culture of Dialogue,* ed. by D. Heitsch and J.-F. Vallée (Toronto: University of Toronto Press, 2004), 229–241
Lamarque, H. *Ovide en France dans la Renaissance* (Toulouse: Cahiers de l'Europe Classique et Néo-Latine, 1981)
Landolfi, L. *Scribentis imago: eroine ovidiane e lamento epistolare* (Bologna: Pàtron, 2000)
Lanham, C. D. *Salutatio Formulas in Latin Letters to 1200: Syntax, Style, and Theory* (Munich: Arbeo-Gesellschaft, 1975)
LeBlanc, Y. *"Va lettre va": The French Verse Epistle (1400–1550)* (Birmingham, AL: Summa, 1995)
Lecercle, F. "Un Pétrarquisme épistolaire: Les *Lettres Amoureuses d'Etienne du Tronchet*," in *La Littérature de la Renaissance,* ed. by M. Soulié and R. Aulotte (Geneva: Slatkine, 1984), 213–25
Lesky, A. "Prose Romance and Epistolography," in: *A History of Greek Literature,* translated by J. Willis and C. de Heer (London: Methuen, 1966), 857–70
Lestringant, F. "De la défloration aux ossements: les jeux de l'amour et de la mort dans les héroïdes d'André de La Vigne et de Clément Marot," in *La Mort dans le texte,* ed. by G. Ernst (Lyon: Presses Universitaires de Lyon, 1988), 65–83
Lewis, C. S. *English Literature in the Sixteenth Century, Excluding Drama* (Oxford: Clarendon, 1954)
Lhote, A. "ESPENCE (Claude TOGNIEL D'), Théologien," in *Biographie châlonnaise avec documents inédits* (Geneva: Slatkine Reprints, 1971), 123–27

Lindheim, S. H. *Mail and Female: Epistolary Narrative and Desire in Ovid's "Heroides"* (Madison: University of Wisconsin Press, 2003)

Loers, V. *Ovidii Heroides et A. Sabini Epistolae* (Cologne: M. Dumont-Schauberg, 1829–30)

Lucas, R. H. "Mediæval French Translations of the Latin Classics to 1500," *Speculum* 45 (1970): 225–53

Lyne, R. "Writing Back to Ovid in the 1560s and 1570s," *Translation and Literature* 13.2 (Autumn 2004): 143–64

Maclean, I. *The Renaissance Notion of Woman: A Study in the Fortunes of Scholasticism and Medical Science in European Intellectual Life* (Cambridge: Cambridge University Press, 1980)

Malquori Fondi, G. "Conversations d'amour par lettres: un recueil méconnu de Le Pays, un roman inconnu de Pradon," in *Art de la lettre, art de la conversation à l'époque classique en France*, ed. by B. Bray and C. Strosetzki (Paris: Klincksieck,1995), 257–70

Mariano, B. M. "Antonii Volsci expositiones in Heroidas Ovidii: alcuni appunti," *Aevum: Rassegna di scienze storiche, linguistiche e filologiche* 67.1 (1993): 105–12

Martin, D. *Signe(s) d'amante: l'agencement des "Evvres de Louïze Labé Lionnoize"* (Paris: H. Champion, 1999)

Martindale, C. "Introduction," in: *Ovid Renewed: Ovidian Influences on Literature and Art from the Middle Ages to the Twentieth Century*, ed. by C. Martindale (Cambridge: Cambridge University Press, 1988)

———. *Redeeming the Text: Latin Poetry and the Hermeneutics of Reception* (Cambridge: Cambridge University Press, 1993)

Massebieau, L. *Schola Aquitanica: programme d'études du collège de Guyenne au XVIe siècle* (Paris: Musée Pédagogique, 1886)

Mathieu Castellani, G., and M. Plaisance (eds.). *Les Commentaires et la naissance de la critique littéraire (Actes du Colloque international sur le Commentaire, Paris, mai 1988)* (Paris: Aux Amateurs de Livres, 1990)

Mayer, C. E. *Bibliographie des oeuvres de Clément Marot*, Travaux d'humanisme et Renaissance 13 (Geneva: Droz, 1954)

McKinley, K. L. *Reading the Ovidian Heroine: Metamorphoses Commentaries 1100–1618* (Leiden: Brill, 2001)

Melville, J. *The Autobiography and Diary of Mr James Melville* (Edinburgh: Printed for the Wodrow Society, 1842)

Meyer, P. "Les Premières compilations françaises d'histoire ancienne," *Romania* 54 (1885): 1–81

Michalopoulos, A. N. "Ovid in Greek: Maximus Planudes' Translation of the Double Heroides," *Classica et Mediaevalia* 54 (2003), 359–74

Molinier, H. J. *Essai biographique et littéraire sur Octovien de Saint-Gelays évêque d'Angoulême, 1468–1502* (Rodez: Impr. Carrère, 1910)

Moore, H. "Elizabethan Fiction and Ovid's *Heroides*," *Translation and Literature* 9.1 (2000), 40–64

Morisset, G. M. "Ovide en France pendant la première moitié du XVIe siècle" (unpublished master's thesis, University of London, 1934)

Moss, A. "The 'Metamorphoses' Transformed: A Survey on Changes in the Latin Commentaries on the 'Metamorphoses' Printed in France up to 1600," in: *Acta Conventus Neo-Latini Turonensis*, ed. by Jean-Claude Margolin (Paris: Vrin, 1980), 187–95

---. *Ovid in Renaissance France: a Survey of the Latin Editions of Ovid and Commentaries Printed in France before 1600* (London: Warburg Institute, University of London, 1982)

---. *Printed Commonplace-Books and the Structuring of Renaissance Thought* (Oxford: Clarendon Press, 1996)

---. *Latin Commentaries on Ovid from the Renaissance* (Signal Mountain, TN: Summertown, 1998)

Most, G. W. (ed.). *Commentaries—Kommentare* (Göttingen: Vandenhoeck & Ruprecht, 1999)

Néraudau, J.-P. "Traduction et création chez Du Bellay, l'exemple de la 'Complainte de Didon à Enée prinse d'Ovide' (*Heroides*, VII)," in *La Naissance du monde et l'invention du poème,* ed. by J.-C. Ternaux (Paris: Champion, 1998), 369–86

Norton, G. P. *The Ideology and Language of Translation in Renaissance France and Their Humanist Antecedents* (Geneva: Droz, 1984)

Pade, M. "The Latin Translations of Plutarch's *Lives* in Fifteenth-Century Italy and Their Manuscript Diffusion," in: *The Classical Tradition in the Middle Ages and the Renaissance,* ed. by Claudio Leonardi and Birger Munk Olsen (Naples: Aux Amateurs de Livres, 1995), 169–83

---. "A Checklist of the Manuscripts of the Fifteenth-Century Latin Translations of Plutarch's *Lives,*" in: *L'eredità culturale di Plutarco dall'Antichità al Rinascimento,* ed. by Italo Gallo (Naples: 1998), 251–87

---. (ed.). *On Renaissance Commentaries* (Hildesheim: Georg Olms Verlag, 2005)

Papathomopoulos, M. "A propos de la métaphrase planudéenne des *Héroïdes* d'Ovide," in: *Philtra: Timetikos Tomos S. G. Kapsomenou* (Thessalonika: 1975), 107–18

Pendergast, W. H. "Sabinus, Imitator of Ovid," *Classical Folia* XXIII (1969): 246–53

Phillippy, P. B. "'Loytering in Love': Ovid's *Heroides,* Hospitality and Humanist Education in *The Taming of the Shrew,*" *Criticism* 40.1 (Winter 1998): 27–54

Polet, A. *Une Gloire de l'humanisme belge: Petrus Nannius (1500–1557)* (Louvain: Librairie universitaire, 1936)

Purnelle, G. *Ovide, "Epistulae heroidum": index verborum, listes de fréquence, relevés grammaticaux* (Liège: C.I.P.L., 1990)

Quain, E. A. "The Medieval *Accessus ad auctores,*" *Traditio* 3 (1945): 215–64

Quicherat, J. *Histoire de Sainte-Barbe,* 3 vols (Paris: 1860–64)

Rackley, S. A. "The Excerpts from Ovid's *Heroides* in the Florilegium Gallicum," *Manuscripta* 36 (1992): 125–35

Rand, E. K. *Ovid and his Influence* (Boston: George G. Harrap, 1925)

Reardon, B. P. (ed. and trans.). *Collected Ancient Greek Novels* (Berkeley: University of California Press, 1989)

Renaudet, A. *Préréforme et humanisme à Paris pendant les premières guerres d'Italie (1494–1517)* (Paris: Honoré Champion, 1916)

Renouard, P. *Bibliographie des impressions et des œuvres de Josse Badius Ascensius: imprimeur et humaniste, 1462–1535,* 3 vols. (Paris: E. Paul et fils et Guillemin, 1908)

Rice Henderson, J. "Humanist Letter Writing: Private Conversation or Public Forum?," in *Self-Presentation and Social Identification: The Rhetoric and Pragmatics of Letter Writing in Early Modern Times,* ed. by T. Van Houdt, J. Papy, G. Tournoy, and C. Matheeussen (Leuven: Leuven University Press, 2002), 17–38

Richmond, J. A. Review, "Wilfried Lingenberg, *Das erste Buch der Heroidenbriefe.* Echtheitskritische Untersuchungen. Studien zur Geschichte und Kultur des Altertums. Neue Folge. 1. Reihe, Band 20. Paderborn: Ferdinand Schöningh, 2003," English (http://ccat.sas.upenn.edu/bmcr/2003/2003-08-17.html: Bryn Mawr Classical Review, 27 August 2003)

Rieu, J. "La Temporalisation de l'espace dans la peinture française du XVIe siècle," in *Le Paysage à la Renaissance,* ed. by Y. Giraud (Fribourg: Éditions Universitaires, 1988), 297–310

Rigolot, F. *Louise Labé Lyonnaise, ou la Renaissance au féminin* (Paris: Champion, 1997)

———. "Problematizing Renaissance Exemplarity: The Inward Turn of Dialogue from Petrarch to Montaigne," in *Printed Voices: The Renaissance Culture of Dialogue,* ed. by D. Heitsch and J.-F. Vallée (Toronto: University of Toronto Press, 2004), 3–24.

Rimell, V. *Ovid's Lovers: Desire, Difference and the Poetic Imagination* (Cambridge: Cambridge University Press, 2006)

Rosati, G. "Sabinus, the *Heroides* and the Poet-Nightingale: Some Observations on the Authenticity of the *Epistula Sapphus,*" *The Classical Quarterly,* New Series 46.1 (1996): 207–16

Ross, J. B. "Venetian Schools and Teachers, Fourteenth to Early Sixteenth Centuries: A Survey and a Study of Giovanni Battista Egnazio," *Renaissance Quarterly* 29.4 (Winter 1976): 521–66

Roy, E. "Charles Fontaine et ses amis: sur une page obscure de la *Deffence,*" *Revue d'histoire littéraire de la France* 4 (1897): 412–33

Sanford, E. M. "Renaissance Commentaries on Juvenal," *Transactions and Proceedings of the American Philological Association* 79 (1948): 92–112

Saulnier, V. L. *Les Elégies de Clément Marot* (Paris: Société d'édition d'enseignement supérieur, 1952)

Schevill, R. "Ovid and the Renascence in Spain," *University of California Publications in Modern Philology* 4.1 (1913): 1–268

Scollen, C. M. *The Birth of the Elegy in France* (Geneva: Droz, 1967)

Shaner, M. C. E. "Meaningful Variations in Marginal Commentaries on Ovid," *Trivium* 31 (1999): 25–31

Sibbald, R. *Scotia illustrata, sive, Prodromus historae naturalis, pt 2, bk 3, chap. 2* (Edinburgh: 1684)

Silver, S. "Le Discours de l'absence amoureuse: l'*Elégie* II de Louise Labé et les *Héroides* d'Ovide," *RLA: Romance Language Annual* 6 (1994): 170–74

Singer, G. F. *The Epistolary Novel: Its Origin, Development, Decline, and Residuary Influence* (Philadelphia: University of Pennsylvania Press, 1933)

Slerca, A. "Octovien de Saint-Gelais traducteur de Virgle et d'Ovide, et la néologie," *Le Moyen Français* 39 (1997): 555–68

Souchal, G. "Le Mécenat de la famille d'Amboise," *Bulletin de la société des antiquaires de l'Ouest* 13 (1976): 485–526, 567–612

Sowards, J. K. "Erasmus and the Education of Women," *Sixteenth Century Journal* 13.4 (1982): 77–89

Spentzou, E. *Readers and Writers in Ovid's "Heroides": Transgressions of Genre and Gender* (Oxford: Oxford University Press, 2003)

Spoth, F. *Ovids Heroides als Elegien* (Munich: Beck, 1992)

Syme, R. *History in Ovid* (Oxford: Clarendon, 1978)

Tarrant, R. J. "The Authenticity of the Letter of Sappho to Phaon (*Heroides* XV)," *Harvard Studies in Classical Philology* 85 (1981): 133–53

Thill, A. "Les 'Héroïdes chrétiennes' en Allemagne aux XVIe et XVIIe siècles," in *Lectures d'Ovide, publiées à la mémoire de Jean-Pierre Néraudau,* ed. by E. Bury and M. Néraudau (Paris: Les Belles Lettres, 2003), 361–70

Tucker, M.-C. "Maîtres et étudiants écossais à la Faculté de Droit de l'Université de Bourges aux XVIe et XVIIe siècles," in *Les Echanges entre les universités européennes à la Renaissance,* ed. by M. Bideaux and M.-M. Fragonnard (Geneva: Droz, 2003), 301–9

Vaillancourt, L. *La Lettre familière au XVIe siècle: rhétorique humaniste de l'épistolaire* (Paris: Champion, 2003)

van Even, E. "Nouveaux renseignements sur le séjour à Louvain de Gui Morillon, sécretaire de Charles-Quint, et de sa famille," *Messager des sciences historiques de belgique* (1877): 136–168

van Marion, Olga. Bibliographical project, *Nederlandse Heldinnenbrieven,* Dutch (http://www.let.leidenuniv.nl/Dutch/Heroides.html: 14 January 2005)

Verducci, F. *Ovid's Toyshop of the Heart: "Epistulae Heroidum"* (Princeton: Princeton University Press, 1985)

Versini, L. *Le Roman épistolaire* (Paris: Presses Universitaires de France, 1979)

Vianey, J. "L'Art du vers chez Clément Marot," in *Mélanges Offerts à Abel Lefranc* (Paris: Droz, 1936), 44–57

Vinay, G. *L'Umanesimo subalpino nel secolo XV (Studi e ricerche),* Biblioteca della societa storica subalpina 148 (Turin, 1935)

White, P. "Ovid's *Heroides* in Early Modern French Translation: Saint-Gelais, Fontaine, Du Bellay," *Translation and Literature* 13.2 (Autumn 2004): 165–80

Wiley, W. L. "Charles Fontaine's Ideas on Poetry," in *Studies in Honor of Alfred G. Engstrom,* ed. by R. T. Cargo and E. J. Mickel (Chapel Hill: University of North Carolina Press, 1972), 197–207

Wilkinson, L. P. *Ovid Recalled* (Cambridge: Cambridge University Press, 1955)

Žižek, S. *Enjoy Your Symptom! Jacques Lacan in Hollywood and Out* (New York: Routledge, 2001)

INDEX OF PASSAGES FROM OVID'S *HEROIDES*

1.1–2, 63, 161, 177, 188, 224–25, 244
1.3, 223
1.33–34, 50
1.53–54, 223
1.59–62, 2
1.98, 4
1.105, 4

2.1–2, 110, 113, 116, 161, 180–81
2.3–5, 179
2.6, 106, 173
2.9, 112 n.42, 176, 177
2.12, 177
2.15, 170
2.18–19, 106, 157 n.32, 175
2.25–26, 181–82, 230
2.27–30, 114
2.29, 116
2.31–32, 112
2.31–34, 179–80
2.33–34, 173
2.34, 110
2.35–42, 114, 180, 234
2.37–38, 110
2.40, 112 & n.
2.41–42, 110–11
2.42, 173

2.48, 114
2.49–51, 115, 180
2.50, 112 n.42
2.52, 111
2.55, 114, 116
2.57, 124
2.61, 106, 114
2.61–62, 175–76
2.63, 112 n.42, 114, 116
2.65, 111
2.67–73, 172
2.69–70, 109–10
2.71–72, 110
2.72, 106
2.74, 166
2.81, 112 n.42, 114
2.83–84, 183
2.83–86, 6
2.85, 6–7, 102, 143, 246
2.85–86, 117–23, 166–67
2.90, 173
2.91, 114
2.93–94, 178
2.94, 111
2.99–100, 114
2.101–2, 112
2.103, 107–8

2.105, 230
2.109, 112 n.42
2.113–14, 171
2.115–20, 111, 172
2.116, 174
2.117, 110, 112 n.42
2.118, 112 n.42
2.120–21, 106
2.121, 110
2.121–30, 116
2.123–34, 179
2.135, 106
2.137, 111
2.141–42, 178
2.147–48, 123–24, 184, 230, 232–33

3.1–2, 55, 144, 161
3.63, 139
3.135, 112

4.1–2, 63
4.3, 161
4.10, 83
4.13–14, 84
4.20, 76
4.53–66, 236 n.74
4.140, 248
4.154, 76

5.7–8, 60
5.29–30, 238
5.31, 239 n.77
5.115–16, 55

6.21, 76, 111 n.41

7.1–2, 45, 108, 115, 162, 172
7.3–4, 158–59
7.4, 172–73
7.6, 152
7.7, 116
7.8, 182
7.11, 173
7.13, 115, 116
7.19–22, 168
7.22, 170
7.23, 152

7.23–26, 161
7.24–25, 107, 157 n.32, 159, 175
7.27, 115, 173
7.28, 152
7.29, 152
7.31, 114, 116
7.32, 111–12, 173
7.33–34, 159
7.35, 167–68
7.36, 168
7.37–40, 178
7.42, 170–71
7.45–46, 176
7.45–60, 103
7.50, 108
7.50–52, 172
7.51–52, 159–60
7.53, 114, 116
7.55, 171
7.57, 115
7.57–58, 174
7.60, 170
7.61, 114
7.64, 168
7.65, 116, 126
7.67, 116
7.85, 106, 168
7.89–92, 103
7.91, 116
7.92, 169
7.95–96, 176–77
7.96, 116
7.97, 106, 116, 126, 169
7.98, 152
7.99–100, 174
7.104, 152
7.109, 116
7.110, 169
7.113, 115
7.113–16, 173–74
7.115, 115
7.116, 115
7.118, 106
7.121, 115
7.123, 174
7.127, 174
7.130, 112

7.133, 106
7.134, 109
7.135, 114
7.136, 234
7.137, 114
7.139, 103, 114, 116, 177
7.141, 114
7.142, 171
7.143–44, 160–61
7.146, 152
7.150, 174
7.153, 115
7.157, 114
7.157–62, 172
7.162, 112
7.165, 171–72
7.166, 112, 114
7.167, 116
7.172, 179
7.178, 171
7.179, 116
7.179–80, 182–83
7.181–82, 103, 159, 169
7.183–84, 162
7.190, 169–70

7.191, 114, 116, 126–27, 180
7.195–96, 184–85

10.9–10, 36 n.57
10.99, 122 n.52
10.131–32, 236 n.74

12.91, 217 n.58

13.1, 63

16.1–378 (*various*), 135–37
16.14, 132–33
16.232, 133
16.293, 236 n.74

17.3–262 (*various*), 138–42
17.80, 135
17.87–88, 135

18.217–18, 189

20.91–92, 58

21.137–38, 58

GENERAL INDEX

A

Abelard. *See* Heloise
accessus, 30, 52–3 & n.21, 64 n.43, 77, 79–80, 81, 117, 151
Achilles, 62, 171, 211 n.52, 214, n.53, 220–1, 225, 239 n.77, 241
Acontius, 58, 61–62, 70, 189, 193, 195 n.18, 238
acrostic, 37, 146, 200 n.29, 205 n.39
Aeneas Silvius. *See* Piccolomini
Agamemnon, 62, 211 n.52, 220–21, 227
Alenus, Andreas, 40 n.64
Alexandre de Villedieu, 51 n.16
"Alexandrian footnote," 247–48
allegorical interpretation, 15, 41, 53, 91
Amboise, Catherine d', 40, 201–2
Amboise, François d', 25
Amboise, Georges d', 201–2
Amboise, J. Marius d', 209
Amboise, Michel d', 8, 22, 27–28, 34, 199–207, 209, 211, 213, 214, 215–41, 247
Apollodorus, 96 n.22
Ariadne, 1, 36 n.57, 59, 96, 107, 112, 122 n.52, 177–8, 182, 216–17, 232, 236 n.74, 247

Aristotle, 45 n.5, 92, 109 & n.
Ascensius. *See* Badius
Aneau, Barthélemy, *Quintil horatien,* 31 n.45, 155 n.28
Ausonius, 124, 165

B

Badius, Jodocus (Josse Bade), 45, 53, 73 n.54, 80, 81, 88, 91, 95, 106, 108, 109, 111, 113, 115–16, 120–22, 126, 129 n.64, 135, 175, 195
Baïf, Jean-Antoine de, 158
Baptista Mantuanus, 38, 200
Barchiesi, Alessandro, 7, 12, 18, 215, 249
Barthes, Roland, 87, 187
Bartolitanus, 88 n.4
Battaleus, Aaron, 88 n.4
Béda, Noël, 50 n.16
Belleau, Remy, 158
Boccaccio, Giovanni, 78–79, 108, 198; *Fiammetta,* 24, 27; *Clarae mulieres,* 38, 124–27, 165; *Genealogia deorum,* 95 n.21, 98 n.28, 125
Boethius, 117
Bouchet, Jean, 34
Boyd, Mark Alexander, 8, 38, 207–43

Briseis, 55, 62, 112, 139, 144–45, 161, 211 n.52, 220–21
Byblis, 44, 58 n.33, 63 n.41

C

Calderinus, Domitius, 88 n.4, 89, 91–93, 192–93
Callimachus, 95 n.21
Camerarius, Joachim, 38
Canace, 163, 220
Catullus, 51, 89, 109 n.39, 177–78, 217, 228, 236 n.74
Celtis, Conrad, 83 n.71
Chaucer, 24, 95 n.21, 125 n.58
Cicero, 11, 29, 50, 53, 55, 59, 79, 90, 91, 107, 111, 117 n.50, 136, 189
Cipelli. See Egnatius
Clericus, Ubertinus, 21, 67, 73, 77–79, 82, 83–85, 88–92, 95, 97–98, 105–6, 108–15, 118–23, 126–27, 129–30, 132–42, 175, 195
commonplace books, 6, 75–77, 85, 111–12
Corrozet, Gilles, 34, 205
Crucius, 88 n.4
Cydippe, 58, 61, 189, 194 & n., 195 n.18, 238, 244

D

Dantonet, P.-C., 209, 210, 213–14
Deianira, 1, 7, 76, 164, 207, 219–20, 222
Deimier, Pierre de, 56, 199
Demetrius, 43, 83
Demophoon, 6, 95–98, 101–2, 107–9, 114–15, 119, 121–23, 166, 177–84, 196–97, 216, 229–36, 239
Derrida, Jacques, 1, 12, 144, 242, dialogue, 13–14, 39, 43, 190–91, 214
Dido, 37 & n., 45, 46 n.9, 48–49, 50 n.15, 59, 79, 95–127, 131, 139, 147, 156–86, 188–89, 191, 196, 213–14, 219, 234, 236 n.74
Dörrie, Heinrich, 23 n.26, 29 n.41, 37–40, 41, 199

Douza, Janus, 221
Dryden, John, 14–15, 19, 24, 182
Du Bellay, Joachim, 31, 35, 107, 127, 147–86, 247

E

Egnatius, Johannes Baptista, 88, 93–94 & n.19
Eliot, T. S., 7
Empedocles, 109
énergie, 154–56
Eobanus Hessus, 38–39
epistolary novel, 25–28, 54
epistolography. *See* Letter, Renaissance theory of
Erasmus, Desiderius, 8, 29, 39, 52, 54, 57–62, 64 n.42, 81, 83, 85, 94, 131, 246
Espence, Claude d', 38–40
Euripides, 128
"exitus acta probat," 6–7, 102, 117–22, 143, 167, 246

F

Fabri, Pierre, 67–71
Fabricius, Georgius, 75–76
Filelfo, Francesco, 54–55
Fontaine, Charles, 4, 34 & n., 35 n.53, 74–75, 82, 101, 103, 107, 121–24, 129 n.64, 130–31, 146–86, 190, 205, 217

G

Genette, Gérard, 13
Golefer, Gilbert de, 207, 219
Gouvéa, André de, 51
Gower, John, 24, 95 n.21, 97 n.26
grammatical commentary, 15, 90–91, 95, 113–16
Guyenne, collège de, 51

H

Habert, François, 35, 39, 202

General Index

Habert, Pierre, 202 n.36
Heinsius, Daniel, 197–98
Heinsius, Nicolas, 192, 197–98, 219
Helen, 36, 48, 60–62, 67, 94, 127–42, 150, 194–95, 224, 236 n.74
Helisenne de Crenne, 27, 34
Heloise and Abelard, 24–25, 27, 38, 187
Hercules, 1, 207, 219–20, 222, 237, 240
Hermione, 59, 112, 214 n.53, 221
Hero, 147, 149–50, 189, 194–95
Heroides: authenticity of, 21–23, 46, 92, 191–98, 247; Christian adaptations of, 35, 38–40, 202; 'double letters,' 19, 22, 26, 46, 48, 92, 127–29, 189, 193–95; textual 'duplicity' of, 3, 13, 19, 30, 32, 47–48, 58, 64, 96, 245; epitaphs in, 12, 33, 96, 123, 166, 183–86, 222–23, 231–34; excessiveness of, 3, 18–19, 78, 103, 117, 126, 145, 165, 205; exemplarity in, 16, 38, 46–47, 61–62, 74, 78–83, 85, 117, 122–23, 139, 142, 166, 169, 190, 206, 211 n.52, 214 n.53, 225, 227, 235–36, 241–42, 246; feminine discourse of, 3, 6, 18–19, 22, 44–49, 59, 64, 77, 87, 96, 101–2, 131, 137–40, 144–45, 187–89, 216, 245–48; feminist readings of, 18–19, 22, 45, 49 n.9, 48–49, 142–43; gendered voice in, 18, 31–33, 44, 46–49, 58, 128–31, 146; imposition of masculine control on, 4, 18–19, 21, 34–35, 45–46, 186, 203–7, 216, 226, 229, 232–33, 238–39; and imposture, 22 n.24, 23, 146, 214; interpolation, 3, 7, 9, 21–22, 106–7, 173–74; intertextuality in, 7, 12, 18–19, 116, 137, 184, 188 n.3, 211 n.52, 219 n.62, 245–46, 247–49; irony in, 5, 7, 12, 18, 46 n.9, 92, 114, 116, 118, 136–37, 140–42, 168, 184–85, 190–91, 207, 225, 241–42, 247–49; masculine rhetoric in, 6, 44, 46–48, 59, 62, 64, 84, 128–31, 135, 216, 232–33, 239; moral readings of, 3, 16–17, 20, 30, 49, 53, 55, 61–62, 74–75, 77–85, 103, 116–27, 133, 137–43, 150–51, 163–70, 174, 185, 206–7, 220, 232, 240; role of perspective, 5–6, 18, 33, 101–2, 206, 245–46; school composition exercises based on, 16, 43–44, 57, 60–62, 85, 246, 248–49; suasive rhetoric in, 16, 43–45, 47, 59–62, 64, 67, 81, 87, 114–16, 119, 128–42, 154; as "supplement," 15, 19, 241–42; syllepsis in, 179, 181–85; as title for the work, 3 n.5, 46, 127–28; and tragedy, 25, 39, 53, 211 n.52, 222, 241, 247
Hinds, Stephen, 22 n.22, 247–49
Hippolytus, 84–85, 164, 191, 196, 220 & n.
Homer, 3, 5, 12 n.1, 55, 128–29, 137, 206, 226 & n., 235, 236 n.74, 244
Horace, 20, 29, 31, 333–34, 51, 73, 74, 94, 111
Hosschius, Sidronius, 198 n.22, 220 n.63
Hypermnestra, 112, 221
Hypsipyle, 76, 112, 191, 196, 213–14, 218–19

I

intention, author's, 3, 7, 21, 30, 49, 77–82, 103, 114, 124–25, 142–43, 165, 186, 245

J

Jahn, J.-C., 198
Jahn, Otto, 196
Jason, 37, 191, 196, 214, 217 n.58, 218–19
Jauss, Hans Robert, 13–16
Jerome, 56
Jesuits, 25, 40, 51, 76–77, 220 n.63
Justinus, 108, 125
Justus Lipsius, 8

K

Knox, Ronald, 215 n.55

L

Labé, Louise, 22 & n., 28 n.38, 32 & n., 34–35, 190
Lacan, Jacques, 1, 19, 142
Laertes, 4
Lando, Ortensio, 28 & n.
Laodamia, 59, 63, 131, 218
La Vigne, André de, 31 n.45, 33, 36, 146, 163
Leander, 46, 147, 149–50, 189, 193, 195
Lefèvre d'Etaples, Jacques, 50 n.16
Lemaire de Belges, Jean, 36
Leto, Pomponio, 89
letter: "A letter always arrives at its destination," 1–7, 11, 249; *ars dictaminis,* 54, 68; classical definition of, 2, 43, 52–53, 145; circulation of, 1–2, 12–13, 15, 187, 242, 245, 249; immediacy of, 4, 6, 163; manuals (vernacular), 27–28, 34, 54, 56, 67–71, 202 n.36; Renaissance theory of, 8, 51–71, 83 & n., 91; true addressee of, 1–4, 11–13, 187–88, 246
Lewis, C. S., 181
Livy, 94, 110
Locher, Jacobus Philomusus, 221
Lotichius Secundus, Petrus, 37
Lucian, 39, 60
Lynceus, 221

M

Macareus, 163, 220, 221–22
Mannerism, 101
Mantuan. *See* Baptista Mantuanus
Manutius, Aldus, 93, 196–97
Marolles, Michel de, 199
Marot, Clément, 29, 31, 33–34, 36–37, 42, 150, 154 n.25, 158, 206
Marquets, Anne de, 40
Martial, 50 n.16, 108

Martindale, Charles, 14–15
Masures, Louis des, 148
Medea, 25, 218–19
Melville, James, 208
Menelaus, 62, 112, 129, 136
Merula, G., 88 n.4, 89
Montaigu, collège de, 50 n.16
moral philosophy, 7, 16, 45 n.5, 46, 78–79, 80, 87, 117, 247
Morillon, Guy, 20–21, 72–74, 79–80, 88, 93–95, 98 n.28, 109, 112, 113, 116, 117–18, 124, 130, 133–41, 193, 194 n.17, 195, 212, 217
Moss, Ann, 17, 41–42, 50 n.16, 80–81, 88, 97, 105, 116, 150
Musaeus, 150

N

Nannius, Petrus, 39, 94
Navagero, 88 n.4
Negri, Francesco, 65–67, 68–70
Nizolius, 88 n.4

O

Oenone, 35, 36, 38, 60, 97, 137, 236–40
Orestes, 214 n.53, 221, 241
Ovid: *Amores,* 21, 23, 30, 92, 111, 112, 145 n.4, 164, 182, 191, 193–97, 229, 237; *Ars Amatoria,* 3 n.5, 11, 23, 35, 58 n.33, 59, 61, 63 n.41, 67, 70, 110 n.40, 111, 112, 130, 132–35, 145 n.4, 164, 217 n.59; *Fasti,* 108, 157, 247; *Ibis,* 92, 94, 110; *Metamorphoses,* 4 n.9, 41–42, 44, 48, 53, 58 n.33, 67, 74, 78 n.60, 90, 110, 111, 112, 145 n.4, 150, 221, 245, 246 n.2; *Remedia Amoris,* 95 n.21, 98 n.28, 101, 110, 112, 145 n.4, 155; *Tristia & Pontics,* 29, 31, 51, 75, 191–92, 194, 196, 237

P

paraclausithyron, 189

paratext, 13, 15, 151, 163–64, 205, 248
Paris (Trojan hero), 6, 36, 46, 61–62, 67, 70, 94, 127–42, 150, 193–95, 197 n.20, 224, 236–40, 244
Parrhasius, Janus, 88 n.4, 117 n.50
Pasquier, Etienne, 28
Paul, Saint, 56, 133
Penelope, 1–5, 12 n.1, 46, 50, 61–62, 67, 70, 76, 80–82, 161, 164, 177, 191–92, 195–96, 213, 214 n.53, 215 n.55, 223–39, 231, 233
Perotti, Niccolò, 54–56, 93, 192
Persius, 23–24, 89
Petrarch, 11–12, 29, 54, 163 n.38, 244
Phaedra, 21, 25, 45, 46, 48, 63, 64 n.42, 74, 76–77, 80, 81–85, 96, 107, 164, 196, 198 n.22, 217, 220 & n., 232, 236 n.74, 248
Phaon, 22, 196, 207, 222–23
Phyllis, 6–7, 24, 48–49, 59, 74, 95–124, 157–86, 191, 196, 213–16, 229–34
Piccolomini, Aeneas Silvius, 26–27, 63 n.41, 70–71, 163 n.40
Pinturricchio, 4 n.10
Pius, J. B., 88 n.4
Planudes, Maximus, 145 & n.
Plato, 56, 128
Pliny the Elder, 107, 108, 111
Pliny the Younger, 55, 59, 93
pluritemporalité, 101
Plutarch, 93 & n., 107–8, 110, 111, 216 & n.
Poe, Edgar Allan, *The Purloined Letter*, 1, 4 n.7, 12, 242
Politian, 59, 87–88 & n.4, 89, 92 n.11
Pontanus, Jacobus, 76–77
Pope, Alexander, 25, 187
Propertius, 37 n.59, 51, 75, 89, 211–12
Protesilaus, 214 n.53, 218
Pygmalion (brother of Dido), 108, 125, 173–74
Pyramus and Thisbe, 66–67, 210

Q

"Quintianus" (ancient poet?), 203
Quintianus Stoa, 88, 203

Quintilian, 71, 77, 111, 119–20 n.51, 245

R

Racine, Jean, 25, 220
Ramus, Petrus (Pierre de la Ramée), 116
Rapin, Nicolas, 209 n.47
Richardson, Samuel, 6 n.11
Rodríguez, Juan, *Bursario,* 145–46
Roman de Troie, 146–47 & n.
Ronsard, Pierre de, 35, 158, 211

S

Sabinus, 8, 16, 23, 26, 92, 98 n.28, 191–99, 203, 209, 211, 215, 220, 223–34, 226, 229–30, 236, 238 n.76, 240–42
Sabinus, Angelus, 93, 192–93, 196, 198, 199
Salutati, Coluccio, 11
Sainte-Barbe, collège de, 51
Saint-Gelais, Octavien de, 16–17, 22, 27, 31 n.45, 35 n.52, 36, 70–71, 72 & n., 97, 146–54, 157, 161–85, 201, 223–34, 230, 240
Saint-Romat, 150 & n.
Sappho, 19, 21–23, 25, 32 n.47, 47, 91–93, 142, 144, 188, 196, 207, 222–23, 244
Scaliger, Julius Caesar, 197
Scoppa, 88 n.4
Sebillet, Thomas, 31, 154–55
Secundus, Johannes, 158
Servius, 53, 96 n.22, 97–98, 126–27
Scève, Maurice, 28 n.38, 34–35
Scoellius, 88 n.4
Seneca the Elder, 19, 43
Seneca the Younger, 29, 55, 56, 189, 220 n.63
Shakespeare, William: *A Midsummer Night's Dream,* 66 n.45; *The Taming of the Shrew,* 49–50
Sichaeus, 106, 108, 125, 127, 169, 173, 174
Sibbald, Robert, 208, 210
Sophocles, 7, 55, 219 n.62

Statius, 92, 108
Stesichorus, 128–29
Strabo, 108

T

Telemachus, 4
Temporal, Jean, 68, 147 n.15
Theseus, 1, 93 n.13, 96, 107, 110, 138, 141, 177, 182, 216–17, 232, 233, 235
Thucydides, 108
Tibullus, 51, 75, 89
Turberville, George, 147, 153, 157 n.33, 181–82, 199
Turpilius, 52, 189

U

Ulysses, 2–4, 12, n.1, 61, 177, 191–93, 195–97, 206, 214 n.53, 223–39

V

Varro, 108

Varus, Cornelius, 209
Villiers, François de, 163
Vinet, Elie, 51
Virgil, 5, 24, 37, 38, 50, 51, 76 n.59, 79, 95–96, 111–13, 116, 124–27, 137, 147–48, 156, 164–65, 168, 174, 178, 184, 188, 219, 236 n.74
Vives, Juan Luis, 8, 62–64, 76, 77, 83
Volscus, Antonius, 21, 71–72, 81, 84, 88–98, 106–14, 118, 121, 123, 126, 129–30, 136–42, 175, 193–95, 217

W

Whitney, Isabella, 219 n.61
Wilkinson, L. P., 19, 44, 53
woodcuts, 4–5, 96–105, 131–34, 202

Z

Zarotus, 88 n.4
Žižek, Slavoj, 1, 12, 18 n.14

www.ingramcontent.com/pod-product-compliance
Lightning Source LLC
Chambersburg PA
CBHW020943230426
43666CB00005B/152